INDIGENOUS RESEARCH

INDIGENOUS RESEARCH

Theories, Practices, and Relationships

EDITED BY

Deborah McGregor,

Jean-Paul Restoule, and

Rochelle Johnston

**CANADIAN
SCHOLARS**

Toronto | Vancouver

Indigenous Research: Theories, Practices, and Relationships
Edited by Deborah McGregor, Jean-Paul Restoule, and Rochelle Johnston

First published in 2018 by
Canadian Scholars, an imprint of CSP Books Inc.
425 Adelaide Street West, Suite 200
Toronto, Ontario
M5V 3C1

www.canadianscholars.ca

Library and Archives Canada Cataloguing in Publication

Indigenous research : theories, practices, and relationships / edited by Deborah McGregor, Jean-Paul Restoule, and Rochelle Johnston.

Includes bibliographical references and index.
Issued in print and electronic formats.
ISBN 978-1-77338-085-8 (softcover).--ISBN 978-1-77338-086-5 (PDF).--
ISBN 978-1-77338-087-2 (EPUB)

1. Native peoples--Research--Canada. 2. Research--Methodology. I. McGregor, Deborah, 1962-, editor II. Restoule, Jean-Paul, 1972-, editor III. Johnston, Rochelle, 1977-, editor

E76.7.I53 2018   305.897'071072   C2018-902699-5
                                                               C2018-902700-2

Cover and text design by Elisabeth Springate
Typesetting by Brad Horning

18   19   20   21   22   5 4 3

Printed and bound in Canada by Webcom

CONTENTS

LIST OF FIGURES AND TABLES

FIGURES

TABLES

ACKNOWLEDGEMENTS

We acknowledge the scholars who created the space for current and future researchers to serve the goals and aspirations of Indigenous peoples, communities, and future generations.

We acknowledge the ancestors, grandmothers, grandfathers, aunties, uncles, Elders, and families who have worked to ensure Indigenous intellectual traditions remain living and enacted. We acknowledge the lands, waters, and relatives that continue to provide substance and knowledge to us to ensure collective well-being.

We acknowledge and respect our collaborators, who have worked patiently with us to see a collective research storytelling effort come to life.

We acknowledge those who have believed in this project and assisted in this journey, including Kerrie Waddington and Karri Yano from Canadian Scholars. We appreciate the editing assistance of Paul Meighan, Steven Whitaker and Barbara Jenni.

Our families have our profound recognition throughout this long journey.

Rochelle would like to acknowledge her family, who grew considerably during the life of this project. Ewan, Kai, and Koen, as well as Lindsay, Sam, Alicia, Aaron, Leen, and Ludo. She'd especially like to thank Mary Ann, and the other women who shared in the mothering and teaching of her children while she supported this work.

Deborah would like to acknowledge her ancestors, community, and family, who continue to inspire her work to ensure a future for generations to come – much love to Steven, Hillary, and Arden.

Jean-Paul would like to acknowledge the many students who took the OISE course in Indigenous Research Methodologies and pushed our thinking on the matter with their brilliant questions, discussions, and papers. Also, for the many SAGE gatherings, symposiums, and writing retreats where methodologies were discussed, *miigwec*. Rochelle and Jean-Paul presented early work on this book at academic conferences and appreciate the kind support and questions encountered there. *Miigwec* to fellow editors, and the editors at Canadian Scholars. Finally, and most significantly, much love and gratitude for the support of family, especially Tara, Vincent, and Myra.

PREFACE

Building upon the theoretical works of Indigenous scholars like Linda Tuhiwai Smith (1999), Shawn Wilson (2008), Margaret Kovach (2009), Kathleen Absolon (2011), and Bagele Chilisa (2012), who explore *what* Indigenous research is, the contributors to this edited collection show *how* Indigenous research is engaged with and practiced. These scholars have created space within the academy for Indigenous approaches to research: through critiquing hegemonic research paradigms that continue to serve colonialist and imperialist ideals; by challenging the homogenization of Indigenous intellectual traditions and expression (Battiste, 2000; Graveline, 1998; Smith, 1999); and by explaining the value of Indigenous knowledges and approaches to research (Absolon, 2011; Kovach, 2009; Lambert, 2014; Mertens, Cram, & Chilisa, 2013; Tuck & McKenzie, 2015; Wilson, 2008). In this volume, we begin to put their insights into practice.

The chapters that follow are grounded in the concrete experiences of each contributor, linking their insights on the practice of Indigenous research to current discussions and debates. Reflections from seasoned and emerging scholars, working within the academy and in their respective communities, describe the diversity of research practices among and within Indigenous nations. The book delves deep into the dilemmas, challenges, and triumphs of its contributing authors. Collectively, they show how varied Indigenous research practices are, reflecting the diversity of Indigenous nations, languages, knowledges, and approaches to inquiry. Each contributor begins their research journey in a different context and place, and pursues a unique path, but those paths cross in revealing and sometimes surprising ways.

This edited collection responds to calls for guidance on how to enact Indigenous research practice, as well as the Truth and Reconciliation Commission of Canada's (TRC) call to make space for Indigenous peoples in education at all levels of society. Principles 7 and 8 of the TRC's final report (TRC, 2015) specifically state that:

> 7) The perspectives and understandings of Aboriginal Elders and Traditional Knowledge Keepers of the ethics, concepts, and practices of reconciliation are vital to long-term reconciliation.
> 8) Supporting Aboriginal peoples' cultural revitalization and integrating Indigenous knowledge systems, oral histories, laws, protocols, and connections to the land into the reconciliation process are essential. (p. 127)

Such imperatives are prompting a growing number of institutional and program initiatives to address Indigenous research priorities and establish research collaborations that serve Indigenous communities. This, in turn, is creating an increasing need for resources that can offer guidance and support to these initiatives.

Responding to the imperative in Indigenous research to serve community (McGregor, this volume), and to create usable knowledge for this purpose (Cormier & Ray, this volume), this book will also be of interest to policy makers, civil servants, and NGOs who are engaged in work with Indigenous peoples, as well as Indigenous communities participating in academic-community collaborations and/or their own research.

Despite the interest in Indigenous research within the academy, many misperceptions remain, and epistemic violence and dominance continues. This volume lends further support to scholars seeking to justify their use of Indigenous research approaches as the academy continues to resist genuine Indigenous scholarship.

There are few venues for the kind of in-depth, reflective, and self-critical writing about Indigenous research included here. For this reason, those researchers already well versed in Indigenous approaches, yet curious about the research journeys of their colleagues, will also find this collection valuable. Similarly, scholars from other critical research traditions may find the approaches to research described here relevant to their work.

This collection was conceived as a space to both nurture and generate nuanced understandings of Indigenous research practices. As editors, we see creating this collection as forming a circle, a relational space for stories. We expect these diverse stories to be received differently by different readers. They may make some readers uncomfortable, some feel transformed, and some perhaps simply relieved that others have shared a similar journey. This is a collection of "truth-telling," in which contributors' stories are celebrated on their own terms. It is in many respects a "safe space" for expressing research practice. We did not ask contributors to conform to traditional academic expectations or conventions, which some scholars have described as a form of epistemic violence itself (Kuokkanen, 2007).

We began, in fact, with an open invitation to scholars and those involved in community-based research to join this circle. The invitation was distributed through relational networks and we endeavoured to create an inclusive space for discussion, rather than begin with predetermined conceptions of what Indigenous research ought to be.

We also debated what diversity meant in the context of this collection. Should we reflect Indigenous research from across the globe? Should we require chapters from different geographical regions or nations? What about other criteria: The researcher's disciplinary home? Their gender? Whether they were Indigenous or non-Indigenous? In the end, we decided that our role was not to impose categories but to provide space, to facilitate dialogue and reflection among those who wished to join the circle.

This volume will thus contribute to the growing circle of scholarship around Indigenous research practice. With the circle formed, we, as editors, faced one more challenge: organizing the collection in a way that would respect the voice of each contributor while facilitating the engagement of the reader. As editors, the chapters we received were experienced by each of us in different ways, illustrating the point made by Luby and colleagues in this collection that each reader takes away something different from a story. The standard approach in edited collections is to organize the volume in predetermined categories or according to themes that chapters appear to fit into. However, in Indigenous (and possibly all) research, many different threads intertwine simultaneously to weave a pattern. Separating out an individual thread provides little insight into the pattern as a whole, and each thread may contribute to more than one component of the pattern. Thus, the contributors' chapters spill out of conceptual boxes. The chapters by Nicole Penak, Karlee Fellner, and Amy Parent, for example, all employ a Trickster as a central focus, while in fact addressing largely dissimilar themes.

The stories in this collection can be described as disruptive, as they vary in their writing structure and form, from so-called "Indigenized" forms such as storytelling and narrative, to a standard academic approach, which can create discomfort when the two are placed alongside each other. In this volume we have embraced this disruption to illustrate that Indigenous research scholarship can and should be inclusive of this variety of forms.

Experiencing different styles of writing in the same volume can be disconcerting, and in some instances startling, as we are trained through formal education to organize our thinking and writing in a linear fashion. However, we take Aman Sium and Eric Ritskes' (2013) point seriously: "Stories in Indigenous epistemologies are disruptive, sustaining, knowledge producing, and theory-in-action" (p. ii). Indigenous scholarship utilizes narrative, poetic, and conventional academic writing styles. There is no single formula for writing or expressing Indigenous research. In Cree scholar Robert Innes' (2010) call for "methodological diversity" in Indigenous studies we find affirmation that there are no "standard" requirements for writing in particular ways to express Indigenous research practice. We acknowledge that these assertions may elicit a degree of discomfort in some, yet we believe the contrasting writing styles are a strength of this book, respecting the unique voices of the contributors and reflecting the diversity of intellectual traditions expressed.

Contributions to this text are organized by section in a way that shows how each chapter connects with multiple themes. The Learning and Reflection Questions at the beginning of each section are intended to give you an idea of how the chapters connect with each other. While some of these questions aim to illuminate relationships between the approaches to research taken by the different contributors, others invite you to reflect on your own practice as an aspiring or experienced researcher.

We recognize that no collection can ever fully capture the range or depth of approaches among Indigenous nations. We would go further and say that it is impractical to represent the diversity *within* a nation, as there are many factors to consider that may impact research practices (for example, whether the context is urban, rural, off-reserve, or on-reserve; and whether the people involved are considered "status" or "non-status," are of a particular gender or age group, or have a certain life experience). To broaden the circle of understanding introduced by this volume, therefore, we have also included a resources section at the end of the collection to provide additional scope and more in-depth guidance to expanding the conversation on research practice.

While the way we have organized this collection provides a map, you are free to plot your own journey through the text, and along the way form your own relationships with the dilemmas, challenges, and triumphs of this circle of scholars. Ultimately, our vision is for you to take what you will from the stories, and apply the lessons learned in a way that you think will provide the most benefit. As stated by Métis scholar Fyre Jean Graveline (1998), "the ultimate value of storytelling is to recreate a situation for someone who has not lived through it, so the listener can benefit from the teller's experience" (p. 168).

The time is ripe for advancing the terms and conditions for intellectually diverse, culturally grounded, and creatively expressed Indigenous research practice. Giving our focused attention to this topic offers a constructive starting point for a journey of reconciliation and Indigenous resurgence.

REFERENCES

Absolon, K. E. (2011). *Kaandossiwin: How we come to know.* Halifax, NS: Fernwood Publishing.

Battiste, M. (2000). Maintaining Aboriginal identity, language, and culture in modern society. In M. Battiste (Ed.), *Reclaiming Indigenous voice and vision* (pp. 193–208). Vancouver, BC: UBC Press.

Chilisa, B. (2012). *Indigenous research methodologies.* Thousand Oaks, CA: Sage.

Graveline, F. J. (1998). *Circle works: Transforming Eurocentric consciousness.* Halifax, NS: Fernwood Publishing.

Innes, R. (2010). Introduction: Native studies and Native cultural preservation, revitalization and persistence. *American Indian Culture and Research Journal, 34*(2), 1–9.

Kovach, M. (2009). *Indigenous methodologies: Characteristics, conversations, and contexts.* Toronto, ON: University of Toronto Press.

Kuokkanen, R. (2007). *Reshaping the university: Responsibility, Indigenous epistemes, and the logic of the gift.* Vancouver, BC: UBC Press.

Lambert, L. (2014). *Research for Indigenous survival: Indigenous research methodologies in the behavioral sciences.* Pablo, MT: Salish Kootenai College Press.

Mertens, F., Cram, B., & Chilisa, B. (Eds.). (2013). *Indigenous pathways into social research.* Walnut Creek, CA: Left Coast Press.

Sium, A., & Ritskes, E. (2013). Speaking truth to power: Indigenous storytelling as an act of living resistance. *Decolonization: Indigeneity, Education & Society, 2*(1), i–x.

Smith, L. T. (1999). *Decolonizing methodologies: Research and Indigenous peoples.* London, UK: Zed Books.

Truth and Reconciliation Commission of Canada (TRC). (2015). *Truth and Reconciliation Canada: What we learned, principles of truth and reconciliation.* Winnipeg, MB: Truth and Reconciliation Commission. Retrieved from www.trc.ca

Tuck, E., & McKenzie, M. (2015). *Place in research: Theory, methodology, and methods.* New York, NY: Routledge.

Wilson, S. (2008). *Research is ceremony: Indigenous research methods.* Black Point, NS: Fernwood Publishing.

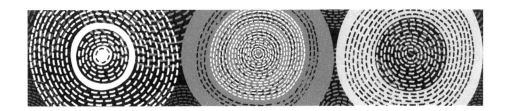

INTRODUCTION

Relationships, Respect, Relevance, Reciprocity, and Responsibility: Taking Up Indigenous Research Approaches

Rochelle Johnston, Deborah McGregor, and Jean-Paul Restoule

Can we speak of a single Indigenous research paradigm? Indigenous research is as diverse as the peoples who engage in the process, yet the varied approaches we collectively refer to as "Indigenous research" share the common feature of being different from other, non-Indigenous, approaches to research (Chilisa, 2012; Mertens, Cram, & Chilisa, 2013; Rigney, 2006; Wilson, 2008). Indigenous research scholarship has been pivotal in clarifying this difference, putting it in context, and providing a theoretical lens through which we can better under-stand and promote research that prioritizes the aspirations, needs, and values of Indigenous peoples and knowledges (Kovach, 2009; Lambert, 2014).

In this volume, we focus on how to put this theory into practice. We ask, "How is Indigenous research practiced?" and "How can it be best carried out in future?" We illustrate some of the many paths one might take on a journey of Indigenous research. To accomplish this, we invited researchers to share their stories of *how* they have applied Indigenous research in their work. The hard work of translating theory into practice provides valuable lessons from which we all can learn.

In this introduction, we provide the context for our contributors' stories by reviewing the theoretical landscape and identifying the touchstones of Indigenous research. In so doing, we challenge "essentialized" or binary conceptions of Indigenous research by creating space for reflections that expose the messiness of what happens in practice (Chilisa, 2012; Rigney, 2006). We then provide a brief overview of the contributors' chapters and make connections between their descriptions and reflections.

The scope of this collection is centred primarily within Canada, yet an effort has been made to illustrate the incredible diversity of Indigenous research across nations. It is unfortunate that, up until now, the overriding need to contrast Indigenous with Western ways of research has tended to mask this diversity. We show that who you are matters, and that Indigenous research practice looks different depending on the variety of factors that define this aspect, including where you are from, your motivations for carrying out the research, your level of accountability to your research participants, your relationships with both participants and partners, and your research location. The approach used depends upon the question(s) being asked and the process used to generate these questions.

The process of answering these questions is, of course, the methodology. What is it about this methodology that makes research Indigenous? Like the concept of Indigeneity itself, the answers are multiple, complex, and contested (Chilisa, 2012; Paradies, 2016), and better approached in context than with fixed definitions. There are some key elements that stand out, however. For example, Indigenous research offers a clear commitment to recognize and support diversity and nationhood – intellectual self-determination, if you will. Indigenous research explicitly recognizes traditional and contemporary Indigenous knowledge traditions, the value of community leadership and support, and the community's ownership of knowledge. Indigenous research holds the potential to regenerate and revitalize the life of Indigenous peoples and communities along with the "knowing" that sustains their ongoing vitality.

In a similar vein, "Indigenist" research, as described by Lester Rigney (2006), is an emancipator, seeking to help "chart our own political and social agendas for liberation from the colonial domination of research and society" (p. 39). According to Rigney, Indigenist research focuses on three principles: "the involvement in resistance as the emancipatory imperative in Indigenous research; the maintenance of political integrity in Indigenous research; and the privileging of Indigenous voices in Indigenous research" (2006, p. 39). Rigney also makes clear that while Indigenist research must benefit Indigenous communities, it is by no means "anti-intellectual" or "atheoretical," nor is it meant only for Indigenous peoples. What it does offer is a clear opportunity for Indigenous voices and perspectives, and thus is a critical starting point for addressing vitally important issues affecting Indigenous and non-Indigenous peoples alike.

INTRODUCING OURSELVES

An important and appropriate place to start applying an Indigenous approach to research is with "self-in-relation" (Absolon, 2010; Graveline, 2000; Kovach, 2009). So let us begin there, by introducing ourselves, the three editors of this volume.

Boozhoo. Jean-Paul Restoule *nintishinikaas* (my name). *Wazhask nitootem* (my clan). *Okikendawt mnissing nitoonci* (my community). *Anishinaabe ndaaw* (my nation). This greeting and introduction in Anishinaabemowin, aka the Ojibwe language, tells a fellow Anishinaabe some key information. It communicates my name, my clan, my community, and my people. In about ten words, I give a knowledgeable Anishinaabe much of what they need to know about who I am and where I come from. Anything else I say afterwards can be contextualized by this standard introduction. This greeting communicates a series of relationships that grow ever wider, from the self, to the clan (family), to the community, to the nation. Extending beyond myself, I am related to all other humans and all living beings in Creation. This greeting embodies a fundamental tenet of Anishinaabe, and Indigenous, worldviews: everyone is related. This is an important consideration when engaging in research relationships. What this introduction left out is that I was raised in Orangeville, a small town northwest of Toronto, Ontario. I began to understand and explore my Anishinaabe heritage while living in Windsor in the early 1990s and I have lived and worked in Toronto for over 15 years.

Hello. My name is Rochelle Nadine Johnston. I was born on Nl'Akapxm Territory in the BC Interior, but my father's parents came to Canada from Scotland and England. My name tells you that through my father's line I am from the Johnston clan of the Scottish lowlands, but the meanings of those European Indigenous institutions have not been passed down to me. My mother's family also came to North America from western Europe. However, they have been here for more generations, have a weaker connection with their European origins, and are more implicated in the colonization of Canada. I am honoured to help with the creation of this book, and being involved has taught me much. My experience with Indigenous research methodologies has been mostly through my work with people indigenous to Africa, especially in the context of doing participatory action research. I have also used Indigenist methods (Wilson, 2008) in my research on how non-Indigenous people stand by and do nothing about genocide here in Canada. So, I come to this work as a learner and as a helper.

Aanii. Deborah McGregor *ndizhnikaaz* (my name). *Wiigwaaskingaa n'doonjibaa* (where I am from). *Mukwa dodem* (bear clan). *Anishinaabe kwe*

(Anishinaabe woman). I am Anishinaabe from the Great Lakes area. I live and work in my traditional territories. My work is informed by my ancestors, family, community, nation, and the lands/waters (relatives) that I come from and continue to work for. I am motivated by my respect for the people and my desire to ensure future generations can enjoy *mnaamodzawin* (a good life).

THE TRANSFORMATION OF INDIGENOUS RESEARCH

Indigenous research methodologies arise from Indigenous worldviews (Geniusz, 2009; Kovach, 2009; Lambert, 2014), but they are also shaped by centuries of struggle to survive and overcome colonialism. Indigenous research seeks to expose epistemic violence and domination (Walker, 2013) and poses a counter-narrative to Western research approaches. We are indebted to the work of Maori scholar Linda Tuhiwai Smith (1999), which explains how research has been used by Europeans to colonize Indigenous peoples around the world. We build on this foundation and focus on the opportunities and challenges of using research as a tool to achieve sovereignty or self-determination. However, Indigenous research methodologies are not simply a response to colonialism; they have existed for thousands of years (Wilson, 2008). Indigenous research methodologies reflect how knowledge is understood and sought in the context of the worldviews, ontologies, and epistemologies of diverse Indigenous nations.

In this introduction, we share key touchstones or themes that resonate with us in the work of those who have practiced and theorized this topic. This chapter serves as an entry point and guide to the burgeoning literature on Indigenous research methodologies and practice that may assist you in your own research path. In acknowledging written sources for the ideas in this chapter, we also respect the wisdom of a community of Indigenous researchers, and the multiple nations that stand behind them.

Much of what has been shared here can be traced to community, the land, and ancestral and sacred sources of knowledge (Tuck & McKenzie, 2015). Indigenous knowledge originates in oral sources (conversations, stories, traditional teachings) in the day-to-day practices of Indigenous peoples (researchers and non-researchers alike) according to Indigenous worldviews and including insights from the spirit world (Walker, 2013; Wilson, 2008). It is our view that Indigenous research contexts, theories, and practices will continue to innovate, while grounded experiences and reflections will assist many in navigating an increasingly complex research terrain. As Oglaka Lakota scholar Keely Ten Fingers (2005) cautions:

Whether researchers choose to utilize indigenous methodologies in upcoming research projects will soon become less and less of a choice, as First Nations increasingly develop our own research ethics and protocols that will apply to all research conducted in our territories and with our people. (p. 62)

DECOLONIZING RESEARCH

Decolonization has become a critical aspect of moving away from the colonizing research that has consistently dehumanized Indigenous peoples over time, and of resisting Euro-Western theories and research (Brown & Strega, 2015). Despite its vital importance, decolonizing research is difficult, uncomfortable, and risky. We must go into the belly of the beast to critique colonialism (Absolon, 2011). This includes taking an honest look at the wrongdoings perpetrated by non-Indigenous people, as well as the ways in which Indigenous people have sometimes participated in our own oppression (Wilson, 2008).

The paradox of decolonizing research arises from having to resist continued attempts to eradicate Indigenous ways of being and knowing, while recognizing the fact that beneficial research can indeed entail cross-cultural encounters, particularly if said research is firmly grounded in an Indigenous paradigm, as Maori education researcher Graham Smith (cited in Kovach, 2009) believes:

> My view was that we needed to put some Indigenous theory tools or, in a New Zealand sense, Maori tools on the wall of the university alongside of all the other theoretical tools and all the other research methodologies, so that we would have a more effective and wider choice of options.... We also now have our own ways of doing things. It is not an either/or situation, and I think this is a really important point to emphasize. (pp. 88–89)

Cross-cultural relationships can cultivate ethical possibilities that foster collaborative research in support of the aspirations of Indigenous communities. These research relationships can create ethical space for research negotiations (Johnson & Larsen, 2013), and, as Deborah McGregor (2013) points out, may respectfully "create space for difference among nations, peoples, knowledges, traditions and values" (p. 162). Collaborative research can also be rooted in Indigenous research traditions that are embodied in treaty relationships (Latulippe, 2015; Luby et al., this volume).

Decolonizing research means designing and carrying out research in ways that honour Indigenous knowledges and communities rather than privilege colonizing institutions, such as the academy. As Anishinaabe scholar Kathy Absolon (2011) explains, "our search for knowledge constitutes a search for power" (p. 55). In an Indigenous research paradigm, Indigenous communities, researchers, and research participants, rather than academic "experts," become the final arbiters of the value of the research. As Kovach (2009) explains, centring power in Indigenous communities could mean following community research protocols, convening community advisory committees, and ensuring research participants have control in their relationship with the researcher.

Currently, most research remains so implicated in the process of colonization that the risk of colonizing anew, no matter how good the researcher's intentions, is enormous. Working within a Western paradigm of research can thwart the efforts of Indigenous people to see the world through Indigenous lenses (Kovach, 2009). We are constantly reminded of the ways research has been used against Indigenous people. While decolonizing research is not easy, many Indigenous researchers agree with Anishinaabek scholars Debby Wilson and Jean-Paul Restoule (2010), who state "that it will be worth the journey" (p. 32).

KNOWLEDGE AND KNOWING

As Cree scholar Shawn Wilson (2008) points out, "all knowledge is cultural" (p. 91). Indigenous knowledge is rooted in, congruent with, and respectful of the "beliefs, values, principles, processes and contexts" of the worldview of a particular Indigenous nation (Absolon, 2011, p. 22). Kovach (2009) writes that, according to Indigenous worldviews, there is a responsibility to transmit Indigenous knowledge from one generation to another. Further, "[l]anguage [in this case, Indigenous languages] matters because it holds within it a people's worldview" (Kovach, 2009, p. 59).

Writing from an Anishinaabe worldview, Absolon (2011) describes knowledge as alive and dynamic because it is "earth-centered and harmoniously exists in relationships with Creation" (p. 49). Similarly, Wilson (2008) speaks of ideas as entities, with Spirit, with whom we can form relationships. Indigenous methodologies are also drawn from the land, as Tuck and McKenzie (2015) point out: "Indigenous knowledges emerge and exist within a universe that is relational and responsive" (p. 95). They add, "Reciprocity in Indigenous methodologies takes a different tenor because of its cosmological connotations, concerned with maintaining balance not just between humans, but with energies that connect and thread through all entities in the Universe" (p. 95). Indigenous knowledge is inseparable from the lived experiences of Indigenous people and so is relevant to our day-to-day lives (Wilson, 2008, pp. 100–101). Knowledge is personal.

Knowledge is also political, because knowledge is power. Further, given Indigenous people's "struggle to live and be well in a society that is opposed to our survival as Indigenous people" (Wilson & Restoule, 2010, p. 33), Indigenous research is a tool of resistance (Brown & Strega, 2015).

Knowledge is bigger than we are, something we can uncover only a part of. It was here before we were: "Knowledge is received or gifted from all living things and from the spirit world" (Wilson & Restoule, 2010, p. 33). According to Absolon (2011), coming to knowledge is an open-ended process; it is difficult to predict where we might end up, what we might come to know. Knowledge is also organic, because it "is cyclical and circular and follows the natural laws of Creation" (Absolon, 2011, p. 31). Indigenous knowledges are derived from land and place (Lambert, 2014; Johnson & Larsen, 2013; Tuck & McKenzie, 2015). Indigenous place-based research methods enable interactions, engagement, and reciprocity in knowledge exchange with the natural world. As Vanessa Watts (2013) points out, "Place-Thought is based upon the premise that land is alive and thinking and that humans and non-humans derive agency through the extensions of these thoughts" (p. 21). In this sense, research is not solely the domain of humans; the land, place, and non-humans also generate knowledge.

Indigenous knowledges are holistic and relational, interconnected and interdependent systems that encompass knowledge of the spirit, heart, mind, and body (Absolon, 2011; Cajete, in Kovach, 2009). As we will discuss below, this has profound implications for the analysis and presentation of knowledge collected through research, a process that risks fragmenting and decontextualizing knowledge from the relationships that give it meaning.

WHY SEEK KNOWLEDGE?

Knowledge is not sought purely for the sake of it – it always serves a purpose, not least because for Indigenous people the struggle for sovereignty is ongoing. Given the brutality and scope of colonization, having an Indigenous person seek knowledge of their own nation is, in and of itself, a powerful rationale for conducting research: "Resistance is a subtext to the journey [in search of knowledge]; resistance to being silenced and rendered invisible, insignificant, uncivilized, inhuman, non-existent and inconsequential" (Kovach, 2009, p. 91).

Indigenous knowledges must be reclaimed from the past, privileged in the present, and transmitted to the next generation (Absolon, 2011). However, reclamation is not just about resisting the extermination of Indigenous knowledges; it is about "stop[ping] it from being misused and misunderstood" (Wilson & Restoule, 2010, p. 35). Part of achieving sovereignty is ensuring that research done *about* Indigenous people is done *by* Indigenous people (Absolon, 2011). Knowledge sovereignty means Indigenous people decide why, what, and when knowledge is being sought and the methods being used to seek it. It also means that Indigenous people are valued as the experts, and Indigenous standards are used to judge whether what is learned is really "true" (Wilson, 2008).

There are other important rationales for such research, including helping communities recover from the effects of colonialism (Cardinal, in Wilson, 2008). Knowledge can be healing for the individual who seeks it, as well as for the community on behalf of which they are working. Such healing can also mean improvements in the material conditions of Indigenous communities (Weber-Pillwax, in Wilson, 2008). Seeking knowledge is not a new enterprise for Indigenous peoples. Indigenous peoples have sought knowledge in systematic ways for countless generations (Lambert, 2014). As such, Indigenous research is not just about healing from colonization (a relatively recent focus); it is more about seeking a path forward that supports "a good life" or overall well-being (Bell, 2013).

HOW DO WE SEEK KNOWLEDGE?

How we seek knowledge, our process, our methodology, is just as informed by an Indigenous worldview as our understanding of what knowledge is. An Indigenous methodology goes beyond conventional intellectual ways of seeking knowledge. Connecting with knowledge through experience allows us to encounter it in context (Kovach, 2009). Indigenous knowledges are highly "embodied," as Jay Johnson and Soren Larsen (2013) explain: "This is research that is embodied and performative: it requires us to walk and to dwell. This entails … an attunement to the embodied landscape as a primary way of coming to know ourselves in relation to others" (p. 15).

As Indigenous peoples holding an Indigenous worldview, we experience our inner world – the world of our thoughts, emotions, dreams, visions, and inspirations – just as strongly as the tangible outer world, and through it gain knowledge. The inner world helps balance the community with the self, the rational with the emotional (Absolon, 2011). It is from the inner world that our motivation for seeking knowledge comes, as well as the meaning we make of the knowledges we connect with (Wilson & Restoule, 2010). Acknowledging the role our inner world plays in our search for knowledge is also an "acknowledgement that the researcher brings to the research his or her subjective self" (Wilson, 2008, p. 59).

Knowledge can also be revealed from the spirit world through dreams, visions, prayers, fasts, ceremonies, and other experiences. Mohawk scholar and professor emeritus Marlene Brant Castellano (2000) writes that "revealed knowledge is acquired through dreams, visions, and intuitions that are understood to be spiritual in origin" (p. 24). In this volume, Anishinaabe scholar Nicole Bell explains that spirit "feeds the work the researcher does." Traditional protocols often manifest spiritual knowledges. An example of a traditional protocol for accessing a spiritual route to knowledge is the offering of tobacco (Wilson & Restoule, 2010).

Of all the forms of Indigenous knowledge discussed, spiritual knowledge is the least accepted in the context of Western research, except perhaps as anthropological data (Kovach, 2009). For this reason, and to protect sacred knowledge from being misused, researchers sometimes resist writing about the spiritual channels they use for accessing knowledge (Kovach, 2009). Others, such as Wilson and Restoule (2010), however, believe that acknowledging these sources of knowledge is a matter of respect and humility:

> Sharing my experience of using tobacco ties as a research methodology creates space for the sacred. Allowing space for the sacred ensures that it continues to expand rather than vanish in an environment that does not readily accept or acknowledge the spiritual significance of Aboriginal worldview and ways of knowing. (p. 43)

Knowledge derived from the spiritual world is highly regarded in Indigenous communities, yet it is also highly vulnerable. Should such knowledge be recorded or written down? What happens to it when it is recorded in this way? Does it lose its power? Stemming from the unfortunate history of how such knowledge has been stolen and misused by academic researchers (Geniusz, 2009), there continue to be debates and discussions regarding when, if, and how such knowledge may be shared, and with whom. Ultimately it is up to the knowledge holders and communities to decide on what terms spiritual knowledge will be shared. As such, many are developing their own research and ethical protocols to help protect their knowledge and guide such decisions (Crowshoe, 2005; Martin-Hill & Soucy, 2005).

As Wilson explains in *Research Is Ceremony* (2008), ceremony is central to the process of reducing the distance, or strengthening the relationship, between another and ourselves, or in this case, between ourselves and the knowledge sought (see Bell's discussion of ceremony as a metaphor for Anishinaabe research theory in this volume). Indigenous languages also play a pivotal role in how knowledge is understood. In the Cree language, for example, what is being researched is not referred to as a noun. Rather, you describe how you might use the research. The emphasis is on describing how you interact with or relate to the knowledge (Wilson, 2008). The relationality of Indigenous knowledge to a particular nation, and/or to a particular place, makes it difficult or inadvisable to generalize it to other contexts (Kovach, 2009). Relational accountability, which will be discussed in detail below, protects that which is being researched – person, place, concept, animal, whatever – from being objectified (Wilson, 2008).

Because of the relational nature of Indigenous knowledge, and indeed Indigenous societies, collective processes of seeking knowledge work well, and receiving guidance, especially from Elders, traditional knowledge keepers, and the spirit world, is often important. Research collaboration may be necessary to revitalize knowledges severed and scattered by colonialism. Permission and ongoing consent of the community as a whole must be sought to use cultural knowledge, or to represent the community through research (Kovach, 2009). Indigenous approaches to seeking knowledge build on the good research that has been carried out before, rather than trying to criticize other researchers (Wilson, 2008). This approach encourages relational accountability and acknowledges that we are all situated differently: what makes sense from where you are situated may not make sense from where I am situated. Building upon, rather than breaking down, the work of others still leaves room for making improvements, a lesson conveyed by Elders, as Wilson (2008) explains:

> Elders never used to directly confront someone about a problem, or offer direct advice. Instead, the Elder would tell a story from their own life, about a time when they faced a similar situation, or about the time when their grandmother used to do the same thing. It was up to the listener to piece together a lesson from the story and to apply the pieces where they fit to help in the current problem. (pp. 27–28)

Indigenous researchers have struggled with the way that Western approaches to analysis fail to respect the relational nature of Indigenous knowledge, by taking knowledge out of the context in which it was shared and reducing it into parts so that it can be further manipulated. Kovach (2009) proposes *interpretation* as a method that is more congruent with Indigenous worldviews. She explains that interpretation reflects the subjectivity of the researcher and the research participants, and eventually of the audience to whom the interpretation is communicated, rather than pretending at objectivity. Research subjectivity is made explicit in Indigenous research, whereas Western research approaches are often positioned as neutral and objective, and thus more valid. Owning one's subjectivity in research is critical in decolonizing research, especially for Western academically trained scholars who tend to privilege Western-produced knowledge over Indigenous knowledges.

RESEARCH AS RELATIONSHIP

Indigenous research methodologies can be understood as processes for establishing, strengthening, and coming into closer relationship with knowledge. However, other relationships – between the researcher and their research participants, between the land the research is taking place on and all its inhabitants, among the people who learn or read about the research once it is completed, between the ancestors and future generations – must also be honoured. Wilson (2008) believes that these two sets of relationships, researcher to knowledge and researcher to the rest of the cosmos, are interdependent. This is consistent with trail blazing Blackfoot academic Leroy Little Bear's assertion that "[t]he function of Aboriginal values is to maintain the relationships that hold Creation together" (cited in Absolon, 2011, p. 49). The researcher is nested in concentric circles of relationships. The researcher must consider their relationship with self, with family, with those that provide guidance in carrying out the research, with the research participants, with the broader community, with the ancestors and future generations, with the environment and land, and with the Creator (Suchet-Pearson, Wright, Lloyd, Burarrwanga, & Hodge, 2013). Because researchers are constituted by their relationships, and their research is the relationship between themselves and the knowledge they are seeking, a researcher must begin by exploring their own location and subjectivities. Learning something of the researcher's personal story may help research participants decide what to share of their own stories, and how to share them (Kovach, 2009, p. 98). As discussed above, knowing the researcher's location allows others to assess the researcher's credibility, and thus the validity of the research. It also makes the researcher conscious of their biases (Kovach, 2009). In this sense, the researcher becomes "knowable" to research participants, thus disrupting the power dynamics inherent in conventional Western research relationships. Locating oneself may involve identifying one's own nation, culture, clan, land, and historical and personal experiences (Absolon, 2011). What usually emerges from locating oneself is an understanding of one's reasons for undertaking the research (Absolon, 2011). Further, self-location is not a one-time act. The process of doing research changes us, as well as the world around us (Wilson, 2008).

Once we understand ourselves in relation, it is possible to carry out research that is true to ourselves. Wilson (2008) talks about the importance of having your own voice in the research, and Absolon (2011) concurs, writing that "I want my words to reflect my way of thinking, being and doing" (p. 15). An extension of this congruency is ensuring the same values inform one's research as inform one's day-to-day life (Kovach, 2009).

From self, one moves to the next level of the concentric circle, which is family. In his book, Wilson (2008) devotes significant attention to the generations that came before (his parents) and after him (his children), and traces how his identity as a Cree man and a Cree researcher is constituted by those relationships. Family relations can also serve as a network through which the researcher connects to those people in the community with whom they need to speak in order to carry out the research (Weber-Pillwax, in Wilson, 2008). Wilson (2008) also mentions that connecting to potential research participants through family members and other intermediaries gives research participants the opportunity to decline participating without having to directly turn down a request. As with self, families have also been colonized. In the process of carrying out her research, Kovach, who was adopted into a white family as a child, furthered her journey to reclaim her Cree-Saulteaux relations. Kovach's (2009) research journey led her back to her traditional territory.

Moving outwards from family, there is community, and within that community there are Elders and traditional knowledge keepers who have expertise in cultural knowledge and ways to access spiritual knowledge. While some researchers, like Wilson and Restoule (2010) engage with Elders as research participants, learning from Elders can be viewed as a critical component of an Indigenous research methodology no matter what the topic (Simpson, 2000).

Research also brings one into relationships through time and space and between material and spiritual worlds. As Nuu-chah-nulth scholar Richard Atleo (2004) describes, the petition that must be made between material and spiritual worlds is embodied in the term *oosumich*. Across time, we have a responsibility to the ancestors and future generations (Absolon, 2011). Tobacco can be used to communicate intentions to the ancestors about the research (Wilson & Restoule, 2010). As Anishinaabeg scholars Deborah McGregor and Sylvia Plain (2014) observe:

> Our teachers in the Anishinaabe tradition include non-human forms such as animals, trees, waters, rocks, etc. They are our relatives and we continue to learn and seek guidance from them as we always have. Recognizing our relatives as a source of knowledge forms an integral aspect of our theoretical

foundation. This means our knowledge is rooted in the Earth and the place we come from: where our ancestors are. (p. 111)

As the above quote connotes, relationships in Indigenous research extend beyond human agents to include all beings, what Western science would call "living" and "non-living." Relational accountability includes literally all relations. Sandra Suchet-Pearson and colleagues (2013) observe that "these relations include not only human relations but limitless 'nonhuman' entities, what are usually described in Western contexts as the elements, animals, trees, landscapes and so on" (p. 33). Haudenosaunee/Anishinaabe scholar Vanessa Watts (2013) adds, "When thinking about agency with reference to Place-Thought, where can it be located? I find it in animals, in humans, in plants, in rocks, etc. How did I come to think that these different entities and beings had agency in the first place? From stories/histories" (p. 25). Research, then, is not strictly a human endeavour. Just as a researcher is accountable to their research participants and community, so they have responsibilities toward the land and all our relations (Wilson, 2008).

THE OTHER Rs OF INDIGENOUS RESEARCH: RESPECT, RESPONSIBILITY, RELEVANCE, RECIPROCITY, AND REFUSAL

We enact relational accountability with all these entities, human and non-human, physical and metaphysical, through research. So then how must we behave in these relationships in order to carry out research in a good way? Restoule (2008), following Kirkness and Barnhardt (1991), takes the four Rs of education – respect, responsibility, relevance, and reciprocity – and applies them to doing research, noting that these actions are inscribed within relationships, a fifth "R," just discussed.

Most fundamentally, the researcher must behave with respect in relationships. Respect is one of the Seven Grandfather Teachings of the Anishinaabek and forms a cornerstone principle in ethical research conduct. While the idea of respect exists in many different cultures and contexts, ways of showing respect seem to differ greatly. Showing respect in the context of carrying out research using an Indigenous approach is similar in many ways to showing respect in our day-to-day lives. While a research relationship is different, it is not that different – the normal courtesies of relating to one another still apply. The researcher must not only strive for egalitarian relationships between themselves and their research participants, but also among the research participants (Wilson, 2008). There is also a burden on the researcher to adapt to the research participants' ways of thinking about and doing things, not the other way around (Wilson & Restoule, 2010). This may require extraordinary patience and flexibility on the part of the researcher.

In showing respect, the researcher must express humility. They must ask permission before doing things and ensure everyone participating in the research is doing so voluntarily. The researcher must also show respect to the individuals and communities they work with by acknowledging the source of the information that is shared, and by ensuring an honest representation of *the individuals' and communities'* knowledge. Unless there is a compelling reason not to, acknowledging the people who participated in the research by name is a way of showing respect and gratitude (Wilson, 2008). However, it is not just people whom researchers must respect. Natural laws that govern the way we relate with all of Creation also need to be honoured (Absolon, 2011).

Responsibility in the context of Indigenous research methodologies is about more than taking responsibility as a researcher; it is about taking responsibility as a human being embedded in a network of relationships. Wilson (2008) calls this being accountable to your relations. Relational accountability is not just about the researcher being responsible to a research participant; it holds the family and community of those two people, and all their other relations, accountable for the research being done in a good way. A researcher must take personal responsibility for the knowledge shared through the research, to ensure it is not misused, as well as for the new knowledge that arises through the research, to ensure that it does not lead to any harm: "The new relationship [that comes with bringing a new idea into being] has to respect all of the other relationships around it" (Wilson, 2008, p. 79). Indigenous research is about relationships and responsibilities. As such, research participants also hold responsibilities.

Research must serve a purpose. Relevance to the community is also a critical concern. Ideally, the research is initiated by an Indigenous community who has requested or expressed a need or desire for research. In some cases, concerns that impact Indigenous communities more broadly are the catalyst for including a particular community or members of that community in the research work. Accountability to the broader community as well as to the particular relationships formed in the course of the research project mean that the work, the questions raised, the outcomes, and the process to undertake the research all have to be relevant to the community. Each of these aspects of the research has to be understood by the community members involved as at least indirectly, or ideally directly, having bearing on their lives.

Reciprocity actualizes the principle of serving the community. The researcher feeding back the results of the research to those who contributed, sharing their own story with the research participants (Kovach, 2009, p. 98), or offering tobacco to an Elder (Wilson & Restoule, 2010) are all forms of reciprocity (Absolon, 2011). However, many Indigenous researchers also aim to have their research improve conditions in Indigenous communities (Kovach, 2009). Reciprocity also makes its way into other aspects of the research process. For example, Kovach (2009) reminds us that when we work through relationships, participants choose the researcher as much as the other way around.

Reciprocity is also a way of maintaining balance in research relationships (Kovach, 2009). As Wilson and Restoule (2010) explain, in the context of tobacco offerings, reciprocity is about establishing a mutual relationship. Further, disrespecting the relationship or acting unethically in the context of research invites the reciprocal process of natural justice: "If a person deliberately mistreats other creatures, that action will invoke natural justice: So they will receive similar treatment either to themselves or their descendants … even to seven generations" (Wilson, 2008, p. 107).

Mohawk scholar Audra Simpson's (2007) seminal work on ethnographic refusal points to questions about what communities and participants in research may *refuse* to disclose or share. Refusal represents sovereignty in research: some matters are "more our business than others" (p. 68). Refusal is a principle of Indigenous research that explicitly recognizes that "the goals and aspirations of those we talk to inform the methods and the shape of our theorizing and analysis" (Simpson, 2007, p. 68). Simpson's insights are critical; they directly challenge the image of the "uncooperative" or "uninformed" research participant. Tuck and McKenzie (2015) add that "[r]efusal is a powerful characteristic of Indigenous methods of inquiry, pushing back against the presumed goals of knowledge production, the reach of academe, and ethical practices that protect the institutions instead of individuals and communities" (p. 148). Indigenous methods and practices are original, varied, and seemingly contradictory, yet they fundamentally base their efforts on Indigenous self-determination in research.

OVERVIEW OF INDIGENOUS RESEARCH: THEORIES, PRACTICES, AND RELATIONSHIPS

We are excited by the depth and originality of the chapters presented in this collection by seasoned and emerging scholars alike. Working within the academy and in the community, they describe the varied research journeys they have taken. The chapters are grounded in the concrete research experiences of each contributor. The contributors link their descriptions and reflections on the practice of Indigenous research to the discussions and debates we have outlined above, and also introduce new and important theories and practices. At the beginning of each thematic section we briefly describe the relationships between the chapters that follow. As noted earlier, chapters often connect equally well with a number of themes. Many of the contributors explain how they have created traditionally grounded paradigms for research and how these have led them to incorporate ceremony and traditional protocols into their research. Expectedly, every chapter deals with relationships in some way, including with whom and with what the research needs to be connected in order to be carried out in a good way. This includes identifying the roles and responsibilities for those in relationship, and relational dynamics.

In the first thematic section, "The Research Is the Process: Research Journeys Inside and Out," Karlee Fellner and Amy Parent both use Trickster tales to explore how the research journey is simultaneously a personal journey, one with the potential to reconcile the researcher's personal and professional selves. Fellner weaves together myth and her research journey by employing a half-coyote, half-wolf creature to help escape the cages of colonization and (re)claim her Cree/Métis "relationality." She arrives at voice as her tool for counteracting the silencing of colonization and in particular the erasure of Indigenous ancestry and language. Similarly, Parent uses her "Raven" stories to shed light on the messiness and riddles of research. While on the one hand raising tensions, Raven also intervenes to ensure balance and harmony in the research process. In the other chapter under this theme, Katrina Srigley and Autumn Varley reflect upon how engaging in Indigenous research also requires "unlearning," to effectively decolonize and build ethical and respectful research relationships.

The chapters under "Making Space for Indigenous Research" address head-on the challenges raised by Smith (1999) in *Decolonizing Methodologies*. In her chapter, Shelly Johnson/Mukwa Musayett holds researchers and research institutions to account for continuing to practice unethical research in Indigenous communities. She then draws from both Western and Indigenous traditions to propose codes of ethics and ethical decision-making models that address these persistent colonial practices. Karen Hall and Erin Cusack follow with their experiences of academic institutions and the process of learning to do research as sometimes spaces for decolonization and healing for both Indigenous and non-Indigenous students. Frustrated by the lack of space within colonized institutions of higher education for Indigenous approaches and people, Paul Cormier and Lana Ray reconnect with their communities to undertake research that promotes positive peace. Within a ceremonial space, they elaborate a research design inspired by the structure of an Anishinaabe fast.

Indigenous communities in Canada are as diverse as the research methods they have produced. The third theme, "Communities We Research With," highlights this diversity, showing how Indigenous approaches can be used with urban and non-urban Indigenous communities. Lorrilee McGregor draws on experiences researching with First Nation communities in northern Ontario to arrive at a comprehensive series of recommendations for researchers, ranging from coming to an understanding of the history and contemporary diversity of a particular First Nation, to approaches to partnership and collaboration, to time frames, to food and incentives, to establishing credibility within the community. Given that most Indigenous peoples in Canada live in urban settings, Angela Mashford-Pringle makes the point that it is important to develop approaches to Indigenous research that work well in the city. Her chapter looks at how the City of Toronto's Aboriginal Advisory and Planning Table on Early Childhood Development is using Indigenous research to try to extend the delivery of culturally sensitive and responsive services to the Aboriginal community in a Toronto suburb. She identifies relationship building, and allowing enough time and space for research to unfold meaningfully, as being key to her approach. Darrel Manitowabi and Marion Maar conclude this section by demonstrating how many of McGregor's recommendations can be put into practice. They share their experiences with community-based participatory research (CBPR), a methodology they see as a decolonizing praxis.

All contributors represented in "Our Tools for Research" reflect on how they have drawn on the knowledges and practices of their particular nation to transform research. Nicole Bell employs three analogies – a Nanaboozhoo story, the bundle bag, and the Medicine Wheel – to describe an Anishinaabe research theory and methodology. The first teaches the Anishinaabe researcher about the challenges they may face, the second provides a theoretical framework to carry out the work, while the third charts a path for conducting Anishinaabe research with integrity. In the next chapter, Georgina Martin shares her experiences working with stories in her research on Secwepemc identities. Weaving together the methodologies of Indigenous storywork and narrative inquiry, she opted to co-create research stories with her research participants/collaborators.

Brittany Luby, in collaboration with her students and emerging scholars Rachel Arsenault, Joseph Burke, Michelle Graham, and Toni Valenti, used Treaty #3 as a template to imagine healthier research relationships between non-Indigenous researchers and Indigenous communities, and between Indigenous researchers and the academy. In their chapter, which both documents and demonstrates the use of a sharing circle to do historical research, the process and the product of Indigenous research are almost indistinguishable. Through trial and error, Paige Restoule, Carly Dokis, and Benjamin Kelly also arrived at sharing circles as the most appropriate methodology in their research with Dokis First Nation, research that simultaneously aimed to protect the water and build community capacity. Further, and like Martin, they use stories, not only to collect data, but also to show how their respective positionalities and wider webs of relations led each of them to experience the research in different ways.

In the last section of the collection, Deborah McGregor describes "knowledge sharing" as a process that allows teachers and learners to transmit, create, and receive knowledge as a community within the context of mentoring and apprenticeship-like relationships. Her chapter focuses on her use of this paradigm over a decade of service to First Nation communities on water governance issues. She explains that knowledge must be shared and learned, rather than extracted. Following from this, McGregor must embody this knowledge by enacting or living out what she has learned, integrating it into her very being.

With the help of Trickster, Nicole Penak tells her tale of storytelling with her racialized classmates in a master of social work program, and how they worked together to restore wholeness and connection. She reframes the idea of the research problem as an imbalance or disharmony, in this case an imbalance caused by colonialism, which she sees as inherent to her field of social work. Penak identifies story as an effective methodology for communicating research to readers, one that moves them to action more readily than other methodologies. Heather Howard is similarly interested in research's potential to restore connections. Conducting research in an urban context, Howard points to how relationalism can empower communities and agencies to make healing and decolonization central to transformative research. As Sarah Hunt explains in the context of her work on gendered violence, witnessing is a decolonizing exercise that humanizes, values, and loves women who trade or sell sex, through acknowledging their stories, experiences, and perspectives. As a witness, Hunt argues, the researcher's goal is not to tell her own story or to speak on behalf of others, but to carry out a culturally sanctioned duty, putting her ego or career second.

CLOSING THOUGHTS, AND QUESTIONS ON THE WAYS FORWARD

Our collective storytelling process, which hopefully brings a richness and diversity of experience with Indigenous research to a potentially new or expanded audience, has been exciting and challenging, but it is in its reception by you, our readers, where the journey will be completed. The values and principles of the six Rs we have outlined should guide any research undertaking with(in) Indigenous communities, no matter the researcher's social location and position relative to the community(ies) participating in research. That being said, each of us will follow a different research path depending upon these locations; we will form different relationships with the Indigenous research approaches and with the Indigenous communities with which we connect.

Entering into research is entering into relationship. It is a relationship with others, human and non-human, micro to macro. Through it all, how the researcher conducts themselves in those relationships is critically important; their approach must consider and embody feelings, values, context, process, and outcome. We should strive to *be* good in our relations and to *do* good in our relations. If research is conducted in the same good way, with the same spirit and intent, then we will have done research that meets a high standard of accountability to all our relations.

REFERENCES

Absolon, K. (2010). Indigenous wholistic theory: A knowledge set for practice. *First Peoples Child and Family Review, 5*(2), 74–87.

Absolon, K. E. (2011). *Kaandossiwin: How we come to know.* Halifax, NS: Fernwood Publishing.

Atleo, R. (2004). *Tsawalk: A Nuu-chah-nulth worldview.* Vancouver, BC: UBC Press.

Bell, N. (2013). Anishinabe Bimaadiziwin: Living spiritually with respect, relationship, reciprocity, and responsibility. In A. Kulnieks, D. Longboat, & K. Young (Eds.), *Contemporary studies in environmental and Indigenous pedagogies: A curricula of stories and place* (pp. 89–107). Rotterdam, The Netherlands: Sense Publishers.

Brown, L., & Strega, S. (2015). *Research as resistance: Revisiting critical, Indigenous, and anti-oppressive approaches.* Toronto, ON: Canadian Scholars Press.

Castellano, M. B. (2000). Updating Aboriginal traditions of knowledge. In G. J. S. Dei, B. L. Hall, & D. G. Rosenburg (Eds.), *Indigenous knowledges in global contexts.* Toronto: University of Toronto Press.

Chilisa, B. (2012). *Indigenous research methodologies*. Thousand Oaks, CA: Sage.

Crowshoe, C. (2005). *Sacred ways of life: Traditional knowledge*. Ottawa, ON: National Aboriginal Health Organization. Retrieved from www.naho.ca/documents/fnc/english/2005_traditional_knowledge_toolkit.pdf

Geniusz, W. (2009). *Our knowledge is not primitive: Decolonizing botanical Anishinaabe teaching*. Syracuse, NY: Syracuse University Press.

Graveline, F. J. (2000). Circle as methodology: Enacting an Aboriginal paradigm. *Aboriginal Policy Research Consortium International (APRCI), Paper 293*. Retrieved from http://ir.lib.uwo.ca/aprci/293

Johnson, J., & Larsen, S. (Eds.). (2013). *A deeper sense of place: Stories and journeys of Indigenous-academic collaboration*. Corvallis, OR: Oregon State University Press.

Kirkness, V., & Barnhardt, R. (1991). First Nations and higher education: The four R's – respect, relevance, reciprocity, responsibility. *Journal of American Indian Education, 30*(3), 1–10.

Kovach, M. (2009). *Indigenous methodologies: Characteristics, conversations and contexts*. Toronto, ON: University of Toronto Press.

Lambert, L. (2014). *Research for Indigenous survival: Indigenous research methodologies in the behavioral sciences*. Pablo, MT: Salish Kootenai College Press.

Latulippe, N. (2015). Bridging parallel rows: Epistemic difference and relational accountability in cross-cultural research. *The International Indigenous Policy Journal, 6*(2). Retrieved from http://ir.lib.uwo.ca/iipj/vol6/iss2/7. DOI: 10.18584/iipj.2015.6.2.7.

Martin-Hill, D., & Soucy, D. (2005). Ganono'se'e yo'gwilode': One who is full of knowledge. *Ethical guidelines for Aboriginal research Elders and Healers roundtable*. Hamilton, ON: McMaster University. Retrieved from www.ihrdp.ca/media/docs/lega4e54fe5d0c807-ethical%20guidelines%20for%20aboriginal%20research.pdf

McGregor, D. (2013). Towards a paradigm of Indigenous–non-Indigenous collaboration in geographic research. In J. Johnston & S. Larsen (Eds.), *A deeper sense of place: Stories and journeys of Indigenous-academic collaboration* (pp. 157–178). Corvallis, OR: Oregon State University Press.

McGregor, D., & Plain, S. (2014). Anishinabe research theory and practice: Place based research. In A. Corbiere, M. A. Corbiere, D. McGregor, & C. Migwans (Eds.), *Anishinaabewin niiwin: Four rising winds* (pp. 93–114). M'Chigeeng, ON: Ojibwe Cultural Foundation.

Mertens, D., Cram, F., & Chilisa, D. (Eds.). (2013). *Indigenous pathways into social research*. Walnut Creek, CA: Left Coast Press Inc.

Paradies, Y. (2016). Beyond black and white: Essentialism, hybridity and Indigeneity. In C. Lennox & D. Short (Eds.), *Handbook of Indigenous peoples' rights* (pp. 24–34). London, UK: Routledge.

Restoule, J.-P. (2008). *The five R's of Indigenous research: Relationship, respect, relevance, responsibility, and reciprocity*. Lecture presented at Wise Practices II: Canadian Aboriginal AIDS Network Research and Capacity Building Conference, Toronto, ON.

Rigney, L. (2006). Indigenous Australian views on knowledge production and Indigenist research. In N. I. Goduka & J. E. Kunnie (Eds.), *Indigenous peoples' wisdom and power: Affirming our knowledge through narratives* (pp. 32–50). London, UK: Ashgate Publishing.

Simpson, A. (2007). Ethnographic refusal: Indigeneity, "voice," and colonial citizenship. *Junctures, 9*, 67–80.

Simpson, L. (2000). Anishinaabe ways of knowing. In J. Oakes, R. Riew, S. Koolage, L. Simpson, & N. Schuster (Eds.), *Aboriginal health, identity and resources* (pp. 165–185). Winnipeg, MB: Native Studies Press.

Smith, L. T. (1999). *Decolonizing methodologies: Research and Indigenous peoples.* New York, NY: Zed Books.

Suchet-Pearson, S., Wright, S., Lloyd, K., Burarrwanga, L., & Hodge, P. (2013). Footprints across the beach: Beyond researcher-centered methodologies. In J. Johnson & S. Larsen (Eds.), *A deeper sense of place: Stories and journeys of Indigenous–academic collaboration* (pp. 21–40). Corvallis, OR: Oregon State University Press.

Ten Fingers, K. (2005). Rejecting, revitalizing, and reclaiming: First Nations work to set the direction of research and policy development. *Canadian Journal of Public Health, 96*(1), 61–63.

Tuck, E., & McKenzie, M. (2015). *Place in research: Theory, methodology, and methods.* New York, NY: Routledge.

Walker, P. (2013). Relationship with humans, the spirit world, and the natural world. In D. Mertens, F. Cram, & B. Chilisa (Eds.), *Indigenous pathways into social research* (pp. 299–316). Walnut Creek, CA: Left Coast Press Inc.

Watts, V. (2013). Indigenous Place-Thought and agency amongst humans and non-humans (First Woman and Sky Woman go on a European world tour!). *Decolonization: Indigeneity, Education & Society, 2*(1), 20–34.

Wilson, D. D., & Restoule, J.-P. (2010). Tobacco ties: The relationship of the sacred to research. *Canadian Journal of Native Education, 33*(1), 29–45.

Wilson, S. (2008). *Research is ceremony: Indigenous research methods.* Halifax, NS: Fernwood Publishing.

PART I

THE RESEARCH IS THE PROCESS: RESEARCH JOURNEYS INSIDE AND OUT

The research journey is a personal one, one with the potential to reconcile a researcher's personal and professional selves, their inner and outer worlds even.

Research journeys can be transformative, so it is no surprise that Tricksters who are shape shifters join many of our contributors on their journeys. Tricksters lead us on paths that are circular, or more accurately, spiralling, rather than linear. This can result in an iterative approach to research: learning through doing research, and then going back and revising the research design based on that new knowledge, as many times as necessary. The research route is determined along the way rather than being fixed in stone and then mechanically followed.

Transformations are not just learning processes, they can be unlearning processes. Colonial ways of thinking and doing may need to be unlearned to make room for Indigenous knowledges and respectful relationships.

With all these twists and turns, research journeys can make for great stories. Through their chapters our contributors demonstrate how Indigenous approaches challenge and change how we communicate about research. The voices in the stories, including the voices of the researcher, research participants, and Elders, are real, embodied, and subjective. They are not the imaginary, disembodied, objective voice we are encouraged to emulate in the academy. How do we tell these research stories? In *Circle Works: Transforming Eurocentric Consciousness* (1998), Métis (Cree) scholar Fyre Jean Graveline utilizes poetry, conversation, and various artistic expressions/depictions in her text to give expression to her voice and consciousness. These types of creative expressions assist researchers to find their own voice and subjectivity. They disrupt European narratives, replacing them with "either a more playful or more powerful new narrative style" (Graveline, 1998, p. 41). In this section, researchers generate knowledge that continues to resist and disrupt an academic tradition that "privilege[s an] objective/linear/rational approach to knowing" (Graveline, 1998, p. 17).

In addition to the chapters in this section by Karlee Fellner, Katrina Srigley and Autumn Varley, and Amy Parent, we recommend reading the chapters by Karen Hall and Erin Cusack (Chapter 5); Angela Mashford-Pringle (Chapter 8); Georgina Martin (Chapter 11); Paige Restoule, Carly Dokis, and Benjamin Kelly (Chapter 13); and Nicole Penak (Chapter 15), which also explore the importance of process in Indigenous research.

LEARNING AND REFLECTION QUESTIONS

1. How can Indigenous research help Indigenous researchers regain knowledge of their culture, history, and identity?
2. How do the mediums adopted by the contributors to relate their research journeys meet with your expectations about how research should be communicated? How do they contrast with academic writing styles and ways of communicating about research that you are familiar with?
3. What do Tricksters have to do with research? What do we learn from Tricksters?
4. What do you need to "unlearn" in order to take an Indigenous approach to research? How can unlearning occur?
5. What do those you are communicating with through your research need to know about you? How might that knowledge change how they understand your research?
6. Why is using creative expression (poetry, art, storytelling) to disrupt the dominant forms of sharing research important? What practices do researchers in this collection engage in to broaden the scope of research writing?
7. What challenges have you encountered in research that you have had to deal with on the fly?
8. How does conducting research alter your relationships? For example, with family, friends, colleagues, your community?

REFERENCE

Graveline, F. J. (1998). *Circle works: Transforming Eurocentric consciousness*. Halifax, NS: Fernwood Publishing.

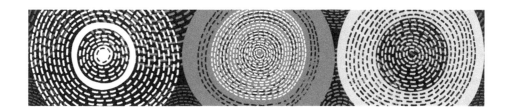

CHAPTER 1

miyo pimâtisiwin: (Re)claiming Voice with Our Original
Instructions

Karlee D. Fellner

Author's Note: Congruent with an oral style of writing, at times I intentionally
remove punctuation between words where it would otherwise stand between
words that I believe ought to flow together, and sometimes use spacing to create
visual/auditory effects.

wayyyyy ya wayyy ya ho way haaaaaaaa
boom   boom   boom   boom

wayyyyy ya wayyy ya ho way aaaaaaaaaaa
boom   boom   boom   boom

wayyyyy ya wayyy ya ho way yahaaaaaaa
boom   boom   boom   boom

my nana and I were picketing a furrier in the downtown eastside   one afternoon
when a young native woman approached us tearfully
"astum   my friend   nistow   go downtown   there is a coyoteperson down there in a
steel cage
she is your sister and she is calling your name"

I wasn't too sure what kind of state my informant was in
but we were getting tired of picketing this rich person's store
and were ready for a crusty bun and some tim horton's soup
so we jumped on the number 22 downtown   got off at west georgia and burrard
actually   to set the record straight   nana had her walker and wasn't jumping anything
and I had sprained my ankle powwow dancing and was wearing a tensor bandage

sure enough   there she was   that incarcerated coyoteperson
in front of the art gallery   she looked sad
the chain-link cage wasn't even big enough for her
to pace back and forth   and there was razor wire around the top

I looked at the coyoteperson   she was not your typical downtown vancouver variety
I knew her kind   âpihtawikosisân   half-breed   coyote father   wolf mother
imagine that   I thought
white with grey markings   bright blue left eye   brown right
I could feel her strong spirit

I felt so deeply for her   I wanted to be with her   to keep her company
I squeezed into the cage with her
initially worried that she would be afraid of me   or bite me   or maybe both
but she seemed at ease when I entered   so was I   being with her filled my heart

I stayed with the coyotewolf in that cage for a few days   getting to know her
I was overjoyed with her   I did not want to leave her   but I knew I had to
so she could be freed   my presence was an enabling mechanism

I climbed the chain-link cage   manoeuvred over the razor wire
eased my way down the other side   my tensor bandage coming unravelled
I looked through the links at her   she told me "you go now my sister   tell the people I
am here"

she said   settler philosophy did not understand that she was not wild
and my freeing her would change things   people would see this was not okay
others would be freed from their cages

For centuries, settlers have been building cages and fences – tobacco sugar cane cotton plantations reserves residential schools Indian status scientific paradigms mental disorders Western methodology the beat goes on. The English language is yet another cage, privileging Western Eurosettler ways of knowing. These cages are so pervasive that it seems impossible to avoid them or find a way out of them. They are clichés – the default position of colonial knowings. On making our way out of one cage, we find ourselves in another. So what are we to do? The caged coyotewolf has shown me that we have to know our original instructions,[1] those instructions that teach us *miyo pimâtisiwin*.[2]

coyotewolf smiles   narrows her eyes   "spirit"   she whispers   her warm breath in my ear
the wind carrying her song   inside me   rustling leaves   rippling water
the shadow of an eagle   kihew   passing across the sun of my dreams
lands on the razor wire   wearing oven mitts
"hey my friend   what are you doing here with my coyotewolf sister
*   you're not from around here"*

"I am pleased to see you healthy my friend   kihew   I was hoping to see you here
čaŋté hówašte wíŋyaŋ   pwâtimowin nitisiyihkason
alberta   ohci niya   I have come to learn"

My spirit name is *miyotehiskwew*.[3] My English name is Karlee Fellner. I am Cree/Métis from central Alberta, where vast fields of wheat barley canola stretch to the ends of the earth beneath a vibrant blue sky. At the time of writing this chapter, I was living as a visitor on Coast Salish territories, where I was completing a PhD program in counselling psychology at the University of British Columbia (UBC). My mother's mother, Nana, is Cree, Métis, Polish, and Norwegian; my mother's father, Poppa, is Swedish. My father's mother was Czech and Hungarian from the former Czechoslovakia, while his father is German and Austrian. I was born on a frosty January morning *kisê-pîsim*[4] in Camrose, Alberta, and raised in the small town of Devon, which rests on the banks of the North Saskatchewan River – about an hour's drive northwest of where *nohkom*[5] Elizabeth Jane Pruden's Métis Scrip was issued near Round Hill. I grew up with a vague sense of my Indigenous ancestry, stories that were tucked beneath my family's dominating narrative of Scandinavian and central European farmers. Despite growing up around my peoples' traditional territories, I was raised with very little knowledge of or connection with my Indigenous cultures or languages. Ironically, it was during my time as a doctoral student, visiting Coast Salish territories, that I began (re)learning my family history and ancestries and found myself on a journey of re connecting in-relation.

coyote was frolicking in the park   digging in the dirt
pouncing on rabbits   letting them go

"hey!"   a booming voice echoed from the bush   "ehhh!"
coyote looked around   a big grizzly mistahaya lumbered out of the trees
"there's somethin funny about you   coyote"   mistahaya sniffed at coyote suspiciously
"oh yeah"   she asked   her eyes darted back and forth
she was apprehensive   she could feel something coming   shifting   transforming

"those others might not see it   but I do"   mistahaya's voice rrrrrrumbbbbbled
"mmm hmmmmmmmmmm"   coyote averted her eyes   ohhh boy
"look at that thick fur coat   bushy tail   those long gangly legs"
mistahaya lumbered   sniffing the air   closer to coyote
she could smell the berries on his breath
"yep   you're a half-breed"   mistahaya grinned at coywolf
patted her on the head   with a paw the size of a frying pan
smiling   humming a grizzly tune   he turned around
and went back to the bush   waddlewaddle   he was gone

now exposed   vulnerable but excited   coywolf ran to a nearby pond
looking at her reflection more carefully
he's right   she thought   all this time I've been acting like a coyote
but I always felt the wolf   always   I knew I was different

she sat quietly   solemnly   at the water's edge   reflecting on mistahaya's insights
she was connecting with the wolf again   there was no turning back

The idea for my doctoral research originated while I was studying for my master's degree in counselling psychology at the University of Alberta. During a project in our multicultural counselling class, I set out to learn how therapists ought to work with clients indigenous to Turtle Island. I had the opportunity to connect with the Aboriginal Student Council (ASC) at the university, attend a seminar held by one of the school's Cree Elders, and attend an Elders' Conference. To this day, I vividly remember the sense of calm spreading through my body as I invited the swirling sage smoke to cleanse me. I entered the Elders' Conference, for the first time exposed to the thunder of the big drum carrying the spirited voices of the singers, bringing the dancers to life. Something awoke inside of me. Through these experiences and my relationships with the students at the ASC, I learned that psychotherapists needed better ways of working with Indigenous clients. The conventional Euro-Western ways we were trained to practice were simply not working. I carried these lessons with me when I went on to do my PhD a couple years later, keen to learn how service providers could better serve Indigenous peoples.

âpakosîs mouse bounded up to coywolf "hey lady! what ya up to"
coywolf's nose was buried in a hole as she dug
âpakosîs could barely hear coywolf's muffled reply "oh ya know just diggin in the dirt"
"what ya lookin for" âpakosîs squeaked
coywolf was so focused on her digging she didn't seem to hear
âpakosîs SQUEAKED LOUDER "I SAAAAAAID what ya lookin for"

coywolf pulled her head from the hole
âpakosîs giggled dirt grass seeds plastic shards paper bits stuck on coywolf's face
coywolf's hair messy matted her brown eye red from some foreign substance
"you look hilarious" âpakosîs giggled "eeehehehehee"
coywolf started giggling "ahhhahaha snorrrrt haha" debris fell from her as her
body shook
"haha yeh I'm sure I DO look hilarious I wanna learn so I've been diggin to find
stuff for days! learned a few things but mosta what's comin up is rubbish" coywolf
motioned to her pile
plastics crumpled receipts metal scraps broken glass a dirty rubber duck with
one eye

âpakosîs giggled "well HECK sis! no wonder! you're not gonna find much in this
tiny cage" she motioned to the cage around them "you gotta get outta here woman!
there's only so much you can learn diggin holes in cages ehhhh and I ain't ever seen
a wolf diggin holes for nothin before"
coywolf looked around blinking her red eye "geez I don't even know how I got in
here"
"yehhhh that's how they get ya distract you with promises of discovery wooo"
âpakosîs rolled her eyes "c'mon you dirtball ehehe let's get you out of here
we'll go see what we can learn in the plains forests rockies ehhhh"

My doctoral studies were the first time I had to think deeply about research. I had worked in a number of research positions, but had never independently designed my own project. Further, none of my previous work had been with Indigenous peoples. Needless to say, I was feeling a bit lost at first. I had a sense of what I was looking for, but had no idea how to look for it. All I knew from conversing with Indigenous friends and colleagues, and from a copy of Shawn Wilson's book *Research Is Ceremony* (2008) that a benevolent professor casually handed me during one of my research positions, was that I had to start with relationship. My doctoral research had started with the relationships formed through my master's project, and needed to continue through cultivating relationships on Coast Salish territories.

When I moved to Vancouver, I immediately connected with the Indigenous community at UBC. I learned that being a good relative begins with knowing whose land I am on and having an understanding of local protocols so as to live in a good way with the people and the other-than-humans of a particular place. Before I speak for myself, I acknowledge the original peoples of the land on which I am speaking (A. Young, personal communication, 2010). Locating myself as a visitor and relative also requires that I situate myself in the context of all my relations. Thus, research with Indigenous peoples necessitates my own understanding of who I am (Absolon & Willett, 2005; Steinhauer, 2001). As I started preparing for my research, I began conversing with my family to learn more about our ancestors and how we came to be where and who we are today.

It was my nana, my maternal grandmother, who spoke with me about our Cree/Métis heritage. As she told me stories of her childhood and her Cree/Métis grandmother, Elizabeth Jane Bruce, née Pruden, who was a traditional midwife, I began to understand my relationships with my ancestors and the land. I realized there had been a fog that had previously clouded my understanding of who I was, where I came from, and where my pull toward Indigenous research came from. As the fog dissipated, I was able to (re)explore the forests, mountains, and prairies that held the wisdom and teachings of my ancestors. Stories from my youth revealed themselves to me as I remembered frolicking in these landscapes, living my original instructions, before the cages of colonization and oppression squeezed them out of my consciousness.

The Western Eurosettler positivist "truth" that was imposed upon me in grade school told me that the spirituality and interconnections with the universe that I felt were not real. I learned that I needed to conform, or I would not succeed in "the world," and would be marginalized as crazy, weird, or some other label denoting inferiority. This "educational homogenization" (Chomsky & Meyer, 2010, p. 46) was reinforced through social interactions with peers throughout my childhood, which demonstrated that being "different" came at great personal cost. Over time, I became socialized into quiet passivity and obedience. I internalized the message that my natural inclinations were inferior, not knowing that this oppression was connected to a much larger, collective experience of colonization on Turtle Island, and the associated Eurosettler/ Indigenous dynamics within myself and my relatives intergenerationally, inter-personally, and intrapersonally.

As I learned about *nohkom* and my other ancestors, the landscapes that held my original instructions stretched before me and I was filled with the overwhelming desire to learn what it meant to be Métis and Cree, and to connect with the land, Cree language, ceremony, and all my relatives. By opening myself to "heart knowledge, blood memory, and the voice of the land" (Holmes, 2000, p. 37) through practices such as quiet reflection, medi-tation, ceremony, and dreams, I have learned that my ancestors and spirit helpers have called me to this work. Generations of coyotes wolves coyote-wolves have been caged in my family, and part of my work is helping past, present, and future generations, as they exist in-relation to myself, transcend these cages. As I set out to explore the landscape of my relationality[6] as a Cree/Métis woman, my dissertation research was intimately intertwined with my personal journey of coming to know.

coywolf trotted through the woods   absorbing all that was around her sights sounds smells
âpakosîs had run off to other commitments   coywolf was enjoying peace quiet

suddenly   a presence   rustling in the trees
coywolf slowed   her eyes narrowed as she scanned the environment
a large shadow darted among trees bushes   stealthy   her brother mahihkan   the wolf
he was trying to sneak up and surprise coywolf   but she had good senses

grinning   coywolf crouched low   meandering through the underbrush
she crawled up behind mahihkan   hehe I'll show him   she thought
but mahihkan   having good senses as well   felt her sneaking up behind him

grinning   he quickly ssspun aroundddd   making a funny face   "grrrruhhhhhh!"
but she was not there   "eeeeeeeyahhhhhhhh!!"   her voice cried out   she pounced at
mahihkan from the side   nearly knocking them both over

"ahhhhhhhhh hahahahahahaha   aaaaaaaaaaa hahahaha"
the two friends doubled over   rolling on the ground   laughing
"ahhhhhhhhh hahahahahahaha   aaaaaaaaaaa hahahaha"

"good to see you brother"   coywolf smiled
they wiped the tears from their eyes   catching their breath
"good to see you too"   mahihkan smiled   "I've been looking for someone to sing with
I thought maybe we could   ssssiiiiinnnnnggggg some songs together"
coywolf's face lit up   beaming heart spirit sun shine
"sure! I've never been much of a singer but I'd love to learn"   she smiled

mahihkan began singing   his heart   drum   beating loudly
"wayyyyyyyyyy hayyyyyyyyyyy   hayyyyyyy   hayyyy   hiiiiiiiiiiiiii"
coywolf listened at first   learning
soon her heart   drum   was beating loudly along with mahihkan's   she sang along

wayyyyyyyyy yahhhhhhhh heyyyyyyyyy yahhhhhhhh heyyyyyyyyyy hiiiiiiiiiiiii
yaaaaaaaaaaa
boom   boom   boom   boom   meandering through forests together boom   boom
boom
*   up down   around   the rocky mountains   the vast open plains   with/in*
between
boom   boom   boom   boom   travelling near and far   boom   boom   boom
boom
wayyyyyyyyy yahhhhhhhh heyyyyyyyyy yahhhhhhhh heyyyyyyyyyy hiiiiiiiiiiiii
yaaaaaaaaaaa

sssinging ssssinginggg singinggg   voices   heart drum beats in harmony   balance
coywolf was beaming   heart spirit body mind   shining
"who knew I could sing!"   she happily proclaimed   mahihkan smiled
the beings around her   all her relatives   were happy to hear her
*   no one had heard a voice quite like this one*
*   half coyote   half wolf*
*   all coyote   all wolf*
*   fullbreed*

As I continue my journey of (re)searching and (re)connecting with my relation-ality as an Indigenous person, voice has emerged as central in decolonizing and Indigenizing myself and my work. Voice is key in ending the intergenerational cycles of silencing among my relatives. Silencing can be seen in the oppression of my natural inclinations as a child, as well as in the silencing mechanisms employed by members of dominating society (including university professors) when I have (re)claimed my voice. Silencing is also observed in my relatives' sup-pression of our Indigeneity, which is connected to the silencing of our ancestors, such as *nohkom* Elizabeth Jane, who was not permitted to pass down the Cree language or her traditional teachings. Looking further in my web of relations, this silencing is shared among many peoples indigenous to Turtle Island (and beyond), not to mention other marginalized and oppressed groups.

As Indigenous peoples of Turtle Island, many of our ancestors were forced to be silent for survival in the face of direct assimilationist policies and practices, while others may have been silent out of a desire to protect their children and grandchildren (McNab, 2007; Wilson, 2004). As the blank pages at the begin-ning of Peter Cole's (2006) book represent, "the voices understandings wisdom rights respect and humanity of the first peoples of canada" (p. 7) have been unac-knowledged by the settlers of Turtle Island in dominating discourses. Thus, voice has been critical to my own decolonizing, Indigenizing, and healing through transforming the English language, integrating Cree language, writing outside of dominating academic structures, and singing and drumming.

coywolf was humming   sauntering through the forest
when she came across a large white wall
she kept moving along   suddenly   she was surrounded
left   right   up   down   middle   side   near   far
*   forests of   chain-link fences   white walls   concrete*
occasional   tree shrub greenery   camouflage

"what in the world are these barriers for"   coywolf wondered out loud
"why   that is easy"   a low voice echoed from all directions
coywolf noticed leaves and vines rustling
*   it was ivy   growing up walls   concrete   in among around fences*

"walls fences will help you and your relatives   we've come to show you a better way
of living
they   will help you stay focused organized controlled
not to worry   it's for the better   we're helping you"

"phhhhhhhh! yer a comedian eh" coywolf chuckled "well gotta jet need to continue my search" coywolf looked around she could not see an exit
    "... so how do I get out of here ..."

ivy chuckled "no no you can't just leave
by walking into this place you've agreed to do things our way"
"no thanks I don't even know how I got here in the first place you appeared out of nowhere"
a vine of ivy crawled up coywolf's leg up her chest wrapping slowly around her neck
coywolf was getting annoyed her brow furrowed a deep growl rumbling from her throat

ivy patted her head "shhhhhh there there don't worry about your search we'll teach you everything you need to know we've discovered superior methods forget the rest"
coywolf felt ivy tighten around her throat her voice strained it was getting hard to breathe
quick to think on her feeeet coywolf began singing
wayyyy ya heyyy ya heyyy hiiiiiii yaaaaaa
    boom boom boom boom

her voice vibrated through vines of ivy they struggled to grip her
thud thud thud thud thud thUD THUDTHUDTHUDTHUD
THUNDERRRRRRRR
THUNDERING in the distance getting closer coywolf's sister paskwâwimostos bison was stampeding toward her sporting two fancy new pairs of exotic western boots
kicking up grass dirt unsuspecting insects her bullhide boots stompin toward coywolf
thudthudthudthunderrrrrr thud thud thud thudthudthudthunderrrrrrrr

ivy tried to trip her no avail vines fell to the ground STOMP
paskwâwimostos grunted urrrrrrrrruhhhhhhhhhhh bison song
thundering bullhide boots reverberating voices ivy could not maintain its hold
vines unravelled from coywolf falling to the ground
paskwâwimostos slowed two steppin trottin toward coywolf
ivy retreated nowhere to be seen

coywolf to paskwâwimostos "ehhhhhhh sister!!!" high paw to high hoof-in-boot
"ehhhhhhhhh sis! urrrrrrrrruhhhhhhhhhhhh" paskwâwimostos grunted
"whassup wit these guys anyways ehhhhhhhhhh"
paskwâwimostos stuck out her long tongue
nudging coywolf with her massive head "don't worry about them ehhhhh
they'll try n scare you shut you up piss you off but don't let em get to ya
you got important work to do gotta help your relatives who knows maybe they'll
learn something too ehhhhh meantime you're strong sis keep the faith you
got this"

paskwâwimostos winked a giant eye turned boots jigging off into the distance
inadvertently knocking off wall chunks breaking fence links chipping concrete
coywolf grinned beaming singing loudly jigging behind her friend

wayyyy ya heyyy ya heyyy hiiiiii yaaaaaa
boom boom boom boom

(Re)claiming Indigenous voice in my doctoral work began with articulating and framing my research. Before narrowing down my research question, I wanted to find a paradigm that fit with my intentions to carry out research that was respectful, reciprocal, relevant, and responsible (Kirkness & Barnhardt, 1991). I felt immense pressure within the academy to use an established Eurocentric approach in my research, but the more I delved into the Indigenous research literature, conversed with my friends in the UBC Indigenous community, and connected with my own Indigeneity, the clearer it became that my paradigm needed to be "inherently and wholly Indigenous" (Kovach, 2009, p. 13). Employing an Indigenous paradigm was not only congruent with my journeying self-in-relation, it was also a responsibility in staying accountable to all my relations and using my privilege in the academy to contribute in some way to Indigenous survivance (Alfred, 2004; Vizenor, 2008; Wilson, 2008). I needed to use my voice.

It has not been easy bringing Indigenous knowledges into a discipline based in a scientist-practitioner training model (Jones & Mehr, 2007) that refuses to acknowledge even its own tenets and roots "that are outside the realm of science" (Hergenhahn, 2005, p. 2). As with other disciplines, many scholars in psychology view Indigenous knowledges as non-scientific and primitive, confining them to "conceptual reservations" (Anderson, 2011, p. 96) outside the field's scope. Rather than feeling discouraged, this tension motivates me to stand strong in asserting Indigenous voices and knowledges in my work. "Psychologists, possibly more than members of any other discipline, have sought to impose their own European definition of reality upon the rest of the world" (Howitt & Owusu-Bempah, 1994, p. 3), and have thus continued to perpetuate cycles of psycholonization (Fellner, 2016) and epistemic violence (Duran, 2006; Gone, 2008; McCabe, 2007; Moodley, 2007). Therefore, creating space for Indigenous voices in psychology, and health more broadly, is imperative if we wish to truly work with Indigenous peoples in healing from the impacts of colonial trauma (Duran, 2006; McCabe, 2007). For me, this requires that I create space for my own Indigenous voice within the academy, articulating an Indigenous paradigm that will open pathways to Indigenous knowledges shaping psychological practice (Kovach, 2009; Wilson, 2008).

wayyyyy ya wayyy ya ho way haaaaaaaa
boom   boom   boom   boom

coywolf was   ssssinging   singgggging   singingggg
trotting through the forest   all around her everything was alive
winged ones   whissssstled   chirrrrrrped   saaaaaaang   melodies echoooing through trees
four-leggeds   scurrrrrrying   rustlllllllling   chatttttttting amongst green undergrowth
six-leggeds   eight-leggeds   crawlers   going about their days

coywolf noticing   the pleasant sounds   feelings of her paws
*   padding along the earth   crunccchhhing   leaves   pine needles*
breathing   fresh   clean air   thick with   aromas of plant people
beneath her   her first mother   the earth   breeeathing deeply calmly
father sky   yawwwwwning   stretching above   flickers of blue among canopies of trees
*   grandfather sun reaching through open spaces*
*   laying his warm   gentle   touch on the grateful beings below*

mistahaya   mahihkan   paskwâwimostos   âpakosîs   were teaching coywolf a lot
she was learning how to be a coywolf   living with/in between coyote and wolf worlds
she was learning to sing with her heartbeat   the heartbeat of mother earth
she was learning to sing   howl   stand tall   strong   when the ivy tried to silence her
she was learning to move swiftly   quietly   with/in between   around
*   the walls fences concrete   where ivy resided*

trotting through the forest   all around her everything was alive
coywolf's   heart full   spirit singing   mind calm   body in rhythm with the earth
wayyyyy ya wayyy ya ho way haaaaaaaa
boom   boom   boom   boom

Indigenous knowledges are diverse and dynamic, emerging through individual and collective experiences in-relation to place (Dei, 2011; Kovach, 2009). Speaking from my own location requires that I articulate a *nehiyaw-otipemisiwak*[7] paradigm in-relation to who and where I am at this particular time in my life (Kovach, 2009). Thus, I do not speak for other Indigenous peoples or for others with Cree/Métis ancestry. Rather, I speak from my current lived experience of *nehiyaw-otipemisiwak* epistemologies in the context of my personal and collective histories, and multiple intersecting past, present, and future relationalities. This framework pulls from the diverse teachings I've learned in various places throughout this journey. As a primarily urban-based, mobile Indigenous person, my Elders and cultural mentors have come from many different nations, including *nehiyawak*,[8] Anishinaabe, Métis, Secwepemc, St'at'imc, Sts'Ailes, Dakota, Lakota, Blackfoot, and Cherokee – many of whom have also had Elders and cultural mentors of diverse nations. I can only speak from the teachings I've received, and I do my best to share where I've received them.

I've chosen to call this paradigm *isîhcikêwin*, which is Plains Cree for the way things are done, ceremony, and culture. *isîhcikêwin* describes the way I approach all aspects of my research from my current understanding in-relation to who and where I am right now. It is holistic, relational, and characterized by particular protocols and culturally sanctioned ways of living. For details on this research paradigm and the methods used in my doctoral research, please see my dissertation (Fellner, 2016). Following *isîhcikêwin*, I've taken what fits for me in the teachings I've received and incorporated it into my ways of knowing, being, and doing. These diverse teachings inform my understanding of *isîhcikêwin*, not unlike my ancestors who blended multiple cultures and languages in who they were. And that included a blend of colonial cultures and languages. So, as a *nehiyaw-otipemisiwak* woman of multiple ancestries, who was born and raised into a colonized society, speaking the colonial language and participating in the colonial system, there inevitably is a blend of Western Eurosettler methods in this paradigm as well – for example, recording and transcribing. The important piece is this paradigm is fundamentally centred in Indigenous ways of knowing, being, and doing, as this is who I am. Further, my own conceptualization of a *nehiyaw-otipemisiwak* paradigm will shift and transform as I shift and transform throughout my life. Acknowledging this honours the contextualized, developmental, relational, and dynamic nature of Indigenous epistemologies (Cajete, 2000; Dei, 2011; Lane, Bopp, Bopp, & Brown, 1984).

In articulating *isîhcikêwin* as a research approach, I questioned the word "research" itself. For me, research is learning, and learning is living. My research journey started before my physical birth in this lifetime, and will continue after I am physically gone. Thus, I see my dissertation research as a ceremony embedded in this larger context of generations of "research." For *nehiyawak*, ceremony is our epistemology and methodology (Makokis, 2005), and as such, provides the basis for our axiology and ontology (Wilson, 2008). Working within her Anishinaabe traditions, in Chapter 10 of this book Nicole Bell also explores ceremony in research. Indigenous ceremonies are centred in building stronger relationships and reaffirming life (Cajete, Mohawk, & Valladolid Rivera, 2008; Wilson, 2008), and are about hearing people's voices (Makokis, 2005). Thus, research as ceremony (Wilson, 2008) resonates for me both in terms of my research intentions, as well as in my deepening relationality with/in my self, family, communities, nations, the natural world, and spiritual and ancestral realms.

I experienced my methodology as intertwined with my personal journey of observing, tracking, and tracing with/in the forests, Rocky Mountains, and plains of Alberta, as well as the other places and landscapes I navigated throughout the journey. My dissertation research was a ceremonial quest for understanding. This conceptualization provided the basis for an emergent paradigm that is holistic, relational, and process-oriented (Wilson, 2008). It required that I open my awareness to physical and metaphysical senses, allowing myself to be guided by knowings through spirit heart body mind (Brant Castellano, 2000; Brown, 1983; Lane et al., 1984). *isîhcikêwin* is fundamentally ethical, grounded in *miyo wicehtowin*[9] that necessitates respect, reciprocity, relevance, and responsibility at all times (Kirkness & Barnhardt, 1991; Wilson, 2008). In my work – and life in general – I am accountable to *kahkiyaw ni wahkomâkanak*[10] *kihci manitow*[11] ancestors *âtayôhkanak*[12] Elders mentors family friends colleagues animals plants insects earth water air all of Creation. At this point in my understanding, *miyo pimâtisiwin* includes the original instructions that provide a guiding framework for how I maintain *miyo wicehtowin* (R. Wright, personal communication, 2015).

Before I continue here, it is important for me to emphasize that in writing about *miyo pimâtisiwin*, I speak from my current understandings as a young adult who has only recently begun learning my original instructions. I know very little and have much to learn, and apologize for any mistakes or offences. The understandings I do have come through my relationships with Elders and mentors of many diverse First Nations who live the teachings they've received, and through participating in ceremony and cultural activities, drumming and singing, learning the Cree language, and opening myself to revealed knowledge "acquired through dreams, visions, and intuitions" (Brant Castellano, 2000, p. 24). Committing to *miyo pimâtisiwin* in all aspects of my life is living Indigeneity and self-determination, which is essential in articulating a *nehiyaw-otipemisiwak* paradigm. For me, this means being true to who I am and acknowledging myself as a "four-direction person" (Makokis, 2005, p. 92) within the teachings of the *nehiyaw* Medicine Wheel (for details of the Medicine Wheel as a conceptual framework, see Hart, 2002; Lane et al., 1984; as well as Nicole Bell's chapter in this volume).

miyo pimâtisiwin requires that my topic, question, and methods be grounded in local ethical protocols and community relationships (Deloria Jr., 1991; Smith, 1999; Wilson, 2008). Thus, in developing and carrying out my research, I continuously engaged in conversations with Elders, mentors, and community members in Vancouver, as well as potential *iyinisiwak*.[13] My topic originated in-relation with the Indigenous community in Edmonton, and continued to be supported by Indigenous community members in Vancouver. As I formulated my research question, I spoke openly of my ideas in many contexts, and through people's feedback and stories, came to understand that my topic was relevant and important. In satisfying the requirements of the dominating Eurocentric structures in the academy, I also situated my topic and rationale in the existing literature, which clearly identified a need for culturally appropriate and relevant research addressing mental health services with Indigenous peoples (McCormick, 2009).

I narrowed down the question and methods of this ceremony through conversations with Indigenous academics and colleagues in the community at UBC. Through several relationally based revisions and iterations, I arrived at the question, "How can mental health services (be shaped so as to) better serve Indigenous peoples living in urban spaces?" Similarly, I articulated my methods in-relation, and allowed them to shift as needed throughout the research process. I also drew on the literature of Indigenous scholars and ventured outside of my department to take courses in Indigenous epistemologies and research. Integrating these learnings with the original instructions I was learning in my personal journey helped me articulate my understanding of an Indigenous approach to *kiskeyihtamowin*[14] and *mahtahitowin*[15] that was grounded in the teachings of *miyo pimâtisiwin* and the *nehiyaw* Medicine Wheel (Lee, 2006).

Voice is integral in how I write about my research. For one, language is important. "Our laws, teachings and ways of life are contained in the nuances contained and held within the Cree language" (Makokis, 2005, p. 119), and are thus critical in our survivance and resurgence (Alfred & Corntassel, 2005; Wilson, 2004). Therefore, I am learning *nehiyawewin*[16] and using it in my writing. Given that I have been colonized with English and am just (re)learning *nehiyawewin*, I am only able to use Cree for certain concepts. Writing primarily in English, I am learning to "use it as I need to for my speaking and writing even if it means I must write chaos chance trickster even if it means I must bring words into existence which thencetofore were naught" (Cole, 2006, p. 22). While using English to articulate Indigenous philosophies is contested, it becomes necessary for translation and inter-knowledge sharing (Dei, 2011). Using both languages enables me to converse with/in both worlds, not unlike my Métis ancestors who integrated the languages of their Cree and settler relatives, creating Michif (Métis Nation of Alberta, 2007).

Another important aspect of (re)claiming my voice comes through spirit heart body mind writing. Rather than continuing to privilege mind writing, I am allowing myself to write in alter/native ways that allow communication to flow naturally through my holistic interconnected being – storying dialoguing experiencing. Writing through embodied holism is more accessible than Academese (P. Cole, personal communication, 2011), and engages a greater diversity of readers in myriad ways. Further, spirit heart body mind writing takes a form more congruent with orality and *nehiyaw pimâtisiwin*,[17] and thus is consistent with *isîhcikêwin*.

Finally, I am (re)claiming my voice through traditional singing and drumming. My ancestors and spirit helpers have called me to the drum, helping me (re)embody my voice and create strength in my journey. Singing and drumming are part of my original instructions. As with the Indigenous ceremonies I participate in in the community, the songs are integral throughout my own research ceremony. They guide me in striving for *miyo pimâtisiwin* in all I do.

miyo pimâtisiwin continues to help me (re)claim my voice in a good way. My original instructions enable me to face the challenges of navigating pathways with/in/between/around the dominating Eurocentric structures of the academy as I continue to use *isîhcikêwin* in my work. It is my hope that sharing my personal story of (re)connecting and articulating an Indigenous research paradigm in the university helps those new to Indigenous research consider how they may conceptualize their own approaches. As I continue decolonizing myself and my scholarship, I hope to carry forth the work of those who have come before me in encouraging current and future generations of diverse Indigenous peoples to find, open, and create spaces for their own voices, knowledges, and ways of knowing, being, and doing in the academy.

ay ay   all my relations

nana and I had had our crusty bun n' soup fix for the day
I was limping along   sans tensor bandage   nana had traded in her walker for an
electric scooter with a basket overflowing with knick-knacks   paddywhacks   give a
dog a bone
I had been strategizing how to help my coyotewolf sister
nana and I decided to stop by   georgia and burrard   the chain-link cage

but my coyotewolf sister was nowhere to be found
in her place   some holes   scraps   a dirty rubber duck with one eye
mouse droppings   the odd clump of dark brown hair   caught in the wire
hmmm   that's strange   must've gotten out somehow   I thought
nana patted me on the arm   "beeze   look around"
*   always reminding me to see the bigger picture*

coyotes   wolves   coywolves   walking sauntering jigging strolling prancing two
stepping
eagles   hawks   spiders   mice   snakes
grizzlies   cougars   bison   elk
all sorts   wearing   hats   glasses   crocs   skinny jeans   tie-dye   bullhide boots
milling   among forests of metal and concrete   where plants grow through the cracks
*   and trees and shrubs   camouflage the walls*

turning toward her nana   coywolf grinned   "ehhhh nohkom   let's go chase rabbits"
nohkomcoywolf's   bluebrown eyes lit up
"you bet I may have a few years behind me   but I've still got it"   she winked
nohkomcoywolf stretched dismounting her scooter
the pair headed for a nearby park   ssssinggggginggg   a coywolf tune
*   dancing   a coywolf jig   dancing*

wayyyyy ya wayyy ya ho way haaaaaaaa
boom   boom   boom   boom

wayyyyy ya wayyy ya ho way aaaaaaaaaa
boom   boom   boom   boom

wayyyyy ya wayyy ya ho way yahaaaaaaa
boom   boom   boom   boom

NOTES

1. This term is used by some Indigenous groups to refer to ways of living with the land that we believe have been given to us by the Creator, and include specific ethics, protocols, and practices that maintain good relationships with the human, other-than-human, natural, and spiritual worlds (Nelson, 2008). For specific details of the original instructions that informed this research project, the reader is referred to my dissertation (Fellner, 2016).
2. *miyo pimâtisiwin:* Plains (y) Cree for "living a good life."
3. *miyotehiskwew:* Plains (y) Cree for "Good-Hearted Woman."
4. *kisê-pîsim:* Plains (y) Cree for "Great Moon" (i.e., January).
5. *nohkom:* Plains (y) Cree for "my grandmother."
6. Relationality is used throughout this chapter as an alternative to the term "identity," as I consider myself-in-relation as opposed to an individual independent of all my relations (Cole, personal communication, 2011).
7. *nehiyaw-otipemisiwak:* Plains (y) Cree for "Cree-Métis" (*nehiyaw* – "Cree person"; *otipemisiwak* – "people who rule themselves").
8. *nehiyawak:* Plains (y) Cree for "Cree people."
9. *miyo wicehtowin:* Plains (y) Cree for "good relationships, harmony."
10. *kahkiyaw ni wahkomâkanak:* Plains (y) Cree for "all my relatives."
11. *kihci manitow:* Plains (y) Cree for "great spirit/great mystery/Creator."
12. *âtayôhkanak:* Plains (y) Cree for "spirit beings/powers/animals/guardians."
13. *iyinisiwak:* Plains (y) Cree for "people who are wise" (plural), i.e., knowledge keepers.
14. *kiskeyihtamowin:* Plains (y) Cree for "coming to know," conventionally referred to as data collection and analysis/synthesis.
15. *mahtahitowin:* Plains (y) Cree for "sharing," conventionally referred to as knowledge translation/dissemination.
16. *nehiyawewin:* Plains (y) Cree for "Cree language."
17. *nehiyaw pimâtisiwin:* Plains (y) Cree for "a Cree worldview/Cree way of life."

REFERENCES

Absolon, K., & Willett, C. (2005). Putting ourselves forward: Location in Aboriginal research. In L. Brown & S. Strega (Eds.), *Research as resistance: Critical, Indigenous, and anti-oppressive approaches* (pp. 97–126). Toronto, ON: Canadian Scholars' Press.

Alfred, T. (2004). Warrior scholarship: Seeing the university as a ground of contention. In D. A. Mihesuah & A. C. Wilson (Eds.), *Indigenizing the academy: Transforming scholarship and empowering communities* (pp. 88–99). Lincoln, NE: University of Nebraska Press.

Alfred, T., & Corntassel, J. (2005). Being Indigenous: Resurgences against contemporary colonialism. *Government and Opposition, 40*, 597–614.

Anderson, J. D. (2011). Space, time and unified knowledge: Following the path of Vine Deloria, Jr. In G. J. S. Dei (Ed.), *Indigenous philosophies and critical education* (pp. 92–111). New York, NY: Peter Lang.

Brant Castellano, M. (2000). Updating Aboriginal traditions of knowledge. In G. J. S. Dei, D. Goldin Rosenberg, & B. L. Hall (Eds.), *Indigenous knowledges in global contexts: Multiple readings of our worlds* (pp. 21–36). Toronto, ON: University of Toronto Press.

Brown, T. (1983). *Tom Brown's field guide: Nature observation and tracking.* New York, NY: Berkley Publishing Group.

Cajete, G. (2000). *Native science: Natural laws of interdependence.* Sante Fe, NM: Clear Light.

Cajete, G., Mohawk, J., & Valladolid Rivera, J. (2008). Re-Indigenization defined. In M. K. Nelson (Ed.), *Original instructions: Indigenous teachings for a sustainable future* (pp. 252–264). Rochester, VT: Bear & Company.

Chomsky, N., & Meyer, L. (2010). Resistance and hope: The future of *comunalidad* in a globalized world. In L. Meyer & B. Maldonado Alvarado (Eds.), *New world of Indigenous resistance* (pp. 41–62). San Francisco, CA: City Lights Books.

Cole, P. (2006). *Coyote & raven go canoeing: Coming home to the village.* Montreal, QC: McGill-Queen's University Press.

Dei, G. J. S. (2011). Revisiting the question of the "Indigenous." In G. J. S. Dei (Ed.), *Indigenous philosophies and critical education* (pp. 21–33). New York, NY: Peter Lang.

Deloria Jr., V. (1991). Commentary: Research, redskins, and reality. *American Indian Quarterly, 15*, 457–468.

Duran, E. (2006). *Healing the soul wound: Counseling with American Indians and other native peoples.* New York, NY: Teachers College Press.

Fellner, K. D. (2016). *Returning to our medicines: Decolonizing and Indigenizing mental health services to better serve Indigenous communities in urban spaces* (Unpublished doctoral dissertation). University of British Columbia, Vancouver, BC.

Gone, J. P. (2008). "So I can be like a whiteman": The cultural psychology of space and place in American Indian mental health. *Culture Psychology, 14*, 369–399.

Hart, M. A. (2002). *Seeking mino-pimatisiwin: An Aboriginal approach to helping.* Halifax, NS: Fernwood Publishing.

Hergenhahn, B. R. (2005). *An introduction to the history of psychology* (5th ed.). Belmont, CA: Thomson Wadsworth.

Holmes, L. (2000). Heart knowledge, blood memory, and the voice of the land: Implications of research among Hawaiian Elders. In G. J. S. Dei, D. Goldin Rosenberg, & B. L. Hall (Eds.), *Indigenous knowledges in global contexts: Multiple readings of our worlds* (pp. 37–53). Toronto, ON: University of Toronto Press.

Howitt, D., & Owusu-Bempah, J. (1994). *The racism of psychology: Time for change.* London, UK: Harvester Wheatsheaf.

Jones, J. L., & Mehr, S. L. (2007). Foundations and assumptions of the scientist-practitioner model. *American Behavioral Scientist, 50,* 766–771.

Kirkness, V. J., & Barnhardt, R. (1991). First Nations and higher education: The four Rs – respect, relevance, reciprocity, responsibility. *Journal of American Indian Education, 30,* 1–15.

Kovach, M. (2009). *Indigenous methodologies: Characteristics, conversations, and contexts.* Toronto, ON: University of Toronto Press.

Lane, P., Bopp, M., Bopp, J., & Brown, L. (1984). *The sacred tree.* Surrey, BC: Four Worlds International Institute for Human and Community Development.

Lee, M. (2006). *Cree (nehiyawak) teaching.* Retrieved from www.fourdirectionsteachings.com

Makokis, J. A. (2005). *ehiyaw iskwew kiskinowâtasinahikewina – paminisowin namôya tipeyimisowin: Cree women learning self determination through sacred teachings of the Creator* (Unpublished master's thesis). University of Alberta, Edmonton, AB.

McCabe, G. H. (2007). The healing path: A culture and community-derived Indigenous therapy model. *Psychotherapy: Theory, Research, Practice, Training, 44,* 148–160.

McCormick, R. (2009). Aboriginal approaches to counselling. In L. J. Kirmayer & G. G. Valaskakis (Eds.), *Healing traditions: The mental health of Aboriginal peoples in Canada* (pp. 337–354). Vancouver, BC: UBC Press.

McNab, D. T. (2007). A long journey: Reflections on spirit memory and Métis identities. In U. Lischke & D. T. McNab (Eds.), *The long journey of a forgotten people: Métis identities & family histories* (pp. 21–37). Waterloo, ON: Wilfrid Laurier University Press.

Métis Nation of Alberta. (2007). *Michif – language of the Métis.* Retrieved from www.albertametis.com/MNAHome/MNA-Culture2/Michif.aspx

Moodley, R. (2007). (Re)placing multiculturalism in counselling and psychotherapy. *British Journal of Guidance & Counselling, 35,* 1–22.

Nelson, M. K. (Ed.). (2008). *Original instructions: Indigenous teachings for a sustainable future.* Rochester, VT: Bear & Company.

Smith, L. T. (1999). *Decolonizing methodologies: Research and Indigenous peoples.* London, UK: Zed Books.

Steinhauer, P. (2001). Situating myself in research. *Canadian Journal of Native Education, 25,* 183–187.

Vizenor, G. (2008). Aesthetics of survivance: Literary theory and practice. In G. Vizenor (Ed.), *Survivance: Narratives of native presence* (pp. 1–23). Lincoln, NE: University of Nebraska Press.

Wilson, A. C. (2004). Reclaiming our humanity: Decolonization and the recovery of Indigenous knowledge. In D. A. Mihesuah & A. C. Wilson (Eds.), *Indigenizing the academy: Transforming scholarship and empowering communities* (pp. 69–87). Lincoln, NE: University of Nebraska Press.

Wilson, S. (2008). *Research is ceremony: Indigenous research methods.* Black Point, NS: Fernwood Publishing.

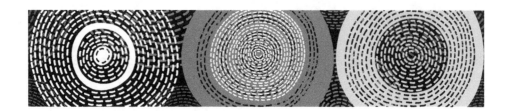

CHAPTER 2

Learning to Unlearn: Building Relationships on
Anishinaabeg Territory

Katrina Srigley and Autumn Varley

INTRODUCTION – IN CEREMONY

One hour before we were set to take the stage to speak at a symposium on
Indigenous education at Nipissing University in March 2016, we sat in the
sacred space with Elder John Sawyer.[1] It was a tradition we had begun earlier
in the year. Prior to speaking engagements, particularly those that might be
stressful, the three of us came together in circle to smudge. In ceremony, we
honoured ourselves, our relationships with one another, and the knowledge we
were set to share. We said *gchi-miigwech* to our ancestors and those who gifted
us knowledge, for the privilege of speaking. We sought balance through conversation and humour. There was a lot of energy in the room that day because
we were about to speak to a large audience, which included the governor general
and an unknown virtual audience.

We were both nervous about the task at hand: we had questions we needed
to ask and concerns we needed to share. Security was everywhere on campus
and we had been briefed about meeting the governor general, but Autumn
wondered, "Do I need to curtsy when we meet? How should he be addressed?"
John calmly reminded Autumn that protocols were important and shared some
thoughts about the customs of the land they were meeting on. John offered her
a *sema* (tobacco) tie and said: "Give this to the governor general and remind him

Figure 2.1: Photograph of John Sawyer, Katrina Srigley, and Autumn Varley at 3MT Competition, Wilfrid Laurier University (April 2016)

Source: 3MT organizers

of the responsibilities and protocols of this territory." Later, while standing in line to meet His Excellency the Right Honourable David Johnston, Autumn held on tightly to the little red tobacco tie. When it was her turn to shake his hand, she offered the *sema* as a welcome to the university and to Nbisiing Anishinaabeg territory. His Excellency graciously accepted the tie and replied warmly: "I am aware of the significance of this gift and I thank you for it."[2] In conversation that morning, Katrina had shared concerns about the request that she, a settler ally, speak about Indigenous education. Why hadn't an Elder such as John, the education director of Nipissing First Nation, or one of her Indigenous colleagues been asked? Wasn't the act of taking the stage to fill the space with her voice at the heart of the problem of education for Indigenous peoples – that privileged white people speak, and Western educational systems teach, and nothing changes?[3] Should she refuse? John shook his head and offered the following to both of us: "You are here for a reason. You have important knowledge to share that we need, all of us. This is an opportunity to do that and it is essential that you do what you do so well, speak honestly and clearly with an open heart. Tell people what you know."

We took John's direction to heart that day, as we do in this chapter. Here we share our stories with you, the reader. In the Anishinaabeg ways of our teachers, we encourage you to pick up what you need to establish relationships, build understanding, and if necessary, "unlearn to learn" on your own educational journeys[4] (Beaucage; Sawyer; Wilson, 2008, pp. 27–28). This might include thinking about your experiences of teaching and learning: Where do we find knowledge? How is knowledge shared? What ethics govern the choices we make in our search for understanding? What do you need to unlearn to learn? Ultimately, our intention is to contribute to Indigenist research by showing how our teaching and learning journeys provided us with answers to these questions.

As we have been taught, we will start by introducing ourselves to give context for the knowledge we share, placing it in relationship with our ancestors, families, teachers, and the territories on which we live. *Aaniin Boozhoo.* Katrina Srigley *ndizhnikaaz. Zhaaganaashkwe ndaaw. Doonjibaa* Mississauga Anishinaabeg territory. *Nbisiing Anishinaabeg Doondaa.* I am thankful to Elder Grandmothers Virginia Goulais and Evelyn McLeod for teaching me how to introduce myself in the Nbisiing Anishinaabeg dialect of Anishinaabemowin. My ancestors are settlers to Turtle Island (the name many Anishinaabeg give North America). From the 18th century onward, they arrived from western Europe and settled in the Toronto area. In 2005, I moved to North Bay to work as an historian at Nipissing University. I am grateful to live on this beautiful territory.

Aaniin Boozhoo. Nongokwe ndizhnikaaz. Anishinaabekwe ndaaw. Kitigan Zibi Anishinabeg doonjibaa. Lafontaine *doondaa.* I am thankful to be able to introduce myself in a good way, acknowledging the many teachers who have been helping me learn Anishinaabemowin. My family comes from Kitigan Zibi Anishinabeg, an Algonquin community in Quebec. I was raised on the shores of southern Georgian Bay in a small community named Lafontaine. In 2013, I decided to make North Bay my home. I am grateful to have built community and learned many important lessons throughout my time on Nbisiing territory.

The process that brought us to ceremony and the Nipissing stage on that March morning, our unlearning and learning journeys, is the subject of this chapter. Autumn was part way through her MA in history, which Katrina was supervising. She was exploring the intergenerational impact of the child welfare system on identity and healing. Katrina was on sabbatical and working in relationship with Glenna Beaucage (culture and heritage manager, Nipissing First Nation) to learn about, document, and share the history of the territory from the perspective of its people. Our choice to begin our day in the sacred space speaks to our relationships with one another and the Anishinaabe worldviews, ceremonies, knowledges, and methodologies that had become central to our post-secondary experiences as teachers and learners. We had both learned and unlearned a great deal, but even when you are well prepared, it is not easy to speak *debwewin* (with truth from the heart) in a large auditorium with your words live streamed, Twitter feeds open, and the governor general in the first row.[5]

LEARNING TO UNLEARN

I (Autumn) arrived on Nbisiing Anishinaabeg territory in the fall of 2013 to begin my third year of my undergraduate degree in history. I spent my first two years at the University of Ottawa. This was the beginning of my relationship with Nipissing University and the territory on which it sits. When I was selecting a university in high school, I did not consider how well an institution supports its Indigenous students. With time, I realized this was essential to a meaningful education for me. In the winter of 2012–2013, Idle No More brought Indigenous resistance and voices to the forefront, not only on Parliament Hill, but also in our classrooms. It soon became apparent that Indigenous voices were not welcomed in this way at the university of my choice (The Kino-nda-niimi Collective, 2014).[6] I started to look elsewhere. An old friend suggested that I consider Nipissing University, the place where he had finished his undergraduate degree and had felt supported as an Anishinaabenini (Anishinaabe man). I visited the campus and the Office of Aboriginal Initiatives once and knew that this was where I would continue my learning.

My third year went very well. While I completed my history degree, I made efforts to take as many Indigenous Studies courses as possible. I advanced my learning in many different ways: Through programs offered by the Office of Indigenous Initiatives, I furthered my traditional knowledge while making connections with other Indigenous students and developing relationships with the land, community leaders, and Elders. In my history courses, I improved my writing skills, honed my analytical and critical mind, and learned how to craft a successful paper.

Things were going well, both in my academic journey and in my personal growth as an Anishinaabekwe; however, the learning I was doing in various spaces and with different people existed in separate spheres and not in relationship. There was a significant disconnect between the teachings I received from Elders, community members, and other students, and those I received from professors. I could not identify it clearly then, but I now realize I had some unlearning and learning to do. In the final year of my undergraduate degree I met Dr. Katrina Srigley and began to learn that many teachings could be part of my educational journey inside and outside the classroom. With the encouragement of a few professors, I applied for graduate school.

When I (Katrina) moved to Nbisiing Anishinaabeg territory in 2005, I had 25 years of educational experience and four university degrees to hang on my wall. Clearly, the mainstream educational system had worked well for me, which is not particularly surprising for a settler child raised by teachers.[7] I had a variety of skills to share in research, writing, teaching, and, through feminist oral history, listening to individual and collective stories in order to restory the past (Srigley, 2010). Unsurprisingly, I brought these interests to my new home, as well as my desire to do deeply local history, to "dig where I was standing" (Olson & Shopes, 1991, p. 202). Yet, when I started to look for ways to use these skills to listen to the stories of Anishinaabekwe on Nbisiing Anishinaabeg territory, I had little success. In fact, my PhD was more of a liability than an asset (Srigley & Sutherland, 2018). This was the beginning of a 12-year process of building relationships to story, people, and territory, which provided me with space to unlearn things I had learned at school, learn about the ways of documenting, sharing, and preserving historical knowledge intrinsic to this territory and its people, and reconnect with my skills and training in ways that allowed me to bring them into relationship in a good way.

My relationship with Claire Clarke is a strong example of my mobilization of feminist oral history methodology and the development of skills that would be relevant to me later on. As this photograph (Figure 2.2) makes clear, we had a close relationship. Establishing meaningful connections with interviewees, connections that create space for sharing and listening to stories in ways that problematize and disrupt power dynamics between interviewers and interviewees, is at the heart of feminist oral history. For a long time now, feminist oral historians have raised questions about relationship in interviews and made self-reflexivity a key aspect of their analysis of memories and interview spaces (Iacovetta, 2000; Sangster, 1994; Yow, 1997). While things have started to change in the last ten or so years, it has been disciplinary historians who have most closely guarded the gates of historical expertise against oral historians (and, of course, "other" ways of doing history), pointing to the bias of relationship and the faulty nature of memory as barriers to the "truth" of the past. One reviewer of my book, *Breadwinning Daughters*, asserted that they were "put off" by the images I included of myself with participants, likening my methodology to the after-effects of a bad meal. Then as now I understand these relationships as an important part of my process of learning about the past, and like all high-quality research, a methodology I acknowledge as part of what I have learned and have to share.

Figure 2.2: Photograph of Katrina Srigley and Claire Clark, Toronto, Ontario (2001)

Source: Personal collection of Katrina Srigley

I formally interviewed Claire five times between 1999 and 2004, but spent countless hours with her, visiting, listening to stories, and scribbling things on little pieces of paper over a nine-year period. Claire was an amazing storyteller and these contexts and moments without a tape recorder taught me how to listen well and build my understanding of her history through our relationship. I wonder now about the greater possibilities of these moments had I understood them as part of my research process and not as off-the-record musings. About once a month, I walked from the university campus to Claire's home at Queen and Bathurst, the place she had lived for most of her life. Along the way, I picked up flowers and the lemon-meringue pie she loved. The last time I saw her it was 2008 and I was pregnant with my first daughter. She was so excited about my expanding belly. Over these years, our relationship developed and was sustained by reciprocity and deep and sustained conversation that taught me a great deal (Beaucage; Benmayor, 1991; Couchie; Cruikshank, 1991; Greenspan, 1998; Sawyer). I now understand my work in relationship with Glenna, John, and many others on Nbisiing Anishinaabeg territory as embedded in the learning I did at graduate school, but I initially saw it as a completely different trajectory. This comes from an epistemological blind spot perpetuated through my learning in the mainstream educational system and my need to put that learning down to unlearn some of its key tenants before I could pick it up again.

When I (Autumn) began graduate school in 2015, I did so because I wanted to learn about my grandmother's experiences in the child welfare system and consider the intergenerational impact of these experiences on my family and my identity as an Anishinaabekwe. I planned to interview my grandmother and other family members for the project. I walked into Katrina's office for the first time in the fall of 2014, while I was still in my fourth year, with the understanding that she was my best resource for oral history at Nipissing University. Together, we worked on the Social Sciences and Humanities Research Council (SSHRC) Joseph-Armand Bombardier Canada Graduate Scholarship and master of arts applications. My first task was to develop a bibliography, so I pulled together sources that reflected what I had learned in my undergraduate history courses. After reviewing the list, Katrina asked, Why not start with the voices and stories of Anishinaabekwe? This question uncovered a world full of Indigenous academics and Anishinaabe voices that had not been visible to me during my undergraduate studies: Kathy Absolon, Kim Anderson, Leanne Simpson, and many others. Katrina encouraged me to listen for histories in multiple places, to drop my assumptions about what constituted legitimate sources for understanding Indigenous women's experiences – novels, plays, poems, visual art, and films brought me to Jackie Traverse and Beatrice Culleton Mosionier. I was beginning to unlearn what I had learned in my courses.

ETHICAL RELATIONSHIPS

Shortly after having been introduced to Indigenous methodologies, I wanted to apply them in an upcoming research paper for my fourth-year seminar with another professor at the university. In the winter of 2014, I came up with a project that would centre Indigenous voices to reflect on Indigenous people's work experiences at Sainte-Marie among the Hurons, a provincially run historic site (Varley, 2014). I wanted to examine the ways in which the portrayal of Indigenous history affected the ways in which visitors interacted with the Indigenous staff. As a previous staff member, I knew from candid conversations with other Indigenous co-workers that there was something to be said about our unique perspectives on how popular and political history shaped our interactions with non-Indigenous visitors. I could count on my prior relationships to be the foundation from which to build these interviews. In accordance with the requirements of Nipissing University's Research Ethics Board (REB), I completed my *Tri-Council Policy Statement: Ethical Conduct for Research Involving Humans* (TCPS 2) test. At the end of December 2015, I was armed with the knowledge of how to conduct interviews ethically and headed home to interview friends, family members, and former colleagues about their experiences working as Indigenous historical interpreters. Keeping with the requirements of my research application, I conducted one interview with each individual. They were no more than an hour in length and were conducted in a space we both agreed upon, generally the participants' homes. All interviews were recorded with my laptop and each interviewee was presented afterwards with a transcript of what they had said. Records of these transcripts and the participant consent forms were to be stored under lock and key in the office of my course instructor for at least five years prior to being destroyed. In the eyes of the TCPS 2 and the REB's requirements, the project fulfilled all aspects of ethical goals.

In the end, my paper, "Selling Ourselves: Indigenous Interpreters at Sainte-Marie among the Hurons," was academically successful. I received a high mark on the final paper for the fourth-year seminar. In addition, I presented it internationally to a receptive and curious audience.[8] For any student, but particularly an undergraduate student, this is a tremendous honour. For those who had participated as interviewees, they remarked that the paper was well written and fairly done. It was not until I had learned to listen to story in other ways, spending time with the resources I had been introduced to in my first meeting with Katrina, that I began to see the flaws in my "successful" paper. When I listened to these first interviews, I could hear the uncertainty and tense responses from both the interviewees and myself. Despite the fact that we were all family members or friends, my list of questions and the recorder changed the nature of our relationship in those contexts. As Lianne Leddy (2010, 2016) has noted in her work, it was as if we could not escape the researcher/researched hierarchies established by the consent form and the ways I was eliciting and listening to story. The conversations were not free flowing. Instead, they were stunted by my questions and the short responses from most participants. In fact, my very first interview only lasted seven minutes. Although I asked approved questions and used sanctioned methods, I managed to hinder trust and negatively impact relationships. Despite my assertion in my own mind and in my paper that I was employing "Indigenous" research methodologies, I wasn't.

At the very heart of Indigenous approaches to knowledge sits the idea of relationships, and the high value placed on relationship building in order to share knowledge. In his work, Shawn Wilson (2008) notes that "concepts or ideas are not as important as the relationships that went into forming them" for understanding (p. 74). It would take me some time to understand that the relationships to stories, people, identities, and ways of knowing that develop through research are more important outcomes than the topic under study. I had relationships with the interviewees prior to our interviews, but the research methodology did not deepen our relationships in any way, or honour Anishinaabeg ways of learning. Rather than truly listening to what my interviewees had to say about the work we had done together at the historical site, they answered *my* questions. I had not yet learned the ethics of listening well in research. I had more unlearning and learning to do.

During the summer of 2015, I (Katrina) sat with Elder John Sawyer in his kitchen. We were having coffee and talking about my work in community on the history of the Nipissing Warriors hockey team and *Gaa Bi Kidwaad Maa Nbisiing*, the stories of Nbisiing (Beaucage & Srigley, n.d.; Srigley with Regan, 2017). In times like these I find space to share, reflect, learn, and strengthen the relationships to people, stories, territory, and spirit that are at the heart of my work. This particular visit, John had something to share with me that acknowledged my research journey. "I have something I want to tell you," said John. "I want you to know that when you first applied to work in community, I was on Council and held the Education portfolio. I rejected your application." I smiled. "You ruined my career." I said teasingly. We laughed. "No," I said. "*Gchi-miigwech.* I wasn't ready. Your decision made possible some of the most meaningful learning of my life."

Ethical and meaningful engagement with Indigenous communities has been at the heart of growing awareness and learning in the academic research community. Chapter 9 of the Truth and Reconciliation Commission of Canada report, first written in 2010 and expanded in 2015, outlines key aspects of that engagement for researchers, including community consultation, cultural awareness, intellectual property rights, and respectful engagement with knowledge holders. This chapter is built from years of experience, listening to and learning from Indigenous peoples and communities. It is shaped by the expertise of Indigenous intellectuals, such as Marlene Brant Castellano, and reflects things that have been said for a very long time by Elders and communities, and documented in the Ownership, Control, Access, and Possession (OCAP) principles and the Royal Commission on Aboriginal Peoples (RCAP).[9]

In 2007, I understood that listening to the stories of Anishinaabekwe and Ininiwiskwew (Cree women) living on Nbisiing Anishinaabeg territory required permission from community, but I was not exactly sure how to go about identifying community for women. I was puzzled by this question, in particular: How do we reconcile the requirement to seek community permission or to engage with communities that no longer are home to many Indigenous women? As I was learning in these years, many of the women whose stories I hoped to listen to and learn from were not from Nipissing First Nation, or had been alienated from community and territory because of status designations under the Indian Act, which determined that they lost status if they married a non-status person (Doerfler, 2015; Lawrence, 2004; Srigley, 2012). It would take relationships and much learning to be able to answer that question and, in the process, flex and push the TCPS. But, at this point, I knew I needed to have community permission. I wrote to then chief Marianna Couchie, and my letter eventually came before Council. As you already know, Council rejected my request to listen to the stories of women on Nbisiing Anishinaabeg territory.

At this time in the early 2000s, more and more research requests from university students and faculty were landing on Chief Couchie's desk. Many of them, like mine, were inspired by the intent to seek community permission, but did not have the relationships and understanding necessary to make meaningful and informed community engagement possible. In writing to the chief, I signalled a lack of understanding of and respect for community governance, akin to writing to the prime minister instead of the minister of Indigenous affairs about Indigenous issues, or, even worse, to this office when you really want to ask about international relations. More importantly, I did not know if there was a need for or interest in this work at Nipissing First Nation (NFN). If I had had relationships in community, I would have learned that a researcher had already spent time on the territory, taken people's stories, never returned, and published representations of women that many found offensive. In 2010, fed up with the flow of requests, Chief Couchie, Laurie Robinson, then executive director of the Office of Indigenous Initiatives at Nipissing University (NU), and the late Dr. John Long began to work on a community engagement plan for researchers at NU.[10] This groundbreaking plan mobilized Chapter 9 on Nbisiing Anishinaabeg territory and became a requirement for any researcher from NU wishing to engage with Indigenous communities or in research likely to impact Indigenous communities or individuals. This development changed the relationship between NU and NFN in positive ways. Through this process and my relationships with Laurie, John L., Marianna, and others, I learned about meaningful community engagement, an important part of my process of unlearning to learn. On Labour Day weekend in 2010, I stood in front of Glenna Beaucage, community historian and then librarian at NFN, with Erin Dokis (Anishinaabekwe, Dokis First Nation) and Lorraine Sutherland (Ininiwiskwew,

Attawapiskat First Nation). We had *sema* and a request – can we have tea to talk about history? Glenna said yes that afternoon. With an open mind, with generosity and a willingness to listen, she gave us her time. We learned from one another, developed a plan, and started to conduct research. As I have spoken and written about elsewhere, this was the beginning of a different kind of research relationship for me, one nurtured and sustained by building trust, honouring reciprocity, and establishing friendship (Srigley & Sutherland, 2018).

As my undergraduate project made clear, I (Autumn) needed to learn more about the ethics of listening well and engaging in Anishinaabe-centred research. Katrina, by this point my supervisor, pushed me to engage even more deeply with literature on Indigenous ways of knowing and learning (Absolon, 2011; Doerfler, Sinclair, & Stark, 2013; Kovach, 2009; Logan McCallum, 2014; Maracle, 2015; Tuhiwai Smith, 1999; Wilson, 2008). In order to learn how to conduct research respectfully in an Anishinaabeg way, I needed to build a relationship with the protocols of sharing and listening in Indigenous research. As Lee Maracle (2015) notes, listening to story is an emotional, mental, physical, and spiritual commitment. To truly listen well, I needed to employ all of my listening skills in these areas. My graduate work not only allowed me to learn about other ways of listening, but also helped me transition and apply my knowledge.

This learning changed the way I approached research. For my major research paper (MRP), I did not bring any questions with me when I sat with people to listen. While I had an idea of what I wanted to talk about, as Elders, storytellers, and family members, it was the individual's decision to set the pace and nature of the story. It is ethical to honour the moments Elders choose and to recognize the story as a gift with obligations through the exchange of *sema*. Over eight months, I wrote down and shared my family's stories. I selected the stories that were passed on as teachings, stories that explained something about our family history. I often spent a few days carefully considering the stories and how best to share them respectfully before utilizing them in my research. Through a review process, my family members read the MRP and approved what I had shared. These are a sample of the ethics of listening that I learned and employed as an Anishinaabekwe. I also employed ethics that are specific to our own family dynamics. I did not change the ways in which I interacted with family members in order to do research. The year before, I had sat down formally and asked questions with a tape recorder. This time, there was no tape recorder and conversations happened on beds while we crafted, in cars as we travelled, in the bush on walks, at pow-wows, over family dinners, and via Facebook or text messages.

While the academy has often challenged Indigenous scholars about our research, our ways of sharing, documenting, and preserving knowledge, calling it unscientific and biased, it is important to remember that Anishinaabeg have their own methodologies (Absolon, 2011; Geniusz, 2009; Kovach, 2009; Leddy, 2010; Simpson, 2011, 2013, 2014; Wilson, 2008). We have listened, learned, recorded, and passed on knowledge in our own ways since time immemorial (Absolon, 2011; Battiste, 2013; Cote-Meek, 2014; Kirkness, 2013). We also have our own research ethics and responsibilities that we expect researchers, both Indigenous and non-Indigenous, to follow. My own research experiences extend discussions about ethics for Indigenous peoples. There is still a need for research councils and institutional policies to understand that relationship building and Anishinaabe ethics are deeply contextual and framed by relationship. For example, NU's Community Engagement Plan requires those who engage in research with Indigenous peoples to engage with the First Nation of those being interviewed.[11] This plan is meant to return the research being generated to the communities, to ensure that communities are aware of the work, and to support relationship development. It also gives community, in this case chief and Council, the power to decide who is permitted to share their story. This specific plan was not helpful for my own research. My family's alienation from Kitigan Zibi territory as a result of the child welfare system meant that it was inappropriate to require approval of chief and Council before I could listen to the stories of my own family members. For our family, community was one another and was situated in southern Georgian Bay, the place we had called home since my grandma arrived in the early 1950s. The meaning of community engagement needed to shift for my work, though I did listen carefully to the importance of acknowledging Kitigan Zibi and our relations there by visiting the territory. In June of 2016, I drove back to Kitigan Zibi Anishinabeg for the first time in almost ten years. I spent time with my grandma's brother, Joe, attended the annual pow-wow, and visited the cemetery to honour my relations. In the future, meaningful engagement with Kitigan Zibi could mean gifting a copy of my research to the community. It did not mean seeking permission to listen to the stories of Anishinaabekwe in my family.

In November 2012, I (Katrina) sat down with John Sawyer and Glenna Beaucage to do my first recorded interview in eight years. We were there to talk about the Nipissing Warriors hockey team. In keeping with the training I had received at university, there were consent forms and I had a digital voice recorder. I would generate a transcript for John and Glenna to review. Unlike in the past, there was ethical and meaningful space for these skills and ways of listening and recording. The understanding and trust in the room was different. We had done this in a few ways. Through my relationships with Nbisiing Anishinaabeg Elders and historians, I had learned how to listen to and learn from stories in ways that honoured their ways of knowing. I did this without recordings, by participating in community and establishing trust. In honouring different ways of listening and learning I disrupted epistemological and methodological hierarchies (Absolon, 2011; Kovach, 2009; McGregor, 2013; Tuhiwai Smith, 1999; Wheeler, 2005; Wilson, 2008). Glenna and I had also established our research plan differently from the way I had been trained. In consultation with community we set research goals, which included writing about and sharing stories of the history of Nbisiing Anishinaabeg on and off the territory. My skills as a feminist oral historian strengthened our ability to do this, but they were not the only way we were going to go about it. This process of unlearning to learn had taken time, it is ongoing, but at this point I understood and could actualize the teaching gifted to me by John that understanding comes from relationships that are deeply contextual. They depend on time and place, the people involved, and the knowledge shared. They are wholistic, including spirit, animals, land, and stories. They are medicine (Absolon, 2011; Anderson, 2011; Simpson, 2011, 2013, 2014; Wheeler, 2005, 2015). Reciprocity is a key element of the success of these relationships and it can come in many forms: a cup of tea prepared the right way, medicines shared appropriately, territorial acknowledgements, listening well, or respect for Anishinaabe ethics. In a one-on-one interview about the Nipissing Warriors hockey team later that year, Elder Larry McLeod extended this teaching. I presented Larry with *sema* and explained our intentions at the outset of the interview. He paused, smiled, and said: "Well now I have to tell you a completely different story!" I had made my understanding of the ceremonial aspects of knowledge exchange and my ethical obligations to that knowledge clear (Doerfler et al., 2013; McLeod; Pitawanakwat, 2013).

CONCLUSION: UNLEARNING TO LEARN

When we sat down on the stage that March morning we had a lot to share about our experiences in Indigenous education. We were set to do so in a good way because of the time we spent together in sacred space that morning and because we had built meaningful relationships and listened well to stories in all their forms. Together we explained: Indigenous education involves all of us; it extends well beyond the walls of our classrooms; it means honouring your own learning journey and who you are, while also building relationships to the ways of gathering and sharing knowledge indigenous to the territory on which you live.

Stó:lō, Anishinaabe, Haudenosaunee, Mi'kmaq, Métis, Innu peoples, and countless others have been learning through relationships since time immemorial. We acknowledge the many Elders, aunties, uncles, and youth, some of whom were sitting in the audience that day, who have long argued that an education system predicated on a single way of knowing continues to do damage to Indigenous, as well as non-Indigenous, peoples. To date, broadly speaking, non-Indigenous peoples have not listened well or unlearned to learn. This extends colonialism and stands in the way of epistemological humility and meaningful education for all Canadians. We, along with other scholars and activists, caution that these are not responsibilities to be taken lightly. As Beth Castle recently noted, researchers have no business getting involved in relationships unless they are prepared to be in them forever.[12] Investing in relationships with Indigenous peoples and communities is an ethical way of doing research and it opens doors to lifelong friendships and commitments. It is thanks to our commitment to ethical research and relationships that our work has been so successful, both professionally and personally. As we continue on our journeys unlearning to learn, we acknowledge that our growth as researchers, friends, and human beings is intrinsically linked to our growth on Anishinaabe territory. The land provided us with the space on which to live, work, and create meaningful relationships.

NOTES

1. We say *gchi-miigwech* to Elder John Sawyer for his guidance. He has reviewed our writing and given consent for us to share the knowledge he has gifted us in this way. While we honour Elders and knowledge keepers as experts by citing them, we do not include dates for the contexts in which we have learned from them. In the Anishinaabeg tradition, our learning is ongoing.

2. For more on Governor General David Johnston's visit to Nipissing University, see: www.nipissingu.ca/about-us/newsroom/Pages/NU-welcomes-Governor-General-of-Canada.aspx. Accessed November 3, 2016.

3. There are many people who have reflected on this issue and the problems with it. This includes government-funded reports: Hawthorne Report, 1967; Royal Commission on Aboriginal Peoples, 1996; Truth and Reconciliation Report, 2015. See also: Battiste (2013); Cote-Meek (2014). We would like to draw attention to the important conversation about white privilege started by Zoe Todd on Twitter: https://twitter.com/search?q=Zoe%20Todd%20white%20privilege&src=typd. Accessed November 3, 2016.

4. While the phrase "unlearning to learn" comes from our own journeys and relationships, we want to acknowledge its use in the wonderful work of Cyndy Baskin (2016) and Sherene Razack (1998).

5. While we have learned a tremendous amount about *debwewin* and stories from the Elders, knowledge keepers, and family members we have worked with, we have also learned from Anderson (2011), Benton-Banai (1988), Cruikshank (1991, 2005), Doerfler et al. (2013), Johnston (1981), Leddy (2010, 2017), Maracle (2015), Simpson (2001, 2004, 2011, 2013, 2014), and Wheeler (2005, 2010, 2015).

6. In January of 2013, there were round dances held in many locations, including the University of Ottawa (uOttawa), as a form of solidarity with the Idle No More movement. Following this demonstration, the University of Ottawa Indigenous and Canadian Studies Students' Association presented a list of five demands essential for the decolonization of the campus to the president of the university. In 2016, the Indigenous Students Association and the Indigenous Law Students Association created both an online petition and a letter to the University of Ottawa Board of Governors that urged the university to commit to reconciliation to uOttawa Indigenous students. The 2016 petition indicates that the University of Ottawa has failed to address the five demands and commit to the decolonization of the campus.

7. I want to acknowledge that my comfort in the educational system also rests in areas that intersect with my settler status, including economic privilege, mental health, my cis identity, and the fact that I did not need to fit my learning strengths into an unwelcoming system. My brother and I share many experiences and spaces in this world, but he had a completely different relationship with the mainstream education system.

8. This paper was presented at the joint Society for American Archaeology and European Association of Archaeology conference entitled "Connecting Continents: Archaeological Perspectives on Slavery, Trade and Colonialism" in Curaçao, November 5–7, 2015.

9. Please see Chapter 9 here: www.pre.ethics.gc.ca/eng/policy-politique/initiatives/tcps2-eptc2/chapter9-chapitre9/; OCAP principles here: http://fnigc.ca/ocap.html; RCAP report here: www.aadnc-aandc.gc.ca/eng/1307458586498/1307458751962. Accessed November 4, 2016.

10. Marianna Couchie recently spoke about this time at a Reconciliation event at Nipissing University: http://live.nipissingu.ca/videos/AI/RBCTLCL.html. Accessed November 10, 2016.

11. Community Engagement Plan: www.nipissingu.ca/departments/aboriginal-initiatives/research/Pages/default.aspx. Accessed November 16, 2016.

12. Elizabeth Castle made this message clear during a talk at the Oral History Association's annual conference in Long Beach, California. She has developed lifelong reciprocal relationships with those she has engaged in research with, such as Madonna Thunder Hawk. We also point to the words of Kim Anderson (2000, 2010, 2011), Winona Wheeler (2005), and Winona LaDuke (2011).

REFERENCES

Elders and Knowledge Keepers

Beaucage, Glenna

Couchie, Marianna

Goulais, Virginia

McLeod, Larry

Sawyer, John

Published Articles and Books

Absolon, K. E. (2011). *Kaandossiwin: How we come to know*. Halifax: Fernwood Publishing.

Anderson, K. (2000). *A recognition of being: Reconstructing Native womanhood*. Toronto: Sumach/ Canadian Scholars' Press.

Anderson, K. (2010). Affirmations of an Indigenous feminist. In C. Suzack, S. Hundorf, J. Perreault, & J. Barman (Eds.), *Indigenous women and feminism: Politics, activism, culture* (pp. 81–91). Vancouver: UBC Press.

Anderson, K. (2011). *Life stages and Native women: Memory, teachings, and story medicine*. Winnipeg: University of Manitoba Press.

Baskin, C. (2016). *Strong Helpers teachings: The value of Indigenous Knowledges in the Helping professions* (2nd ed.). Toronto: Canadian Scholars' Press.

Battiste, M. (2013). *Decolonizing education: Nourishing the learning Spirit*. Saskatoon: Purich Publishing.

Beaucage, G., & Srigley, K. (n.d.). *Gaa-be kidwaad maa Nbisiing:A-kii bemaadzijik, e-niigannwang/The stories of Nbisiing: The land, the people, the future*, under community review.

Benmayor, R. (1991). Testimony, action, research, and empowerment: Puerto Rican women and popular education. In S. B. Gluck & D. Patai (Eds.), *Women's words: The feminist practice of oral history* (pp. 159–174). London: Routledge.

Benton-Banai, E. (1988, 2010). *The Mishomis book: The voice of the Ojibway*. Minneapolis: University of Minnesota Press.

Cote-Meek, S. (2014). *Colonized classrooms: Racism, trauma and resistance in post-secondary education*. Halifax: Fernwood Publishing.

Cruikshank, J. (1991). *Life lived like a story: Life stories of three Yukon Native Elders*. Vancouver: UBC Press.

Cruikshank, J. (2005). *Do glaciers listen? Local knowledge, colonial encounters, and social imagination*. Vancouver: UBC Press.

Doerfler, J. (2015). *Those who belong: Identity, family, blood, and citizenship among the white Earth Anishinaabeg.* Winnipeg: University of Manitoba Press.

Doerfler, J., Sinclair, N. J., & Stark, H. K. (2013). Bagijige: Making an offering. In J. Doerfler, N. J. Sinclair, & H. K. Stark (Eds.), *Centering Anishinaabeg studies: Understanding the world through stories* (pp. xv–xxvii). East Lansing: Michigan State University Press.

Geniusz, W. (2009). *Our knowledge is not primitive: Decolonizing Anishinaabeg botanical teachings.* Syracuse, NY: Syracuse University Press.

Greenspan, H. (1998). *On listening to Holocaust survivors: Recounting and life history.* Westport, CT: Praeger Publishers.

Iacovetta, F. (2000). Post-modern ethnography, historical materialism, and decentering the (male) authorial voice: A feminist conversation. *Histoire Sociale/Social History, 33,* 275–293.

Johnston, B. (1981). *Tales the Elders told: Ojibway legends.* Toronto: Royal Ontario Museum.

Kino-nda-niimi Collective. (2014). *The winter we danced: Voices from the past, the future, and the Idle No More movement.* Winnipeg: ARP Books.

Kirkness, V. (2013). *Creating space: My life and work in Indigenous education.* Winnipeg: University of Manitoba Press.

Kovach, M. (2009). *Indigenous methodologies: Characteristics, conversations and contexts.* Toronto: University of Toronto Press.

LaDuke, W. (2011). Winona LaDuke on Redemption. Sacred Land Film Project. Retrieved from https://www.youtube.com/watch?v=TfD5WaHM04E.

Lawrence, B. (2004). *"Real" Indians and others: Mixed-blood urban Native peoples and Indigenous nationhood.* Vancouver: UBC Press.

Leddy, L. (2010). Interviewing Nookomis and other reflections of an Indigenous historian. *Oral History/Forum d'histoire orale, 30,* 1–18.

Leddy, L. (2016). "Mostly just as a social gathering": Anishinaabe Kwewak and the Indian homemakers' club, 1945–1960. In K. Burnett & G. Read (Eds.), *Aboriginal history: A reader* (pp. 352–363). Oxford: Oxford University Press.

Leddy, L. (2017). Dibaajimowinan as method: Environmental history, Indigenous scholarship, and balancing sources. In J. Thorpe, S. Rutherford, & A. L. Sandberg (Eds.), *Methodological challenges in nature-culture and environmental history research* (pp. 93–104). New York: Routledge.

Logan McCallum, M. J. (2014). *Indigenous women, work, and history, 1940–1980.* Winnipeg: University of Manitoba Press.

Maracle, L. (2015). *Memory serves: Oratories.* Edmonton: NeWest Press.

McGregor, D. (2013). *Nishnaabe research, theory and place-based research.* Nishnaabewin Niiwin, Sault Ste. Marie, March 2013.

Olson, K., & Shopes, L. (1991). Crossing boundaries, building bridges: Doing oral history among working class women and men. In S. B. Gluck & D. Patai (Eds.), *Women's words: The feminist practice of oral history* (pp. 189–204). New York: Routledge.

Pitawanakwat, B. (2013). Anishinaabeg studies: Creative, critical, ethical, and reflexive. In J. Doerfler, N. J. Sinclair, & H. K. Stark (Eds.), *Centering Anishinaabeg studies: Understanding the world through stories* (pp. 363–377). East Lansing: Michigan State University Press.

Razack, S. (1998). *Looking white people in the eye*. Toronto: University of Toronto Press.

Sangster, J. (1994). Telling our stories: Feminist debates and the use of history. *Women's History Review, 3*(1), 5–28.

Simpson, L. (2001). Aboriginal peoples and knowledge: Decolonizing our processes. *The Canadian Journal of Native Studies, 21*(1), 137–148.

Simpson, L. (2004). Anticolonial strategies for the recovery and maintenance of Indigenous knowledge. *American Indian Quarterly, 28*(3/4), 373–384.

Simpson, L. (2011). *Dancing on our Turtle's back: Stories of Nishnaabeg re-creation, resurgence and new emergence*. Winnipeg: ARP Books.

Simpson, L. (2013). *The gift is in the making: Anishinaabeg stories*. Winnipeg: Highwater Press.

Simpson, L. (2014). Land as pedagogy: Nishnaabeg intelligence and rebellious transformation. *Decolonization: Indigeneity, Education & Society, 3*, 1–25.

Srigley, K. (2010). *Breadwinning daughters: Young working women in a Depression-era city, 1929–1939*. Toronto: University of Toronto Press.

Srigley, K. (2012). "I am a proud Anishinaabe Kwe": Issues of identity and status in northern Ontario after Bill C-31. In J. Brownlie & V. Korinek (Eds.), *Finding a way to the heart: Feminist writings on Aboriginal and women's history* (pp. 241–266). Toronto: University of Toronto Press.

Srigley, K. (Director) with E. Regan. (2017). *The Nipissing Warriors*. North Bay, ON: Regan Pictures. Retrieved from https://vimeo.com/154408816

Srigley, K., & Sutherland, L. (2018). Decolonizing, Indigenizing and Biiskaaybiiyang in the field: Our oral history journey. *Oral History Review, 45*(1).

Tuhiwai Smith, L. (1999). *Decolonizing methodologies: Research and Indigenous peoples*. Otago, New Zealand: University of Otago Press.

Varley, A. (2014). Selling ourselves: Indigenous interpreters at Sainte-Marie among the Hurons (Unpublished paper).

Wheeler, W. (2005). Reflections on the social relations of Indigenous oral history. In D. McNab (Ed.), *Walking a tightrope: Aboriginal people and their representations* (pp. 189–214). Waterloo, ON: Wilfred Laurier University Press.

Wheeler, W. (2010). Cree intellectual traditions in history. In A. Finkle, S. Carter, & P. Fortan (Eds.), *The West and beyond: New perspectives on an imagined region* (pp. 47–61). Edmonton: Athabasca University Press.

Wheeler, W. (2015). Narrative wisps of the Ochēkiwi Sipi past: A journey in recovering collective memories. In K. Llewellyn, A. Freund, & N. Reilly (Eds.), *The Canadian oral history reader* (pp. 285–296). Montreal, QC & Kingston, ON: McGill-Queen's University Press.

Wilson, S. (2008). *Research is ceremony: Indigenous research methods*. Halifax: Fernwood Publishing.

Yow, Valerie. (1997). Do I like them too much?: Effects of the oral history interview on the interviewer and vice-versa. *Oral History Review, 24*(1), 55–79.

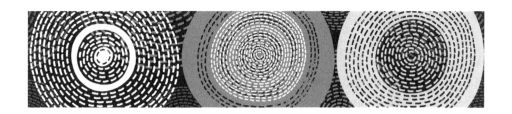

CHAPTER 3

Research Tales with Txeemsim (Raven, the Trickster)

Amy Parent

LOCATION

My traditional name is Nox Ayaa Wilt (translated as "one who is close to her mother"). On my mother's side, I am from the Nisga'a Nation in northwestern British Columbia. I am a member of the McKay family from the House of Ni'isjoohl, and belong to the Ganada (Frog) Clan. On my father's side, I am French and German. I am also a mother to two children (Willow and Max). I have been involved both personally and professionally with the Urban Native Youth Association (UNYA) in East Vancouver over the last 14 years. Most importantly this organization motivated me to do my master's research on the impacts that community-based education has on the lives of Aboriginal youth and to share the important knowledge that I learned from the youth with community members, educators, and policy makers. Since writing this chapter, I have completed my PhD in education at the University of British Columbia (UBC) and am now an assistant professor at Simon Fraser University.

RESEARCH OVERVIEW

This work is drawn from my master's research, which explored the opportunities and challenges of wholistic[1] educational practices provided by non-profit

Aboriginal youth organizations located in Vancouver, British Columbia (Parent, 2011).[2] Through a sharing circle and open-ended interviews with youth and an Elder from these organizations, I sought to understand the role of Indigenous knowledges (IK) and effective practices that support the youth who utilize programs within these organizations. Our conversations revealed that urban Aboriginal youth are finding new ways to explore their Indigeneity and cultural traditions. The youth overwhelmingly state that IK is important in their daily lives and detail the various community processes that facilitate their deeper understanding of this ancient wisdom. The youth also describe how Aboriginal youth organizations are meeting their needs for a wholistic education. These findings suggest future directions for programming planning and development of Aboriginal youth organizations (Parent, 2011).

An Indigenous methodological approach that incorporates a wholistic framework informed the theoretical lens and data-gathering processes for my thesis. I also worked with Verna Kirkness and Ray Barnhardt's (1991) seminal article on the four Rs (respect, responsibility, relevance, and reciprocity), and an additional, fifth "R," relationships, as an ethical code for my research. According to Marsden (2005), the four Rs "are increasingly becoming a vital ethical element to Indigenous research and scholarship" and have been employed by mainstream Canadian regulatory research bodies and numerous Indigenous scholars who are working with Indigenous methodologies (Marker, 2004; Pidgeon, 2008; Wimmer, 2016). Somewhere along the way, a familiar teacher and friend, Txeemsim (Raven), also joined me on my research journey.

MY RESEARCH STORY

As Jo-ann Archibald (1997) reminds us, "our Elders first teach us to understand and appreciate our environment before letting the journey begin" (p. 68). I therefore begin by describing a learning process that highlights some of the methodological considerations and concerns related to being a Nisga'a researcher working in an urban Aboriginal community setting. In doing so, I do not seek to provide all of the answers to the ethical problems and responsibilities of conducting such research; rather I hope to take you (the reader) on my personal journey exploring the educational and community landscapes and relationships of my community and research environment. I hope this research story contributes to the advancement of a transformational pedagogy that is both practical and useful for other sojourners in similar landscapes.

Like Archibald (2008) and Nicole Penak in Chapter 15 of this volume, who write about Coyote, the omnipresent Trickster who travelled with them on their research journeys, I have come to know this Trickster character as Txeemsim. The Trickster character in Aboriginal stories has multiple meanings. Trickster has the ability to shape shift and transform into other beings. According to Archibald (2008), "The English word 'trickster' is a poor one because it cannot portray the diverse range of ideas that First Nations associate with the Trickster … who sometimes is a shape shifter, and who often takes on human characteristics" (p. 5). In my culture Txeemsim (Clemsum) means Trickster, or miracle worker. According to Bert McKay (1993), "Txeemsim displays the best of what humankind should strive for. But he is an approachable demi-god, full of human failings, even as he demonstrates how these failings can be conquered" (cited in Rose, 1993, p. 15). In many of the stories, the Trickster character also teaches us how to create balance and harmony in our lives; in this way Txeemsim demonstrates how I have attempted to create a wholistic research project. Aboriginal stories often have implicit meanings, and Archibald (2008) reminds us that it is up to the learner to find the theories embedded in stories. Thus, I understand Txeemsim as playing with different levels of metaphors, reflexivity, and analysis. I leave it to you to find and create your own meaning from the three tales about Txseemsim that have shaped my research story.

ELDER SELECTION: WHAT KIND OF AN ELDER AM I?

Before I began my study, I consulted with my research supervisor, community members, and the executive directors of the organizations that I worked with to select an Elder to guide my research process. According to Alannah Young (2007):

> In many Indigenous contexts, Elders are considered leaders, consultants and teachers. The collective of Elders in a community are considered the authoritarian body because of their combined expertise and wisdom. Not all old people are Elders as many Elders are the ones who know the protocols associated with cultural teachings and demonstrate them in appropriate ways. (p. 8)

As such, Elders have considerable cultural knowledge and expertise, and are highly respected because of their actions and leadership in a community. Age is not a factor in order for one to become an Elder. Elders become accepted by the community because they are deemed to have good speaking skills, are listened to, and share their cultural knowledge with others (Archibald, 2008; Young, 2007). Archibald (2008) notes, "A researcher who enters a First Nations cultural context with little or no cultural knowledge is viewed as a learner. Entering a teacher/learner relationship requires time and practice of various cultural protocols before teaching and learning can really occur" (p. 38).

My teacher/learner relationship with Jerry Adams began seven years ago when I met him at the Urban Nation Youth Association, where he was both the executive director and a mentor to me. Jerry has spent almost 30 years working and serving the Vancouver urban Aboriginal community in various professional capacities. Jerry and I also come from the same Nation and I felt it was important to work with an Elder from my cultural community for this project. I approached Jerry to guide this study after receiving advice from several people in the urban Aboriginal community that he *should* be asked to begin stepping into a role as an Elder. Jerry is best known for his sense of humour and his care and attention in attending to other people's needs. As Archibald (2008) and Young (2007) have already noted, age is not always a factor in determining who is an Elder. It is here that Txeemsim enters the story. Below is an excerpt from my research journal (February 12, 2009):

> Jerry and I chatted for a bit about our current work projects. After speaking about his work for a while, Jerry asked me how my MA was going. I let him know that was why I had come to visit him, because I had just received my ethics approval for my research. I briefly explained that I would like to do a sharing circle workshop with youth so that I could "give back in my research" by creating an atmosphere where youth could learn more about IK and wholism in their lives. Following the workshop, I would conduct interviews with the youth to determine whether or not Aboriginal youth organizations were meeting their wholistic needs. I then followed up with "and this is why I am really here" with a short giggle. "I am here because I would like you to be my Elder for this research." I presented him with my "Elder Letter of Contact."
>
> Jerry looked at me with a bewildered look and said, "Am I an Elder?" To which I responded, "Yeah, I think you are." It was at this moment that I realized I should have been more sensitive in my approach. I had not thought about the fact that Jerry might not view himself as an Elder yet, since people had only recently told me that he should start being called upon to act as an Elder. I realize now that there was a bit of dissonance between the fact that people should start treating Jerry like an Elder and the fact that Jerry might not consider himself to be an Elder. Oops! Thankfully Jerry humorously responded

by asking me what kind of an Elder he should be, "an old dirty elder" or an "Elder"? I told him maybe we could call him an "Elder in training," to which I garnered a roar of laughter. He quickly followed up again with, "Well, I don't want to be one of those dirty Elders." He then added, "I am only 61," to which I suggested, "That is why we can call you an 'Elder in training.'" To which we both started laughing.

This was the first research lesson I was to receive from Txeemsim. While this implied request could have been considered a transgression, Txeemsim interjected to teach me that I need to be more careful in future requests to "Elders." I am extremely grateful for Jerry's willingness to share his knowledge with me. He has assisted me in developing an enriched awareness about IK and my family (in particular the important role that my mother has assumed as our family matriarch). He has also guided the unfolding of this research story.

CONSENT BY WHOM AND FOR WHOM?

Txeemsim once again peeked her nose out and revealed herself to me one week before the Introduction to Indigenous Knowledge Sharing Circle Workshop that Jerry and I hosted to provide the youth participants the opportunity to co-construct a deeper understanding of IK in their lives. Txeemsim gleefully pranced along my research terrain to demarcate the power differential between me and my research participants, all the while shrieking an ominous warning. These power imbalances have also been noted by Smith (1999), who suggests that a researcher cannot be excused from dealing with power, nor does it excuse them of the responsibility of deciding how to use that power. Rather, it is how the researcher negotiates the process that truly matters, for the lives of the participants and for themselves. I have chosen to outline how I have negotiated some of these power imbalances in the story below.

> I went to one of the youth centres that I partnered with to host an information session to invite youth to participate in my research study. One underaged [under 18 years old] youth in the group, who no longer lived with her parents, wanted to sign her own consent form. In my research journal entry that day, I wrote:
>
> > Mary, the only girl in the group announced, that she didn't have a family and would sign her own form. Thankfully, Andrina (one of the youth workers) suggested that Mary contact her social worker by sending her the form

electronically, or get her aunty to sign it for her. Mary disregarded Andrina and proceeded to sign her own form. I let [Mary] know that I was approaching the signing of the consent forms by the honour system and then grew silent. Mary chose not to hand me her form after this but decided a little later to give me her email address. I approached Andrina in private and asked her how I should speak with Mary if she came to the workshop with a forged document. Andrina told me to send the consent form to Mary electronically and ask her to send it to her social worker. Andrina told me if I did not get an email from her [social worker] or her aunty that I should be firm with Mary because it was "not too difficult" for her to get the document signed. In some cases, Andrina informed [me,] it would be difficult for some youth to get a guardian to sign the form, but not in Mary's case. (March 3, 2009)

Speaking with Andrina was my first strategy in trying to resolve the dilemma. I also went to class and shared this story with my classmates and professor. The class suggested that I try to make an amendment to my ethics application so that I could add an "emancipated youth" consent form. I would have followed this advice but I did not have the time to make an amendment to my ethics application because my sharing circle workshop was scheduled six days later. My final strategy was to send Mary an email and ask her to forward the consent form on to her social worker or have her aunty sign it for her. In the end, Mary did not come to the youth centre on the day of the workshop. None of the other youth who participated in the study were emancipated minors. Nevertheless, this dilemma could have been avoided if I had taken the advice of my research supervisor some months previous and had included an "emancipated minor" consent form in my ethics application.

My concerns with consent forms did not end with Mary, however. I continued to experience a great deal of unease with the process of obtaining consent from the youth. I felt a huge weight and moral responsibility inscribed onto me as I watched the youth sign their consent forms. I felt that some youth signed their consent forms based on a certain level of trust and acceptance of me. For those youth that did not know me, I feel that they may have based this trust on their first impressions of me and the relationships that I had formed with other youth workers whom they knew and trusted. A few of the youth in the information sessions signed their consent forms for the honoraria provided (although none of these youth ended up attending the sharing circle workshop or interviews). None of the youth seemed concerned about their legal rights, or questioned my responsibilities as a researcher.

At the information sessions, most of the youth took a quick glance at the consent form, signed it, and wanted to hand it back to me immediately. It was only after I suggested that they may want to keep the form until the day of the workshop so that they could read it, that some of the youth decided to keep the forms. Some of the youth declined, however, and handed the form back to me without fully reading it.

The youth's apparent nonchalance toward the forms was disconcerting for me. It has made me question what would happen to these youth if another researcher came along with different motivations. Indigenous peoples have a sordid history of having research done *on* them instead of *with* them. Even today, I am not sure if all researchers do the latter. I also question whether a consent form can truly protect research participants if they do not fully recognize the importance of such documents.

Trying to obtain "informed consent" has therefore made me keenly aware of the power imbalances between the participants and myself. If we were to have a truly equal relationship, should the youth not provide me with their own consent forms for me to sign? Or more cynically, shouldn't I have put a disclaimer from Txeemsim on the consent form that said "Warning, the researcher is now signing off on her responsibilities, participate at your own risk". I also wonder how the honoraria I provided signified a power differential. Even though I followed the UBC Ethics Review Board's rules for the provision of honoraria to participants, I felt strong conflicting emotions when some of the youth told me they signed their consent forms because they were interested in the honoraria. Was the provision of honoraria in this situation coercive given that many of the youth would find the Safeway gift cards useful for their day-to-day living and survival? I offered the honoraria as a way to honour and respect the youth for their time and sharing, yet I worried it might not seem this way. I discussed these concerns with Jerry, who told me that the honoraria should be viewed as a way of paying the youth to "witness" the research. In Chapter 7, Lorrilee McGregor also discusses the cultural basis for gift giving in research.

I can't say that I have fully resolved my conflicting emotions over the consent forms, but I did my best to go over the implications of the forms at the beginning of my sharing circle workshop, and I made sure I asked the youth if they had any questions throughout the process. I also outlined my and Jerry's philosophies and responsibilities on a piece of flipchart paper. I placed the youth's rights underneath our responsibilities and invited them to add to the flipchart paper any other items they thought were important. Later, I went over the same information with each of the youth in their individual interviews.

Unfortunately, the tensions I experienced with "free and informed consent" persisted. Upon completion of my master's degree, I partnered with the UNYA Youth Photo Club to create three large photo mural panels to represent Aboriginal youth's perspectives of Indigenous knowledge in Vancouver. The photo club asked my permission to include quotes about IK (borrowed from participants in my thesis) and layer them onto the photo mural panels. This might not seem like a problem according to conventional ethical standards given that the youth had originally agreed on their consent forms that any materials they produced could be used again in future publications. Nevertheless, as Piquemal (2001) states, while

> [f]ree and informed consent is accepted in most circles, what often goes unquestioned is that free and informed consent may have different meanings and implications in cross-cultural situations, particularly when doing research in Native communities. (p. 65)

According to Piquemal's assertions, this meant that I could not conclude with a single piece of paper that consent was given. I have been told by Elders and other members of the community that a piece of paper can easily be burned. I took this to mean that paper means nothing – ongoing consent requires that a researcher follow the five Rs (respect, responsibility, relevance, reciprocity, and relationships). It also hints at the tensions between orality and text. As a result, I felt it was my responsibility as a community member and as an Indigenous researcher to respect participants by asking for their permission a second time to ensure their ongoing consent. All of the youth were happy to have their quotes about the importance of IK in their lives used on the photo murals. Most youth stated "of course" and indicated a desire to move on to another conversation topic.

LEARNING FROM TXEEMSIM'S RIDDLES ABOUT INDIGENOUS KNOWLEDGE

Throughout the research process, the various methods that Jerry and I utilized in working with the youth in this study provided an intergenerational learning experience about IK that was transformative, inspiring, and serendipitous for all. These methods helped the youth to realize that they have a considerable amount of cultural knowledge and wisdom to share with each other. For some youth this experience may have evoked a critical understanding about the contradictions and challenges IK can represent in community and academic contexts.[3] Nevertheless, all of the youth learned or experienced some new knowledge about IK from the sharing circle workshop and activities. Despite many of the pariticipants' positive affirmations about the importance of IK in their lives,[4] Txeemsim revisited me at the end of my research to confront me with unsolvable riddles and lessons (see next section below). Jerry helped me to untangle these riddles after I sought further clarification from him about the importance of IK. In his view, IK was only "somewhat important," and the concept itself was problematic:

> I am old school and feel IK is another term for scholars to study us Indians. If it is to encourage the youth to look at what it means to them yes, if it is only scholastic I would be less inclined to support it. I guess I am somewhat evasive. I don't have a clear answer because I don't know what it means. Sorry kiddo. (personal correspondence, May 25, 2009)

These comments added a layer of complexity to my understanding of IK and allude to implicit tensions in the concept. I was troubled by Jerry's wariness and lack of familiarity about IK (as a concept) and my first reaction was a desire to quell the tension. I wondered if I had not been clear when I let Jerry know why I was going to introduce IK to the youth, and if that was the case, how we had ever put together a sharing circle workshop that taught youth about IK. After I reflected on his comments I responded with the following email:

> Thank you for getting back to me and sharing your thoughts about this "troubling term." One of the things I realize is that I did not share with you, why IK is being used in certain contexts.
>
> IK as a concept has been used by Indigenous scholars to overcome the systemic discrimination that has been created by European knowledge frameworks. It is an articulated vision that is being used by Indigenous people to call attention to the rapid global change that is occurring on their knowledge, lands and languages by dominant knowledge systems. It was also created to share a common language with European systems of thought to discuss the effects of colonization.
>
> I use this term in hopes that one day all learning environments will incorporate its various aspects (experiential learning, storytelling, Elders, songs, stories, land, spiritual knowledge, dreams, intuition, holism) into their curriculum. I feel that these aspects are useful to help Aboriginal youth learn more about their identity and cultural heritage. (personal correspondence, May 26, 2009)

Jerry was unmoved by the systemic reasoning outlined in my email and explained that the purpose of IK was to facilitate a personal process of self-discovery for the learner through the reclamation of traditional teachings:

> You did tell it is my memory bank that gets emptied too quickly. I still think that we are dependent on too many labels throughout history. Yet things seem to recycle themselves again. It is traditional teachings we are talking about which are oral traditions in many cases for our people. I think that if rediscovery of self is the end result like it did in your story then it is good. That in the end your IK was right in front of you through your mother. Self-discovery is not new but just plain old traditional teachings that are happening again for our children and youth.
>
> Good luck Kiddo! (personal correspondence, May 27, 2009)

My correspondence with Jerry did not give me the insights I was hoping to find. Yet, I now realize that without them, my research story would be unbalanced and incomplete. I have therefore outlined the tensions, which the correspondence revealed in the form of Txeemsim Riddles, below:

- IK is difficult to separate from the individual and be codified into a definition.
- Indigenous people have become suspicious of the labels created by European systems of knowledge. Some Indigenous people may be resistant to use new categories and labels to describe their cultural teachings and knowledge (even when they are being used by Indigenous peoples).
- It is hard to capture the meaning of IK in a European format because it is process based and evades categorization. The sources of IK are also often experiential and cannot always be explained through text alone.
- IK is not a uniform concept across all Indigenous peoples; it comprises a diversity of knowledge that is spread among different peoples.

Jerry's input throughout the course of my research taught me that IK can be difficult for an individual to define and codify. As Battiste and Youngblood Henderson (2000) notes, "those who have knowledge use it routinely, perhaps every day, and because of this, it becomes a part of them and unidentifiable except in a personal context" (p. 36). This suggests that IK is often expressed unconsciously rather than intentionally through an individual's actions. As a result, it may be difficult to discern in the words that they use. Further, the comments made by Jerry and several other Indigenous scholars invoke the challenges faced by Indigenous researchers and explain why some Indigenous people are suspicious of research (Kuokkanen, 2007; Lawrence, 2004; Pidgeon, 2008; Smith, 1999). Even though I knew of these tensions at the outset of my research, Txeemsim was certain that I must experience these tensions personally. Indigenous research has only recently been introduced to academia and Western research practices. Western research practices by "outsiders" have put forth negative constructions of Indigenous people, which contain a plethora of debilitating labels (Shields, Bishop, & Mazawi, 2005; Smith, 1999). Therefore, translating IK into Western academic practices poses significant challenges and the language that Indigenous scholars and educators use to describe Indigenous peoples continues to be contested, debated, developed, and refined in academic, political, educational, and community contexts. It is important that these discussions continue.

In striving to understand the meaning of IK I have learned that it needs to be taught within a specific community context at a personal level; otherwise, the concept may alienate learners. IK must remain grounded in specific cultural origins of knowledge and be taught in a way that maintains its spiritual and cultural integrity. Many Indigenous cultures also have their own distinct ways of knowing and it is necessary to acknowledge them in order to facilitate a greater wholistic understanding of the concept. At the same time, I believe it is necessary to address the dominant knowledge system's discrimination against IK; delineating the interconnections between Indigenous knowledge systems throughout the world is one means of actively resisting this discrimination (Battiste & Youngblood Henderson, 2000; Little Bear, 2000; Smith, 1999).

Further, it is salient to note that knowledge can be untidy and unclear. The English language's propensity for linear representation often tidies up that which tends to be messy in verbal and cognitive constructs (Little Bear, 2000; Youngblood Henderson, 2000). Indigenous languages do not put so much value in linear representations. As a result, Western educational institutions' reliance on Western languages and the written word inevitably devalues the experiential learning that is so fundamental to place-based Indigenous knowledge. Researchers and educators (such as myself) therefore struggle to express the components of Indigenous cultural systems that have been sustained through oral traditions and Native languages in modern literary and academic contexts. Translating the nuanced details of gestures, facial expressions, and voice intonations to written text is particularly challenging (Marker, 2003). Working within a Western academic institution therefore requires the researcher to critically analyze ways to represent the meaning of IK with regard to its many sources (including spiritual experiences, dreams, visions, and stories.) This process will clarify appropriate contexts for teaching IK that are of value to the learner.

Despite the emergence of these riddles, it must be emphasized that the youth did not have difficulty integrating IK into their discourse. Although some of them preferred to speak about their specific nation's cultural knowledge, they seemed to recognize the value and importance of using IK as part of a shared vision.

I realize I will not be able to solve all the tensions that I encounter as a researcher and educator. Nevertheless, I am thankful that Txeemsim presented me with her riddles. They need to be communicated and explored so that individuals can make their own meaning out of them. I also appreciate Jerry's comments about "perceived dualisms" because they will help me to address the contradictions that arise from using IK in various contexts. As Battiste and Youngblood Henderson (2000) so aptly states, "IK is a way of living within contexts of flux, paradox and tensions, respecting the pull of dualism and reconciling 'perceived opposing forces'" (p. 42). In other words, I must learn to live in the question and embrace the journey rather than the destination.

CONCLUSION

I had many unexpected moments throughout the research process when Txeemsim swooped down in front of me to caw her cacophonic song. Sometimes Txeemsim's songs were loud and easy to understand, while other times they were cryptic and required more patience and deeper listening for me to hear the message. Despite the dissonance of Txeemsim's songs, none of her messages left me unchanged. These haphazard, funny, and sometimes "troubling" moments significantly influenced my master's research journey. I therefore chose to interweave these moments throughout the body of my thesis and to share them with others wishing to conduct research in Indigenous community contexts. I realize that research done in a "good way" requires one to be transparent about the messiness and riddles encountered throughout the research process. Sharing some of Txeemsim's teachings is my way of describing how I worked with feelings of doubt, familiarity, surprise, and uncertainty through the data gathering and analysis process as I traversed along this research path. Bringing research riddles to light allows them to be seen and explored so that Aboriginal communities and researchers can make their own meaning out of them.

NOTES

1. The spelling of "wholistic" with a "w" is intentional and reflects the interconnections and interrelation-ships that are important components of Indigenous epistemologies. A wholistic understanding of suc-cess ensures that a student's physical, intellectual, emotional, and spiritual needs are met by their schooling and life experiences (Pidgeon, 2008). The concept also emphasizes strong interconnections between students' families and communities throughout their schooling and life experiences. This spelling also ensures there is no confusion with the Western humanistic definition of "holistic."

2. This research was based on my eight years of volunteerism, employment, and personal experience as a visitor and researcher in unceded and overlapping territories of the Musqueam, Squamish, and Tsleil-waututh Nations. Alannah Young (2007) refers to this as the "informal pre- study phase" of Indig-enous research, which is premised on understanding the cultural, social, and historical background of the people and places with whom one is to do one's research. The informal pre-study phase involved discussing the relevance of a research study with the executive directors of Aboriginal community orga-nizations, Aboriginal child and youth advocates, Aboriginal youth workers, Elder Jerry Adams, Aboriginal youth (whom I knew from previous work at UNYA), and my research supervisor to see if there was indeed interest for such research in the community. I then wrote a research proposal for the project. Following the completion of my proposal, I met with the executive directors of four Aboriginal organizations and an Aboriginal child advocate to present my proposal and receive feedback from them. Next, following the advice provided by the executive directors of the Urban Aboriginal Youth Association, I conducted a pilot sharing circle workshop using a structured experience model, as outlined by Charters-Vaught (1999), wherein she states that a structured experience workshop allows the "participant to discover for himself [or herself] the learning being offered by the experiential process" (p. 65). Taking part were seven Aboriginal youth workers and a manager from one of the partner organizations. I incorporated their feedback from the pilot session to prepare a sharing circle workshop template to be used for my MA workshop with youth participants and Jerry. I hosted a pilot interview with an Aboriginal youth worker, who had also participated in the pilot sharing circle workshop that I had previously conducted, to refine my interview skills and learn how to draw meaning from the stories that she shared with me. For further methodological details, please see Parent (2011).

3. For more information about the methodology and findings of the study, please see Parent (2011). Our discussion of Indigenous knowledges with the youth involved the following: (1) Youth were asked to articulate how they would describe their specific Aboriginal culture and knowledge to someone from another planet through a scenario-based small-group question. (2) Next, Jerry and I both discussed how we understood IK from a Nisga'a cultural background. (3) Finally, during a sharing circle, youth were encouraged to express their understandings about IK and wholism that were connected to their Aboriginal cultural background.

4. The youth's perceptions of Indigenous knowledge are discussed in detail in my master's thesis (Parent, 2009).

REFERENCES

Archibald, J. (1997). *Coyote learns to make a storybasket* (Unpublished doctoral dissertation). Simon Fraser University, Vancouver, BC.

Archibald, J. (2008). *Indigenous storywork: Educating the heart, mind, body and spirit*. Vancouver: UBC Press.

Battiste, M., & Youngblood Henderson, J. (2000). *Protecting Indigenous knowledge and heritage*. Saskatoon: Purich Publishing.

Charters-Vaught, O. (1999). Indian control of Indian education: The path of the upper Nicola Band. *Canadian Journal of Native Education, 23*(1), 64–90.

Kirkness, J., & Barnhardt, R. (1991). First Nations & higher education: The four R's – respect, relevance, reciprocity & responsibility. *Journal of American Indian Education, 30*(3).

Kuokkanen, R. (2007). *Reshaping the university: Responsibility, Indigenous epistemes and the logic of the gift*. Vancouver: UBC Press.

Lawrence, B. (2004). *"Real" Indians and others: Mixed-blood urban Native peoples and Indigenous nationhood*. Vancouver: UBC Press.

Little Bear, L. (2000). Jagged worldviews colliding. In M. Battiste (Ed.), *Reclaiming Indigenous voice and vision* (pp. 77–85). Vancouver: UBC Press.

Marker, M. (2003). Indigenous voice, community, and epistemic violence: The ethnographer's "interests" and what "interests" the ethnographer. *International Journal of Qualitative Studies in Education, 16*(3), 361–376.

Marker, M. (2004). The four Rs revisited: Some reflections on First Nations and higher education. In L. Andres & F. Finlay (Eds.), *Student affairs: Experiencing higher education* (pp. 171–188). Vancouver: UBC Press.

Marsden, D. (2005). *Indigenous wholistic theory for health: Enhancing traditional based Indigenous health services in Vancouver* (Unpublished doctoral dissertation). University of British Columbia, Vancouver, BC.

Parent, A. (2011). "Keep us coming back for more": Urban Aboriginal youth speak about wholistic education. *Canadian Journal of Native Education, 34*(1), 28–50.

Pidgeon, M. (2008). *It takes more than good intentions: Institutional accountability and responsibility to higher education* (Unpublished doctoral dissertation). University of British Columbia, Vancouver, BC.

Piquemal, N. (2001). Free and informed consent in research involving Native American communities. *American Indian Culture and Research Journal, 25*(1), 65–79.

Rose, A. (1993). *Nisaga'a: People of the Nass River*. Vancouver: Douglas & McIntyre.

Shields, C., Bishop, R., & Mazawi, A. (2005). *Pathologizing practices: The impact of deficit thinking on education*. New York: Peter Lang.

Smith, L. T. (1999). *Decolonizing methodologies: Research and Indigenous peoples.* Dunedin, NZ: University of Otago Press.

Wimmer, R. J. (2016). The "4 Rs revisited," again: Aboriginal education in Canada and implications for leadership in higher education. In L. Shultz & M. Viczko (Eds.), *Assembling and governing the higher education institution: Democracy, social justice and leadership in global higher education.* London: Palgrave Macmillan.

Young, A. (2007). *Elders' teachings on Indigenous leadership: Leadership as a gift* (Doctoral dissertation). University of British Columbia, Vancouver, BC. Retrieved from UBC Electronic Theses and Dissertations: http://hdl.handle.net/2429/5600

Youngblood Henderson, J. (2000). Postcolonial ghost dancing: Diagnosing European colonialism. In M. Battiste (Ed.), *Reclaiming Indigenous voice and vision* (pp. 57–77). Vancouver: UBC Press.

PART II

MAKING SPACE
FOR INDIGENOUS RESEARCH

Research can be dangerous. In particular, research can entrench positions of power. The academy is created by, and in turn helps to recreate, a colonial system that has dehumanized Indigenous peoples. It is no surprise that universities remain mostly inhospitable to Indigenous scholars and scholarship, and are difficult places from which to build research relationships with Indigenous peoples and communities who have been harmed by research in the past. Unscrupulous researchers continue to launch their careers off the backs of Indigenous peoples and their communities with little or no benefit to those communities (Smith, 1999; Mihesuah & Wilson, 2004). Researchers, whether non-Indigenous or Indigenous, are in positions of power, and are privileged relative to the "researched," and so risk replicating inequitable power relations through research.

Decolonization and respectful research starts with the individual and can be facilitated by interpersonal relationships, particularly between Indigenous professors and their Indigenous and non-Indigenous students. However, research decolonization also needs to happen on a larger scale. Disciplinary bodies of knowledge and research methods that effect epistemic violence against Indigenous peoples must be challenged. Effective systems for holding researchers accountable for unethical work with Indigenous communities, particularly ones grounded in Indigenous ethics, must be established and implemented. Finally, the overall purpose of the academy, something rarely considered by those who labour within it, should be re-evaluated. Yet, despite there still being such a long way to go, Indigenous students and scholars are carving out safe spaces to learn, relate, teach, and practice within the academy.

In addition to the chapters in this section by Shelly Johnson, Karen Hall and Erin Cusack, and Paul Cormier and Lana Ray, the chapters by Karlee Fellner (Chapter 1), Amy Parent (Chapter 3) and Sarah Hunt (Chapter 17) address power, colonization, and decolonization.

LEARNING AND REFLECTION QUESTIONS

1. When should the Indigenous community the research is about become involved in the research process?
2. How can research be "with" Indigenous peoples rather than "for" or "about" them? How do you know?
3. Why is it important for research to change the material realities of Indigenous communities/society?
4. What sorts of practices do researchers feel compelled to follow in order to advance their careers? How can these be harmful to Indigenous communities?
5. How do the contributors in this collection protect themselves, restore balance, and stay connected in the midst of violent experiences within the academy? How do you?
6. What would you do if you were to encounter a micro-aggression or instance of unethical research?
7. Given these challenges, is Indigenous research worth pursuing from within the university? What are your limits?
8. How is the role of academic expert or researcher challenged by Indigenous worldviews?
9. How does relational accountability in an Indigenous community differ from institutional accountability within a university?
10. What power differences exist among Indigenous peoples?
11. How can research be re-imagined through traditional research processes like drumming, singing, storytelling, returning to land for instruction, and ceremony?

REFERENCES

Mihesuah, D., & Wilson, A. (Eds.). (2004). *Indigenizing the academy: Transforming scholarship and empowering communities*. Lincoln, NE: University of Nebraska Press.

Smith, L. (1999). *Indigenous methodologies*. London: Zed Books.

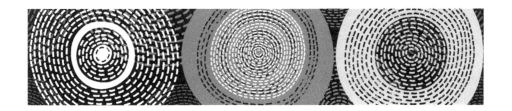

CHAPTER 4

Wise Indigenous Woman Approaches to Research:
Navigating and Naming Jagged Ethical Tensions
and Micro-Aggressions in the Academy

Shelly Johnson/Mukwa Musayett

PERSONAL AND POLITICAL: SETTING A SAULTEAUX WOMAN WITHIN THE "IVORY TOWER"

My Saulteaux naming ceremony remains a powerful and foundational life experience that continues to shape my ways of being, knowing, doing, and naming in academia. Four Saulteaux uncles took me deep into the forest to visit with Saulteaux Elders; both within their summer home, and with dozens of intergenerational family and community members gathered in huge ceremonial teepees. Conducted entirely in our Saulteaux language, one uncle told the Elders stories of my life, and shared collective observations of my actions from the perspectives of family and community members. Praying, feasting, drumming, storytelling, and singing began late in the evening and lasted long into the early morning hours of a new day. It is within this ceremony that I received my traditional name, colours, and instructions on the ways in which to care and give thanks for my name, Mukwa Musayett. In our Saulteaux language it translates as "I'm walking with bears" or "Walking Bear" depending on the dialect used. The teachings of respect, responsibility, reciprocity, taking action to help other beings, and assisting the well-being of the land, sky, and waters are integrally connected with the inherent right to be known in this way.

It is these specific foundational teachings that accompanied me into academia, and have helped to shape my decisions to listen, name, and take action to make relevant change. For example, with respect to land in the Canadian jurisdictional and legal context, "unceded territories" refers to lands that Indigenous peoples have not relinquished to Canada through treaty, war, or surrender. This chapter takes the position that the Canadian occupation of unceded First Nations lands in British Columbia constitutes political, economic, and social aggression against First Nations people, and is enforced and maintained by the power and muscle of Canadian government, police, and military. Canadian aggression against Indigenous peoples is further influenced by judicial and business self-interests, and maintained through the absence of Indigenous history taught from Indigenous perspectives in the Canadian educational curriculum. All of these facts contribute toward the creation of interpersonal tensions between and among First Nations and non–First Nations peoples in Canada and BC. For relevant change making to occur, we must name these tensions and the core principles or teachings that link and assist us to move toward truth-telling and reconciliation.

The tensions inherent in this jurisdictional quagmire also exist in academic institutions located upon ceded and unceded territories in Canada, and are reflected in research activities and micro-aggressions within the "ivory tower." This chapter is written from the standpoint of a Saulteaux woman researcher who has worked within three academic institutions located on unceded territories in BC. Some cities, such as Vancouver, publicly admit location on unceded Musqueam territories (City of Vancouver, 2014, pp. 14–15; Meizner, 2014). This chapter is one opportunity to struggle with the question, "How is Indigenous woman identity and research impacted by the ways in which colonial, racialized, and gendered micro-aggressions and political tensions unfold inside academia?" The consideration of what "exists" as enacted within colonial academic institutions must also include examples of Indigenous naming, action, and resistance to political aggression, unethical research, and micro-aggressions.

The first step begins with critical self-questioning, because complex constitutional and adversarial tensions extend into research relationships. For example, what does it mean to be employed by a university that economically and politically benefits from research conducted upon unceded Indigenous territories and from its location of unlawful occupation? What does it mean to work in academia, where micro-aggression, racism, and gender-bias are barriers to listening to understand, being respectful, and acting in reciprocal ways to benefit both the local First Nations and the institution? Finally, how are academics held to account for jagged ethical research tensions and micro-aggressions in the academy and community, if at all?

This chapter centres one example of what I describe as "wise Indigenous woman approaches to research." It includes "her-Indigenous-voice centring" to make new space for Indigenous woman voice and presence in ethical research within the academy, and upon contested and unceded Indigenous territories. It troubles uncomfortable questions such as "How do we ensure that academic institutions, particularly those located on unceded territories, change unethical research practices with Indigenous peoples?" This profoundly personal and political work is predicated upon additional factors inherent in a gendered colonial history, a specific Indigenous worldview, extended family relationships, and ongoing tribal/cultural responsibilities (Kovach, 2009; Mihesuah & Wilson, 2004; Wesley-Esquimaux & Calliou, 2010; Wilson, 2008). The next section identifies one macro example of "unwise" practices, conducted upon Nuu-Chah-Nulth people by a former University of British Columbia (UBC) professor, and its long-term implications.

FEEDING FROM INDIGENOUS VEINS: HISTORICAL "BAD BLOOD" CONTROVERSY ON UNCEDED TERRITORIES

Learning from stories for teaching purposes is something that Sto:lo academic Jo-ann Archibald (2008), a First Nations academic at UBC, terms "storywork." One example of Indigenous storywork, in a research context, involves vials of blood taken from the Nuu-Chah-Nulth First Nation people in a 1980s research project conducted by Dr. Richard Ward of UBC, and funded by Health Canada for $330,000 (Wiwchar, 2000a). Nuu-Chah-Nulth people have lived for millennia, or since time immemorial, on unceded lands on the west coast of what is now known as Vancouver Island. Ward was the son of a medical doctor and was born in England. In the 1980s, of 1,878 Nuu-Chah-Nulth people surveyed by Ward's research team, 833 voluntarily gave blood samples for a study on arthritis, a serious health issue affecting many in their communities. Without reporting the inconclusive results of the study to the Indigenous research participants, Ward left UBC for the University of Utah in the United States, and later became a professor at the prestigious University of Oxford in England. Ward took the Nuu-Chah-Nulth blood samples with him and received $172,000 in new grant funds from the US Department of Justice to use the Nuu-Chah-Nulth blood samples for various genetic anthropology research studies, without the consent of the participants (Brunger, 2013; Shields et al., 1993; Steel, 2008; Wiwchar, 2000a, 2000b).

While employed as a tenured professor at Oxford, Ward expressed regret through the Nuu-Chah-Nulth newspaper *Ha-shilth-sa* "if his actions caused harm" to the research participants. He was subsequently forced to return the samples to the Nuu-Chah-Nulth for disposal (Steel, 2008; Wiwchar, 2000b). However, he did so only after the genetic research findings were published in an eminent scholarly journal (Shields et al., 1993); a significant benefit to him and his academic career. The Nuu-Chah-Nulth people did not benefit from Ward's arthritis research (Steel, 2008; Wiwchar, 2000a), except to learn to be cautious of academic research and researchers. They termed their experience with Ward as the "bad blood" controversy and have since established Research Ethics protocols meant to protect them from future unethical research and researchers (Steel, 2008).

Ward died suddenly in 2003 at age 59, still pondering the return of yet more blood samples to another Indigenous people, the Yanomami of the Amazon in the global South. Ward's obituary appeared as an article in the *American Journal of Human Genetics*. His colleague in blood research, Weiss (2003), wrote that "Indigenous peoples are understandably suspicious that we feed our careers from their veins" (p. 1081). Indeed, it is a lesson that the Nuu-Chah-Nulth people learned from their experience with Ward. The decision to share this "bad blood experience" and to name both the research and researcher is meant to increase research safety for other Indigenous peoples and academics.

WHAT'S THE DIFFERENCE BETWEEN AN INDIGENOUS AND A NON-INDIGENOUS ACADEMIC?

As members, citizens, and descendants of First Nations, Métis, and Inuit communities, Indigenous academics must address ethical research considerations on a level that is far more complex than the decision-making of mainstream academic research ethics boards (REB). For example, if non-Indigenous academics participate in unethical research, they may be reprimanded by university sanctions up to and including suspension or dismissal, or they may simply leave of their own volition. Ward was born in England, gathered his research in the "colonies" with Indigenous groups, and returned to Oxford as a full professor, thus demonstrating how research and grants are used as important credentials to apply for positions at prestigious universities (Steel, 2008; Wiwchar, 2000a, 2000b).

However, if Indigenous academics participate in, or conduct, unethical research with Indigenous peoples, we are subject to additional sanctions. For example, if possible, many Indigenous academics choose to remain close to extended family and community; this means that any potential unethical practices risk not only our own reputations, but those of our families and communities. Second, effects of unethical research such as that conducted by Ward are long-lasting (Smith, 1999; Steel, 2008). If unethical research were to be conducted by Indigenous academics, and become known to their family or community, relationships will rupture. From an Indigenous worldview, relationships are critically important. Unlike non-Indigenous academics who may seek another academic position far from harmed research participants, we can never "apply" for another family or community, nor can our actions escape community memory. The fact that other Indigenous peoples will know if we conduct harmful research has more power to encourage ethical research approaches by Indigenous academics than any university REB sanction, or moving far away, can ever achieve.

As a result of difficult research experiences, Indigenous academics are challenged by Indigenous organizations, communities, and peoples to do more than submit institutionally based ethics forms to REBs, or serve on institutional REBs. An unspoken expectation is that we must do more than provide "Indigenous perspectives" on research advisory committees, conduct research with Indigenous peoples, or teach research classes in academic institutions (Kovach, 2009; Smith, 1999; Wilson, 2008). These are important roles. However, Indigenous academics are also tasked to take leadership roles to teach Indigenous community members about ethical research practices and their research rights (Johnson, De Finney, Brown, Green, & McCaffrey, 2014).

ARE INDIGENOUS COMMUNITIES BEING PROTECTED BY TODAY'S ETHICAL RESEARCH STANDARDS?

History and stories are good teachers, and the recent Nuu-Chah-Nulth experience with blood research may be able to help inform other Indigenous people about questionable research ethics and the extremely limited power of REBs to enforce ethical academic conduct. It is an experience that highlights that unethical research can, and is, conducted by tenured, published faculty from "elite" institutions. Autonomous academics have access to large grants, a span of control, and influence over research assistants and contractors. In addition, as in the Ward example, proof of unethical research seems to have no impact on their academic livelihood or institutional ability to secure additional funds (Weiss, 2003). Indigenous communities, in comparison, have a long institutional memory of being recipients of injustice (Miller, 1996; Milloy, 1999) and unethical research (Smith, 1999; Steel, 2008).

From the perspective of Indigenous peoples, too many times the road to ethical and meaningful research is fraught with potholes, road closures, detours, and strategically placed stop signs. Unnecessary ethical fatalities litter research processes and are caused by a lack of Indigenous knowledge about rights in research practices, and research rage, also known as micro-aggressions. Trauma stories and anecdotes continue to be told by Indigenous peoples hurt in the research process, as evidenced by this recent conversation with a Cree Elder who participated in an unethical community-based health research project. He said, "I told that White researcher that what she'd done to the Elders in that research project, was worse than anything that happened to them at residential school" (Elder, personal communication, March 2, 2012). When I asked the Elder if he or the other Elders were aware of the *Tri-Council Policy Statement on Ethical Conduct for Research Involving Humans* (TCPS, 2010), or if they were aware of section 9, which specifically addresses researcher ethics with First Nations, Inuit, and Métis peoples, he said no. I asked if the researchers offered any type of access to trauma counselling once they learned of the harm to the Elders. Again, he said no. At that point, I shared section 9.16, Privacy and Confidentiality, of the TCPS and asked that he share it with people in his community. The section specifically notes that "research undertaken with participants who have suffered traumatic experiences (e.g., former residential school students) poses a risk of re-traumatizing participants. Researchers should anticipate such risks in the research design, and adhere to cultural protocols for determining participant needs and access to trauma counselling" (TCPS, 2010, p. 127).

It was in 2012 when the Elders in this project asked for their words, their "research data," back from researchers, and were told no. When I intervened at the Elders' request, I was told to file a complaint with the institutional REB. Further, I was encouraged not to be surprised to experience consequences for *my* actions, and the Elders could expect the same. The threat was shared with the Elders, who decided to withdraw their request, rather than risk their safety or mine. It was shortly after this experience that I resigned from the academic institution, found employment elsewhere, and supported the decision of the Elders to disengage with the research project and the institution.

As Indigenous academics and researchers, it is important to consider realistic options that exist to address unethical or disrespectful research processes in Indigenous communities. Certainly, the first step is to help educate Indigenous peoples and communities about research protocols; their rights, roles, redress options, responsibilities, and what they can reasonably expect from research relationships. This work is currently underway by a number of Indigenous research bodies, including the Siem Smun'eem: Indigenous Child Welfare Research Network (2013) located at the University of Victoria. The network offers a series of workshops designed and led by Indigenous academics to help Indigenous people understand their rights within research processes. However, not every person or community has the benefit of this knowledge. Due to costs associated with travel and child care, or to competing responsibilities, not every person in an Indigenous community has the opportunity to attend research sessions.

The reality is that unethical research and researchers exist despite the presence and work of the TCPS (2010) and institutional REBs. Research undertaken through funding provided by the Canadian Institutes of Health Research (CIHR), Natural Sciences and Engineering Research Council of Canada (NSERC), and Social Sciences and Humanities Research Council of Canada (SSHRC) are accountable to the TCPS standards. So is research funded by Health Canada and myriad other funding bodies. Yet unethical research persists, and concerns are expressed about the fact that academic REB processes are not without their own inherent flaws or lack of understanding of Indigenous research issues (Thunderbird Circle, 2013). Indigenous peoples are wise to understand that their ability to hold researchers to account for unethical practices is limited.

In social work practice, a belief exists that it is better to erect a gate or barrier at the top of a cliff, rather than wait at the bottom of the cliff with an ambulance. Hence, one starting place might be to ensure that all Indigenous peoples are aware of and have opportunities to engage with section 9 of the TCPS (2010) prior to entering into any research projects. Some Indigenous agencies and communities in BC have already developed and expect adherence to existing research protocols, principles, and political review processes conducted by in-house ethics review committees. These are required due to the complexity of issues and requests for research coming before them. In addition, Indigenous agencies and communities are increasingly seeking ways to deal with the federal, provincial, and territorial governments' ability to conduct "in-house reviews" or "consultations," or research done by regulatory bodies without an independent academic oversight or ethics review process.

Indigenous organizations and agencies must also recognize the autonomy of Indigenous peoples to participate in research, or not. In some instances, existing protocols already adhere to organizational or agency or political ethics review processes. In addition, some First Nations may already adhere to other guidelines or processes for research with Indigenous peoples. The recent and unanimous Supreme Court land claim decision supporting the Aboriginal title position of the Tsilhqot'in peoples to 1,700 square kilometres of land in central BC (Hasselback, 2014; *Tsilhqot'in Nation v. British Columbia*, 2014) may also trigger sovereign decision-making regarding future research with Tsilhqot'in citizens. Conversely, this legal precedent may also provide opportunities to address long-standing political research inequities on other unceded or ceded Indigenous territories. However, in the meantime, Indigenous people must contend with existing research realities, that in most academic institutions do not include an Indigenous research ethics board for any researchers seeking permission to conduct research with, on, or about Indigenous peoples.

RESPONSES THAT ARE NOT HELPFUL: FEAR, THREATS, QUICK FIXES, AND MICRO-AGGRESSIONS

Indigenous academics continue to point to unhelpful ways that research institutions respond when unethical research issues are brought forward by Indigenous peoples. Stories are privately shared among Indigenous peoples regarding institutional tendencies to react with "quick fixes" to make complaints "go away." However, these responses typically do not address recurring or chronic issues with specific individuals or institutions. Another common story told in communities is about researchers who resort to "fear tactics," or threats to file lawsuits against Indigenous peoples for "defamation of character" if complaints about poor research practices go forward to institutional REBs. Many of these responses result in the same outcome: Indigenous peoples are silenced, vote with our feet, and share concerns about specific research projects or researchers via the "moccasin telegraph." These are some ways used to protect Indigenous communities and others from unethical processes. The next section of this chapter links micro-aggressions to unethical research, and names the emotions and considerations behind both.

LINKING MICRO-AGGRESSIONS AND UNETHICAL RESEARCH IN AN INDIGENOUS ETHICAL DECISION-MAKING MODEL

One threat to the mental well-being of Indigenous academics is the reality of racial micro-aggressions within the academy, and their cumulative effects. Racial micro-aggressions are brief, commonplace, and occur in three forms: micro-assaults, micro-insults, and micro-invalidations. They can include, daily verbal, behavioural, or environmental indignities, whether intentional or unintentional, that communicate hostile, derogatory, or negative racial slights and insults toward people of color. Perpetrators of micro-aggressions are often unaware that they engage in such communications when they interact with racial or ethnic minorities. (Sue et al., 2007, p. 271)

My own experience within the academy includes micro-aggressions from both Indigenous and non-Indigenous academics. The first that I can recall was from an Indigenous male academic and occurred early in my academic career, when he learned I was thinking of applying for a Tri-Council grant. His comment, made when there was no one else within hearing, was, "You shouldn't apply now when I'm applying with [two senior Indigenous academics]. You don't have a chance to compete with us." As a result, I did not apply. They did, but their Tri-Council grant application was unsuccessful.

Another common micro-aggression is the inference that Indigenous community-based research skills are "less prestigious than" quantitative research skills of non-Indigenous researchers. Instead it seems that Indigenous researchers are expected to lend our Indigenous identity and provide our CV as "credence" or to "provide proof of Indigenous support" to the applications of non-Indigenous or senior researchers. For example, one non-Indigenous researcher told me, "We are applying for this Aboriginal health research grant. It would be great if you added your CV to it, Shelly. Your CV, while it isn't that strong by itself, would really strengthen our application because you are Aboriginal" (Personal communication, March 15, 2010).

I declined that specific research "invitation" and many others, where my contributions appeared only required in order to "tick the Indigenous box" or provide an Indigenous "stamp of approval" to support the "more important" work of non-Indigenous researchers. A non-Indigenous researcher, upon learning that I planned to apply for my first SSHRC grant, actively discouraged me: "Applying for a SSHRC is so competitive. You'll only be disappointed and it's early in your career. It's better that you participate on someone else's grant, learn how to do the research from people much more experienced and knowledgeable than you" (Personal communication, October 1, 2012). This same colleague did not respond to a congratulatory group email sent a few months later by another colleague after I was awarded the SSHRC grant. Upon learning that I was the only applicant and sole Principal Investigator, the academic said to me, again outside the hearing circle of others, "Huh! SSHRC must not have had many applications when you applied" (Personal communication, May 30, 2013). During a faculty meeting following the announcement, another non-Indigenous faculty member stated, "She got this SSHRC grant on her first application ever. Why, I didn't even do that!" (Personal communication, May 2013). The inference by all was that I was somehow given an advantage as an Indigenous person that was not available to a non-Indigenous academic.

When I was awarded a second SSHRC grant, another non-Indigenous colleague commented, in an incredulous voice during an open faculty meeting, "What? *You* got another SSHRC grant? Really? *You?*" I did not respond to the comment, nor did I break the silence that followed. Once the meeting ended, I learned of a conversation between two more colleagues that included the comment, "SSHRC must have a quota of grants that have to be given to Aboriginal people. That's the only way she could get one." The inference was that I could not possibly be successful in an open competition with either of them as more senior, accomplished, and white academics.

Indigenous capacity building in largely non-Indigenous research institutions remains a challenging process, just like capacity building in community. In academic institutions, capacity building is further encumbered by numerous ongoing examples of racial micro-aggressions. Questions remain about how to "make spaces" for Indigenous peoples to name the micro-aggressions and expect resolution in timely and helpful ways. An analysis of the micro-aggressions aimed at me leads to a deeper examination of the inherently hostile, derogatory, and negative intentions. These comments strategically attack my mental and emotional sense of well-being and competence, and serve to undermine my sense of belonging in the academy by an almost daily reminder of my "insignificant, token place" within it. It is one example of the ways in which micro-aggressions perpetrated "against" Indigenous faculty link with the experiences of unethical research practices "on" Indigenous peoples. Both result in harm to Indigenous peoples.

UNDERSTANDING THE LINKAGE BETWEEN MICRO-AGGRESSIONS AND UNETHICAL RESEARCH

There is a paucity of literature related to understanding the link between micro-aggressions and unethical research. There is a specific and marked absence of Indigenous ethical decision-making models related to research concerns, and an absence of Indigenous ethical decision-making models or boards in academia in general. This does not mean the models do not exist among the rich diversity of Indigenous peoples living on Turtle Island (North America). It simply means that little is currently written from Indigenous perspectives to guide Indigenous academics about what we can do within academic institutions when we experience micro-aggressions or become aware of unethical research behaviours with Indigenous communities. However, a review of traditional Aboriginal codes of ethics and ethical decision-making models used in social work helps us to consider ways in which Indigenous people or Indigenous academics could raise concerns.

In 2013, the *Workers Compensation Act* (1996) was amended to create new legislative requirements to prevent and reduce bullying and harassment in the workplace. The requirements resulted in new obligations for employers to provide training about bullying and harassment to all academic faculty and staff (including students as paid employees by the university, and students on unpaid practicum as part of their academic program). As a result, some academic institutions in BC created a 15-minute online training course and six questions to fulfill this legislated requirement (UBC, 2014).

As with the decision by research participants about whether to become involved in research processes, there are serious questions to consider in linking micro-aggressions in academic institutions with unethical research. Questions to consider might include: Do academic institutional policies exist that adequately address micro-aggressions, unethical research, harassment, or bullying? Are there sufficient numbers of Indigenous people at senior levels in academic institutions across Canada to mentor or guide processes to challenge poor research practices? If junior Indigenous academics speak up to question the linkage, might that hurt our chances of tenure or promotion by committees largely composed of white, tenured colleagues? These are questions that we need to ask and consider for *our Indigenous selves*. For some Indigenous academics this process may lead to questioning whether tenure in a non-Indigenous educational institution should even be our goal. For others the questions and answers may provide even more impetus for resistance to unethical research done to Indigenous peoples, and determination for change. The next section of the chapter identifies codes of ethics and policies that may assist in the examination and actions arising from the linkage between micro-aggressions and unethical research.

AN ETHICAL INDIGENOUS PLACE TO BEGIN

Fortunately, there are many pathways available to guide Indigenous academics through jagged ethical tensions and to deal with micro-aggressions enacted within the academy. This chapter began in a personal way with the description of my own public naming ceremony and the decision of a collective of relatives to influence it with truth-telling about me, and my actions. The process of naming micro-aggressions and unethical research practices can begin with one person, and as in the example, it then becomes the responsibility of the collective to take it forward in public ways using the traditions and norms of the institution to bring it to a resolution. The harassment and bullying polices of our worksites offer some assistance, as does the *Traditional Code of Ethics* (2006) formulated by the Assembly of Manitoba Chiefs Youth Secretariat. This document provides guidance and direction as to our true purpose as human beings and reminds us of our original instructions, no matter which venue we are working in or living upon. It is important to understand the code in its wholistic form in much the same way that the Seven Grandfather Teachings of the Ojibway people is understood as a wholistic path to living a good life.

Indigenous ethical decision-making frameworks or models exist in diverse Indigenous contexts. They function in connection with the specific Indigenous peoples, lands and places, values and beliefs. It is critical to understand these interdependent relationships (or relational accountability) because they are what guide Indigenous research or ethical decision-making actions in ways that may differ from processes used by non-Indigenous peoples. Therefore it is critical to understand that there must be differences in ethical decision-making models when Indigenous concerns are raised about unethical research practices, or micro-aggressions in relationships. This is not an easy task given that Indigenous peoples often hold competing roles as relatives, academics, friends, and leaders in Indigenous contexts and other junior employment roles in non-Indigenous contexts.

A PROCESS TO ADDRESS MICRO-AGGRESSIONS AND UNETHICAL RESEARCH IN ACADEMIA

Finding or developing local ways to skillfully address micro-aggressions and unethical research in the academy invites the participation of many people. The following five steps are offered as a place to continue the conversations, name the processes, and take action to address the harmful effects.

First, Indigenous peoples negatively affected by micro-aggressions and/or unethical research with Indigenous peoples, or those interested in addressing them in academia, could benefit from an engagement process or conversation at the nation, community, or institutional level. For example, conversations could begin by sharing this chapter with others. People could be encouraged to discuss examples of witnessing or experiencing disrespect, lack of reciprocity, and lack of safety within the academy, as well as instances where respect, reciprocity, and safety were demonstrated. Making space for truth-telling is a key component of this first step and process.

Second, the discussion could evolve to include an understanding of how the nation, community, or institution has formulated its own ways of addressing micro-aggressions, or its own research ethics and approval processes. A guided circle discussion could expand on what exists generally, what is specifically missing, and the people or resources that are required to move the issues forward.

Third, a visual decision-making map and timeline could be constructed to determine a clear path to identify how the micro-aggression or unethical research practice developed. For example, borrowing on the process developed by the College of the Rockies, its research development process led to identification of two research committees: one that focuses on research methodology, and a second that provides ethics approval. In other institutions, the process may lead to the development of an Indigenous research ethics committee or an Indigenous micro-aggression resolution process. Resources to pay Indigenous community-based researcher representatives to participate, or appointment of an Elder to an adjunct professor position, may be required to ensure adequate and meaningful participation.

Fourth, an Indigenous scholar from the institution must be invited to participate in the ethics committee as well as the micro-aggression resolution process. Fifth and finally, the nation and institution can agree to work toward the joint development of a training and dispute-resolution process for research or micro-aggressions arising within the community or research project. Nations or institutions may look to peacemaking circle processes as one example of a process meant to repair harms. Due to the significant diversity among nations and institutions, these processes must be site specific and culturally appropriate.

CONCLUSION

This wise Indigenous woman approach to navigating ethical research tensions and micro-aggressions in the academy is difficult work because of the resistance to addressing racism and political aggressions against Indigenous peoples in Canada and, by extension, within the academy. Addressing unethical research practices and micro-aggressions takes time, awareness, education, knowledge, and commitment to change. It also requires the willingness of those in positions of power to take meaningful steps to address disrespect toward Indigenous peoples and to change our experiences in community and academia. Until this occurs, perhaps this five-step model can be of some assistance to begin a conversation amongst Indigenous and non-Indigenous academics about one way to address the jagged tensions within the academy.

REFERENCES

Archibald, J. (2008). *Indigenous storywork: Educating the heart, mind, body and spirit.* Vancouver: UBC Press.

Assembly of Manitoba Chiefs Youth Secretariat. (2006). *Traditional code of ethics.* Retrieved from www.umanitoba.ca/student/asc/media/Pamphlet_02a.pdf

Brunger, F. (2013, October 19). Research abuse of Aboriginal children: Not just a consent issue. [Web log message]. *Canadian Bioethics Society.* Retrieved from www.bioethics.ca/blog.html?Step=2&MB=305

City of Vancouver. (2014). *Regular Council meeting minutes.* Retrieved from http://former.vancouver.ca/ctyclerk/cclerk/20140624/documents/regu20140624min.pdf

Hasselback, D. (2014, June 26). Supreme Court paves way for aboriginal title claims. *Financial Post.* Retrieved from http://business.financialpost.com/2014/06/26/supreme-court-paves-way-for-aboriginal-title-claims/

Johnson, S., De Finney, S., Brown, L., Green, J., & McCaffrey, S. (2014). Siem Smun'eem (Respected children): A community-based research training story. In C. Etmanski, B. Hall, & T. Dawson (Eds.), *Learning and teaching community-based research: Linking pedagogy to practice* (pp. 93–112). Toronto: University of Toronto Press.

Kovach, M. (2009). *Indigenous methodologies: Characteristics, conversations and contexts.* Toronto: University of Toronto Press.

Meizner, P. (2014, June 25). City of Vancouver formally declares city is on unceded Aboriginal territory. *Global News.* Retrieved from http://globalnews.ca/news/1416321/city-of-vancouver-formally-declares-city-is-on-unceded-aborginal-territory/

Mihesuah, D., & Wilson, A. (Eds.). (2004). *Indigenizing the academy: Transforming scholarship and empowering communities.* Lincoln, NE: University of Nebraska Press.

Miller, J. (1996). *Shingwauk's vision: A history of Native residential schools.* Toronto: University of Toronto Press.

Milloy, J. (1999). *A national crime: The Canadian government and the residential school system, 1879–1986.* Winnipeg: University of Manitoba Press.

Shields, G., Schmiechen, A., Frazier, B., Redd, A., Voevoda, M., Reed, J., & Ward, R. (1993). mtDNA sequences suggest a recent evolutionary divergence for Beringian and northern North American populations. *American Journal of Human Genetics, 53*(3), 549–562.

Siem Smun'eem: Indigenous Child Welfare Research Network. (2013). Retrieved from http://web.uvic.ca/icwr/

Smith, L. (1999). *Decolonizing methodologies: Research and Indigenous peoples.* London: Zed Books.

Steel, D. (2008, July 17). Blood taken for research destroyed. *Ha-shilth-sa.* Retrieved from www.hashilthsa.com/archive/news/2013-07-22/blood-taken-research-destroyed

Sue, D., Capodilup, C., Torino, G., Bucceri, J., Holder, A., Nadal, K., & Esquilin, M. (2007). Racial microaggressions in everyday life: Implications for clinical practice. *American Psychologist, 62*(4), 271–286. DOI: 10.1037/0003-066X.62.4.271

Thunderbird Circle. (2013). Position statement of the Thunderbird Circle. Retrieved from https://caswe-acfts.ca/position-statement-of-the-thunderbird-nesting-circle-iswen/

Tri-Council Policy Statement (TCPS). (2010). *Canadian Institutes of Health Research, Natural Sciences and Engineering Research Council of Canada, and Social Sciences and Humanities Research Council of Canada, Tri-council policy statement: Ethical conduct for research involving humans.* Retrieved from www.ethics.gc.ca/pdf/eng/tcps2/TCPS_2_FINAL_Web.pdf

Tsilhqot'in Nation *v.* British Columbia, SCC 44. (2014). Retrieved from scc-csc.lexum.com/scc-csc/scc-csc/en/item/14246/index.do

University of British Columbia (UBC). (2014). *Bullying and harassment prevention at UBC.* Retrieved from bullyingandharassment.ubc.ca/

Weiss, K. (2003). Obituary. Richard H. Ward, Ph.D. (June 7, 1943–February 14, 2003): Wild ride of the Valkyries. *American Journal of Human Genetics, 72*, 1079–1083. Retrieved from www.ncbi.nlm.nih.gov/pmc/articles/PMC1180261/pdf/AJHGv72p1079.pdf

Wesley-Esquimaux, C., & Calliou, B. (2010). Best practices in Aboriginal community development: A literature review and wise practices approach. Retrieved from http://communities-4families.ca/wp-content/uploads/2014/08/Aboriginal-Community-Development.pdf

Wilson, S. (2008). *Research is ceremony: Indigenous research methods.* Halifax: Fernwood Publishing.

Wiwchar, D. (2000a, June 21). Genetic researcher uses Nuu-chah-nulth blood for unapproved studies in Genetic Anthropology. *Ha-shilth-sa.* Retrieved from www.hashilthsa.com/archive/news/2013-07-22/genetic-researcher-uses-nuu-chah-nulth-blood-unapproved-studies-genetic-anth

Wiwchar, D. (2000b, October 5). Ward responds. *Ha-shilth-sa.* Retrieved from www.hashilthsa.com/archive/news/2013-07-22/ward-responds

Workers Compensation Act. (1996). Retrieved from www.bclaws.ca/civix/document/LOC/complete/statreg/--%20W%20--/Workers%20Compensation%20Act%20%5BRSBC%201996%5D%20c.%20492/00_Act/96492_01.xml

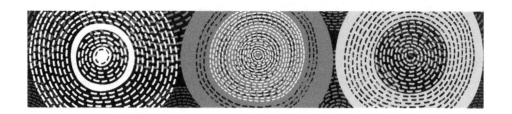

CHAPTER 5

Healing and Transformative Learning through
Indigenous Methodologies

Karen Hall and Erin Cusack

INTRODUCTION

Our academic journeys began at Dalhousie University, in Halifax, Nova Scotia,
where we both completed a bachelor of science in health promotion policy and
research. This first leg of our journey began our respective transformative experiences as students and women. The health promotion program was grounded in
the social determinants of health perspective, and emphasized a critique of the
broad social institutions that structure health and social inequities. Our worldviews had been completely altered by the time we graduated, both finishing the
program with questions we had not known needed answers. Though our personal
and academic journeys are markedly different, we now speak from this shared
experience as co-learners, colleagues, and friends.

In this chapter, we explore the concepts of decolonization in our lives and
in our work. In our stories we see parallels and contrasts in our learning, experiences, and applications of a decolonizing lens. As we have continued to walk
intersecting paths on our academic pursuits, our many parallels stem from our
shared undergraduate education in health promotion, guidance from the same
graduate supervisor, and taking a Critical and Indigenous Methodologies graduate course together. Ultimately, we approach the topic of decolonization from
differing epistemologies, one Indigenous and one non-Indigenous. We explore

and unpack the meaning of a decolonizing lens in our work, and our perceptions of our respective roles in decolonization processes in the academy. We will focus on our learning in the Critical and Indigenous Methodologies class and how it has manifested itself in different ways in our lived experiences and in our research. We reflect on our educational trajectories, and our shared and individual roles in decolonizing processes; however, we recognize that our learning and negotiation of these roles is ongoing and lifelong. In this chapter, we aim to describe the complex relationship of walking a path to a decolonizing approach together, as Indigenous and non-Indigenous women.

MAKING SPACE: TRANSFORMATIVE LEARNING (ERIN)

My narrative centres on my experiences as a non-Indigenous woman learning in university about the damaging legacy of colonialism, and how these experiences changed my worldview. I am grateful for the opportunity to share my story in this volume, and would like to acknowledge the intellectual and emotional labour of the Indigenous scholars, professors, colleagues, and friends that have shaped my transformative learning experiences. I believe it is important to understand how my history, upbringing, and identity shape my experiences, perspectives, and opportunities. I was born and raised outside of Halifax, Nova Scotia, in Mi'kma'ki, the ancestral and unceded territory of the Mi'kmaq people. My family heritage is Irish, English, and Scottish; however, my family identity is most prominently shaped by the Irish Catholic roots of my family name, Cusack. My Cusack ancestors first settled in New Brunswick in the late 1700s. I was raised by feminist parents in a predominantly white, suburban neighbourhood.

I attended public school, where I was taught a "white-washed" version of Canadian history that focused on the French fur traders and Acadian settlements of Atlantic Canada: "My schooling gave me no training in seeing myself as an oppressor, as an unfairly advantaged person, or as a participant, in a damaged culture" (McIntosh, 1989, p. 10). Until my undergraduate studies, not only had I not been given "training" to see myself as a member of an advantaged group, at the disadvantage of others, this discussion of privilege and oppression was markedly absent. In the third year of my undergraduate program at Dalhousie University, I took a class called Multicultural Health Promotion Policy in Canada, with Dr. Debbie Martin. It was in this class that I began to "unpack the invisible knapsack" of my white privilege beginning with Peggy McIntosh's (1989) often cited essay. For the first time in all of my schooling I learned about the realities of the forced assimilation of Indigenous peoples in Canada through colonization, the

Indian Act, residential schools, Indian hospitals, the child welfare system, and the ongoing disparities in federal funding for Indigenous communities. I became aware of the ongoing legacy of colonialism in this country that is perpetuated by the failure to accurately teach the history of Indigenous peoples' oppression.

In 2010, in this small, elective class of only six students, I learned for the first time about how the silence around the detrimental effects of colonization and the resulting inequities pathologize Indigenous peoples, and allow white privilege to go unaddressed while more deeply entrenching systemic racism (Weber-Pillwax, 2012). Dalhousie's health promotion program is rooted in a social determinants of health perspective focused on addressing the roots of health inequities, but where were the concepts of colonization, cultural assimilation, intergenerational trauma, and systemic racism on the list of social determinants of health? How is it that I had come this far in my education without learning that mainstream understandings of Indigenous communities are based on historical inaccuracies? These burning questions have changed how I see and interact with the world around me. The glaring, pervasive, and harmful colonial thinking in the media; the ideologies of our elected politicians; misinformation of service providers; and opinions of my friends and my family are formulated on intentional silence about the detrimental effects of past and ongoing colonial processes of which we are all a part. So now, as a white person indicted as a participant in the system that continues to oppress Indigenous peoples, what is my role? How do I engage in processes of decolonization as I continue in academia?

Dr. Martin's class was a transformative learning experience that changed my view of myself, of academia, and of the Canadian political context. One of the major ideas I took away from that class was the power of research and "data" to pathologize and disempower groups of people, as has been the case with Indigenous peoples in Canada. This class compelled me to engage in issues of Indigenous health research and policy, but based on the understanding that research processes, as well as outcomes, must do no harm. I am not an Indigenous person, nor am I connected with Indigenous communities in ways that allow me to engage in meaningful research driven by the voices of these communities. I became invested in topics of Indigenous health, but knew that I was not the person to conduct this research given my position. In my final year of my undergraduate degree I completed an honours thesis in what I considered at the time to be an unrelated topic: my qualitative study examined the relationship between social support and health and wellness for young, queer women in rural communities.

After completing my undergraduate degree in 2011, fuelled by a passion for health equity issues, I moved to Victoria, British Columbia, to pursue a master's degree in an interdisciplinary program, under the supervision of Dr. Charlotte Loppie. Although recognized for her seminal work related to the social determinants of Indigenous health, I sought Charlotte's guidance for her background in and passion for sexuality studies. At the University of Victoria I reconnected with Karen, also a graduate student of Charlotte's but in another program of study. In the winter of 2012, along with a small group of fellow graduate students, Dr. Loppie and Dr. Jeffrey Reading arranged a special topics research methodology class to satisfy the need for many of their students to explore Indigenous and decolonizing methodologies, both as a course requirement and as a requirement to conduct meaningful research with the Indigenous communities they were engaging with. My research topic – exploring socio-cultural influences on young women's sexual agency – was very different from my classmates'. However, Dr. Loppie had designed the class to allow us to meet the methodology course requirements of our respective programs. At the time, no other methods course offered at the University of Victoria explored the application of critical, feminist theory in qualitative research methods to health promotion and public health topics. This course offered me the freedom to tailor my reading list to inform my methodology chapter for my master's thesis.

While I was the only student not specifically working with Indigenous people, it was in this Critical and Indigenous Methodologies class that I found answers to some of the questions I had begun exploring in my undergraduate work about my role as a non-Indigenous person in processes of decolonization. As I was not personally delving into Indigenous health research in my thesis work, the course offered me a position to listen, learn, and engage as an outsider with the key readings informing my colleagues' Indigenous research paradigms by authors such as Absolon (2011), Smith (2012), Kovach (2009), and Sinclair (2004, 2007). I continued to proceed as though these seminal readings in Indigenous methodologies were not relevant to me in my work. Yet my perception of the disjuncture between colonial issues and my area of study began to dissolve as I formulated my master's research proposal through the course assignments. I began to better understand how the impacts of Eurocentric ways of knowing have imposed a pervasive and detrimental bias into research paradigms and research questions. It became apparent that the sexuality, gender, and women's sexual and reproductive health issues I was exploring were also inherently colonial issues. These topics cannot be explored without consideration of the Western notions that privilege the biomedical aspects of sexual health, heteronormativity, and a rigid gender binary that, at best, ignores the experiences of so many, and at worst, pathologizes and causes harm.

In my research proposal I began to operationalize a decolonizing lens by deconstructing and challenging Western perspectives on gender, sexuality, and sexual orientation. This meant shifting my focus away from comparing the experiences/outcomes of different groups of women based on social identity or location (for example, queer vs. straight, racialized vs. white, or trans vs. cisgendered women). I came to realize that classifying or stratifying women in this way only further entrenches the false dichotomies and binaries of the Western perspectives of gender and sexuality. Instead, I engaged with critical feminist methodologies that allowed me to examine and displace heteronormative and (cis)gendered structures that (dis)advantage young women differently. An important aspect of this shift in focus was realizing that I cannot disentangle myself from the research. I then built processes into the research design that allow me to reflect on my position within the structures I am examining in order to attempt to interpret the stories of other women who occupy very different locations within the same structures.

Through my interactions with my classmates and friends in this class, I began to understand that as a non-Indigenous student, I had to extend my decolonizing lens beyond my writing. My Indigenous classmates stressed the importance of recognizing Indigenous knowledge not just as a research methodology, but as a paradigm in its own right (K. Summers, personal communication, March 2012). As such, this paradigm comes from a worldview that cannot simply be adopted by non-Indigenous people operating within the dominant structure. This teaching from my classmates was an important crux in my understanding of decolonization processes. I began to understand that my goal was not to understand an Indigenous paradigm, but rather to acknowledge and make space for Indigenous ways of researching.

I struggled and continue to struggle with knowing how to make space for Indigenous ways of knowing as it varies in different physical and social contexts. In the context of the class, I began very simply by listening and being cognizant of not dominating conversations. I tried to literally clear the airways and hear voices of my Indigenous colleagues who often discussed the manifestations of colonization in their lives, their families, and their communities. As a non-Indigenous, white person my worldview is reflected and privileged in academic settings that are based upon Western epistemology. I attempted to help create an academic space that centred on Indigenous perspectives by remaining silent, listening, and making a concerted effort to (un)learn from my classmates and colleagues. When I did engage in critical discussions with my classmates, I did so with the understanding that my role was to acknowledge, respect, and value my classmates' Indigenous perspectives. I looked for ways to contribute that leveraged their discussions, rather than sidelining them by drawing comparisons between Western and Indigenous paradigms. Situated as I was on the periphery in this class, I quickly became privy to the tensions between the Indigenous and non-Indigenous students, particularly non-Indigenous students engaging in Indigenous health research. These tensions arose in the process of attempting an intercultural dialogue, and Indigenous and non-Indigenous students came away with vastly different interpretations of these academic experiences, including some of our class discussions. The non-Indigenous students experienced this dialogue as a positive learning opportunity that helped inform their work and research with Indigenous peoples that comes from a place of good intentions. Some of the Indigenous students, however, were confronted with deeply ingrained and institutionalized colonial perspectives of an academic setting. Specifically they articulated the challenges of conducting decolonizing research intended to initiate healing from the effects of colonization while operating within the academy, which privileges Eurocentric values and priorities, and Western markers of success. Our class discussions focused on the teachings of Absolon, Smith, Denzin and Lincoln, Kovach, Sinclair, and others about the irreducibly complex relationships between Indigenous and non-Indigenous ways of knowing. Even in the space of this class, where the classmates shared a common interest in countering oppression imposed by dominant Western structures, comparing and contrasting Indigenous and non-Indigenous paradigms was inherently problematic. This process of taking a decolonizing lens to research from within the academy meant decentralizing the power and privilege of the Western approach. The focus must not be solely on reducing the inequities facing Indigenous peoples, but also on opposing the dominant structures that created them. In this class, my Indigenous colleagues and friends taught me about their challenges in critiquing these structures when their resistance disrupted the comfort of those in positions of privilege.

As a non-Indigenous person, who was not conducting research with Indigenous peoples or communities, I felt uniquely positioned to sidestep some of the tensions in the class when engaging with my colleagues. I became uncomfortably aware of my privileged position to speak in the class. When I engaged in dialogue about my non-Indigenous classmates' Indigenous health research projects, my words were often not met with the same discomfort or defensiveness as when Indigenous classmates would do the same. As a member of the "mainstream" I had the privilege of speaking out against these dominant forces without the legitimacy of my culture or perspective being called into question.

This privilege was not shared among my Indigenous colleagues, many of whom had personally felt the effects of colonial oppression. One Indigenous colleague (and friend) described feeling the burden of being a "teacher" to her non-Indigenous classmates in educating them about Indigenous issues and perspectives. This expectation reinforced the dominance of Western perspectives as she was called upon to act as a representative for Indigenous peoples and provide "proof" to legitimize the realities of her Indigenous experience. Through these interactions, I began to better understand how Western and Indigenous identities are political and create power dynamics, even in a space intended for decolonizing dialogue and despite the non-Indigenous students' best intentions to learn.

Taking part in decolonizing processes, including recognizing and deconstructing my position as a white woman afforded the privileges of belonging to a dominant group, has ultimately meant getting uncomfortable. I am coming to understand the importance of leaning into this discomfort in order to resist the structures that create what McIntosh (1989) refers to as my "unfair advantage." In my own research this has meant reflection on and acknowledgement of not only the detrimental effects of colonial processes, but the ways I operate within these processes that comply with oppressive forces. This requires building processes into my study design that allow for continual reflection on my location within the dominant social structures as a cisgendered, white, heterosexual woman, how I benefit from this, and how this shapes my research. Essentially, I must "write myself into" the analysis first, before trying to interpret the stories of other women who may occupy very different spaces within the same structures.

I am still unsure of my role in mobilizing and supporting decolonizing action. What I have learned is that decolonization requires resisting and dismantling the dominant model that unjustly advantages me while disadvantaging others (Wilson & Yellow Bird, 2005). In my work as a student, this means starting with making space for the voices of my Indigenous colleagues to define and guide the relationships between Indigenous and non-Indigenous peoples in decolonizing the social, political, cultural, and physical space we share. Understanding my role as a non-Indigenous person in decolonizing academic spaces is a continuous learning journey that requires an ongoing process of decolonization. I have begun this journey by quieting my own voice to listen to and prioritize the voices of Indigenous people speaking to Indigenous research and perspectives. I aim to recognize and challenge my own entrenched Western views, and how they impact the dynamics of academic spaces for others. When appropriate, I respectfully engage in discussions of Indigenous issues in ways that attempt to leverage Indigenous priorities and offer a critique of oppressive structures.

KAREN'S STORY OF LEARNING

While Erin speaks to her transformative decolonizing experience as a non-Indigenous woman coming to the realization of Canada's history and the inherent privilege this history affords her, I offer my perspective as a Dene woman within this colonial context. I speak from a place that understands the joys and pains of being an Indigenous person. Joy, in terms of my sense of belonging when I practice my culture and ceremonies, and pain brought on by my experiences as a racialized woman in a country that has inadequately educated its citizens about the true history of Canada. My own colonial story of being raised in a predominantly non-Indigenous environment has strongly shaped my sense of Indigenous identity – causing deep-rooted issues of belonging within both Dene and non-Indigenous contexts. The realities of Canada's colonial legacy and policies of assimilation are my lived experiences, and this chapter provides the opportunity to acknowledge that pockets of decolonized spaces are occurring within academic institutions. Recognizing and acknowledging these spaces is critical for the decolonization movement, promoting Indigenous methodologies, and ultimately disrupting hegemony within these settings.

> All my life I have been searching: for those cultural mirrors, for like-minded Spirits, for kindness in the world, for a sense of belonging, for acceptance and for knowledge. Oh how thirsty I was to learn about what happened to our people. It was like I was born into a time where the cyclone had hit and the people were still walking around in states of trauma. No one could explain to me what happened. No one could connect the dots between my personal chaos and the political, institutional and cultural attacks against Indigenous peoples in Canada. (Absolon, 2011, pp. 17–18)

To find a quotation such as this, that reflects so strongly my reality, is like a gift. It affirms and puts words to the inner struggles I have felt for much of my life. It seems ironic that the academic institution, largely criticized for perpetuating homogeneity, is the very place I learned of Canada's shameful history, its totalizing dominance over Indigenous peoples, and how this history has shaped my own life. However, upon further reflection, it was not so much the institution itself that facilitated my healing journey, but rather the intersection of caring Indigenous scholars, relationships, and safe spaces. I identify this intersection as a key component to the decolonizing efforts within the academy. Specifically, I use the Critical and Indigenous Methodologies class to exemplify a decolonized space facilitating self-discovery of identity, belonging, healing, and connection. Kovach (2010) makes the statement that "identity and education always intersect" (p. 5), and as someone who has gained so much from the stories of other Indigenous methodologies scholars, particularly those of Kovach and Absolon, I would not be honouring them or my own story if I did not share it too.

My colonial story begins before I was born. It begins with my mother, who was born and raised on the land by my Etsi (grandmother) and Etsé (grandfather), around Great Bear Lake in the Sahtu region of Denendeh (Northwest Territories). My grandparents raised my mother in an environment full of love and laughter, strong values and respect for all Creation, to work hard (it was a matter of survival), and to honour the gift of life provided by the Creator. Born with the gift of healing, my Etsé, a medicine man, began training my mother as a small child. The secure and loving upbringing would change for my mother when she was forced to attend residential school at a young age. Within that confinement, she endured years of abuse and was punished for an identity imposed upon her, that categorized her as "Other." The "Othering" of my mother affected the trajectory of her life, and ultimately mine. A number of years after I was born, my mother made the difficult decision to leave me in the care of my father as she went on her healing path. My father, full of love and pride for his daughter, raised me in a secure, loving home. My father, who is non-Indigenous, eventually remarried a non-Indigenous woman and I became a big sister to two.

I lived a privileged life in this environment. I have no doubt this arrangement contributed to the achievements and successes I enjoy today, but I must acknowledge two things that occurred as a result of my childhood. One is that my achievements and successes are measured within Western standards – I have been trained all my life to succeed in a dominant Western society. The second is that the arrangements of my childhood affected my sense of identity and belonging as a Dene woman. The formative years of my life were shaped by not being primarily raised in my Dene culture. My accomplishments as a Dene woman measured within Dene standards are unbalanced. And because of this I have felt unbalanced as a person.

It would be unfair to say that I have not been exposed to my Dene culture – most of my vacation time was spent with my mother. Some of my best memories are of being on the land, going to drum dances, learning how to sew moccasins, and assisting in ceremonies. But these times were intermittent throughout my life. I have come to understand that part of my healing journey is to reveal, and not feel guilty for revealing, that I struggled emotionally and spiritually because my mother was not in my life on a constant basis. I struggled with being a Dene person in a dominant non-Indigenous environment and questioned my worth as a Dene child, youth, and adult. The older I became, the more uncomfortable I felt in my skin – I felt like a fraud calling myself a Dene person because my culture felt so foreign to me. I did not know how to embrace my culture when all I knew was how to live primarily as a non-Dene. Despite this, I learned how to live with this discomfort, although unable to identify what it was about my life that made me feel like an outsider.

When I began the bachelor of science in health promotion policy and research program at Dalhousie University, the discomfort remained. At least in Somba K'e (Yellowknife), where I had lived most of my life, I was surrounded by many Indigenous people. Halifax and the university environment were quite the opposite. I felt, for the first time in my life, aware of my skin colour. As Indigenous issues were brought up in class, and as the sole Indigenous student, I was immediately looked upon as the expert by my peers. An indication of the failure of the school system to educate Canadians about their history, this further fuelled my feeling of inadequacy as a Dene woman for not knowing the answers.

In the second year of my program I met Dr. Charlotte Loppie, who at that time was a professor within the health promotion program. My transformative and healing journey really begins at this point. It was Dr. Loppie who introduced me to the social determinants of Indigenous peoples' health, and the implications of colonialism. As I began to understand the history of Canada, I started to piece together how the residential school impacted my mother's life, and took every opportunity to explore this history in my coursework. I felt a deep, meaningful connection with this new knowledge – it was exciting to find subject matter that fuelled my passion and gave me a sense of purpose. At the same time, as I progressed through my undergraduate degree, the world of Indigenous health research began to unfold in front of me. I began attending graduate summer institutes and gatherings for students conducting research in Indigenous health, and learned very early in my research training about the ethics of conducting research with Indigenous communities. As an Indigenous student planning on conducting research in my own community some day, I learned that my pre-existing relationship with my home community of Somba K'e (Yellowknife) was an asset and something to be valued. However, this was also a reminder that I did not feel connected to my Dene heritage, and having spent several years on the east coast, I felt even more disconnected.

Once I completed my undergraduate degree, I started an interdisciplinary master's degree to continue working with Dr. Loppie, now teaching at the University of Victoria, located on the traditional territory of the Lekwungen and

WSÁNEC Nations. At that point I felt confident in the training I had received in Indigenous health research and looked forward to applying my work in this new program. I did not anticipate that my confidence would quickly dissipate throughout my coursework. My graduate program is grounded in critical theory and analysis (Studies in Policy and Practice Program, 2014), which I found extremely informative, particularly that hegemonic discourses render certain members of society powerless. Yet, I found the dynamic of my program's classes extremely uncomfortable as, once again, the only Indigenous student. My values and beliefs did not fall within the critical paradigm, yet I could not articulate this. I felt pressured and moulded into a direction that was uncomfortable, which did not feel right. Critical theorists are considered close allies of Indigenous knowledge systems (Kovach, 2010), but their roots remain firmly planted in a Western paradigm that privileges Western voices within that realm.

It was not until I took the Critical and Indigenous Methodologies class one year later as an elective that I began piecing together the roots of my discomfort both inside and outside the academy. My analysis brought me to this conclusion: the intersection of existing relationships with fellow graduate students and scholars teaching the methodologies course, coupled with a "safe" learning environment, created a decolonized space. Half of the students were Indigenous (including both professors), with a small class size of six students, four of whom I had personal relationships with. The course was delivered in the Centre for Indigenous Research and Community-Led Engagement, a space I was very familiar and comfortable with. This decolonized space was critical to my discovery of the healing element inherent within Indigenous methodologies. It afforded me a sense of security and assurance that no judgment would be cast upon my opinions. Until that point, I had not experienced an academic environment where I felt safe or comfortable expressing my opinions with my peers. The academic setting privileges Western knowledge systems and evidence-based research characterized by objectivity, not subjectivity. From my position and experiences as a Dene woman and student, with a passion for research involving Indigenous knowledge and healing systems, I often felt pressured by Western parameters to legitimize my research and work.

The most instrumental discussions leading to the discovery of healing within Indigenous methodologies were class discussions around epistemology. At the heart of Indigenous methodologies are our epistemologies and worldviews. Examining epistemologies requires that we begin our research with an examination of self and reflection on our Indigenous epistemologies. Because there is tremendous diversity of Indigenous cultures in Canada, so exist the possibilities for many different Indigenous methodologies. And just as Indigenous cultures are heterogeneous, so are Indigenous methodologies. For example, in our class, the other two Indigenous students explored Anishinaabe and Gitxsan values and worldviews (epistemologies) and how their respective methodologies would unfold from them.

How is this healing? Despite sharing a colonial history, each Indigenous person experiences the roots of colonialism according to their own personal and subjective lived experiences. As we walk our individual paths in this life-time we may be presented with the opportunity to begin resolving and making sense of our personalized colonial story. For those of us who have selected the path of academia, Indigenous methodologies can serve as a healing mechanism due to their emergence from our own cultural epistemology. In other words, to incorporate an Indigenous methodology within our research, we must turn to our specific cultural teachings. Once this was understood, I realized that my Indigenous methodology would be shaped by my experiences and worldview as a Dene woman, which in turn led to some powerful moments of understanding where my own issues of identity and belonging stem from.

My healing process involved allowing myself to let go of the guilt I have felt for being disconnected from my culture. I now understand this was largely out of my control and part of a wider colonizing agenda. Questioning my identity as a Dene woman gives power to and feeds into the very system that requires dismantling, whereas voicing my struggle and colonial story destabilizes it. As I reflected on my past, it also dawned on me how connected I am to my mother, her teachings, and my ancestors. Ever since I was a young girl, my mother's teachings have been consistent: that my grandparents and ancestors are always watching over me; to pray to them and the Creator to lead me on a good path; and that she loves me unconditionally as my grandparents loved her. I also learned of the Dene laws, developed by the great medicine man, Yamoria. These laws appear simple, but they organized Dene society around concepts of survival, compassion, and respect:

- Share what you have
- Help each other
- Love each other as much as possible
- Be polite
- Be respectful of Elders and everything around you
- Sleep at night and work during the day
- Young children should behave respectfully

- Be happy as much as possible
- Pass on the teachings

As I became familiar with the Dene laws, I realized how intrinsic these values are to my identity, adding to my confidence as a Dene woman and, in turn, shaping my Indigenous epistemology. My specific Dene epistemology, wrapped in my own personal and subjective experiences throughout my life, gives meaning to my research interests of examining how dominant health care ideologies perpetuate inequities for Indigenous peoples. Specifically, I am interested in disrupting biomedical, individualistic, and depoliticized discourses within health care through critical pedagogy of those operating within this sector. Educating service providers on the social determinants of Indigenous peoples' health intends to counter commonly held stereotypes of Indigenous peoples (Greenwood & de Leeuw, 2012). Employing an Indigenous methodology for my research is useful as it implicitly highlights the historical implications of dominant health care discourses; however, my reasons for choosing this methodology have a much deeper significance. I choose to incorporate a Dene Indigenous methodology for what it represents to me, as a Dene woman – self-discovery of identity, belonging, healing, and connection.

CONCLUSION

The transformation we underwent as a result of this decolonized space meant we had two very different outcomes. The process allowed Erin to reflect on her position of privilege, while allowing Karen to voice her struggles in life and within academic institutions. The power in this story reminds us that spaces of decolonization within the academy are occurring; these sites may be overt or subtle, but the impacts are profound because they reveal power dynamics, fostering deconstruction and self-reflection for members of the dominant white society, while bringing voice and healing to Indigenous students. As scholars, our ongoing transformative learning and healing experiences will inform our research and work we produce. We aim to contribute to a growing body of literature that displaces the taken for granted "truths" of a Western research paradigm. For Erin this means using critical research methodologies to resist Western notions of objectivity in research that mask underlying colonial power structures of patriarchy, heteronormativity, and gender binaries. This approach to research involves acknowledging and dissecting subjective experiences of power and position in order to inform change. For Karen, understanding that

Indigenous methodologies arise from Indigenous epistemology sheds light on how her colonial story is embedded within her research interests. Subjective experiences cannot be removed from the research process. As a methodology falling outside the Western paradigm and its discursive power, the process of reading, writing, and discussing Indigenous methodologies is political. But these methodologies also represent the beauty and diversity of Indigenous cultures and may serve as a gateway to healing ourselves.

REFERENCES

Absolon, K. E. (2011). *Kaandossiwin: How we come to know*. Halifax: Fernwood Publishing.

Greenwood, M. L., & de Leeuw, S. N. (2012). Social determinants of health and the future of Aboriginal children in Canada. *Paediatrics & Child Health, 17*(2), 381–384.

Kovach, M. (2009). Being Indigenous in the academy: Creating space for Indigenous scholarship in the academy. In A. Timpson (Ed.), *First Nations, first thoughts – new challenges* (pp. 51–76). Vancouver: UBC Press.

Kovach, M. (2010). *Indigenous methodologies: Characteristics, conversations, and contexts*. Toronto: University of Toronto Press.

McIntosh, P. (1989, July/August). White privilege: Unpacking the invisible knapsack. *Peace and Freedom*, 10–12.

Sinclair, R. (2004). Aboriginal social work education in Canada: Decolonizing pedagogy for the seventh generation. *First Peoples Child & Family Review, 1*(1), 49–61.

Sinclair, R. (2007). Identity lost and found: Lesson from the Sixties Scoop. *First Peoples Child & Family Review, 3*(1), 65–82.

Smith, L. T. (2012). *Decolonizing methodologies: Research and Indigenous peoples*. London: Zed Books.

Studies in Policy and Practice Program. (2014). *General information*. Retrieved March 23, 2017, from http://web.uvic.ca/calendar2014/GRAD/GPROGS/SiPoaP/index.html

Weber-Pillwax, C. (2012). *Proceedings from the National Colloquium on Racism, Cultural Safety, and Aboriginal Peoples' Health*. Ottawa: Canada.

Wilson, S. (2008). *Research is ceremony: Indigenous research methods*. Black Point, NS: Fernwood Publishing.

Wilson, W. A., & Yellow Bird, M. (Eds.). (2005). *For Indigenous eyes only: A decolonization handbook*. Santa Fe, NM: School of American Research Press.

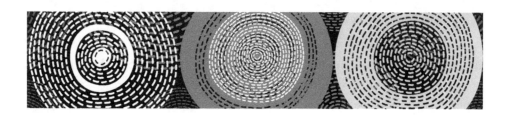

CHAPTER 6

A Tale of Two Drums: *Kinoo'amaadawaad Megwaa Doodamawaad* – "They Are Learning with Each Other While They Are Doing"

Paul Cormier and Lana Ray

Long ago and yet not so long ago, the Ojibwe and Sioux peoples were at war with each other. Warrior societies flourished and around the village campfires the talk was always of war. Only the women, children and old men were making up the village. The men and available youth were on the war path, even though most of the people forgot what they were fighting about.

In one of the main villages, there lived a little girl. Tired of war, she decided to fast to seek guidance. On the seventh day of her fast, a Grandmother appeared to her and told the little girl that the men were so busy with the war that they forgot how to connect with their hearts. She showed the little girl how to make a drum and told her that if the drum is given to the men, they would once again connect with their hearts.

The little girl took the finished drum to the men who were fighting. They accepted the drum and began to use the drum and use their voices as medicine prayers. They started connecting with their hearts, and soon all thought of war left their minds. Peace came into the people's hearts. (Adapted from the Sheshegwaning Women's Hand Drum Group, n.d.)

We choose to begin with an origin story about the drum because as Anishinaabe peoples we recognize the relevance and resonance of traditional stories to contemporary realities. As with our ancestors, Anishinaabe researchers are faced with hostile environments that disconnect us from our families, communities, and hearts. Although we enter the academy to become "word warriors" (Turner, 2006) it is easy to be consumed by the politics and power struggles of academia. Herrera (2011) corroborates this understanding, explaining that the intact belief systems of Indigenous students collide with the non-malleable walls of the academy, causing students to become lost.

Like the little girl described above, we must have courage and strength to promote peace while recognizing the central role of ceremony in this vision. Thus, we will present our own metaphorical drum tales to connect with our hearts from the unique perspective of community members, friends, researchers, and peace makers. We assume that when we are connected to our hearts in research, it will be ethical and can be used as a peace process where positive peace (explained below) is the ultimate goal. By "learning with each other while we are doing," there is no expert, there is no researcher, there are only people working and learning together on our personal peace journeys to improve the lives of our community and ourselves through ceremony. "The purpose of any ceremony is to build stronger relationships or bridge the distance between our cosmos and us. The research that we do as Indigenous peoples is a ceremony that allows us a raised level of consciousness and insight into our world" (Wilson, 2008, p. 137).

Using examples from our individual research projects, each narrative will discuss the use and meaning of land, the importance of relationships, the open-ended and dynamic nature of our process, and our personal journeys for peace by reconnection to our homeland through ceremony and community – which we believe form part of a holistic and ethical approach to research in Indigenous contexts (Ray & Cormier, 2012). Our individual narratives will provide readers with an explanation of how sacred space through connection to community relationships guided our paths toward personal and community peace through research. The discussion will conclude by utilizing a fasting ceremony as a framework to summarize learning and lessons to eliminate violence from research approaches.

WARRIOR SOCIETY: VIOLENCE, RESEARCH, AND THE ACADEMY

Perhaps naively, we began our academic journeys believing higher learning through research and formal education could provide understanding in our lives and possible solutions to the problems of our communities. However, as we progress through our academic careers what we discover are negative stories about power imbalances, academic jealousy, intellectual property theft, and competition for jobs, money, and recognition. LaRocque (2010) writes, "I have experienced Canada's archives, libraries, cathedrals, martyrs' shrines, museums, movies, forts, and university hallways—all places that reflect Eurocentrism—as places of exile" (p. 35) for Aboriginal peoples.

The academy continues to be a societal structure embedded with a culture of violence (Cormier, 2010). It remains a sanctuary of Western thought and structure (Ray, 2012) that is individualistic-centred, power driven, and competitive in nature (Herrera, 2011). Unfortunately these experiences are corroborated by historical analysis of Aboriginal post-secondary education (Stonechild, 2006), clear contemporary data on academic success rates of Aboriginal peoples in Canada (Statistics Canada, 2008), and narratives of other Indigenous academics, such as Waterfall (2008) and Herrera (2011), who discuss systemic lateral and epistemic violence.

In 2011 we co-authored an article for publication in the *Canadian Journal of Native Education* titled "Killing the Weendigo with Maple Syrup: Anishnaabe Pedagogy and Post-Secondary Research," in which we corroborated Cajete's (1994) view that urged for the resurgence of Indigenous pedagogies, suggesting that they are relevant within institutional settings, providing new insights and approaches to good relationships in the academy through ethical research.

Critical of the Eurocentrism present in the academy, we also posed an important question for Indigenous researchers based on Battiste's (2009) discussion of cognitive imperialism: how do we as Indigenous researchers avoid the trappings of cognitive imperialism within our work with Indigenous communities? Battiste's (2009) definition of cognitive imperialism suggests an imposition of one worldview over another, with the imposed worldview considered superior. In the context of colonialism in Canada and its impact on Aboriginal lives, cognitive imperialism is at the root of the violence. That violence is embedded in the structures of Canadian society, manifesting itself in unequal life chances, unequal distribution of wealth, poverty, and violence. The evidence of structural violence exists in Western countries not meeting everyday basic needs (clean water, health care, and education) of some resident minority populations (Galtung, 1990). Described as cultural violence, this violence exists in those aspects of culture that can be used to legitimize direct or structural violence, making it look or even feel right.

Galtung (1969) originally described this type of violence in the context of peace studies, suggesting that peace "has two sides: *absence of personal violence*, and *absence of structural violence*. We shall refer to them as *negative peace* and *positive peace* respectively" (p. 183). Clearly, positive peace should be the goal of peace researchers in the field of peace and conflict studies, like Paul. Similarly, for those of us who work in subjects like Indigenous studies, as Lana does, should we not model our beliefs? How do we accomplish this? Given the history of research and structures that support formal research in the academy, is it possible to remove the violence from the process? Is it possible to have an Indigenous research paradigm or are we just being tricked into believing we can?

As Berger and Luckmann (1967) remind us, although institutions and structures appear to be void of human influence, outside the control of individuals, it is individuals who in fact are responsible for the construction of institutions. This viewpoint is consistent with the Anishinaabe governance structure and a relational worldview. In the Anishinaabe governance structure the individual is present in the centre circle and is surrounded by rings that represent family, clan, community, and nation (Watts, 2006). In this respect the governance circle, like water, is subject to a ripple effect. This occurs because everything is interrelated.

Our responsibility as scholars is to promote a ripple of peace instead of perpetuating violence. Because the structures of the academy are inherently violent toward Indigenous thought, we must turn to our Indigenous ways of knowing to promote peace in our work, and "the only way to work exclusively within Traditional knowledge systems is for 'methodologies' to emerge from and be defined by our experiences and languages" (Ray, 2012).

CONNECTING TO OUR HEARTS: INDIGENOUS KNOWLEDGE, LAND, THE ACADEMY, AND LIVING PEACE

In Ojibwe the drum is called *o'dewegan*, which translates to "the tool that makes the heart sound" (Oginii Kwe, personal communication, 2004, as cited in Goudreau, 2006). Drumming is a celebration, a spiritual expression that can be shared with others who take part by listening, dancing, or drumming along. It awakens our spirits and is a tool used to connect to the Creator, Mother Earth, and all our relations. Through the drum, synchronicity, peace, and contentment can be achieved (Goudreau, Weber-Pillwax, Cote-Meek, & Wilson, 2008, p. 78). Duncan Cameron (1804), an employee of the fur trade, wrote in 1804 that a drum or two must always follow the Indigenous people of our traditional area, "for it would be as difficult for an Indian to do without his drum as it would be to go without a gun" (p. 255).

Historically many non-Aboriginal peoples and missionaries forbade the use of the drum because they thought it could start wars and contained evil spirits (Vennum, 1982). Similarly, today there is a resistance to heart knowledge (Gehl, 2012). Algonquin scholar Lynn Gehl (2012) explains that heart knowledge is both personal and spiritual and that wholistic truth, or *debwewin*, is derived from the connection of mind knowledge to heart knowledge. A lack of understanding and appreciation of the sophistication of Indigenous knowledges has resulted in its overwhelming absence within the confines of the academy. As Tobasonakwut Kinew once told Paul, white men never understood that our laws are contained within our drums and songs. When we sing and play the drum, we are enacting the laws of our people, the laws given to us by the Creator. This is why it is so important for us to practice ceremony, play our drums, sing, and celebrate (personal communication, July 21, 2006).

What we have come to understand throughout our life journeys is that the more we know about our sacred items and our ceremonies, "the more we will know about ourselves and how to obtain and maintain balance amongst the four elements of our being" (Goudreau et al., 2008, p. 79). Elder Norm, who was our guide during a fasting ceremony, taught us that the sweat lodge is a symbolic representation of Mother Earth's womb and the sweat lodge ceremony provides safety, comfort, and nourishment to us like it did before we were born. When we play the drum in the sweat lodge it connects us to the spirit of the land, our past relatives and friends who returned to the spirit world.

Mother Earth has a profound meaning to Anishinaabe people. The land, our mother, is more than a resource. It is our identity and culture (Adelson, 2007; Mills, 1994; Oakes, Riewe, Bruggencate, & Cogswell, 2009) and provides continuity between the past and present (Carlson, 2010; Christie, 2009) while giving food and nourishment—both physically and spiritually. It can also be a data source, a teacher, and spiritual guide. Returning to the land (our mother), returning to our teachings, has been our way of managing research with people whose experiences have been built on power and abuse. We have decided to show them and give them the experience of research relationships built on respect. As Ross (2006) suggests, "This means you have to involve them in the processes built on real-life manifestations of respectful relationships, not simply talk about them" (p. 156).

USING OUR VOICES AS MEDICINE PRAYERS: A TALE OF TWO DRUMS

Similar to other Aboriginal academics such as Atleo (2004), LaRocque (2010), and Absolon (2011), we struggle with the question of how to conduct research respectfully and reconcile our responsibilities to Indigenous families and communities while still fulfilling our requirements as academics. Through "learning with each other while we are doing," research has become, as Wilson (2008) describes, a ceremony, with relationships and relational accountability at the core

Paul's Drum Tale

Boozhoo, Paul Cormier is my given name, *Maiingan nindizhnikaaz. Opwaaganasiniing nin-doonjibaa. Maiingan n'dodem.*

I was invited to my first pow-wow when I was in my early 20s. As I sat and absorbed the sights, sounds, colours, and symbols of the ceremony, my heart felt heavy. The drumming resonated with my spirit, producing images of my grandmother sitting in her chair, softly singing. Ojibwe words flowed from her mouth in the rhythm of chanting. Looking up from my perch, knee-high coloured socks and familiar long, flowing skirt dancing in the sunlight, I felt undeniable love. The tears suddenly started flowing from my eyes, blurring the images of the dancers, leaving me saddened and lonely.

Years later, upon describing my first pow-wow experience to a Mi'kmaq Elder named Donna, she would explain to me, "You felt sad because the drum represents the heartbeat of Mother Earth and you feel the earth and her people are sick." She then handed me a drum and continued, "When you feel that sadness, play this drum and you will feel better. It is a healing drum and I've been carrying it for you."

of our approaches. Below we describe how our journeys began – only the Creator knows how and where they will end ...

We begin our stories with a traditional introduction because situating ourselves reminds us of who we are, and more importantly what our responsibilities are to ourselves, our families, and our communities.

My research journey took me back to my home – a place where I didn't want to conduct my PhD research. Although my PhD studies started in 2008, I believe my preparation started years ago with that first pow-wow experience and the emotions I felt that day hearing a traditional drum for the first time. My preparation included teachings from many Elders, members of various Aboriginal cultures in Canada, over many years. In this regard my research ceremony fits definitions of action research from a tradition emphasizing "cyclical, dynamic, and collaborative approaches to investigation" (Stringer, 2008, p. 13), finding appropriate data sources while pursuing a question in a seemingly meandering route while systematically documenting and data gathering.

I agree with Denzin and Lincoln's (2008) assertion that critical Indigenous qualitative research is always already political and that it must consider how research benefits, as well as promotes, self-determination for research participants. It begins with the concerns of Indigenous peoples and is assessed in terms of the benefits it creates for them. In this type of research, "researchers are directly accountable to

Indigenous persons" (Denzin & Lincoln, 2008, p. 2). My research must be useful to my community. It must be developed with community members, based on their localized needs, and recognize the political nature of Aboriginal lives in Canada and research in general. "The performative is always pedagogical, and the pedagogical is always political" (Denzin & Lincoln, 2008, p. 5).

I choose for my research to focus on process; *"Kinoo'amaadawaad Megwaa Doodamawaad* – 'They Are Learning with Each Other While They Are Doing'" is about learning. It is research on research, being both a research process and a peace process, which I argue are synonymous. Despite being from my community, I do not believe it is my role to make inferences about the daily lives of my family and friends. Wilson (2008) corroborates this view by suggesting researchers cannot possibly know all the relationships that brought other people to their present state and point of view. Without that knowledge you cannot judge another, the conclusions they make, or draw conclusions for them. This is not possible since conclusions are also relational (or relative).

Knowledge is a sacred gift from the Creator (Ray & Cormier, 2012). As such, our challenge as researchers is to consistently question why we've been given specific knowledge or experience. Thus, I endeavour to be more self-reflective in my writing and use my findings for wider audiences (Zeni, 1998) than simple academic requirements. That first pow-wow and the kindness my new friends showed me that day started me on a path to sharing that led me to reintroducing ceremony to members of my community through traditional knowledge in the form of stories, dreams, and ceremonies that Simpson (2000) describes as Anishinaabe ways of learning.

Lana's Drum Tale

Boozhoo, Lana Ray nindizhnikaaz. Red Rock nindoonjibaa. Oshowkinoozhe n'dodem. Waaskone Giizhigook Anishnaabe noswin.

Unlike Paul, my pursuit of a doctoral degree took me far away from home. I began to drive toward this new opportunity overwhelmed with excitement. But as this excitement began to wear, it was replaced by a heavy weight. It was the weight of being a 24-year-old female in a classroom of people (mostly men) double my age, coming from a small northern community and working among people from "big cities" with world experience, being the first in my family to attend any sort of graduate studies, and being amidst people with connections and credentials. It was the weight of self-doubt.

I hoped this weight would lift when my program commenced, but instead it was validated on a number of occasions. This included being mistaken for an assistant or someone's daughter, being singled out in class and asked if I knew what a word meant, hearing comments about my refinement and appearance by fellow students, it being assumed that another student was mentoring or helping me, and being asked to do clerical work related to my courses and program when this was not asked of classmates.

At times I wondered, How did I get into the program? Was there some sort of mistake? It felt loud and clear to me that I didn't belong. Yet, as the first in my family to pursue doctoral studies, I desperately wanted to succeed and I knew that belonging was essential to this success. I bargained with myself that it would be best to keep up appearances, and that this change would only be superficial, it would only be short term. However, as Homi Bhabha explains, through mimicry I was playing a dangerous game, one which can work to maintain colonial power structures (Swanson, 2012, p. 572). As I assumed my new persona, I forgot about humbleness and kindness, and engaged in theoretical conversations that were far removed from my family and community.

I am thankful that on a long weekend my mother came to visit and I took her to an academic function with my new circle of "friends." After a short while my mother told me that she was leaving. When we got home my mother told me she was disappointed in me, suggesting I had forgotten who I was. After this wake-up call I made the conscious decision to separate myself from the circle. This was not received well and I quickly became an outsider or "black sheep" in my department, encountering lateral and structural violence on a regular basis. It was debilitating and consumed the majority of my time and energy.

During this time I became close with a traditional woman from a nearby First Nation community. She taught me many things, including beading, and I became her helper. Like I had experienced growing up, there was a sense of love, respect, relevance, and groundedness to the learning. This experience created a space where I could heal and be filled with peace. I found the sacred space I needed, bringing a new level of self-awareness, and I realized I wanted to incorporate these experiences in my research but did not have the words.

A while later I came across the term *Kinoo'amaadawaad Megwaa Doodamawaad* in a document from my community. I was granted permission to use the term, not knowing Paul was also using this in his dissertation. When I found out that he was using the concept, I anticipated having to find a new description of my journey, but instead he was very supportive, sharing that this would only benefit our community. Since then we have grown to be friends and have participated in ceremony together, and I have moved home, reconnecting with family and friends and my traditional land base. All of these actions have further contributed to my understanding of "learning with each other while we are doing."

MOVING FORWARD THROUGH VISION: FASTING AS A FRAMEWORK FOR RESEARCH

Ceremony is the purest form of Indigenous methodology, defined by Evans, Hole, Berg, Hutchinson, and Sookraj as "research by and for Indigenous peoples, using techniques and methods drawn from the traditions and knowledges of those peoples" (as cited in Denzin & Lincoln, 2008, p. x). In honour of the gift of learning given on our journey, we conclude by summarizing our research ceremony according to the structure of a fast we both participated in. That ceremony is generally structured as follows:

Choosing the Site

Ceremonial site selection is as much about trusting your feelings, searching for physical signs, or following a dream as it is about the pragmatic aspects of safety, accessibility, and timing. Similarly, in designing ethical research in Indigenous contexts, researchers must be allowed to follow their hearts. This can present itself in the form of dreams, experiences, and/or friendships. The pragmatic tools of Eurocentric research (Creswell, 2009; Palys, 2003) are important. However, for Indigenous researchers, reconnecting to traditional homelands allows familiarization with local community and landscapes that define their personal research ceremony.

Preparing for the Fast

An Elder or guide leads the preparation by teaching and emotionally preparing participants. The Elder instructs participants on the gathering of tools and medicines, explains what they can expect, and questions what they hope to learn during the ceremony. Formal research similarly provides guides who share their experience, advise us on proper techniques and tools, and point us toward the right literature/data sources. Since beginning our research ceremonies, we have discovered that the physical environment surrounding our community contains many symbols that trigger the memories of our people. Book knowledge is important; however, the stories of our community members on the land provide a richer understanding of our circumstances.

The Sweat Lodge Ceremony – "Entering the Spirit World"

Preparing for the sweat lodge involves participatory learning that requires teachings as the lodge is constructed. Every element used is a symbolic representation of ancient teachings that act as memory devices for the transmission of knowledge across generations. All are accompanied by ancient lessons in the form of narratives. The ceremony begins with honouring those that have come before and we ask that they watch over us during the difficult journey of denying our bodies of food and water for four days. Despite the perception that formal research is a solitary endeavour, many people participate in the journey with us, including family, friends, communities, authors, and academics coming before us. We recognize their contribution to learning by acknowledging their work. In this way we build on the past, respectfully connecting the past, present, and future.

Entering the Fasting Site

Once entering the fasting site, participants receive knowledge in the form of dreams, physical symbols (animals, flora), or personal reflection. The ceremony happens over a number of days, with each day bringing new challenges, personal doubts, and learning. As each day passes, participants are asked to reflect on personal aspects of their lives (good and bad), a vision, and questions that require guidance. Participants are encouraged to walk around and connect to their environment, searching for messages and signs. We learn to relinquish control and trust the process. We reflect and acknowledge work that supports our hypothesis, critically analyze work that opposes, and most importantly, listen to signs that reaffirm our research paths or lead us in a different direction.

The Sweat Lodge Ceremony – "Returning from the Spirit World"

Returning from the spirit world, we give thanks for the love, support, and ongoing relationships of our family, friends, and community. We acknowledge the incredible accomplishment of completing our fast. We know that in the days, weeks, and years to come we will reflect on our experience. Many of the lessons we were given during our ceremony will only become clear after many hours of critical reflection. Similarly, in formal research, projects can occur over great lengths, with some patterns only becoming visible after many hours of reading, reflection, discussion, and experience. In Indigenous contexts, we give thanks by ensuring we conduct research relevant to our community and recognizing the contribution of others.

Gift Giving and Sharing of the Meal

Gift giving and sharing of the meal requires community participation. All those present are given gifts for their support before, during, and after the ceremony. A sharing circle is held so participants can share with community members what they learned during the fast. For us, giving back meant returning to our home areas, fasting for our community, maintaining ties with those who helped along the way, and ensuring our completed products are helpful in other ways than just fulfilling our degree requirements.

CONCLUSION: "LET THE DRUMS BE YOUR HEART / LET THE SONGS BE YOUR SOUL" (JERMEY, 1996, P. 145)

Research started out for us as a process learned from books through Eurocentric eyes, conducted according to the rules of the academy into which we were (or are) slowly being assimilated. While we find the violence embedded in the structures of the academy unchanged, we believe we can be accountable for our own promotion of internal peace which, in turn, will have a ripple effect on the violent structures that support formal research. Wilson (2008) asserts, "If research doesn't change you as a person, then you haven't done it right" (p. 135). In Indigenous contexts, this change should also occur on a community level. Conducting a research ceremony is a relational process conducive to a dynamic context of mutual knowledge exchange, allowing the emergence of learning that embodies the physical, the metaphysical, and their shared space, unearthing a natural ethos along the way (Ray, 2012, p. 96).

Like the traditional story of the little girl who fasted for guidance, we have also fasted for direction toward a path of peace. As Aboriginal academics we constantly struggle with the symptoms of power-based relationships where we feel the sting of cognitive imperialism and structural violence. Searching for personal answers, the ceremony we organized and participated in has had an influence on other community members who assisted and who now want to participate in a fast. The ripples are already beginning to create change and we sincerely hope others can learn from our experiences. While this chapter is a tale of two drums, we believe ultimately it is the voice of our community that clearly resonates through the words of our research like the heartbeat of Mother Earth. It has become a journey of healing, a peace process for our community and individually – male and female, like the two halves of the peace pipe, separated by many years but becoming good friends.

REFERENCES

Absolon, K. E. (2011). *Kaandossiwin: How we come to know*. Halifax: Fernwood Publishing.

Adelson, N. (2007). *Being alive well: Health and the politics of Cree well-being*. Toronto, ON: University of Toronto Press.

Atleo, R. (2004). *Tsawalk: A Nuu-chah-nulth worldview*. Vancouver, BC: UBC Press.

Battiste, M. (2009). Maintaining Aboriginal identity, language, and culture in modern society. In M. Battiste (Ed.), *Reclaiming Indigenous voice and vision* (pp. 192–208). Vancouver, BC: UBC Press.

Berger, P., & Luckmann, T. (1967). *The social construction of reality*. New York, NY: Double Day.

Cajete, G. (1994). *Look to the mountain: An ecology of Indigenous education*. Skyland, NC: Kivaki Press.

Cameron, D. (1804). *The Nipigon Country 1804*.

Carlson, K. T. (2010). *The power of place, the problem of time: Aboriginal identity and historical consciousness in the cauldron of colonialism*. Toronto, ON: University of Toronto Press.

Christie, J. J. (2009). *Landscapes of origin in the Americas: Creation narratives linking ancient places and present communities*. Tuscaloosa, AL: University of Alabama Press.

Cormier, P. (2010). Indigenous youth conflict intervention: The transformation of butterflies. *First Peoples Child & Family Review, 5*(3), 23–33.

Creswell, J. W. (2009). *Research design: Qualitative, quantitative, and mixed methods approaches* (3rd ed.). Thousand Oaks, CA: Sage.

Denzin, N. K., & Lincoln, Y. S. (2008). Preface; Introduction. In N. K. Denzin, Y. S. Lincoln, & L. T. Smith (Eds.), *Handbook of critical and Indigenous methodologies* (pp. ix–xv; 1–20). Thousand Oaks, CA: Sage.

Galtung, J. (1969). Violence, peace, and peace research. *Journal of Peace Research, 6*, 167–191.

Galtung, J. (1990). Cultural violence. *Journal of Peace Research, 27*(3), 291–305.

Gehl, L. (Gii-Zhigaate-Mindoo-Kwe). (2012). Debwewin journey: A methodology and model of knowing. *AlterNative 8*(1), 53–65.

Goudreau, G. (2006). *Exploring the connection between Aboriginal women's hand drumming and health promotion (Mino Bimaadiziwin)* (Unpublished master's thesis). University of Alberta, Edmonton, AB.

Goudreau, G., Weber-Pillwax, C., Cote-Meek, S., & Wilson, S. (2008). Hand drumming: Health-promoting experiences of Aboriginal women from a northern Ontario urban community. *Journal of Aboriginal Health, 4*(1), 72–83.

Herrera, M. (2011). *Red earth, brown earth: Walking in two worlds, the journey of Indigenous women in academia* (Unpublished doctoral dissertation). Canadian Institute of Integral Studies, San Francisco, CA.

Jermey, J. J. (1996). To be Native. In J. T. Maki (Ed.), *Let the drums be your heart: New Native voices* (p. 145). Vancouver, BC: Douglas & McIntyre.

LaRocque, E. (2010). *When the other is me: Native resistance discourse, 1850–1990.* Winnipeg, MB: University of Manitoba Press.

Mills, A. (1994). *Eagle down is our law: Witsuwit'en law, feasts, and land claims.* Vancouver, BC: UBC Press.

Oakes, J. R., Riewe, R., Bruggencate, R. T., & Cogswell, A. (2009). *Sacred landscapes.* Winnipeg, MB: Aboriginal Issues Press, University of Manitoba.

Palys, T. (2003). *Research decisions: Quantitative and qualitative perspectives.* Scarborough, ON: Thomson Canada Limited.

Ray, L. (2012). Deciphering the "Indigenous" in Indigenous methodologies. *AlterNative, 8*(1), 85–98.

Ray, L., & Cormier, P. N. (2012). Killing the Weendigo with maple syrup: Anishinaabe pedagogy and post-secondary research. *Canadian Journal of Native Education, 35*(1), 163–176..

Ross, R. (2006). *Returning to the teachings: Exploring Aboriginal justice.* Toronto, ON: Penguin Books.

Sheshegwaning Women's Hand Drum Group. (n.d.). *How the drum came back to the Ojibwe people.* Retrieved from http://sheshdrumgroup.tripod.com/drumstory/drumstory.html

Simpson, L. (2000). Stories, dreams, and ceremonies – Anishinaabe ways of learning. *Journal of American Indian Higher Education, 11*(4). Retrieved from www.tribalcollegejournal.org/stories-dreams-ceremonies-anishinaabe-ways-learning [Accessed Feb 13, 2018]

Statistics Canada. (2008). *2006 census: Aboriginal peoples in Canada 2006: Inuit, Métis and First Nations, 2006 census: Findings.* Retrieved from www12.statcan.ca/census-recensement/2006/as-sa/97-558/index-eng.cfm [Accessed April 1, 2010]

Stonechild, B. (2006). *The new buffalo: The struggle for Aboriginal post-secondary education in Canada.* Winnipeg, MB: University of Manitoba Press.

Stringer, E. (2008). *Action research in education* (2nd ed.). Upper Saddle River, NJ: Pearson/Merrill Prentice Hall.

Swanson, K. (2012). The noble savage was a drag queen: Hybridity and transformation in Kent Monkman's performance and visual art intervention. In M. Fitzgerald & S. Rayter (Eds.), *Queerly Canadian: An introductory reader in sexuality studies* (pp. 565–576). Toronto, ON: Canadian Scholars' Press.

Turner, D. (2006). *This is not a peace pipe: Towards a critical Indigenous philosophy.* Toronto, ON: University of Toronto Press.

Vennum, T. (1982). *The Ojibwa dance drum: Its history and construction.* Washington, DC: Smithsonian Institute Press.

Waterfall, B. (2008). *Decolonizing Anishinabec social work education: An Anishinabe spiritually infused reflexive study.* Retrieved from ProQuest Dissertations and Theses (Doctoral dissertation). (NR39929)

Watts, V. (2006). *Towards Anishnaabe governance and accountability: Reawakening our relationships and sacred Bimaadiziwin* (Unpublished master's thesis). University of Victoria, Victoria, BC.

Wilson, S. (2008). *Research is ceremony: Indigenous research methods*. Black Point, NS: Fernwood Publishing.

Zeni, J. (1998). A guide to ethical issues & action research. *Educational Action Research, 6*(1), 9–19.

PART III

COMMUNITIES WE RESEARCH WITH

In Indigenous research we frequently refer to "community," but what exactly do we mean by it? What constitutes community, or to what scale or level are we referring? Traditional institutions and values structure community. Dene community is different from Nisga'a community, is different from Cree community, and there are further differences within the communities of those nations. Community also means something different in an urban context than on-reserve or in rural or remote communities. Some communities share the same geographic space, have a land base, have traditional or colonial governments and institutions, while others may not. Yet all these communities share common concerns and aspirations.

In the introduction we explain that Indigenous and traditional knowledges, often developed over thousands of years, are governed by communities, and specific protocols must be observed to work with these types of knowledges. Researching these knowledges in a good way demands that the researcher do more than work with community members and their knowledge respectfully. The researcher may be required to actively participate in traditional activities and experience knowledge in embodied ways. Many Indigenous knowledges are lived in community, rather than being taught in a decontextualized way. The academy has devalued Indigenous knowledges and ways of knowing, and thus the reclaiming and resurgence of these knowledges remains a critical aspect of research endeavours (Kuokkanen, 2007; Tuck & McKenzie, 2015).

Communities, of course, expect cultural protocols to be followed by researchers no matter what topic is being researched. It is expected that researchers do research that is useful to the community and that they share that knowledge back to the community rather than just with an external academic audience. Indigenous research has the potential to assist Indigenous scholars in reclaiming their identity and culture.

In addition to the chapters in this section by Lorrilee McGregor, Angela Mashford-Pringle, and Darrel Manitowabi and Marion Maar, we recommend you read Paige Restoule, Carly Dokis, and Benjamin Kelly's chapter on community research (Chapter 13).

LEARNING AND REFLECTION QUESTIONS

1. Which of the contributors' approaches and recommendations for working with Indigenous communities surprised you? Do you have any of your own recommendations to add?

2. Angela Mashford-Pringle, Darrel Manitowabi, and Marion Maar invested substantial time and resources in building relationships among organizations and staff involved in the research and in ensuring consensus about the design of the research. Was this time well spent?

3. How do your personal interests overlap with your interests as a researcher?

4. Why might Indigenous communities wish to engage in academic research? Why might they not?

5. What decisions about the research were made jointly with people and organizations in the community? What were the effects of sharing decision-making?

6. How does engaging with existing institutions, Indigenous and non-Indigenous, affect how the researchers carry out their research?

7. Why might one establish a research steering committee?

8. Each of these researchers' experiences reflect the specific Indigenous communities they worked with. Are their learnings about working with communities useful to someone doing research with a different community? How would you go about finding out?

9. How are the opportunities and challenges of conducting research with Indigenous people similar and different in urban and non-urban contexts?

10. How can we evaluate whether community engagement or even the research itself was successful?

REFERENCES

Kuokkanen, R. (2007). *Reshaping the university: Responsibility, Indigenous epistemes, and the logic of the gift.* Vancouver: UBC Press.

Tuck, E., & McKenzie, M. (2015). *Place in research: Theory, methodology, and methods.* New York: Routledge.

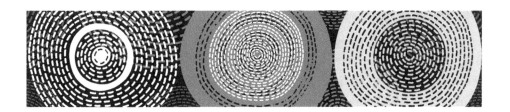

CHAPTER 7

Conducting Community-Based Research in First Nation Communities

Lorrilee McGregor

INTRODUCTION

In keeping with Indigenous discourse I will introduce myself in my language. *Giiziptot ndiznakaaz. Wagaskinaga n'donjaba. Makwa dodem.* My name is Lorrilee McGregor, I'm from Whitefish River First Nation, and I belong to the bear clan. I come from a family of chiefs and academics and a community rich in beauty and culture. I am fortunate that I know my family and community history and can trace my ancestry as far back as Chief Shawanosoway (a renowned medicine man), whose daughter, Pichins, married a Scottish trader named Captain Alexander McGregor circa the mid-1800s. As an Anishinaabe[1] researcher with 25 years of experience working with First Nation communities, I offer my advice to researchers who wish to work with First Nation communities. My aim is to clarify appropriate conduct and inspire a dynamic and rewarding research process that benefits Indigenous peoples.

RESEARCH IS A DIRTY WORD

To survive and thrive, Indigenous peoples have always been engaged in research and knowledge generation through observation and experimentation. Outsider research has a negative reputation in many Indigenous communities due to unethical practices, irrelevant topics, and incorrect assumptions. Numerous times researchers have parachuted into communities, extracted data, and left without sharing the results with the community. Furthermore, often such research did not lead to improvements in community health and well-being. Linda Tuhiwai Smith (1999) articulates the reaction many Indigenous peoples have when confronted with the word "research":

> The word itself, "research," is probably one of the dirtiest words in the indigenous world's vocabulary. When mentioned in many indigenous contexts, it stirs up silence, it conjures up bad memories, it raises a smile that is knowing and distrustful.... The ways in which scientific research is implicated in the worst excesses of colonialism remains a powerful remembered history for many of the world's colonized peoples.... It galls us that Western researchers and intellectuals can assume to know all that it is possible to know of us, on the basis of their brief encounters with some of us. It appals us that the West can desire, extract and claim ownership of our ways of knowing, our imagery, the things we create and produce and then simultaneously reject the people who created and developed those ideas and seek to deny them further opportunities to be creators of their own culture and own nations. (p. 1)

For many years, Indigenous peoples were the subjects of studies that did not strengthen their culture, identity, or well-being. Fortunately, Indigenous peoples have been asserting their role in research processes, and taking charge of the research agenda. Marlene Brant Castellano (2004) describes this development:

> Aboriginal Peoples in organizations and communities, as well as universities and colleges and some government offices, are now engaged in transforming Aboriginal research into an instrument for creating and disseminating knowledge that once again authentically represents ourselves and our understanding of the world. (p. 98)

Various social movements among Indigenous peoples – partly in response to the federal government's publication of the *Statement of the Government of Canada on Indian Policy* (Minister of Indian Affairs and Northern Development Ottawa, 1969), also known as *The White Paper* – spurred participatory approaches to research such as land use studies and needs assessments (Jackson, 1993). Other types of research that Indigenous peoples have employed include program evaluations and community polls. These studies are not necessarily published in academic journals but are intended to inform decision-making at the community level.

Another response to negative research experiences has been the development of community research ethics protocols aimed at ensuring respect for local values and protecting the community from unethical research practices. Examples of Indigenous community ethics guidelines and/or processes include:

- *Protocol for Review of Environmental and Scientific Research Proposals* (Akwesasne Task Force on the Environment, 1996)
- *Code of Ethics: Guide for Interveners and Users of the Pathways to "Miupi-maatisiiun" Services* (Cree Board of Health and Social Services of James Bay, 2009)
- *Guidelines for Ethical Aboriginal Research* (Aboriginal Health Research Review Committee, 2003)
- *Code of Research Ethics* (Kahnawake Schools Diabetes Prevention Project, 2007)
- *Mi'kmaw Research Principles and Protocols* (Mi'kmaw Ethics Watch, 1999)
- *Protocols & Principles for Conducting Research in a Nuu-Chah-Nulth Context* (Nuu-chah-nulth Tribal Council, 2008)

These guidelines are publicly available for other communities who wish to adapt them for their own use.

A DECOLONIZING FRAMEWORK

Indigenous peoples' negative experiences with research are connected to colonization. Consequently, Smith (1999) advocates for a decolonizing research methodology, or

> [a] process which engages with imperialism and colonialism at multiple levels. For researchers, one of those levels is concerned with having a more critical understanding of the underlying assumptions, motivations and values which inform research practices. (p. 20)

Smith (1999) also suggests using Indigenous methodologies when conducting research with Indigenous peoples. The chapters by Paul Cormier and Lana Ray, Shelly Johnson, and Karen Hall and Erin Cusack in this volume each explore the decolonizing process in the context of research. Bartlett and colleagues (2007) have developed a process framework for decolonizing research that is "iterative, culturally based, and process-oriented." There are six processes in this framework: rationalizing, enabling, facilitating, experiencing, accepting, and enacting (Bartlett, Iwasaki, Gottlieb, Hall, & Mannell, 2007). A decolonizing framework is a meaningful way to guide community-based participatory action research because it "challenges traditional western ways of doing research, and requires the reformulation of underlying assumptions and methods" (Bartlett et al., 2007, p. 2371). Important principles of this framework include: negotiating research relationships, utilizing Indigenized methods, recognizing reciprocal capacity building, and crediting Indigenous knowledge.

RECOMMENDATIONS FOR CONDUCTING RESEARCH IN FIRST NATION COMMUNITIES

Devising recommendations for research approaches that will work with all Indigenous populations is challenging because of cultural, linguistic, historical, and geographical heterogeneity among and within Indigenous communities. Because my work experience has primarily been with Anishinaabe communities in northern Ontario this chapter draws examples from this region.

Awareness of History

Before working with an Indigenous community, researchers must appreciate that vibrant cultures existed in North America prior to colonization and that these communities continue to thrive. They must also understand how colonization impacts Indigenous peoples' experience of the research process (Bartlett et al., 2007; LaVeaux & Christopher, 2009). Manifestations of colonization include the dispossession of land, replacement of traditional forms of government, interruption of language transmission, prohibition of ceremonies, and disruption of family continuity, especially through the residential school system and the Sixties Scoop, when many Aboriginal children were seized and placed in foster care.

Cultural Diversity

Given the diversity of Indigenous communities, researchers must be mindful of differences in cultures, languages, dialects, and beliefs. Other differences may be a result of ideology, values, attitudes, lifestyles, gender, age, and social class

(Bartlett et al., 2007). Researchers must also be aware of local customs and protocols, and expect diverse perspectives even within the same community. For example, in Anishinaabe communities, offering tobacco, which is considered a sacred medicine, symbolizes an invitation to a reciprocal relationship. However, some community members may be uncomfortable with this offering, particularly if they strongly identify with Christian beliefs. Prior to a presentation, researchers must determine whether tobacco is appropriate to offer so they do not offend the person and embarrass themselves. This is just one cultural norm that may differ among and within First Nations communities.

Relationship Building

Kristen Jacklin and Phyllis Kinoshameg (2008) noted that, while Kinoshameg was a member of the community in which they were doing research, Jacklin had to establish a relationship with the community of Wikwemikong before gaining permission to conduct her dissertation research. Similarly, Marion Maar and her colleagues (2011) discuss the importance of building rapport with communities for successful engagement. Additionally, Judith Bartlett and her colleagues (2007) state that "the research process began well in advance of submitting our research proposal to the funding partner" with early team meetings, telephone calls, and emails among the community partners and academic investigators (p. 2377).

I would suggest there are different levels to relationship building in First Nation communities – namely, with the leadership, with band administration and staff, and also with community members. These relationships may take years to nurture and develop, and evolve over time (Schinke et al., 2008). In relationship building, it is important to join with the community for events other than research. For example, one community encouraged academic investigators to attend community events to meet community members (Zehbe, Maar, Nahwegahbow, Berst, & Pintar, 2012).

Community Champions

For researchers, a good strategy is to engage the assistance of a champion who can lobby within the community for a study and also connect the researcher to key people. For example, Jacklin notes that it was Kinoshameg who helped smooth the transition when there was a change in political leadership (Jacklin & Kinoshameg, 2008). Likewise, in three remote Ontario First Nation communities, the support and assistance of senior management was critical to the success of Bruce Minore and his colleagues' (2004) participatory action research project on continuity of care. Maar and colleagues (2011) also note the importance of local champions in recruiting research participants. A community champion can help a researcher get a meeting with the chief and Council, introduce the researcher to key staff members, identify community members for a research steering committee, and help navigate the ins and outs of a First Nation community. A community champion can be a gatekeeper in that they may have the power to control or limit research being done in the community, but the role of a community champion differs from that of a gatekeeper in that they actively support and promote research.

Community Leadership

Most Band Councils have a two-year term of office, and once elected, a new chief and Council could withdraw support for research already in progress. During Jacklin's dissertation research with Wikwemikong Unceded Indian Reserve, Jacklin and Kinoshameg (2008) noted that it was challenging to work amidst the turnover in political and health centre leadership. They saw the need to engage the newly elected Council in a dialogue about an ongoing research project; however, like other researchers, they found the chief to be extremely busy addressing local, regional, national, and international issues. For researchers, it is crucial to cultivate good working relationships with the chief, the Band Council, and the band administration and staff, as getting time with them, though difficult, is extremely valuable.

Before commencing a study in a First Nations community, researchers must obtain permission from the elected leadership. In the case of Haudenosaunee[2] communities where authority structures are complex, researchers may also need permission from traditional governing entities.

Partnerships and Collaboration

Fundamental to community-based research are research partnerships (Jacklin & Kinoshameg, 2008; LaVeaux & Christopher, 2009; Maar et al., 2011). Here the community negotiates its level of involvement based on available human and financial resources. For the researcher, this means giving up absolute control and collaborating during all research phases. A research steering committee can greatly facilitate this process.

For its part, the community can negotiate benefits such as capacity building, economic incentives through research positions, and ensuring the allocation of some of the research budget in the community. This is in addition to the benefit of generating knowledge that is important to the community.

Research partnerships can be formalized through a research agreement that outlines details such as: how to obtain informed consent; data collection methods; data storage and who will have access to data; and how results will be reported back to the community and disseminated (Canadian Institutes of Health Research [CIHR], 2007).

Research Topic

Community partnerships and collaboration help ensure that research topics are relevant to the community. Often a researcher approaches a community with a research topic that is not a priority for the community, and sometimes the community agrees to the research simply to avoid missing an opportunity. Other times, a research topic is generated organically through discussions between researchers and the community. Such was the case for research on human papillomavirus in northwestern Ontario (Zehbe et al., 2012). Another example was in the community of Wikwemikong, where Robert Schinke and his colleagues (2008) developed a long-term research relationship and the community began to identify the research they wanted and worked with Dr. Schinke to develop the study. Identifying a community's research priorities through a partnership and engagement process can also generate relevant research topics. The Manitoulin First Nations Diabetes Care and Prevention Research Project, for example, was initiated by six First Nation communities and three health boards (Maar, Gzik, & Larose, 2010). Several different diabetes research projects were developed as a result of this engagement process.

Data Collection Methods

The researcher, in collaboration with the community, should develop the most appropriate method for collecting data. For example, Maar and colleagues (2011) were informed that lengthy questionnaires might not work well in Aboriginal communities, especially if the survey was not culturally sensitive or offered insufficient response options. In some cases, oral interviews may be preferable to written surveys, and here researchers could offer to conduct interviews at the community health centre if participants do not want a researcher visiting them at home.

Biological sampling is viewed with a high degree of caution because, according to some Indigenous philosophies, every part of the body, including tissue samples, is considered sacred (CIHR, 2007). Furthermore, because of past unsanctioned uses of biological samples, concerns remain about how researchers could potentially be using the samples for other purposes, such as genetic patenting (Maar et al., 2011).

Ethical Research

Genuine community-based research must also be ethical. Brant Castellano (2004) interprets Leroy Little Bear's view: "human action, to achieve social good, must be located in an ethical, spiritual context as well as its physical and social situation" (p. 103). Research is human action, and since community-based research aims to make a constructive difference in the world, it can be seen as "achieving social good." Similarly, Zehbe and colleagues (2012) discuss the intersection of public health and Aboriginal holistic health approaches and the ethical space between the two which creates an opportunity for a dialogue.

Research with Indigenous peoples should include a formal or informal community ethics review process in conjunction with an institutional (i.e., university or hospital) review, where applicable. If community processes are not available, then the *Tri-Council Policy Statement 2* (Interagency Advisory Panel on Research Ethics, 2014), Chapter 9, on "Research Involving the First Nations, Inuit and Métis People of Canada" should be the minimum standard that is adhered to. For consultation purposes, other community-specific Aboriginal research ethics guidelines are also publicly available – for example, the *Guidelines for Ethical Aboriginal Research* (Aboriginal Health Research Review Committee, 2003) developed on Manitoulin Island.

Data Analysis and Interpretation

Data analysis and interpretation can be the most challenging aspect of community research. There is always a danger that only one lens will be applied – that of the researcher, who has certain experiences as well as the time and resources to do it. However, there are ways to ensure data is interpreted within a cultural context (LaVeaux & Christopher, 2009). Bartlett and her colleagues (2007) had a researcher manage the initial data handling, conducting content analysis and coding key statements. However, community members were involved in this process by clustering themes. Schinke and his colleagues (2008) used a similar process in Wikwemikong, where the community research team led the data analysis process.

Knowledge Translation and Action

The co-generation of knowledge results from shared understandings between researchers and Indigenous communities, and both contribute to the resulting body of knowledge (Wilson, 2001). Bartlett and her colleagues (2007) refer to this as "reciprocal capacity building," which is more about process than a product (e.g., a report).

Translating results into meaningful information that Aboriginal communities can act upon is a critical phase of community-based research. For example, results of a needs assessment in Wikwemikong were used to support funding proposals and to develop a strategic plan for the health department (Jacklin & Kinoshameg, 2008). Sometimes exploratory research leads to the development of a large-scale study (Zehbe et al., 2012), or a new study can build on a completed study (Schinke et al., 2008).

Finally, researchers must communicate results to the community before publishing them. First Nation community members dislike being the last to hear about study results.

Food and Incentives

Food is an important aspect of culture, and for Indigenous communities sharing food is about more than meeting nutritional needs. Food is about sharing time and connecting with others. To indicate respect for attendees' time and attention, research meetings and presentations should always have food available. If a researcher visits a community member at home, they may be offered tea as a gesture of hospitality. Drinking tea, or sharing a meal with your hosts, is considered good manners.

Gift giving in Indigenous communities perpetuates a historical custom of interacting with others. As such, incentives such as honorariums or gifts are expected as acknowledgement for sharing information with a researcher (Maar et al., 2011). The researcher must discuss appropriate gifts and levels of compensation with community contacts.

Expect Lengthy Time Frames

After obtaining community consent, researchers can expect matters to move more slowly than in other settings. Expect lengthened time frames when scheduling activities such as getting on the Band Council agenda, meeting with staff, and arranging community meetings. Staff are typically too busy to drop everything to assist a researcher, and their schedules must be accommodated. Researchers may hear the term "Indian time," which means things will happen when they are meant to happen. Furthermore, if there is a death in the community expect that meetings and data collection will be postponed.

Communication Styles

The communication style of Indigenous people who grow up on the reserve can be perceived as passive and quiet. Researchers may notice subjects are silent for a while before responding to questions. Researchers should not be tempted to fill this quiet time with more questions or with their own thoughts. The best course is to be silent and wait patiently.

Meetings among First Nations people tend to be informal with much joking and laughter. Researchers need to be able to laugh at themselves, not take themselves too seriously, because most Indigenous people like to tease. In fact, teasing is a sign of acceptance. Finally, in First Nation communities, the dress code tends to be relaxed.

Credentials

While researchers may feel the need to reassure the community they are well qualified by listing their degrees and extensive experience, in First Nation communities they must resist the urge to do this unless pressed for details. Humility and modesty are the preferred conduct in First Nations communities, and volunteering unsolicited information about credentials may be perceived as arrogant or boastful.

Confidentiality

The kinship network is vast within and among First Nation communities, so kinship relationships are important. Research, especially focus groups and interviews, can become complicated or constrained due to concerns about anonymity and confidentiality. The researcher may need to negotiate data storage arrangements with considerations for limiting access to maintain anonymity and confidentiality. If, for example, raw data was going to be stored at the band office, research participants might be concerned that anyone working at the band office might have access to their data. The solution might be to ensure that data is stored in a locked filing cabinet with restricted access and that research participants are aware of this.

SUMMARY AND DISCUSSION

As an approach, community-based research allows Indigenous communities to direct and control the research agenda. Due to the diversity among Indigenous populations in culture, ideology, values, attitudes, lifestyles, gender, age, and social class, the research process must be specific to the community. Numerous recommendations situate community-based research within a decolonizing framework. Based on a review of community-based research with First Nation communities, the following approaches can be recommended:

- being cognizant of Canada's colonial history and its impact on Indigenous populations;
- appreciating the diversity of Indigenous populations;
- recognizing community leadership as critical for community consent;
- collaborating with community champions who can facilitate the research process;
- developing partnerships and collaborating with the community;
- negotiating a research topic;
- using appropriate data collection methods;
- creating an ethical space for dialogue and respecting community ethics;
- involving the community in data analysis and interpretation;
- ensuring that knowledge translation and action are research outcomes; and
- providing food and incentives to the community.

This is not an exhaustive list of recommendations, but a starting point for respectful and ethical community-based research. Community-based research is a dynamic research approach that can empower and engage a community and also affect researchers positively. Research becomes more than a transaction between researcher and community; it is about relationships and processes that culminate in long-term benefits for both parties. Research should also inspire action that makes a difference in the lives of Indigenous peoples.

NOTES

1. Anishinaabe refers to a language and cultural group that has been referred to as Ojibway, Ojibwe, Chippewa, or Algonquin, but also includes Odawa and Potawatomi.

2. Also known as Onkwehonwe or Iroquois.

REFERENCES

Aboriginal Health Research Review Committee. (2003). *Guidelines for ethical aboriginal research.* Little Current, ON: Noojmowin Teg Health Centre. Retrieved from www.noojmowin-teg.ca/Shared%20Documents/GEAR%20-%20FINAL.pdf

Akwesasne Task Force on the Environment. (1996). *Protocol for review of environmental and scientific research proposals.* Hogansburg, NY. Retrieved from https://sites.google.com/site/atfeonline/documents

Bartlett, J. G., Iwasaki, Y., Gottlieb, B., Hall, D., & Mannell, R. (2007). Framework for Aboriginal-guided decolonizing research involving Metis and First Nations persons with diabetes. *Social Science & Medicine, 65*(11), 2371–2382.

Brant Castellano, M. (2004). Ethics of aboriginal research. *Journal of Aboriginal Health, 1*(1), 98–114.

Canadian Institutes for Health Research. (2007). *CIHR guidelines for research involving Aboriginal people.* Retrieved from www.cihr-irsc.gc.ca/e/29134.html

Cree Board of Health and Social Services of James Bay. (2009). *Code of ethics: Guide for interveners and users of the pathways to "Miupimaatisiiun" services.* Chisasibi, QC. Retrieved from www.creehealth.org/library/online/corporate/cbhssjb-code-ethics-201

Interagency Advisory Panel on Research Ethics. (2014). *Tri-council policy statement 2.* Ottawa: Government of Canada. Retrieved from www.pre.ethics.gc.ca/eng/policy-politique/initiatives/tcps2-eptc2/chapter9-chapitre9/

Jacklin, K., & Kinoshameg, P. (2008). Developing a participatory Aboriginal health research project: "Only if it's going to mean something." *Journal of Empirical Research on Human Research Ethics, 3*(2), 53–67.

Jackson, T. (1993). A way of working. In P. Park, M. Brydon-Miller, B. Hall, & T. Jackson (Eds.), *Voices of change: Participatory research in the United States and Canada,* (pp. 47–64). Westport, CT: Bergin & Garvey.

Kahnawake Schools Diabetes Prevention Project. (2007). *Code of research ethics.* Kahnawake, QC. Retrieved from www.ksdpp.org/elder/code_ethics.php

LaVeaux, D., & Christopher, S. (2009). Contextualizing CBPR: Key principles of CBPR meet the Indigenous research context. *Pimatisiwin: A Journal of Aboriginal and Indigenous Community Health, 7*(1), 1–25.

Maar, M., Gzik, D., & Larose, T. (2010). Beyond expectations: Why do Aboriginal and Euro-Canadian patients with type 2 diabetes on a northern, rural island demonstrate better outcomes for glycemic, blood pressure and lipid management than comparison populations? *Canadian Journal of Diabetes, 34*(2), 127–135.

Maar, M. A., Lightfoot, N. E., Sutherland, M. E., Strasser, R. P., Wilson, K. J., Lidstone-Jones, C. M., … Williamson, P. (2011). Thinking outside the box: Aboriginal people's suggestions for conducting health studies with Aboriginal communities. *Public Health, 125*(11), 747–753.

Mi'kmaw Ethics Watch. (1999). *Mi'kmaw research principles and protocols.* Cape Breton University, NS. Retrieved from www.cbu.ca/mrc/ethics-watch

Minister of Indian Affairs and Northern Development Ottawa. (1969). *Statement of the Government of Canada on Indian policy.* Ottawa: Queen's Printer. Retrieved from www.aadnc-aandc.gc.ca/eng/1100100010189

Minore, B., Boone, M., Katt, M., Kinch, P., & Birch, S. (2004). Addressing the realities of health care in northern Aboriginal communities through participatory action research. *Journal of Interprofessional Care, 18*(4), 360–368.

Nuu-chah-nulth Tribal Council. (2008). *Protocols & principles for conducting research in a Nuu-Chah-Nulth context.* Retrieved from www.fnehin.ca/uploads/docs/NTO_Research_Protocol.pdf

Schinke, R. J., Hanrahan, S. J., Eys, M. A., Blodgett, A., Peltier, D., & Ritchie, S. D. (2008). The development of cross-cultural relations with a Canadian Aboriginal community through sport research. *Quest, 60*(3), 357–369.

Smith, L. T. (1999). *Decolonizing methodologies: Research and Indigenous peoples.* New York: Zed Books.

Wilson, S. (2001). What is an Indigenous research methodology? *Canadian Journal of Native Education, 25*(2), 175–179.

Zehbe, I., Maar, M., Nahwegahbow, A., Berst, K., & Pintar, J. (2012). Ethical space for a sensitive research topic: Engaging First Nations women in the development of culturally safe human papillomavirus screening. *Journal of Aboriginal Health, 8*(3), 41–50.

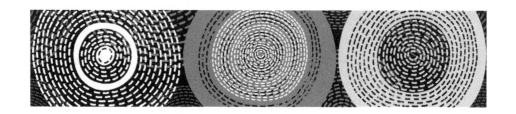

CHAPTER 8

Aboriginal Children in Toronto:
Working Together to Improve Services

Angela Mashford-Pringle

INTRODUCTION

This chapter examines how the City of Toronto's Aboriginal Advisory and Planning Table on Early Childhood Development attempted to engage with the south Etobicoke Aboriginal community (herein referred to as the "Table"). The Table worked with an Algonquin researcher and community partners to determine where Aboriginal families reside and which programs and services could be of benefit to them. The end goal of the research was to provide Aboriginal children in Etobicoke access to culturally relevant, affordable early childhood care and education in an area that had previously been underserviced; at the time of the research, there were few Aboriginal-specific services for Aboriginal people in Etobicoke. As such, there was a need to determine how to engage the Aboriginal families in south Etobicoke in order to understand their needs and receive valued input from the community.

According to Statistics Canada (2008b), there are approximately 31,000 self-identified Aboriginal people in the city of Toronto, whereas McCaskill, FitzMaurice, & Cidro (2011) estimated from their research that there may be as many as 80,000 Aboriginal people. Additionally, the *Toronto Aboriginal Research Project Report* (TARP) (McCaskill et al., 2011) and *Little Voices Report* (Native Child and Family Services of Toronto, 2011a) estimated approximately 80,000 Aboriginal people reside in the city of Toronto. When looking at Etobicoke specifically, there are 113,905 residents in Etobicoke and, of these residents, 1,450 are self-identified Aboriginal people (Statistics Canada, 2008a). The Aboriginal population in south Etobicoke is primarily First Nations and Métis. If the numbers reported by Aboriginal organizations themselves are accurate, then the number of Aboriginal people and families in south Etobicoke may be much higher. For instance, research has shown that due to economic conditions, many Aboriginal people often report living in areas that have low rents and high numbers of low-income families, such as south Etobicoke (City of Toronto, 2008; Environics Research Group, 2011; McCaskill et al., 2011; Native Child and Family Services of Toronto, 2011a, 2011b). The discrepancy in Aboriginal population estimates deserves further study, but was beyond the scope of the current project.

Based on early reports, the members of the Aboriginal Advisory and Planning Table (henceforth known as Table members) wanted to determine the programs and services available for Aboriginal children and families in the south Etobicoke area of the city of Toronto; the belief held by the majority of the members was that there were no culturally appropriate services in place for them. As the lead researcher, I developed a work plan to conduct primary research with Table members, front-line staff, managers, and senior management at south Etobicoke organizations that provide programs and services to children and families in order to determine what currently exists in the area for any child and family.

The Table members agreed that, in order to improve the lives of Aboriginal children and their families, it is important to provide quality, culturally sensitive, and responsive programs and services. By providing Aboriginal-specific programs and services to Aboriginal families and their children, there is also a chance to revitalize and reclaim their culture and worldview (Mustard & McCain, 2002). However, as highlighted previously, determining where Aboriginal families reside in large urban centres and what programs and services would be of benefit becomes a more difficult task as not all Aboriginal people self-identify in the census or with mainstream service providers.

SITUATING MYSELF

For Indigenous people, part of a greeting is to know more about the person you are talking to. Often Indigenous people will provide their name, the nation/tribe they identify with, and a little information about themselves or their connections (Ten Fingers, 2005; Wilson, 2008). In keeping with Indigenous greetings, my name is Angela Mashford-Pringle from Timiskaming First Nation in northern Quebec.

I am a first-generation urban Algonquin woman, and I have lived in or near the city of Toronto for most of my life. My connections to the Toronto Aboriginal community are varied, and have allowed me to form relationships with individuals and organizations that provide Aboriginal programs and services, especially those working in the fields of early childhood development and education. It is through these connections that I came to the project I will discuss in this paper.

BACKGROUND INFORMATION

As noted in the introduction, there are an increasing number of Aboriginal people living in Toronto. McCaskill and colleagues (2011) and Environics Research Group (2010) found that Aboriginal people move to cities for education, employment, or to be with family members, but they do not necessarily have the same social support networks that they would have in their home communities. There is a growing body of research with regard to urban Aboriginal people; however, it is still sparse and often limited to specific towns or cities (Peters, 2011).

In the city of Toronto, there is more than 40 years' history of Aboriginal organizations that have sought to assist Aboriginal people with their social, physical, emotional, and spiritual needs. As the number of Aboriginal people migrating to Toronto rises, there has been a corresponding increase in the programs and services available for them. However, as many of the Aboriginal organizations developed to assist Aboriginal people in Toronto are centrally located in the downtown core, there are few organizations (Aboriginal or non-Aboriginal) that provide culturally relevant and specific services outside of this core. There have been improvements in some areas, like Scarborough, but funding is limited and, at times, finding non-Aboriginal partners to work with has been challenging. Aboriginal organizations have not been able to reach out to determine which other neighbourhoods in Toronto have large Aboriginal populations and there have been limited attempts to engage the community through non-Aboriginal organizations. Funding for such research has not been readily available, and often Aboriginal organizations find their staff are already overloaded in the work they are funded to provide (personal communication with Tanya Paquette, 2012). Many of the Toronto Aboriginal organizations have a representative on the Aboriginal Advisory and Planning Table. In informal discussions, Table members and Aboriginal people in the Toronto area often state that it is difficult to access the social services system and, conversely, Aboriginal organizations do not know how to locate their target population, which is not easily identifiable or in one concentrated area like other ethnic minorities. There is limited data about where

Aboriginal people reside in Toronto as census data is based on self-identification and Indian Registry data includes status or registered "Indians" only. Both data sources are flawed in that some Aboriginal people may not self-identify because of the socio-political history between Aboriginal people and the government, while others may be registered but migrate often between Toronto and another location, like their home community, and may not identify or seek services in Toronto (Peters, 2006). It was through informal discussions with Table members that I heard about these issues. Hence, this project's aim was to provide necessary information for improvements in program delivery in all of the Toronto area for early childhood development, education programs, and services to Aboriginal children and families. I was tasked with speaking with various organizations providing early childhood education and care, as well as those that provided family services like the Community Action Program for Children and parenting groups. It was necessary to see what was available and how Aboriginal-specific services could be delivered.

HOW THE RESEARCH BEGAN

The Toronto Child and Family Network was developed for the Best Start program funded by the province of Ontario in the early 2000s. Building upon the existing Best Start Network for the City of Toronto, the Toronto Child and Family Network was created to promote positive outcomes for children and families, and to engage a wide range of community organizations across the city. The Toronto Child and Family Network has continued to develop since its inception. The City of Toronto, through this network, has been committed to providing services that meet the needs of the wide diversity of children within the city limits. The Aboriginal Advisory and Planning Table is one committee of a larger Toronto-area Early Childhood Development Table. To this end, the Aboriginal Advisory and Planning Table on Early Childhood Development was implemented in order to work toward improving the programs and services available to Aboriginal children in the city. The Table has members from a number of different Aboriginal and non-Aboriginal organizations in the city that provide Aboriginal-specific services to Aboriginal children and families. The information and statistics provided by the member organizations and the City of Toronto have shown that there are gaps in services provided to Aboriginal children (Native Child and Family Services of Toronto, 2011a). As mentioned, many of the programs and services for Aboriginal children are located in the downtown core of Toronto, which creates issues for Aboriginal families living in areas like Scarborough, Etobicoke, and North York.

My involvement with the Toronto Aboriginal Advisory and Planning Table came about through my previous working relationship with the co-chair, Ms. Laurie Hermiston. The Table was interested in gaining knowledge about the Etobicoke Aboriginal community based on previous reports like *TARP* (2011) and the *Little Voices Report* (2011a). The Toronto Aboriginal Advisory and Planning Table understood that an Aboriginal community existed in the south Etobicoke area, primarily in Mimico and Long Branch. The Table is composed of representatives from a number of child care and child welfare organizations in the city of Toronto that provide services to Aboriginal children and families. Some of the organizations are considered Aboriginal, with the remainder being non-Aboriginal organizations that have Aboriginal-specific programs or services.

I attended some of the Table's meetings regarding planning and research. During these meetings, I became an *ex-officio* member of the Table; I was invited to the meetings, but did not have any voting power and could not propose any new items for the agenda. The Table members were certain that some programs and services were already in existence for Aboriginal families, but they wanted to know exactly what these were, who was involved in the delivery of the programs, how often these programs or services were provided, and where Aboriginal families could access these services. After discussions regarding the existing programs and services (often located in the central downtown core of Toronto), it was apparent to the Table members and to me that the needs of Aboriginal children and families outside of the downtown core may be underserviced. Nonetheless, Table members did not have established relationships with non-Aboriginal organizations in south Etobicoke in order to discuss and collaborate on how to provide the services to Aboriginal children and families.

Working closely with the Toronto Aboriginal Advisory and Planning Table through telephone conversations, email, and with the co-chair, questions for the project began to emerge. There was a clear understanding that the project should follow Indigenous research methodologies. The traditional meanings and teachings associated with the Medicine Wheel were used as a basis for looking at the following four variables: available programs and services, including access and availability in south Etobicoke; culture and language activities and/or events provided in the area; recruitment and assistance of Aboriginal families; and levels of collaboration or connections with Aboriginal people and/or organizations in the Greater Toronto Area.

To this end, I developed a Medicine Wheel conceptual framework as shown in Figure 8.1. As an Aboriginal scholar and researcher who has been grounded in the Medicine Wheel teachings, I find it easy to relate the many

Figure 8.1: Medicine Wheel Framework for Toronto Aboriginal Early Childhood Project

Note: ECD = early childhood development; ECD/E = early childhood development and education

teachings about the four directions to the variables of a project like this one. They help me to examine the project in a non-linear way while ensuring that I am using Indigenous ways of knowing and being. Using the teachings of the Medicine Wheel, I often analyze data with the teachings of each direction and examine the data for different connections that may not be apparent in a linear analysis. For example, Aboriginal families require affordable and safe services, and these are provided by most organizations that work with families. However, Aboriginal families may also require financial advice or assistance and wish to be connected to other Aboriginal families through the types of social events that have not taken place at the organization in the past. Each aspect of the Medicine Wheel has unique and vast teachings that take a life-time to learn. However, using the knowledge of each aspect may illustrate a different way of viewing data and the ensuing connections between said data, partners, stakeholders, and analysis. Other Indigenous scholars have written about the use of the Medicine Wheel as a conceptual framework that can assist with an Indigenous view of analysis (see Dapice, 2006; Lavallee, 2009; and MacDonald, 2008).

It was of great concern to the Table members and myself that the research represented the four aspects of self, or the four directions of the Medicine Wheel: physical, spiritual, emotional, and mental. The variables were placed within the direction, or aspect, that the Table members and I felt best represented the variable. For example, access to programs and services is a physical concern and is very related to individuals and families; however, it is also a concern for society and requires the wisdom or mental aspect to ensure that programs and services are provided in a "good way" which is culturally appropriate and sensitive to the needs of the Aboriginal children and families who will attend. After consideration and contemplation, each of the initial variables were placed in their respective aspect/direction. Further use of the Medicine Wheel as a framework occurred during the analysis of the data prior to the written report.

The Table members also wished that the research follow the Seven Grandfathers Teachings: humility, honesty, bravery, love, truth, respect, and wisdom. Bouchard and Martin (2009) have written about the Seven Grandfathers Teachings and the need for Anishinaabe people to not only live by these teachings, but to ensure that they try to instill these beliefs in all aspects of their lives. As an urban Algonquin person and researcher, I often use the Seven Grandfathers Teachings in my research as I try to represent these qualities in how I conduct myself and how I develop and conduct my research. The Medicine Wheel framework and the Seven Grandfathers Teachings were discussed as the questions for the qualitative interviews were developed and again after the initial analysis was completed. These Indigenous frameworks were used as overarching "signposts." The use of two-eyed seeing, where both an Indigenous perspective and Western perspective are used to examine all aspects of the research plan development, implementation, conduct, and analysis, was part of providing an additional Aboriginal lens and voice. As such, linear and non-linear views of the project, data, and analysis could bring about unique solutions that would reflect both Western and Aboriginal organizations who provide (or would provide) programs and services to Aboriginal families in south Etobicoke.

THE PROJECT

As the project was developing, I began to foster personal relationships with Table members to understand what each of them wished to "get" from the research. Correspondingly, over the passing of months I began to understand what each member was looking for and how it related back to their organizations, and in some cases, to the individual Table member. Smith (1999) states that this relationship building is essential in using Indigenous research methods, and I would agree that it was necessary to understand the motivations of the Table members.

Ten Fingers (2005) argues that to provide an Indigenous voice in research, Indigenous people must be consulted. Almost half of the Table members were of Aboriginal descent, which provided input from some Indigenous peoples throughout the design and planning of the research, and all of these members were parents or caregivers with children of varying ages. It was anticipated that as Aboriginal families were engaged in the research through focus groups, further input would be garnered. The Toronto Aboriginal Advisory and Planning Table accepted that Aboriginal input may change the questions or the design of the research as it unfolded, and they believed that it would make the research stronger and more impactful if there was community input throughout the research. As there were many difficulties in locating and engaging Aboriginal families in south Etobicoke, the research team and the Table members used Elders and those Aboriginal members of the Table to provide an Aboriginal voice and direction for the research.

The Aboriginal Table members were very interested in finding out what programs and services were already in existence or where Aboriginal families were accessing programs and services for their children. The non-Aboriginal Table members were interested in determining how partnerships with local community organizations could be established and what their home organizations would have to provide in order to ensure Aboriginal families in south Etobicoke received Aboriginal-specific programs and services. The differences amongst the committee members were reflected in the questions developed for the research. It is interesting to note that the Table members did not discuss culture or language separately, but rather were concerned that there were culturally appropriate and sensitive programs and services available to Aboriginal children and families in south Etobicoke. Thus, the Table members had a preconceived sense of what constituted an Aboriginal program or service for Aboriginal children and their families, which would include culture and language as well as a knowledge of the socio-political history of Aboriginal people and their struggles in urban centres.

The Table members consistently stated that there must be culturally appropriate, sensitive programs and services for Aboriginal children and their families, and when questioned what that meant, the answer was often that the front-line staff must be knowledgeable about the history of Aboriginal people in order to not further oppress or colonize, or worse, perpetuate a path of assimilation in the programs and services offered.

A set of questions was designed for interviews with local south Etobicoke service providers through extensive consultations with Table members and an Elder who was associated with Aboriginal early childhood development from the Toronto area. Initial meetings were set up by the co-chair of the Toronto Aboriginal Advisory and Planning Table, as the Table also wanted to introduce itself and the possibility of partnership to each community organization contacted for an interview. It was fortunate there was an established coalition of child and family organizations in Etobicoke that met frequently to discuss service provisions and programming decisions. I was invited to attend two meetings in order to meet the organizations' representatives and convey what the project would entail. Using existing relationships assisted with conducting the interviews at the south Etobicoke organizations and the downtown Aboriginal organizations. All of the organizations, Aboriginal or non-Aboriginal, were very receptive to the research and possible partnerships that may come from this project.

In the first meeting, it was determined that none of the Etobicoke organizations were currently providing Aboriginal-specific programming to children or their families. This finding led to a secondary set of questions and interviews with key members of the Etobicoke coalition. From my discussions with the Toronto Aboriginal Advisory and Planning Table, I knew the members would be interested in what was available for Aboriginal children and families, as well as whether Etobicoke coalition organizations were willing to partner with the Aboriginal organizations in the downtown Toronto area in order to provide Aboriginal-specific programs and services. The Etobicoke organizations had questions about partnerships, but showed a greater interest in learning more about Aboriginal peoples, cultures, and languages in relationship to the families they could potentially serve.

Short telephone interviews were conducted with Etobicoke coalition members and it was determined that they did know about the Aboriginal population in south Etobicoke. However, they were unsure how to provide Aboriginal-specific programs and services as they did not have staff with the required knowledge. Some Etobicoke participants asked me questions as an Aboriginal parent and researcher regarding issues such as how Aboriginal families may access programs and services, self-identification, and what would encourage families to attend existing programs and services. This exchange altered the research from a clinical qualitative interview to more of a kitchen-table conversation. The change from the traditional method of a formal interview to a two-way conversation is in keeping with Aboriginal ways of being; everyone has knowledge and information, and many traditional teachings suggest that when people have conversations, more is learned than having one "expert," which is contrary to Western research methods of conducting qualitative interviews. The conversations allowed the south Etobicoke participants to receive some information that may have helped with developing partnerships and/or providing programs and services to Aboriginal children and families. These conversations also allowed for some key ground-level analysis of who was accessing their programs and services and where partnerships could be essential in helping Aboriginal families in south Etobicoke.

Additionally, Etobicoke coalition members were very interested in partnering and gathering knowledge about Aboriginal children and families as they believed that outreach to these families was necessary and would benefit the entire community. Unfortunately, given there were no specific programs and services already established for Aboriginal children and families, Etobicoke coalition members were unsure how we could reach the Aboriginal population in a short period of time to conduct the focus groups. Suggestions and possible collaborations were given to me during the interviews with south Etobicoke coalition participants. Nonetheless, many of the participants were eager to learn about Aboriginal children and their families in a holistic way and their enthusiasm was evident in their responses and interaction with me.

After I spoke with Table members, Aboriginal organizations participants, and the south Etobicoke coalition participants, an analysis of the responses yielded several themes: partnership and collaboration is necessary and desirable; focus groups with Aboriginal children and families are necessary to fully understand the needs of the south Etobicoke Aboriginal community; and there is a need for cultural competency and awareness training to assist with partnering and providing services to Aboriginal families in a culturally sensitive manner. From these initial findings, it was agreed that further discussions and possible events, in partnership with the Toronto Aboriginal Advisory and Planning Table and its representatives, were the first actions required, which could then lead to providing Aboriginal social events in south Etobicoke that could engage the Aboriginal children and families. It was also agreed that contacting the Aboriginal community in south Etobicoke would take more time than the current project had allotted for. The time of year and funding for the project (December to March) limited the ability to plan and recruit Aboriginal families for focus groups. All the organizations, Etobicoke and downtown, were unsure of how to contact Aboriginal families, especially those not already accessing any programs and services (regardless of the location). Therefore, I made a recommendation to the Toronto Aboriginal Advisory Committee that a first step would be to provide training to the south Etobicoke front-line workers about working with Aboriginal people. I believed that if front-line workers understood the cultural nature of certain programs and services they might be helpful in engaging south Etobicoke Aboriginal families. A second recommendation was hosting an Aboriginal social event in south Etobicoke to encourage Aboriginal children and families to meet the south Etobicoke coalition organizations.

WHERE ARE WE NOW?

The Toronto Aboriginal Advisory and Planning Table has received a brief report with a number of recommendations. Connections have been made between the Etobicoke child and family organizations, the Toronto Aboriginal Advisory and Planning Table, and other Aboriginal organizations. I have continued to discuss next steps with the Table and it is anticipated that workshops will be provided to south Etobicoke staff about Aboriginal people and how to work with this unique community.

At this time, I have tried to continue to nurture the relationships in south Etobicoke, with organizations, and with the Toronto Aboriginal Advisory and Planning Table, in order to continue to work toward providing Aboriginal children and families with the programs and services that they require. While the project did not necessarily end with specific information from the Aboriginal community in south Etobicoke, the Toronto Aboriginal Advisory and Planning Table is more aware of what is available there for Aboriginal families and can now work toward "filling the gaps" in programs and services. By waiting to develop a respectful relationship with Aboriginal families in south Etobicoke, the true needs of the Aboriginal community will be met in time and with Aboriginal input.

The relationships developed in, and with, Aboriginal communities are of great importance and take time, continual nurturing, and cultivation. After relationships are established, researchers can begin to work with Indigenous communities to plan research in a respectful and culturally appropriate manner. I have been a part of the Toronto Aboriginal community for most of my adult life as the community has helped me to reclaim more of my Indigeneity through teachings, events, and socialization. Any researchers wishing to work with an Aboriginal community, regardless of where they are situated, must establish and build a relationship that is likely going to continue long after the research is complete. Most Aboriginal communities do not want to be a "project" that a researcher comes to, completes, and leaves without staying connected. That is not the Indigenous way. In my case, I had previous relationships with committee members and organizations; I conducted the research, and will remain a part of the Toronto Indigenous community in a variety of ways. The circle continues for me and the research that I will conduct in partnership with the community is evolving with some of the partners that were part of this project. Continuing to build and nurture relationships is important to me as an Algonquin scholar, but also as an Algonquin person who is away from my traditional territories and enjoys being with other Aboriginal people to continue my personal journey in life.

REFERENCES

Bouchard, D., & Martin, J. (2009). *Seven sacred teachings: Niizhwaaswi gagiikwewin*. Vancouver: More Than Words Publishers.

City of Toronto Social Development Finance and Administration Division. (2008). *Toronto Aboriginal persons demographic snapshot, 2006*. Retrieved from www1.toronto.ca/city_of_toronto/social_development_finance__administration/files/pdf/aboriginal-affairs-cttee-presentation.pdf

Dapice, A. (2006). The medicine wheel. *Journal of Transcultural Nursing, 17*(3), 251–260.

Environics Research Group. (2010). *Urban Aboriginal peoples study: Toronto report*. Retrieved from http://uaps.ca/wp-content/uploads/2010/02/UAPS-Toronto-report.pdf

Environics Research Group. (2011). *Urban Aboriginal peoples study: Main report*. Retrieved from http://142.132.1.159/wp-content/uploads/2010/03/UAPS-Main-Report_Dec.pdf

Lavallee, L. (2009). Practical application of an Indigenous research framework and two qualitative Indigenous research methods: Sharing circles and Anishnaabe symbol-based reflection. *International Journal of Qualitative Methods, 8*(1), 21–41.

MacDonald, C. (2008). Using components of the medicine wheel to develop a conceptual framework for understanding Aboriginal women in the context of pap smear screening. *Pimatisiwin: Journal of Aboriginal and Indigenous Community Health, 6*(3), 95–108.

McCaskill, D., FitzMaurice, K., & Cidro, J. (2011). *Toronto Aboriginal Research Project (TARP) final report*. Retrieved from http://abdc.bc.ca/uploads/file/09%20Harvest/TARP-FinalReport-Oct%202011.pdf

Mustard, J. F., & McCain, M. N. (2002). *The early years study: Three years later*. Toronto: Founders' Network.

Native Child and Family Services of Toronto. (2011a). *Little voices child and family centres: A framework for the delivery of Native children's services in the city of Toronto*. Toronto.

Native Child and Family Services of Toronto. (2011b). *Native child and family services of Toronto: Framework for an Aboriginal child and family centre*. Toronto.

Peters, E. (2006). "[W]e do not lose our treaty rights outside the ... reserve": Challenging the scales of social service provision for First Nations women in Canadian cities. *GeoJournal, 65*, 315–327.

Peters, E. (2011). Emerging themes in academic research in urban Aboriginal identitites in Canada, 1996–2010. *Aboriginal Policy Studies, 1*(1), 78–106.

Smith, L. T. (1999). *Decolonizing methodologies: Research and Indigenous peoples*. Dunedin, New Zealand: University of Otago Press.

Statistics Canada. (2008a). *Aboriginal children's survey, 2006: Family, community and child care*. (89-634-X No. 001). Ottawa: Minister of Industry.

Statistics Canada. (2008b). *Aboriginal peoples in Canada in 2006: Inuit, Métis and First Nations, 2006 census*. Ottawa: Statistics Canada.

Ten Fingers, K. (2005). Rejecting, revitalizing, and reclaiming: First Nations work to set the direction of research and policy development. *Canadian Journal of Public Health, 96 (Supplement)*, S60–S63.

Wilson, S. (2008). *Research is ceremony: Indigenous research methods*. Halifax: Fernwood Publishing.

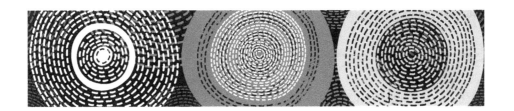

CHAPTER 9

Applying Indigenous Health Community-Based Participatory Research

Darrel Manitowabi and Marion Maar

One of the Seven Anishinabek Teachings is *mnaadendiwin*, or respect. In our experience, *mnaadendiwin* is demonstrated not in words one says or ideas one writes, but by the conduct and behaviour in one's relationship "with" and "in" community. Research praxis that is informed by *mnaadendiwin* involves the centring of Indigenous epistemology, ontology, and practice. Praxis in *mnaadendiwin* is necessary for demonstrating an understanding of this Teaching.

INTRODUCTION

Indigenous peoples in Canada have poorer health outcomes than the general population (Gracey & King, 2009; Smylie, 2009). In the following chapter, we focus on the methodology of community-based participatory research (CBPR) examining the impact of socioeconomic interventions on Ojibwa/Anishinabek[1] First Nations health and well-being. More specifically, we provide our experiences applying the CBPR approach to a research project in collaboration with five Anishinabek First Nations in northeastern Ontario. In doing so, we demonstrate how CBPR methodologies engage upon a decolonizing praxis advocated by the Indigenous anthropologist Beatrice Medicine (Harrison, in Medicine, 2001, p. xv).

SETTING AND BACKGROUND

Our research study took place in the Algoma, Manitoulin, and Sudbury Districts of northeastern Ontario, an area of the province home to 14 First Nations (Union of Ontario Indians, 2016). We invited six First Nations in this region to collaborate on our study and five accepted our invitation.

The participating northeastern Ontario First Nations share a common economic history. The natural resource economy provided most employment in the past, mainly in the mining and forestry sectors (Buse & Mount, 2011). Most current economic opportunities are in public administration, health, and social services, and to a lesser extent in the natural resource economy and small businesses (Statistics Canada, 2013a–c). In general, the First Nations employment rates, average income, and post-secondary completion are below the provincial average (see Table 9.1).

Since the 1990s, First Nations have delivered their health care services through the 1986 federal Indian Health Transfer Policy (Maar, 2004; Warry, 2007). Each of the five First Nations in our study offers illness prevention and nursing services in a community health clinic. Since 1994, First Nations people in Ontario have had access to additional specialized provincially funded services through the Aboriginal Healing and Wellness Strategy (AHWS). By the year 2000, three

Table 9.1: Sociodemographic Profile of First Nations in the Districts of Algoma, Sudbury, and Manitoulin Compared with the Province of Ontario in 2011

	FIRST NATIONS IN ALGOMA	FIRST NATIONS IN SUDBURY	FIRST NATIONS IN MANITOULIN	ALL OF ONTARIO
Population:	13,145	13,045	5,295	12,651,795
Population >15:	9,980	10,300	3,875	10,473,670
No High School:	32.7%	25.7%	34.5%	18.7%
High School:	22.8%	23.7%	20.8%	26.8%
Post-Secondary:	44.4%	50.5%	44.9%	54.5%
Employment Rate:	45.0%	56.9%	46.3%	60.1%
Average Income:	$27,687	$32,937	$23,119	$39,667

Note: "Post-secondary" means the percentage of the population that has completed a certificate, diploma, or degree.

Source: Statistics Canada (2013a–d)

AHWS Aboriginal Health Access Centres were in operation in northeastern Ontario: N'Mninoeyaa Health Access Centre, Algoma District; Noojmowin Teg Health Access Centre, Manitoulin District; and Shkagamik-Kwe Health Centre, Sudbury District (Association of Ontario Health Centres, n.d.).

In 1989, the Waubetek Business Development Corporation opened to provide economic development and business services for Indigenous peoples in northeastern Ontario (Waubetek, 2017). As of 2015, it had invested $65 million in over 3,000 Indigenous businesses in its catchment, and 94 percent were still in operation (Madahbee, 2015, p. 26).

SUMMARY OF RESEARCH FINDINGS

In light of the above-noted enhancements in First Nations health and economies we undertook a study guided by the following research question: How is health and well-being in First Nations communities influenced by socioeconomic factors at the individual, community, nation, and service systems levels? Our study incorporated a focus group methodology with 88 total participants in the health and economic sectors in five First Nations. Based on a qualitative analysis of focus group transcripts, our research findings suggest the devolution of federal and provincial services is problematic. While there is increasing access to programs and services, these have reduced community solidarity; have led to higher unemployment, and a reliance on materialism, technology, and social welfare; and have resulted in divisions between those who are employed and unemployed (Manitowabi & Maar, 2013). Our focus in this chapter is a description of our research methodology. Before doing so, we next provide a background on our disciplinary approach and CBPR framework.

SITUATING MEDICAL ANTHROPOLOGY AND COMMUNITY-BASED PARTICIPATORY RESEARCH

The academic researchers are anthropologists and engage in medical anthropological research. Anthropologists have a long and at times controversial history of studying Indigenous peoples. Maori scholar Linda Smith (2008) states, "The ethnographic 'gaze' of anthropology has collected, classified and represented other cultures to the extent that anthropologists are often the academics popularly perceived by the indigenous world as the epitome of all that is bad with academics" (pp. 66–67). The discipline of anthropology has historically focused on cultural difference and the assumption of the assimilation of Indigenous peoples, and thus focused on "capturing" and "describing" for archival and museum purposes, preserving a record for future generations (cf. Medicine, 2001, p. 4). Deloria Jr. (1971) characterized this approach to research as a "[c]ompilation of useless knowledge 'for knowledge's sake' [that] should be utterly rejected by the Indian people. We should not be objects of observation for those who do nothing to help us" (p. 94). Though Deloria Jr.'s commentary was critical of anthropologists, not all Indigenous academics have felt the same way. Dr. Beatrice Medicine (Lakota) in particular was a pioneering Indigenous anthropologist with a decolonizing anthropological praxis and subaltern analysis focus, transforming anthropology from its earlier colonial roots (Harrison, in Medicine, 2001, p. xv).[2]

The anthropological praxis of Medicine's time coincided with a transitional and growth period of medical anthropology. In the 1970s its focus was the comparative study of medical systems throughout the world; in the 1980s it transitioned to clinical settings, and by the 1990s an increasing number of medical anthropologists focused on global and public health (Good, Fischer, Willen, & DelVecchio Good, 2010, p. 3). Today medical anthropology is theoretically rich and its application cosmopolitan, with new directions as collaborators with local institutions and organizations (Good et al., 2010, p. 2).

Our approach in medical anthropology uses a CBPR framework in which community members are a part of the research project, with the purpose of engaging in research leading to community empowerment or self-determination (Jacklin & Kinoshameg, 2008). The focus of CBPR is the incorporation of community research partners in ways that recognize their knowledge, facilitate their decision-making, and enhance community capacity (Minkler & Wallerstein, 2003). The CBPR approach in Indigenous health research is an emerging framework for both Indigenous and non-Indigenous researchers (e.g., Jacklin & Kinoshameg, 2008; Tobias, Richmond, & Luginaah, 2013). In the following chapter, we detail our experience applying CBPR Indigenous health research in northeastern Ontario.

APPLYING COMMUNITY-BASED PARTICIPATORY RESEARCH

We have either collaborated in research projects or conducted independent research projects in northeastern Ontario for about two decades, and in the process we have developed community networks and community contacts in several of the First Nations. Moreover, one of us (Manitowabi) is an Indigenous anthropologist who was raised and still resides in the area. In this section of our chapter, we outline the development of a seven-phase CBPR process informed by *mnaadendiwin*, the Anishinaabe Teaching of respect, explained at the start of this chapter.[3]

EXPLORATORY DIALOGUE (PHASE 1)

In 2007 a health director nearing retirement from one of the First Nations health authorities in the Manitoulin District shared with us his career-long observation of First Nations having varying levels of health despite investments in social programs, infrastructure, and economic development initiatives. This conversation led to the planning of exploratory research meetings involving the health director, the authors, other university academics, and health and economic First Nations stakeholders in northeastern Ontario. Our first meeting took place at the Northern Ontario School of Medicine in Sudbury, Ontario, and we agreed to have follow-up exploratory meetings, alternating in First Nations and university locations. In these exploratory meetings, we held roundtable discussions and discussed academic and community-based perspectives on the poor health status of northeastern Ontario First Nations and the link to economic inequality. Furthermore, we discussed the tremendous amount of economic development taking place over the last 15 years and First Nations control of health, law enforcement, education, employment supports, child welfare, and child care in the participating First Nations. We collectively raised the question, "Do we know if all of this development is having an impact on health within our First Nations population?" (Meeting Minutes of December 18, 2008). At this exploratory stage, all stakeholders made in-kind contributions in the form of time and travel since we did not have research funds.

ESTABLISHING PROJECT GOVERNANCE (PHASE 2)

At subsequent meetings in 2009, we began the process of focusing our exploratory research dialogue by discussing potential First Nations community research participants, research funding, and steps required in the research process (Meeting Minutes of April 16, 2009; Meeting Minutes of June 2009; Meeting Minutes of July 20, 2009). The series of meetings in 2009 led to a commitment to invite health and economic First Nation stakeholders to a two-day workshop to formally explore a health and economic development study in First Nations communities in northeastern Ontario. This workshop took place in December 2009 with a grant of $10,000 from the First Nations and Inuit Health Branch, Health Canada. This grant covered meals, travel, and a small honorarium for community member participants. First Nation health and education stakeholders participated as part of their employment through in-kind contributions by their First Nation.

Seventeen people, including First Nations health and economic stakeholders from five First Nations, a First Nations political organization, a First Nations economic body, academics, and graduate students attended the December 2009 workshop. The objective was to propose a research project to the First Nations stakeholders based on our initial exploratory meetings and to determine if there was sufficient support to pursue the research. Another objective was to create space for dialogue to acquire feedback from each First Nation to guide the research formulation and process. The workshop consisted of formal presentations with group discussions on the state of First Nations health and economics in the region and perspectives on ethical research with Indigenous communities. By the conclusion of the workshop, all First Nations representatives had agreed to pursue a research project formally. First Nation stakeholders perceived a strong relationship between economic development and health. First Nations participants also formulated the project title, *Exploring First Nation Wellbeing and Prosperity through Health and Economic Indicators: Anishinaabe Mno-Bimaadiziwin.*[4] Furthermore, First Nations stakeholders set the conditions of the research relationship by emphasizing the need for transparency, collaborative research administration, and the establishment of a research steering committee. A draft research methodology comprising community profiles, focus groups, key informant interviews, and a survey, as well as potential funders, took place. Furthermore, there arose a decision that each First Nation should contribute $1,000 toward the research process and submit a Band Council Resolution (BCR)[5] to formally demonstrate their support. This workshop resulted in the creation of a research project management framework. It consisted of one group of First Nations and university stakeholders collaborating on administration of the project, including securing permissions and seeking funding sources, and another group focusing on management of the project, including appropriate implementation of the project and data collection (see Figure 9.1) (Whaley & Vuckovic, 2009). At the conclusion of the December 2009 workshop, we reached a decision that another workshop was required in January 2010 to refine research questions, agree upon research funders, and devise a research timeline.

PROJECT PLANNING (PHASE 3)

The January 2010 meeting became a productive planning meeting. It attracted senior-level First Nations political leaders from northeastern Ontario. The political leaders provided a critical voice in workshop discussions, demanding equity in the research collaboration. One of the First Nations passed a BCR in preparation for the workshop, and others had initiated the process of planning BCRs. The authors reported at the meeting that they had, in collaboration with one

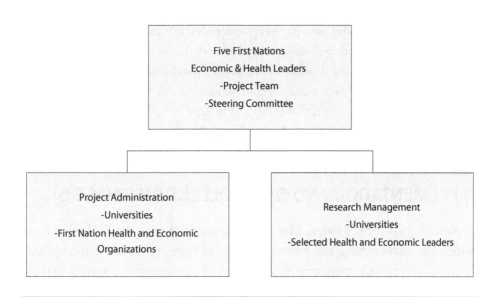

Figure 9.1: Research Project Management Framework

Source: Modified from Whaley and Vuckovic (2009)

of the stakeholders, successfully secured a pilot study research grant from the Indigenous Health and Research Development Fund amounting to $25,000. The funds were to cover expenses related to a literature review and community focus groups with the anticipation that our results would inform a more comprehensive future study. We chose the focus group methodology since it is an appropriate and cost-effective approach to collecting a variety of community perspectives. A portion of the workshop focused on drafting focus group questions. This exercise resulted in 14 draft questions on health, 31 on economic development, and 4 on education. Workshop participants furthermore identified research process steps and delegated research leadership to Maar and Manitowabi in the pilot study.

PREPARING FOR IMPLEMENTATION OF THE PROJECT (PHASE 4)

The next phase consisted of completing an ethics review and coordinating with research management group members on the acquisition of BCRs. Teleconference research meetings took place with the research management team periodically for the remainder of 2010. It became challenging to hold regular meetings given that the busy First Nation members' work schedules were often competing with the heavily structured schedules of the academic researchers. In some cases, there were gaps of several months in between teleconference calls, and at other times the teleconference meetings were not well attended.

By the start of 2011, all research ethics approval and BCRs were in place, and each First Nation made a $1,000 contribution to this research project. Focus group questions, recruitment, and composition were complete. This next research phase shifted from regular research meeting updates to working with each First Nation to plan focus groups.

IMPLEMENTATION AND DATA COLLECTION (PHASE 5)

In planning for focus groups, Maar and Manitowabi took the lead from First Nations in determining the optimum time, location, and composition. Each First Nation research management member booked focus group venues as their in-kind contribution and recruited focus group members based on the criteria of having knowledge and experience with economic development and health in the community in the past and present.

We scheduled our first focus groups in the Algoma District First Nation for May 2011. In our initial plan for focus groups, we designed four; two each day, the first taking place from 10 a.m. to 12 p.m., the second from 1 p.m. to 3 p.m. This choice was to provide lunch for all participants by a local First Nation caterer. Another reason for this format was to accommodate travel time for the researchers. In planning the composition of focus group participants, we decided to group community members and First Nation administration employees separately. The reason for this choice was that we expected differing perspectives between community members and administrators and we wanted to encourage open dialogue. For example, an administrator's viewpoint may include operational costs for programs and unique experiences of program delivery, while community members may not necessarily share the same experience of health and economic issues; instead, they represent the perspectives of clients, patients, or small business owners.

On our first day of focus groups, we held focus groups with economic development administrators and political leaders in the morning and community small business owners and Elders familiar with community economic history in the afternoon. In consultation with the local First Nation research team members, we revised our original economic and education questions to ten. Topics included the current and past picture of the community, the impact of recent developments (as applicable to the First Nation), the connection between economics and health, and the state of well-being in the First Nation. Manitowabi facilitated the economic development focus groups given his previous research experience in the area; seven participated in the first focus group, and four in the second.

On the second day, we followed the same format, having health administrators and providers in the first focus group, and community members and Elders in the second. Maar facilitated this day of focus groups and asked ten revised questions from the original health questions with a focus on past and present health and its relation to social programs and economic development.

In conducting the focus groups, we had participants write their names on folded heavy-duty paper to display each member's name to demarcate the voice of each participant. Maar and Manitowabi hired a research assistant to help with focus groups, setting up voice recorders and making notes of each person's voice to ensure that the comments aligned with the correct participant during transcriptions.

At the conclusion of each focus group, Manitowabi consulted one-on-one with some participants to get information on knowledgeable community members who were not present. Using this method, known as "snowballing" (cf. Bernard, 2011, p. 148), he later returned to the First Nation to conduct one key informant interview with the one First Nation member who agreed to the invitation.

ITERATIVE IMPROVEMENT APPROACH TO IMPLEMENTATION (PHASE 6)

After the initial round of focus groups, we reflected upon the experience and the participation rates. In hindsight, we determined that it would have been sufficient to hold two focus groups, the first combining both health and economic development administrators and the second combining the health and economic development community members. Furthermore, the First Nation was larger than some others, and thus if we followed the original format, we projected we would have fewer participants with four focus groups. We thus decided to modify to one day, having two for the balance of First Nation research sessions.

In the next round of focus groups, we experienced an unexpected delay. With the conclusion of the first round, summer arrived, and many First Nation members had scheduled vacations and could not accommodate focus groups. We thus delayed until the fall, and at that time, none of the remaining four First Nations could participate. The year 2012 worked in our favour, and we completed the remaining focus groups (for a summary, see Table 9.2).

REPORTING BACK TO THE COMMUNITY (PHASE 7)

At the conclusion, our research assistant transcribed the focus groups, and we did a thematic analysis of the transcripts using NVivo 10, qualitative data software. We produced draft individual reports for each First Nation and offered public

Table 9.2: Focus Group Totals

FIRST NATION LOCATION	DATE OF FOCUS GROUP	NUMBER OF PARTICIPANTS IN EACH FOCUS GROUP		
		Administration	Community	Total
Algoma	May 19–20/11	11	20	31
Manitoulin A	Feb. 1/12	8	3	11
Manitoulin B	Mar. 23/12	10	10	20
Manitoulin C	June 12/12	14	4	18
Sudbury	July 12/12	4	4	8
Total		47	41	88

Note: "Administration" refers to those participants in administrative and leadership positions such as economic development officers, health directors, and social service providers. "Community" refers to those who do not work in administration and includes small business owners, community members with chronic illnesses, and Elders.

presentations of findings to each First Nation. In all but one First Nation, there was general agreement with the findings, and some focus group participants were present to add additional commentary to findings. In the First Nation presentation with elements of expressed disagreement, concerns were over the choice and comprehensiveness of the methodology and line of inquiry. After some extended conversation on the background of the first community workshops and the consensus reached to do an initial less comprehensive pilot study focusing on health and economics, the majority reached consensus on the relevance of a focus group methodology and health and economics. In the conclusion of all reports, we recommended the following as the next research priorities:

1. Conduct detailed social histories of each First Nation to trace social changes;
2. Collect and analyze economic and health data in the past and compare with contemporary data sources;
3. Study and consult with comparative Indigenous communities pursuing self-determination and cultural restoration initiatives for insight on "wise practices"[6]; and
4. Consult with community members to develop a framework and implementation plan to achieve self-determination and cultural restoration, and improve community health and well-being.

We emphasized these final points with each community and had an extensive dialogue on initiatives that were either underway or anticipated in the future.

Table 9.3: Phases of Indigenous Health CBPR

PHASE	METHOD
1.	Exploratory Dialogue: Consult with First Nations research stakeholders.
2.	Establish Project Governance: Form collaborative research steering committee.
3.	Project Planning: Determine methodology with research steering committee.
4.	Prepare for Implementation of the Project: Acquire First Nations formal permission to conduct research and undertake an ethics review.
5.	Implementation and Data Collection: Recruit participants and begin research.
6.	Iterative Improvement Approach to Implementation: Refine or revise participant recruitment and methods if there is limited participation.
7.	Report Back to Community: Analyze data, present draft findings to First Nation, and integrate feedback (if applicable) in the final research report.

DISCUSSION AND CONCLUSION

Our focus of this chapter has been to share our experience applying CBPR in Indigenous health research and detailing lessons we have learned. In this section, we link the principles of CBPR with our experience and examine the rewards and challenges of CBPR. We also provide an update on the current state of our work and situate the contemporary context of this research within anthropological research with Indigenous peoples in general.

Jacklin and Kinoshameg (2008) have stressed community integration, empowerment, and self-determination as important overarching principles in CBPR in Indigenous health. In our project, the research ideas originated with the community, demonstrating important CBPR principles such as self-determination. However, how we can effectively maintain these ideals throughout the lifespan of projects is not immediately apparent.

Maar and colleagues (2015) emphasize the need for purposeful dialogue between academic researchers and community stakeholders during specific phases of research, including design, data collection, and knowledge translation. This discussion is necessary in order to facilitate bidirectional learning between researcher and community stakeholders. Further, the dialogue session requires engaging a cooperative spirit between Indigenous peoples and Western-trained researchers, an outcome that Indigenous scholar Ermine (2007) termed the "partnership model of the ethical space" (p. 203). Similarly, the strength of our experience of maintaining CBPR principles throughout our study was the ongoing meaningful stakeholder dialogue followed by successful integration of community voice and agency in the development of each phase of this research project. We experienced a productive synergy in the initial meetings, and we nurtured an equal community voice in situating the current economic challenges in First Nations and the connections to health outcomes. In doing so, as researchers we benefited from First Nations stakeholders, who are most knowledgeable of their communities, to educate the investigators. In turn, researchers shared the process of research planning, research ethics, and funding to determine the feasibility of a research project. Once establishing feasibility, we collaborated to recruit other First Nations and held workshops to develop a CBPR framework to inform our project. This process is constructive since we reached interview questions by consensus, determined a timeline, and formed a research management group to oversee the process.

On the matter of empowerment and self-determination, it is our observation that First Nations exercised empowerment and self-determination in this process by collaborating and influencing all phases of the research process. Self-determination was not only in the workshop collaborations but also in the employment of the administrative and management committees (Figure 9.1), which ensured that community stakeholders with the relevant expertise were in decision-making positions. We acknowledge this is an observation, and we did not ask community stakeholders if they held the same opinion.

However, we faced many challenges as well. The participation in our research project faded as time passed and new priorities emerged for academics and community stakeholders. After our workshops, we had less than ideal participation in teleconference planning meetings. Furthermore, there were significant gaps in communications and scheduled meetings due to the delay in responses and availability of community and academic representatives. We attribute this to the fact that First Nation members are busy with their employment commitments to their First Nation, and collaborative research is additional work and therefore must be a secondary priority. Further, during the academic year, researchers have limited availability until summer, when their schedules allow more flexibility for research activities. This situation does not fit well with community stakeholders, since vacations are often scheduled during this time.

All of the above leads to the question: Did our research findings lead to increased empowerment in participating First Nations? This question is hard to answer since we did not ask if this took place as a result of this exercise. We can say that part way through our research study the significant funding opportunity identified for follow-up research was not available. Consequently, none of the First Nations followed up with us to formally explore our research recommendations for a further study. However, we found that the communities in some way or other were engaging in courses of action related to our propositions in a community-based way, without our involvement. In one First Nation, an administrative division had independently undertaken a consultation very similar to ours and had come up with similar findings, and they were already engaged in the next steps. In this instance, this administrative division did not know members of their administration had consulted with us to plan this research project. At the least, this coincidence was an unforeseen triangulation that supported the validity of our findings.

Although the First Nations did not pursue our recommendations in a linear step-by-step fashion, at the time of writing, new research collaborations did emerge based on this research. One First Nation is interested in developing a new training and education program to address secondary school completion rates and the need for employment training. Results from our research report were used to justify these as holistic community wellness issues. In this instance, Manitowabi collaborated with the First Nation in planning and writing an education and training grant, and he has agreed to facilitate a knowledge exchange with community members on university studies as a pathway.

More recently, occupational health and safety researchers at Laurentian University have engaged in a collaborative exploration of research examining issues related to Indigenous communities. Two of the First Nations who participated in this study responded favourably to Manitowabi's invitation to explore a research project in this area. Findings from this study have informed the research rationale for this possible research in Indigenous worker health and safety. Though this original research project has come to an end, the implications of the findings remain relevant since First Nations are or plan on addressing portions of our research, such as education, training, and community needs.

CBPR AS DECOLONIZING PRAXIS IN ANTHROPOLOGY

Returning to the contemporary role of anthropology and the application of CBPR, our collaborative approach to medical anthropology does not fit the critiques of Deloria Jr. (1971) or Smith (2008). In many ways, our CBPR research demonstrates that anthropological approaches are not claimed to be *a priori* disempowering to Indigenous peoples; instead, anthropological approaches can even be in opposition of these critiques. Our approach contributes to Beatrice Medicine's (Harrison, in Medicine, 2001, p. xv) application of anthropology as a decolonizing praxis. We have done so by employing a research approach that recognizes research in Indigenous communities must orient to a logic that equalizes the relationship between First Nations and researchers and understands their voice is central to all decision-making processes. We are striving toward a decolonizing praxis in the discipline of anthropology advocated by Beatrice Medicine by continuing a dialogue with First Nations and giving back by informing other initiatives and collaborating in other related research projects. We have not abandoned these First Nations at the conclusion of our study, but *respectfully* recognize we may be collaborators in the future, and this is indeed taking place at the time of writing.

ACKNOWLEDGEMENTS

Doug Graham (formerly of Mnaamodzawin Health Services Inc.), Dr. Harry Cummings (University of Guelph), Dawn Madahbee (Waubetek Business Development Corporation), and Tony Jocko (Union of Ontario Indians) undertook instrumental roles in the early formation of this research. This research project would not have been possible without a grant from the Indigenous Research and Development Program and the First Nations and Inuit Health Branch, Health Canada. We also acknowledge all First Nation stakeholders who informed our methodology and verified our findings. We are grateful for the helpful comments by reviewers. Any errors of interpretation are those of the researchers.

NOTES

1. Anishinabek has various translations, one of which is "the people" (Anishinabek Nation, 2009).

2. We recognize that the academic relationship between anthropologists and Indigenous peoples remains a contentious topic (cf. Moreton-Robinson, 2016, p. 6). Rather than focus our energies on critiquing the relationship between anthropology and Indigenous peoples, our academic approach is to invest in meaningful academic collaborations with Indigenous communities to address health issues.

3. Compare the nine principles of Indigenous CBPR by LaVeaux and Christopher (2009). Our approach differs by focusing on an Anishinabek case study CBPR methodological phase approach.

4. This phrase means "good health," and there are various renditions and translations of this term. Our spelling is the preference of workshop participants; compare, for instance, the spelling by the Anishinabek Nation (2009), *mino-bimaadiziwin*.

5. A Band Council Resolution is a formal decision made at a scheduled meeting of the chief and Council leadership.

6. "Wise practices" is a variant of "best practices." Wise practices are reflective of Indigenous epistemologies and ontologies, recognizing culturally appropriate and community-specific knowledge (see Thoms, 2007, p. 9).

REFERENCES

Anishinabek Nation. (2009). *Health Secretariat: Good health for our people*. Retrieved from www. anishinabek.ca/policy-unit.asp (accessed July 14, 2016).

Association of Ontario Health Centres. (n.d.). *Aboriginal Health Access Centres*. Retrieved from www.aohc.org/aboriginal-health-access-centres (accessed August 22, 2016).

Bernard, R. (2011). *Research methods in anthropology: Qualitative and quantitative approaches* (5th ed.). Toronto: Alta Mira Press.

Buse, D., & Mount, G. (2011). *Come on over!: Northeastern Ontario, A to Z*. Sudbury, ON: Scrivener Press.

Deloria, Jr., V. (1971). *Custer died for your sins: An Indian manifesto*. New York: Macmillan.

Ermine, W. (2007). The ethical space of engagement. *Indigenous Law Journal, 6*(1), 193–203.

Good, B., Fischer, M., Willen, S., & DelVecchio Good, M. (2010). *A reader in medical anthropology: Theoretical trajectories, emergent realities*. Maldon, MA: Wiley-Blackwell.

Gracey, M., & King, M. (2009). Indigenous health part 1: Determinants and disease patterns. *The Lancet, 374*(9683), 65–75.

Jacklin, K., & Kinoshameg, P. (2008). Developing a participatory Aboriginal health research project: "Only if it's going to mean something." *Journal of Empirical Research on Human Research Ethics, 3*(2), 53–68.

LaVeaux, D., & Christopher, S. (2009). Contextualizing CBPR: Key principles of CBPR meet the Indigenous research context. *Pimatisiwin: A Journal of Aboriginal and Indigenous Community Health, 7*(1), 1–25.

Maar, M. (2004). Clearing the path for community health empowerment: Integrating health care services at an Aboriginal health access centre in rural north central Ontario. *Journal of Aboriginal Health*, January, 54–64.

Maar, M., Yeates, K., Barron, M., Hua, D., Liu, P., Lum-Kwong, Moy, M., ... & Tobe, S. (2015). I-RREACH: An engagement and assessment tool for improving implementation readiness of researchers, organizations and communities in complex interventions. *Implementation Science: IS, 10*, 64. Retrieved from http://doi.org/10.1186/s13012-015-0257-6 (accessed March 11, 2017).

Madahbee, D. (2015, July 26). Everyone benefits when Aboriginal enterprise succeeds. *Northern Ontario Business, Aboriginal Business*.

Manitowabi, D., & Maar, M. (2013). The impact of socioeconomic interventions on Anishinaabeg health and wellbeing. In A. Corbiere, D. McGregor, & C. Migwans (Eds.), *Anishinaabewin niiiwin: Four rising winds* (pp. 97–112). M'Chigeeng, ON: Ojibwe Cultural Foundation.

Medicine, B., with S. Jacobs (Ed.). (2001). *Learning to be an anthropologist & remaining "Native": Selected writings*. Urbana, IL: University of Illinois Press.

Meeting Minutes. (2008, December 18). *First Nation Research Project Economic Impact: Health Outcomes Roundtable Discussion*. Northern School of Medicine [sic], Room 215.

Meeting Minutes. (2009, April 16). *Economic Impact: Health Outcomes.* Waubetek Business Development Corporation boardroom, Whitefish River First Nation.

Meeting Minutes. (2009, June). *Economic Development: Health Impacts Study.*

Meeting Minutes. (2009, July 20). *Economic Development: Impacts on Health.* Northern Ontario School of Medicine boardroom.

Minkler, M., & Wallerstein, N. (2003). *Community-based participatory research for health.* San Francisco: John Wiley.

Moreton-Robinson, A. (2016). Introduction: Locations of engagement in the first world. In A. Moreton-Robinson (Ed.), *Critical Indigenous studies* (pp. 3–16). Tucson: The University of Arizona Press.

Smith, L. (2008). *Decolonizing methodologies: Research and Indigenous peoples.* New York: Zed Books.

Smylie, J. (2009). The health of Aboriginal peoples. In D. Raphael (Ed.), *Social determinants of health: Canadian perspectives* (2nd ed.) (pp. 280–304). Toronto: Canadian Scholars' Press Inc.

Statistics Canada. (2013a). *Algoma, DIS, Ontario (Code 3557)* [table]. *National Household Survey (NHS) Aboriginal population profile, 2011 National Household Survey.* Statistics Canada Catalogue no. 99-011-X2011007. Ottawa, ON. Retrieved from www12.statcan.cg.ca/nhs-enm/2011/dp-pd/aprof/index.cfm?Lang=E (accessed August 9, 2016).

Statistics Canada. (2013b). *Sudbury, DIS, Ontario (Code 3552)* [table]. *National Household Survey (NHS) Aboriginal population profile, 2011 National Household Survey.* Statistics Canada Catalogue no. 99-011-X2011007. Ottawa, ON. Retrieved from www12.statcan.gc.ca/nhs-enm/2011/dp-pd/aprof/index.cfm?Lang=E (accessed August 9, 2016).

Statistics Canada. (2013c). *Manitoulin, DIS, Ontario (Code 3551)* [table]. *National Household Survey (NHS) Aboriginal population profile, 2011 National Household Survey.* Statistics Canada Catalogue no. 99-011-X2011007. Ottawa, ON. Retrieved from www12.statcan.cg.ca/nhs-enm/2011/dp-pd/aprof/index.cfm?Lang=E. (accessed August 9, 2016).

Statistics Canada. (2013d). *Ontario (Code 35)* [table]. *National Household Survey (NHS) 2011 census.* Statistics Canada Catalogue no. 99-004-XWE. Ottawa, ON. Retrieved from www12.statcan.cg.ca/nhs-enm/2011/dp-pd/prof/index.cfm?Lang=E (accessed August 9, 2016).

Thoms, J. M. (2007). *Leading an extraordinary life: Wise practices for an HIV prevention campaign in Two-Spirit men. 2-Spirited People of the 1st Nations.* Retrieved from http://2spirits.com/PDFolder/Extraordinarylives.pdf (accessed September 27, 2017).

Tobias, J., Richmond, C., & Luginaah, I. (2013). Community-based participatory research (CBPR) with Indigenous communities: Producing respectful and reciprocal research. *Journal of Empirical Research on Human Research Ethics, 8*(2), 129–140.

Union of Ontario Indians. (2016). *Health overview.* Retrieved from www.anishinabek.ca/departments/health-secretariat-2/overview/ (accessed July 7, 2016).

Warry, W. (2007). *Unfinished dreams: Community healing and the reality of Aboriginal self-govern-ment*. Toronto: University of Toronto Press.

Waubetek Business Development Corporation. (2017). *Who we are*. Retrieved from www.wau-betek.com/who-we-are (accessed March 2, 2017).

Whaley, D., & Vuckovic, K. (2009, December 8–9). Unpublished report from Workshop on Health and Economic Development Study in First Nations Communities.

PART IV

OUR TOOLS FOR RESEARCH

Although we use the term "Indigenous research," the theories, methodologies, tools, and approaches to research vary with each nation and in different contexts. Many of our contributors are working to align research methodologies with their nation's traditions. Sometimes they borrow theories and methods that are congruent with Indigenous worldviews – for example, feminist, post-structural, postcolonial, qualitative, participatory, autoethnographic, and critical approaches. Most importantly, though, the researchers support the resurgence of Indigenous research processes that help them connect to themselves, humanity, and the wider cosmos; using research to heal. They do this by adapting traditional tools for seeking knowledge to fit their research needs, such as storytelling, circles, witnessing, drumming, returning to land for instruction, and ceremony. They use analogy and metaphors to adapt lessons from traditional teachings for academic research purposes, for example, Medicine Wheel teachings, Trickster Nanabozoo stories, treaties, and two-eyed seeing. Finally, they also use Indigenous protocols to create a space where sensitive topics can be safely and caringly researched.

In addition to the chapters in this section by Nicole Bell; Georgina Martin; Brittany Luby, Rachel Arsenault, Joseph Burke, Michelle Graham, and Toni Valenti; and Paige Restoule, Carly Dokis, and Benjamin Kelly, Nicole Penak's chapter (Chapter 15) deals extensively with methodology.

LEARNING AND REFLECTION QUESTIONS

1. Why is it important to distinguish between Indigenous research broadly and the research approach taken by a specific Indigenous nation/cultural group?

2. Are there particular stories from your tradition that might describe and give life to your research? Are there particular ceremonies or teachings? What analogies can you draw from these stories, ceremonies, and teachings? Note: These questions do not apply only to Indigenous people; all communities have stories, traditions, and ceremonies in some form.

3. How do the research methods discussed by the researchers ensure respectful research relationships?

4. Circles as a methodology are frequently utilized and adapted to Indigenous research. When is this appropriate, and how do you think sharing or talking circles should be used? What are the protocols?

5. How does the language you use in research, or whether you are using oral or written language, affect the meaning of the knowledge you are sharing?

6. What are the different roles and responsibilities of people involved in these research projects?

7. What can collaboration in research look like? How about cross-cultural collaboration?

8. What dynamic tensions have you experienced in research?

9. Why do researchers utilize different writing styles when communicating their research?

10. From where do you seek guidance when you face a dilemma in your research?

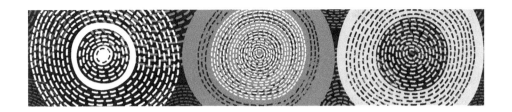

CHAPTER 10

Anishinaabe Research Theory and Methodology
as Informed by Nanaboozhoo, the Bundle Bag,
and the Medicine Wheel

Nicole Bell

This chapter presents a discussion of Anishinaabe[1] research theory and methodology as informed by three analogies: Nanaboozhoo storytelling, items contained in a bundle bag, and the Medicine Wheel. I am focusing on "Anishinaabe research" rather than "Indigenous research" or even "Aboriginal research." This is because I can only start from where I am in my understanding of what research means to me as an Anishinaabe person, and that means looking at what it means to be an Anishinaabe re/searcher. While parallels may be drawn, this chapter does not claim to address doing research in other Indigenous contexts.

This analysis of what Anishinaabe research theory and methodology is begins with the story of how Nanaboozhoo saved Nookomis. I use this story and the analogies it contains to describe and give life to Anishinaabe research.

All researchers need a theoretical framework that articulates their theory, methods, practical tools, epistemology, and ontology. This raises the question: What is the "toolkit" for Indigenous research? Which in turn leads to the question: What are the tools I can draw on as an Anishinaabe researcher to inform the work that I do and to pursue knowledge? I believe Anishinaabe tools are the sacred objects used to manifest teachings in ceremonies. I therefore use the metaphor of the bundle bag and the sacred objects it contains to provide the guidance and thus the theory of Anishinaabe research.

To break the theory down into actual methodology, I use the symbol of the circle and the teachings of Medicine Wheels. The encapsulating messages of wholeness, interrelationship, interconnectedness, and balance contained in Medicine Wheels speak to the need for research methodology to be informed by its theory. I therefore use Medicine Wheels as a metaphor for the actual implementation of Anishinaabe research.

SITUATING ANISHINAABE RESEARCH THEORY AND METHODOLOGY

The retelling of a Nanaboozhoo[2] story, as found in *Tales of Nanabozho* by Dorothy Reid (1963), illustrates the dilemma Indigenous researchers find themselves in as they attempt to do research that respects Indigenous knowledge through culturally relevant theory and method.

> Many Indigenous researchers have struggled individually to engage with the disconnections that are apparent between the demands of research, on one side, and the realities they encounter amongst their own and other Indigenous communities, with whom they share lifelong relationships, on the other side. There are a number of ethical, cultural, political and personal issues that can present special difficulties for indigenous researchers. (Smith, 1999, p. 5)

Nanaboozhoo was always plagued by the evil ways of the Windigoes.[3] On one particular occasion in the fall season, the Windigoes were plotting to kill Nookomis (Nanaboozhoo's grandmother). While the Windigoes were devising their evil plan, a flying squirrel happened by and heard the entire plot. The flying squirrel immediately went to Nanaboozhoo to share the Windigoes' plan, which he was able to do once Nanaboozhoo stopped ignoring him so as not to disrupt his slumber. The flying squirrel also shared with him a safe place where Nanaboozhoo could hide Nookomis from the Windigoes. It was a grove of maple trees located beyond a great waterfall, and the trees could be reached by crossing the waterfall on a narrow log. Nanaboozhoo took Nookomis to this safe place and proceeded to search out the Windigoes to teach them a lesson. But the Windigoes had their own ways of knowing things and knew where Nookomis was and went to her. Once they arrived at the waterfall all they could see through the mist of the falls was a fire (the maple trees in colour), and they decided that Nookomis must have died in the fire and so they left. Once Nanaboozhoo learned of how the maple trees protected Nookomis, Nanaboozhoo rewarded them.

Nanboozhoo represents the Anishinaabe researcher whose job it is to find, learn from, and protect Anishinaabe knowledge (which is Nookomis). However, Nanaboozhoo's (the researcher's) job is complicated by the fact that powerful Windigoes, which represent some conventional research theory and practice, try to wreak havoc on Nanaboozhoo by trying to kill his Nookomis (Anishinaabe knowledge). The Windigoes (conventional research) can arise from negative values such as greed and jealousy, dichotomies of inferiority/superiority, and fear. These breed the desire for power and control, and result in colonization and the view that research should only be done within the frameworks of the colonizers.

The flying squirrel represents the dreams and vision that Nanaboozhoo needed to be able to save Nookomis. Just as Nanaboozhoo needed the squirrel to provide the knowledge of the Windigoes' scheme, so too does the Anishinaabe researcher need the vision to be able to see the negative implications of some conventional research methods (the Windigoes). Nanaboozhoo's ignoring of the squirrel represents how easy it is for an Anishinaabe researcher to remain blind to the Eurocentrism in conventional research methods, especially if the researcher is engaged in the re/searching process – searching for, finding, and following the cultural trail of the grandmothers and grandfathers – after being socialized into a colonial culture. Thus Nanaboozhoo ignoring the squirrel represents the need for the Anishinaabe researcher to "wake up" from his/her colonization and the potential traps in conventional research (the Windigoes) that may result in him/her breaching Anishinaabe protocols and pursuing knowledge in inappropriate ways.

The safe place that Nanaboozhoo (the researcher) brings Nookomis (Anishinaabe knowledge) to represents ceremony. It is in ceremonies that Anishinaabe people create places for their personal growth and healing as well as that of the Anishinaabe community. The falls that Nanaboozhoo and Nookomis crossed to set up a new and safe camp represents life, as water is the lifeblood of the earth and it is through ceremony that Anishinaabe people keep themselves alive as a spiritual people. The narrow log that was used to cross over the falls represents the Anishinaabe road and how important it is for them to stay straight on that road for their survival as Anishinaabe people.

The coloured leaves of the maple trees were seen as "fire" by the Windigoes. Fire in Anishinaabe ceremonies represents the spirit – spirit is manifested in the use of fire in ceremonies. For Anishinaabe research, this speaks to the need for spirit to be present in the work that they do so that it "feeds" the people. As shared with me by Elder Edna Manitowabi (personal communication, 1992–2007), the coloured leaves also speak to the hard work that Mother Earth does to put on her most beautiful dress of colour. This parallels the hard work Anishinaabe researchers need to do to break free from the constraints of conventional research, or the Windigoes.

It seems ironic that this story is called "Nanaboozhoo Saves Nookomis" when in actuality it isn't Nanaboozhoo who saves Nookomis, as the Windigoes knew where she was and Nanaboozhoo was not present to save her anyway. Therefore, it really is not the researcher (Nanaboozhoo) who can save or keep alive Anishinaabe knowledge (Nookomis), but only the spirit (the fire/coloured leaves) that feeds the work the researcher does. It is only if the research has spirit that it will live. To light the fire, just as Mother Earth changes the colour of the leaves, is very hard work.

ANISHINAABE RESEARCH THEORY

The spirit of Anishinaabe people is kept alive through ceremony. Carried within the bundle bag[4] are sacred objects for ceremonial or spiritual purposes, which serve as metaphors for the thinking I feel should stand behind the work I should be doing as an Anishinaabe researcher. Theory can be defined as "an account of the world which goes beyond what we can see and measure. It embraces a set of interrelated definitions and relationships that organizes our concepts of and understanding of the empirical world in a systematic way" (Marshall, 1998, p. 666). Sacred objects in a bundle bag brought to and used in Anishinaabe ceremony provide a metaphor for concepts and interrelated definitions of Anishinaabe research theory.

The medicines[5] and thus the smudging[6] with the medicines in the bundle bag represents the need and responsibility of the Anishinaabe researcher to create a personal space for taking away the bad and situating him/herself positively (sage), finding his/her strength (sweetgrass), giving continuous thanks (tobacco), and cleansing his/her spirit (cedar) both before and during his/her research endeavour and ultimately in his/her daily life.

The fire (represented by matches or flint in the bundle bag) is a symbol of "spirit" representing past spirits, present spirits, and future spirits. It is essential that Anishinaabe research contain spirit. This occurs through the use of spirit in the methodology, the connection of the researcher to the topic being studied at a spirit level, and the fostering of the Anishinaabe spirit in the community through the research product.

The feather represents the messenger (usually the eagle). By putting thoughts into the feather, the spirit of the eagle (as the bird that flies the highest) takes the messages or prayers to the Creator or spirit world. Anishinaabe research should serve as a message that would be well received by the grandmothers and grandfathers in the spirit world.

Contained in the pipe are the seven Original Teachings. All Anishinaabe research should adhere to these seven teachings: wisdom, love, respect, bravery, honesty, humility, truth.

The teaching of the little boy waterdrum[7] speaks to the healing power of that drum (for an in-depth discussion of the drum in relation to Anishinaabe research, see Paul Cormier and Lana Ray's chapter). Because the Anishinaabe researcher is a member of an oppressed people and may consider him/herself to be an oppressed person, it is imperative for the Anishinaabe researcher to have done enough of his/her own healing work in order to be able to research with integrity. As discussed by Rochelle Johnston, Deborah McGregor, and Jean-Paul Restoule in their introduction to this book, the Anishinaabe researcher is required to act in ways during his/her research and to produce a product that will bring healing to the community in some capacity.

The drum that is made, cared for, and used in ceremonies represents the heart of the people. All Anishinaabe research must contain the heart of the people for the good of the people. Anishinaabe research cannot be called "Anishinaabe research" if the heart of the Anishinaabeg has not been captured.

The water that is brought to ceremony and prayed for by the women represents the cleansing process in doing Anishinaabe research. It is essential that the Anishinaabe researcher keep his/her heart and spirit as pure as possible to ensure the greatest benefit to the community. A continuous cleansing process helps to achieve this purity of heart and spirit.

The berries in ceremony are medicine and provide nourishment to feed the spirit of the Anishinaabe researcher and the community. The earth's giving of the berries and the giving of thanks represents the give-and-take dynamic that is essential in Anishinaabe research, to include "reporting back to the people and sharing knowledge. Both ways assume a principle of reciprocity and feedback" (Smith, 1999, p. 15).

The shaker or rattle symbolizes the first sound of Creation and can represent in Anishinaabe research the "first voice" (Graveline, 1998) of the Anishinaabeg. This voice must be sounded powerfully and authentically. Just as one in ceremony must learn in increments the songs that are sung in ceremony, so too does the Anishinaabe researcher need to continually check his/her "singing" (representation) of the knowledge shared.

Medicine Wheels, either visually represented in ceremony or implicitly through the praying to the four directions, symbolize the need for balance in

Anishinaabe research. This includes a balance between the researcher's physical, mental, spiritual, and emotional aspects of his/her being. All of these aspects must be employed in the research process and must be done so in balance.

Often Anishinaabeg will have representations of colour, usually ribbon or cloth, which symbolize meaning to them either individually or collectively. The colours usually represent gifts or strengths of that individual. For the Anishinaabe researcher, this means knowing what one's strengths and gifts are and using them to achieve his/her fullest potential for the benefit of his/her community. The knowing of one's strengths and weaknesses assists the Anishinaabe researcher in analyzing his/her conceptual as well as emotional and other forms of baggage (Kirby & McKenna, 1989).

A clan[8] symbol is usually contained in a bundle bag and symbolizes for the Anishinaabe researcher his/her guidance and support. The Anishinaabe researcher must be connected to the world around him/her, and one of the ways to do this is through recognizing and understanding his/her clan. The Anishinaabe researcher then comes to realize that the work he/she does for the community is made possible by the spirit helpers of his/her clan.

Just as the ceremonies of the Anishinaabeg will keep the Anishinaabe people alive, so too will the Anishinaabe researcher's bundle bag keep the Anishinaabe people alive. The constant acknowledgment through praying to the four directions in Anishinaabe ceremony speaks to a fundamental paradigm: the symbol of the circle and the teachings of Medicine Wheels are powerful teachers and helpers not just in ceremonial practice, but also in life activities, including research.

ANISHINAABE RESEARCH METHODOLOGY

I believe integrity is the foundational core of Anishinaabe research and is essential to conducting Anishinaabe research. While there are many teachings contained in Medicine Wheels, the illustration in Figure 10.1 presents those learnings with respect to doing Anishinaabe research with integrity.

Starting in the east, the Anishinaabe researcher obtains *vision* with respect to the research journey by being able to *see* and *identify* the task at hand. This vision can be obtained through personal fasting, sharing/talking circles, or speaking with an Elder. Then *time* must be spent relating *to* the topic of the research. This *time* spent in the south requires that the researcher get to a place of being able to feel the research topic that has been visioned. At a feeling level, the Anishinaabe researcher begins to be able to *express* with a degree of genuineness the topic of study. Following this, in the west, *reason* begins to take form as the Anishinaabe researcher begins to *figure out* what has been learned and reflects on his/her personal

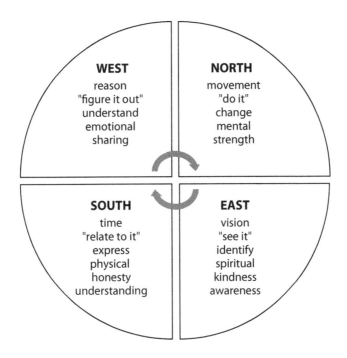

Gifts of the four directions: vision, time, reason, movement
Actualizing the four gifts: see it, relate to it, figure it out, do it
Creating change or healing process: identify, express, understand, change
Fours aspects of a person: spiritual, physical, emotional, mental
Core cultural values: kindness, honesty, sharing, strength
Learning process: awareness, understanding, knowledge, wisdom

Figure 10.1: Researching with Integrity[9]

experiences and learning. It is at this point that the Anishinaabe researcher can say that he/she begins to *understand* the information about the topic being considered. In the north the Anishinaabe researcher is able to *move* with the information that has been gathered to be able to *do* something with it to create *change*. Let's not forget that all of these steps in the research process must reflect the foundations of Anishinaabe worldview as manifested in ceremony.

In order for Anishinaabe research to be done with integrity, it must implement within its methodology methods that reflect what the Elders term "core values." Methods must promote *kindness, honesty, sharing,* and *strength* in both the researcher and the community he/she is serving. These values are imperative to ensuring integrity and thus balance in the research process. Maintaining personal and community integrity requires working from an Indigenous world-view grounded in cultural values. Leona Makokis (2001) also speaks of the values of kindness, honesty, sharing, and strength in the research process. Makokis defines these as natural laws that "help the researcher to understand the importance, validity, and sacredness of the information being shared" (Makokis, 2001, p. 79). Makokis shares these definitions as applied to Indigenous research:

- Love/Kindness – before we can be humble, we have to be kind, and that we must feel with our heart, not just our mind.
- Honesty – refers to being aligned and straight. We are to lead honest lives. For whatever we do, we must do it in complete honesty with ourselves and others. This keeps our heart, mind, and spirit full of integrity.
- Sharing – to help, having everybody involved.
- Strength – refers to strength and determination in the body. (Makokis, 2001, pp. 96–97)

The implementation of these values into research also addresses the emotional engagement often required by the Anishinaabe researcher when doing research. Often, the work of Anishinaabe researchers stems from a topic that they are emotionally attached to; one that they can say they are passionate about. Eber Hampton (1995) clarifies this:

One thing I want to say about research is that there is a motive. I believe the reason is emotional because we feel. We feel because we are hungry, cold, afraid, brave, loving, or hateful. We do what we do for reasons, emotional reasons. That is the engine that drives us. This is the gift of the Creator of life. Life feels.... Feeling is connected to our intellect and we ignore, hide from, disguise, or suppress that feeling at our peril and at the peril of those around us. Emotionless, passionless, abstract, intellectual, academic research is a goddam lie, it does not exist. It is a lie to ourselves and a lie to other people. Humans – feeling, living, breathing, thinking humans – do research. When we try to cut ourselves off at the neck and pretend an objectivity that does not exist in the human world, we become dangerous, to ourselves first, and then to people around us. (p. 52)

However, the complementarity of Medicine Wheels teaches the balance in all things, including research. The researcher must balance objectivity and subjectivity to ensure integrity in his/her work.

To complete the research process with integrity, the Anishinaabe researcher must engage every aspect of his/her being in the process. This requires that the researcher establish a *spiritual, physical, emotional,* and *mental* connection with the research being done. While it is not particularly difficult to imagine how a researcher might establish a mental connection to the research, it is more difficult for the conventional research community to imagine how a researcher might establish a spiritual, physical, and emotional connection. In fact, some schools of Western thought would argue that these connections create researcher bias and therefore make the findings invalid. However, from an Anishinaabe perspective, research without a spiritual connection is a "dead" piece of work – one which cannot provide life to the people it should be serving. Research without a physical connection (a physical sacrifice or physical engagement) produces "shallow" understanding and analysis. Research without an emotional connection does not have "heart," and so will have difficulty convincing the audience it is intended for and producing any significant change or betterment. It is thus imperative that the Anishinaabe researcher be balanced at a personal level in relation to the topic being studied.

Because Anishinaabe researchers are emotionally attached to the research they do, they engage in the research process with the hope that they can create some change. They are emotionally attached to the Indigenous experience and therefore use their research skills to address their experiences and create positive change. This need to create change and therefore *act* through research is validated by Cora Weber-Pillwax (2001) when she states that

> unless we realize that knowledge in actuality through integration into our own ways of being and knowing and doing, our studies have no life. [...] If my work as an Indigenous scholar does not lead to action, it is useless to me or anyone else. I cannot be involved in research and scholarly discourse unless I know that such work will lead to some change *(out there)* in that community, in my community. (p. 169)

Shawn Wilson (2001) identifies key questions Indigenous researchers need to ask to ensure that positive relationships are maintained through the research process. They are:

1. What is my role as a researcher, and what are my obligations?
2. Does this method allow me to fulfill my obligations in my role?
3. Does this method help to build a relationship between myself as a researcher and my research topic?

4. Does it build respectful relationships with the other participants in the research? (Wilson, 2001, p. 178)

The need for establishing and maintaining a healthy relationship is foundational to Anishinaabe research. This idea of relationship, however, goes beyond physical relationships, as Wilson (2001) states:

> [T]o me an Indigenous methodology then becomes talking about relational accountability. As a researcher you are answering to all your relations when doing research. You are not answering questions of validity or reliability or making judgments of better or worse. Instead you should be fulfilling your relationships with the world around you so your methodology has to ask different questions: rather than asking about validity or reliability, you are asking, "Am I fulfilling my role in this relationship? What are my obligations in this relationship?" The axiology or morals need to be an integral part of the methodology so that when I am gaining knowledge, I am not just gaining in some abstract pursuit; I am gaining knowledge in order to fulfill my end of the research relationship. This becomes my methodology, an Indigenous methodology, by looking at relational accountability or being accountable to all my relations. (p. 177)

Weber-Pillwax (1999) also addresses the importance of relationship in Indigenous research and presents the following principles that need to be considered when implementing Indigenous research methodology:

1. The interconnectedness of all living things,
2. The impact of motives and intentions on person and community,
3. The foundation of research as lived indigenous experience,
4. The groundedness of theories in indigenous epistemology,
5. The transformative nature of research,
6. The sacredness and the responsibility of maintaining personal and community integrity, and
7. The recognition of languages and cultures as living processes. (pp. 31–32)

By implementing methods in the east that establish clear *vision*, a *spiritual* connection, and *kind* strategies, an *awareness* with integrity will result. This *awareness* will in turn become an *understanding* with integrity through methods that provide *time* in which the Anishinaabe researcher can *relate to* the research topic through *expression* and a *physical* connection. This understanding will become *knowledge* through *reasoning* and *figuring out* which methods to employ to establish an *emotional* connection. True *wisdom* is achieved through methods that *move* the learning to a place of being able to create *change* that is in the best interest of Anishinaabe people. The framework of a Medicine Wheel provides a visual representation of a path for doing Anishinaabe research with integrity. While I have addressed each quadrant in isolation with each of its characteristics, as well as holistically, Anishinaabe methodology as articulated by a Medicine Wheel is more interactive than this. There is a constant cross-over and interconnection going on all the time.

Research has an important role to play in the decolonization of Anishinaabe people. Through research, and particularly through research based on culturally relevant theory and methods, Anishinaabe people can begin to tell their story with authentic voices and create meaningful change. In addition, through the ongoing articulation of Anishinaabe research theory and methodology, a place for Anishinaabe research practice is created. Cultural teachings and constructs can help frame Anishinaabe research theory and methodology. As an Anishinaabe re/searcher I use the teachings of Nanaboozhoo, sacred objects used in ceremony, and the Medicine Wheel to inform my research.

NOTES

1. Anishinaabe is the word used by many Algonquian nations to name themselves in their language.
2. Nanaboozhoo is the traditional teacher/Trickster of the Anishinaabe people.
3. The Anishinaabe people call evil spirits Windigoes.
4. A carrier of sorts that contains sacred objects for ceremonial or spiritual purposes.
5. Natural plants that are believed to have been given to the Anishinaabe people by the Creator and are therefore considered sacred.
6. Washing the body with the smoke of the burning medicines.
7. Sacred drum used for ceremonial purposes.
8. A group of people represented by an animal who have shared responsibilities. A person is born or adopted into a clan. Everyone from a clan is considered family.
9. The use of "understanding" in the south and "understand" in the west represent two separate processes. "Understanding" in the south is part of the learning process along with awareness, knowledge, and wisdom. "Understand" in the west is part of the healing process along with identify, express, and change.

REFERENCES

Graveline, F. J. (1998). *Circle works: Transforming eurocentric consciousness.* Halifax, NS: Fernwood Publishing.

Hampton, E. (1995). Memory comes before Knowledge: Research may improve if researchers remember their motives. *Canadian Journal of Native Education, 21*, 46–54.

Kirby, S., & McKenna, K. (1989). *Experience, research, social change: Methods from the margins.* Toronto, ON: Garamond Press.

Makokis, L. (2001). *Teachings from Cree Elders: A grounded theory study of Indigenous leadership* (Unpublished doctoral dissertation). University of San Diego.

Marshall, G. (1998). *Oxford dictionary of sociology.* New York, NY: Oxford University Press.

Reid, D. M. (1963). *Tales of Nanabozho.* Toronto, ON: Oxford University Press.

Smith, L. T. (1999). *Decolonizing methodologies: Research and Indigenous peoples.* New York, NY: St. Martin's Press.

Weber-Pillwax, C. (1999). Indigenous research methodology: Exploratory discussion of an elusive subject. *Journal of Educational Thought, 33*(1), 31–45.

Weber-Pillwax, C. (2001). What is Indigenous research? *Canadian Journal of Native Education, 25*, 166–174.

Wilson, S. (2001). What is an Indigenous research methodology? *Canadian Journal of Native Education, 25*(1), 175–179.

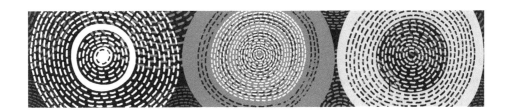

CHAPTER 11

Storytelling and Narrative Inquiry:
Exploring Research Methodologies

Georgina Martin

Weytk, Georgina Martin *ren skwekwst.* Hello, my name is Georgina Martin. I locate myself as a Secwepemc woman from Williams Lake, in the interior of British Columbia. I grew up in the community of T'exelc, also defined as the Williams Lake Indian Band under the *Indian Act.* Sandy (2011) notes, "T'exelc, is a place where the salmon charge up the river" (p. 2). Another name for T'exelc is Sugar Cane, which "comes either from the sweet tall grass that grows there or from a story of sugar falling off a pack mule as a pack train travelled through" (Sandy, 2011, p. 2). T'exelc is one of the 17 communities comprising the Secwepemc nation.

In this chapter I outline two distinct methodologies I wove together for my doctoral research into Secwepemc identities. The specific methodologies are Indigenous storywork, created by Jo-ann Archibald (2008), and narrative inquiry, developed by Jean Clandinin and Michael Connelly (2000). Being Indigenous, I am cognizant of the sensitivities and approaches required while occupying research space within an Indigenous community. In my particular case extra care was needed to engage with my home community and in the appropriate handling of individual stories. The path and process complied with both university ethics and community protocols. Indigenous storywork validated the stories of the participants, while narrative inquiry sanctioned the retelling of my personal story. Validation is crucial for personal self-empowerment because Indigenous peoples were involuntarily denied or stripped of their autonomous identities, a term I coined as "legislated interference." This research is one example of how Indigenous people and scholars have the power to reclaim their cultural identities. Due to the heartfelt and emotional nature of the research topic the strength of the two methodologies supported the emotional and relational work involved in my inquiry.

My interest in examining my Secwepemc identities is personal; it evolved from the fact that Aboriginal peoples' identities were disrupted by *Indian Act* legislation and colonial policies. These realities caused my identities to feel suspended at birth. I was born in an Indian hospital where Canadian Indigenous people were institutionalized by the federal government to quarantine the infected who had tuberculosis. For this reason, my mother was in the Coqualeetza Indian hospital in Sardis, BC. It was not until my PhD research that I had the courage to explore my turmoil about identities that resulted from legislated interference. This interference contributed to my lost sense of belonging. To address my longing to belong, I began my study with my autobiographical narrative and then continued exploring Secwepemc identities alongside an Elder and a youth from my T'exelc community.

Accordingly, I articulate the importance of capturing the participants' narratives in order to maintain their truths. I describe my approaches of weaving together the two methodologies in my PhD study. It is imperative to locate oneself when conducting research in your home community, as I am. Working from an Indigenous paradigm with Indigenous people is paramount. As Shawn Wilson (2001) states, "Indigenous research needs to reflect Indigenous contexts and worldviews: that is, it must come from an Indigenous paradigm rather than an Indigenous perspective" (p. 176). In order to be faithful to an Indigenous paradigm, I selected a process that supported my Indigeneity, an approach that sustains my Secwepemc worldview.

My dissertation rejects the colonially legislated characterization of *Indian Act* identity and emphasizes life and lived-experiences of the Secwepemc people. To achieve this I needed to utilize an appropriate research approach. Bagele Chilisa (2012) identifies this as a way to challenge and resist "the blind Euro-Western application of methodologies across all cultures" (p. 190). This method cultivates ways for the colonized and marginalized to write about themselves and rewrite what is negatively written by the colonizer.

Chilisa (2012) advocates for members of the colonized/marginalized to approach writing from multiple positions. She recommends the researcher consider events and practices that are ethically responsible and will not compromise the researcher's transformative journey. I realized I needed to be ethically responsible to ensure that my research approach was for the people and not about them. I engaged with community representatives to establish how the study could benefit the community and I continued to work alongside an advisory group for input and guidance. I purposefully built trust to ensure that the community understood that I was conducting my research to engage in a symbiotic mutual exchange to understand intergenerational cultural identities. These standpoints require "knowledge production approaches that are multiple, interconnected, and sensitive" (Chilisa, 2012, p. 190). Some Indigenous researchers may prefer dominant Euro-Western standards, while others resist and seek alternative methodologies that support Wilson's (2001) shift to an Indigenous paradigm. I knew when I decided to research the delicate substance of identities, I needed to apply methodology(ies) that kept the sensitivity at the forefront. This is what drew me to the strong relational aspects of Indigenous storywork and narrative inquiry. Both Indigenous storywork and narrative inquiry support the creation of respectful, trusting relationships with my community and participants. These approaches are complementary in that narrative inquiry facilitates the powerful connection to place, traditions, Indigenous ways of knowing, the passing on of traditional ways, and recovering them through lived-experience, while Indigenous storywork shrinks the epistemic divide between Western and Indigenous methodologies. By explaining and relating to Indigenous knowledge using Indigenous storywork, I am able to exhibit the importance of incorporating a Secwepemc worldview that aligns with the cultural values of the people. The methodologies also share non-prescriptive features. Indigenous storywork does not have a set storyline; rather the stories are interpreted through the lenses of both the teller and the listener. Narrative inquiry is based on stories told and retold that can erupt anywhere along the continuum of an individual's life cycle. The non-prescriptive approaches of Indigenous storywork refer to the way stories can be told to share histories or teach an important lesson. The sharing and learning happens in order for the listener to make meaning of the story; there is no finite plot. An example given by both Linda Smith (1999) and Jo-ann Archibald (2008) is when stories unfold the receiver may not form an interpretation until years later, or they may never find meaning in the story. Similarly, narrative inquiry is non-prescriptive, as the telling and retelling of lived-experiences can be told from any point in the person's experience.

METHODOLOGICAL DISCUSSION

Michael Crotty (1998) defines the basic elements involved in the qualitative research process as methods, methodology, theoretical perspective, and epistemology. All of these elements are interrelated and linked. My intention is to describe how I came upon the methods and methodologies I chose and to identify how the research process supports my cultural identity inquiry. An important aspect of Wilson's (2001) concept is the difference between paradigm and perspective. He states, "Some methods and strategies have inherent in them more relationship building and relational accountability than others and therefore may be more attractive in an Indigenous paradigm" (Wilson, 2001, p. 39). In the next section, I explore Crotty's basic elements of research within the context of Wilson's Indigenous paradigm.

LOCATING THROUGH A SECWEPEMC PARADIGM

To create a Secwepemc paradigm I return to my personal relational experience and speak from a position of embodiment, which Clandinin and Connelly (2000) refer to as "embodiments of lived stories." In my study, I claim Indigenous and Secwepemc as my preferred identity references because Indigenous includes all our people at a global level and my genealogy is Secwepemc. My attraction to a Secwepemc framework solidified in response to the negative assaults hurled against Indigenous identities by colonialism, residential schools, and the *Indian Act*. This reinforced negativity contributed to the urgency for many Indigenous people to self-define their identities; the negative attacks on Indigenous identities promoted the importance of drawing on Indigenous knowledges (IK). IK offers strength to the Indigenous researcher and helps them regain their confidence in articulating their worldview within a Eurocentric research context, especially while addressing deeply personal and sensitive topics such as identity. The aim of my knowledge creation is to work from an Indigenous research paradigm through utilizing self-location, storytelling, and community-relevant protocols. A mainstay of my Secwepemc cultural identity interest is to understand my sense of belonging. This sense of belonging involves connections to the land, family, and community; life is organized as a collective.

Upon deciding to research what it means to be Secwepemc, I needed to develop a process that would be meaningful and reciprocal for my community and me. Two key images persistently consumed me during my preparation: my grandfather reminding me to never forget where I come from, and the beckoning of my hand drum. To share my research path and how I am situated within an Indigenous paradigm, I analyze how I have shape shifted through Crotty's research elements to find a Secwepemc paradigm.

Methodology

According to Crotty (1998), "methodology is the strategy, plan of action, process or design lying behind the choice and use of particular methods and linking the choice and use of methods to the desired outcomes" (p. 3). For my methodology, I found that I needed to engage in my own form of telling and retelling my lived experiences. I embarked on an autobiographical narrative to learn how my childhood memories of separation contributed to my lingering loss of identities. While narrative inquiry supports the researcher to safely return to traumatic experiences, doing so was challenging because of the very deep and personal nature of my topic. Through a narrative inquiry approach, I was able to limit the return to memorable events to ones that I could emotionally and psychologically handle. This methodology is respectful and relational and promotes an ethic of care in the way it is applied. The intent is to heal and transform rather than injure. The emotional safety to tell, retell, live, and relive the stories is made possible by the relational and aesthetic qualities of narrative inquiry. An example is when reliving and retelling the stories of the effects of residential school, I would not reveal conditions that would harm anyone. I strove to uphold the stories as teaching stories rather than intensify the deeply rooted emotional scars that the mere mention of the schools can arouse. The intent of narrative inquiry is to learn from these experiences and advance to a point where the storyteller can "re-story" the experience in a healing way. My identity detachment arose from the lost maternal connection to my mother at birth due to her containment in an Indian hospital. This experience shaped my wonderings about my identities, especially my lost sense of belonging. I deemed narrative inquiry to be the best methodology to support my inquiry into my lived-experience.

As explained by Clandinin and Connelly (2000), narrative inquiry focuses on what they call the four directions: inward and outward, backward and forward. Inward means looking at the internal conditions, "such as feelings, hopes, aesthetic reactions, and moral dispositions" (p. 50). Outward includes external conditions, such as the environment. Backward and forward is "temporality – past, present, and future.... We wrote that to experience an experience – that is, to do research into an experience – is to experience it simultaneously in these four ways and to ask questions pointing each way" (Clandinin & Connelly, 2000, p. 50). Connelly and Clandinin (1990) advise that researchers who pursue narrative need to follow their nose and, after the fact, reconstruct their narrative of inquiry. Put simply, narrative inquiry is a way to understand experience (Clandinin & Connelly, 2000).

Writing and thinking narratively, my stories speak to temporal issues (my loss of identity) by looking at events in the past, present, and future. I began my inquiry by writing about my cherished lived-experiences with my grandparents, and I struggled to elicit the childhood memories of how my lost sense of connection to Secwepemc identities occurred. I moved through a maze of confusion because I enjoyed several fond experiences growing up and being raised by my grandparents. Yet I could not overcome the fact that I did not have a lasting mother/daughter relationship, and this tugged at me especially because I fostered the inability to feel or show affection toward my children and loved ones. The lost sense of emotional bonding became a survival mechanism. I learned that if I did not have a deep emotional attachment then I could maintain a high level of emotional detachment and not be hurt. The lack of emotional connection still haunts me and deprives me of the healthy, caring relationships that are characteristic of our people. For my research project I am in the midst of formulating four stories derived from my lived-experiences utilizing what Clandinin and Connelly (2000) refer to as the personal and social (interaction); past, present, and future (continuity); and notion of place (situation) in narrative. I am also beginning to relate to the inward and outward, backward and forward movement of what is a very complex and thorough process.

In addition to the challenges of the narrative construction process is the challenge of handling and releasing appropriate stories. Given that many Indigenous communities are ravaged by external assaults, I refuse to conduct my research in any form that could re-traumatize the people. Doing so required another protective layer of care, so I brought my hand drum and Indigenous storywork into the fold.

My use and reconciliation of storytelling and narrative inquiry are directed and guided by Kirkness and Barnhardt's (1991) influential four Rs – respect, relevance, reciprocity, and responsibility. The four Rs refer to "the need for a higher educational system that *respects* them [the students] for who they are, that is *relevant* to their view of the world, that offers *reciprocity* in their relationships with others, and that helps them exercise *responsibility* over their own lives" (Kirkness & Barnhardt, 1991, p. 1). In addition, the four Rs represent respect for First Nations' cultural integrity, relevance to First Nations perspectives and experiences, and reciprocal relationships and responsibility through participation. These four Rs form the moral and ethical foundation of my Secwepemc identity study. Like many Indigenous scholars, I utilize the four "R" principles of Indigenous education in an Indigenous research context because the principles are relevant for community engagement.

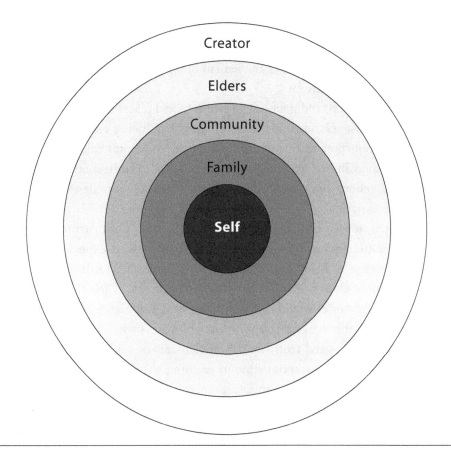

Figure 11.1: Circle Image

Archibald (2008) expanded the four Rs to embrace the seven principles governing the practice of First Nations stories and storytelling for educational purposes. The seven principles are: "respect, responsibility, reciprocity, reverence, holism, interrelatedness, and synergy" (p. ix). Holism is described by Archibald (2008) as an Indigenous philosophical concept of "interrelatedness between the intellectual, spiritual (metaphysical values and beliefs and the Creator), emotional, and physical (body and behaviour/action) realms to form a whole healthy person" (p. 11). Holism is represented by the image of the circle, which shows the synergistic influence and our responsibility for all generations (Archibald, 2008). I apply the circle image by situating myself in the centre surrounded by the four additional rings of family, community, Elders, and the Creator, as shown here.

To speak from a relational position is the best way to describe who I am, because I embody the five spheres outlined in the circle – self, family, community,

Elders, and Creator. The holism, synergy, and interrelatedness amongst them are equally vital. They are all interconnected and related within my Indigenous paradigm. This interconnectedness is an element of distinction between Secwepemc and Euro-Western worldviews.

Archibald's (2008) Indigenous storywork model places additional emphasis on respectful trust relationships. She clarifies that "being culturally 'worthy' or 'ready' is important to understanding the fundamental values of respect, reverence, responsibility, and reciprocity in relation to Indigenous storywork" (p. 108). Indigenous storywork allows "First Nations storytellers to use their personal life experiences as teaching stories in a manner similar to how they use traditional stories" (Archibald, 2008, p. 112). Thus, both narrative inquiry and Indigenous storywork focus on participants' lived-experience; however, they diverge in how participants' stories are used. While situating my lived-experiences alongside my two participants' stories, I felt the divergence between how our stories would be let out. My lived-experience as a Secwepemc person prompted me to exercise appropriate protocols when sharing stories to ensure that the voices and truths of the participants be told. I understood why Archibald dedicated substantial time in learning about story from her Sto:lo Elders in order to invoke appropriate protocols. She shared how her understandings formed through the learning relationships with Elders and she was challenged by the experiential story wanderings with Coyote the Trickster. Within this Indigenous tradition, "sharing can take the form of a story of personal life experience and [it] is done with a compassionate mind and love for others" (Archibald, 2008, p. 2). I felt that I needed the extra protection of Indigenous protocols to oversee and support my interaction with the community and participants. I did not want to be perceived as a threat given the history and experience many Indigenous communities have faced with the extraction of research and data for the wrong purposes. According to Secwepemc scholar Ron Ignace (2008), it was painful for the Secwepemc people when their words about the ancient past were discharged as irrelevant by anthropologists. He told of how the ancestors' stories were further stripped of any consciousness of history and edited in narratives and treated as "folklore." The historical misperception of non-Indigenous researchers taught me to maintain a stronger reciprocal relationship with my community. To exercise care, I drew from my hand drum to metaphorically guide the study. A Secwepemc framework, an Indigenous methodology based on the spiritual and physical properties of the hand drum, safeguards my relationality. The hand drum is a sacred and revered component of Secwepemc identity. The whole is signified by its parts, the wood from the tree and the hide from the animal. The Secwepemc people believe that we are connected to the spirit world through both animate and inanimate objects. The lives of the trees and animals are sacrificed, and in turn they are honoured by how one takes responsibility and cares for the hand drum. Ultimately, the hand drum comes from the land and the drumbeat represents the heartbeat of Mother Earth.

METHODS

To appropriately gather data that reflects my Secwepemc worldview, I sought techniques or procedures that were consistent with my relationship with my community. The methods needed to be relational. I believe this is why I was drawn to both Indigenous storywork and narrative inquiry. Given that identity formation is a deep and personal process I realized that respect was needed to honour the participants in the sharing of stories. My intergenerational identities project includes me, an Elder, and a youth. To adhere to community protocols, the Elder was chosen by the advisory committee based on her cultural experiences, her knowledge of the language, and her work experience counselling Indigenous students in the public school system. The criteria for the youth participant were male (for gender balance) and between the ages of 19 and 23. The youth participant was also identified and selected by the community advisory group. I collected stories from the participants twice independently, and in the final session we met as a collective. On each occasion, I borrowed from Clandinin and Connelly (2000) the concept of photographs and artefacts to assist the participants in composing their stories. Each participant meeting was at a location that gave them comfort. I offered nutrition and a monetary gift. Prior to meeting with the participants I asked them to bring an important photograph or artefact that connected them to their Secwepemc identity. Narrative inquiry does not require a set of questions; rather, the researcher engages in conversations with the participants. When the story sharing began, the Elder shared special photographs of her grandparents to help her with her childhood memories. The photographs triggered memories and the stories evolved. During the second meeting, the Elder focused on a series of handcrafted baskets handed down through generations to share the richness of her history and traditions. My interaction with the youth was similar. He reflected on an important family photograph as his connection to identity. He relied on his memory, as he forgot to bring the physical photo during our first conversation. The second time we met he had the photograph on his cell phone because he was afraid he would forget the photo again. The photos and artefacts were used to prompt the conversations and generate reflexive lived-experiences. As the researcher I did more listening than talking and simply permitted the stories to be told.

As I began analyzing my data, I felt storywork and narrative inquiry diverging. I found that narrative inquiry worked for analyzing my personal stories, but it felt uncomfortable applying the same technique to the participants' stories because narrative inquiry requires "self-critical reflexivity" (Rosborough, 2012, p. 40). I analyzed my own stories or narratives by applying narrative inquiry, but I could not apply the same method to the participants' stories because analyzing did not wholly sustain the words of the participants in speaking their truths. Therefore, to keep the participants' stories intact, I needed to adopt an appropriate method. In my view, Indigenous storywork did this. I shifted from co-composing stories with my participants to co-creating their stories. Applying a narrative inquiry approach would have meant that I would compose the stories and invite the participants to review and amend or add to the text after the stories are written. By co-creating, I have written the stories as they are shared in the transcripts to contribute to the fullness of Secwepemc identities. Co-creating is back and forth movement that ensures the meanings of the stories are authentic. I reviewed and correlated the transcripts into story form as I heard them. The stories were then shared with the participants for accuracy and affirmation of intent. I feel that the participants' voices are stronger when the stories are co-created rather than co-composed.

THEORETICAL PERSPECTIVE

The philosophical position informing my methodologies, which, as outlined by Crotty (1998), is "the philosophical stance informing the methodology and thus providing a context for the process and grounding its logic and criteria" (p. 3), aligns with Indigenous storywork protocols and Indigenous knowledges. Archibald's (2008) storywork research model initiates a respectful trust relationship that coincides with IK. Archibald "incorporates [the principles of] cultural respect, responsibility, reciprocity and reverence" (p. 38). It is mandatory for researchers to adhere to ethical guidelines, and to be particularly sensitive about the implications of conducting research with Indigenous people and communities. It is also important for the research to be relevant to the community and respect the knowledge and traditions being shared and/or experienced. According to Kathy Absolon (2011), "the awareness and knowledge we have about ourselves [Indigenous scholars] in relation to Creation is integrated into our methodologies as we locate and story ourselves into our search processes" (p. 58). We are informed by who we are and where we come from. I agree with Absolon that for many of us our research is about "finding our way home" (Absolon,

2011, p. 110). Through my doctoral journey, I searched for more cultural knowledge, history, traditions, stories, and identities. Absolon states that "Indigenous Knowledge and methodologies enable us to conduct our searches" (Absolon, 2011, p. 110). I realized this early on and this is why I reached for my hand drum to keep me anchored and connected in many ways. Much like Absolon (2011), Archibald (2008), Battiste (2000), Kirkness and Barnhardt (1991), and Smith (1999), I did not want to be absorbed into the academy.

My hand drum serves as my connection and anchor to IK in several directions. The hand drum itself represents the same rootedness expressed by Steinhauer (2001). She explains:

> Trees have roots that are firmly rooted in the ground. Their creation and growth involves a long nurturing process.… I think of how solidly the roots are rooted in the ground and how they provide the life food, the knowledge, for the rest of the tree. I see these roots as representing our ancestors. (p. 186)

For me, as for Paul Cormier and Lana Ray, who have also contributed to this volume, the hand drum bears important cultural meaning. In particular it can be my metaphorical and theoretical framework for my research. It symbolizes connectedness and respect. Connectedness is in the natural materials used for the drum and its circular shape. The materials reflect the rootedness of the tree; the frame of the drum is made from cedar. The drum itself is made from deer or moose hide. The drum is handled with utmost care and respect; the Secwepemc people honour animate beings as well as inanimate objects, as they believe that all things deserve respect. As an emerging hand drummer I heed important protocols when handling the drum. I possess two hand drums. I was gifted my first drum by my lifelong friend, and my second drum was given to me by my community as I prepared for a conference presentation in Cairns, Australia, in 2010. I understand responsibility transfers from the person/party giving the drum to the receiver, and the responsibility to take care of and honour the drum is immediate. The person is expected to know the details and the meaning of the parts of the hand drum. The receiver sets out and carefully prepares to honour the drum. I observed Secwepemc hand drummers approach the drum in harmony. They set any negativity aside as the drumbeat keeps time with the heartbeat of Mother Earth, who sustains life. The actions are sacred. My actions are guided by cultural integrity as I engage with my community and participants in research. I extend the same honouring of the hand drum to the acceptance and sharing of my participants' stories.

EPISTEMOLOGY

My Secwepemc worldview anchored by my hand drum translates into my epistemology. The drum forms the epistemological element introduced by Crotty (1998), which is "the theory of knowledge embedded in the theoretical perspective and thereby the methodology" (p. 3), and it becomes the anchor for cultural protocols. I am learning to bring who I am and what I represent into my search to find, enjoy, and be proud of my cultural identities and reject external labels. My PhD project was definitely a healing journey. I am drumming my way home. Indigenous storywork and narrative inquiry are the tools that helped me move through various phases of my study and my personal journey. This process has given me the strength to share my story in a good way, as a teaching story. I chose to focus on the positive aspect of identity formation rather than remain stuck in the colonized text where many Indigenous people can remain trapped.

REFERENCES

Absolon, K. E. (2011). *Kaandossiwin: How we come to know.* Halifax, NS: Fernwood Publishing.

Archibald, J. (2008). *Indigenous storywork: Educating the heart, mind, body, and spirit.* Vancouver, BC: UBC Press.

Battiste, M. (2000). Maintaining Aboriginal identity, language, and culture in modern society. In M. Battiste (Ed.), *Reclaiming Indigenous voice and vision* (pp. 192–208). Vancouver, BC: UBC Press.

Chilisa, B. (2012). *Indigenous research methodologies.* Thousand Oaks, CA: Sage.

Clandinin, D. J., & Connelly, M. (2000). *Narrative inquiry: Experience and story in qualitative research.* San Francisco, CA: Jossey-Bass.

Connelly, F. M., & Clandinin, D. J. (1990). Stories of experience and narrative inquiry. *Educational Researcher, 19*(5), 2–14.

Crotty, M. (1998). *The foundations of social research: Meaning and perspective in the research process.* London, UK: Sage.

Ignace, R. (2008). *Our oral histories are our iron posts: Secwepemc, stories and historical consciousness* (Unpublished doctoral dissertation). Simon Fraser University, Burnaby, BC.

Kirkness, V., & Barnhardt, R. (1991). First Nations and higher education: The four R's – respect, relevance, reciprocity, responsibility. *Journal of American Indian Education, 30*(3), 1–15.

Rosborough, P. C. (2012). *K̓angex̌tola sewn-on-top: Kwak'wala revitalization and being Indigenous.* University of British Columbia. Retrieved from https://circle.ubc.ca/handle/2429/42965

Sandy, N. H. (2011). *Reviving Secwepemc child welfare jurisdiction*. University of Victoria, BC. Retrieved from http://ezproxy.library.ubc.ca/login?url=http://search.proquest.com/docvie w/940892709?accountid=14656

Smith, L. T. (1999). *Decolonizing methodologies: Research and Indigenous peoples*. New York, NY: Zed Books.

Steinhauer, P. (2001). Situating myself in research. *Canadian Journal of Native Education, 25*(2), 183–187.

Wilson, S. (2001). What is an Indigenous research methodology? *Canadian Journal of Native Education, 25*(2), 175–179.

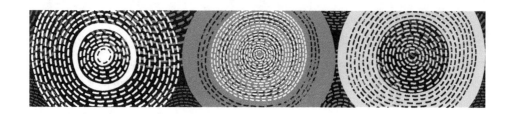

CHAPTER 12

Treaty #3: A Tool for Empowering Diverse Scholars to Engage in Indigenous Research

Brittany Luby with Rachel Arsenault, Joseph Burke, Michelle Graham, and Toni Valenti[1]

On September 30, 1873, Crown and Anishinaabe negotiators gathered at Northwest Angle on Lake of the Woods to make a treaty. Four days later, they concluded Treaty #3 (Canada, 1871–1874/1966).[2] Anishinaabe Elders envisage(d) Treaty #3 as a land sharing agreement. In return for annuities, carpentry tools, farming equipment, reserve lands, and educational support, the Anishinabeg would allow "Her Majesty's subjects" to settle among them. Anishinaabe Elders sometimes note that there is no word for "cede" in Anishinaabemowin to support this position. By contrast, the written English version of Treaty #3 suggests that the Anishinabeg ceded their lands, "embracing an area of fifty-five thousand square miles [approximately 14,244,935 hectares]," to the Crown (Canada, 1871–1874/1966, p. 4). Crown and Anishinaabe negotiators have yet to agree on a single interpretation of Treaty #3, particularly the division of land and natural resources.

And yet, both parties agree(d) that Treaty #3 established a relationship between non-Indigenous settlers and the Anishinabeg living in what is now known as southeastern Manitoba and northwestern Ontario. As early as 1859, Simon J. Dawson recommended that the Crown open a dialogue with the Anishinabeg. A friendly relationship, Dawson believed, could diminish the threat of violence east of Red River. He wrote that "cultivat[ing] a good understanding, and tak[ing] such measures … would prevent the possibility of a collision with them [the Anishinabeg]"

(Dawson, 1968, p. 16). Dawson feared that the Crown might struggle to suppress violence in the region as "the Indians [were] said to be increasing" and a stable food supply "enable[d] them to collect in numbers sufficiently great to be formidable" (Dawson, 1968, p. 16). Much like federal employees, the Anishinabeg also had reason to fear violent conflict: non-Indigenous traders, missionaries, surveyors, and road workers entered the territory in increasing numbers after 1793.[3] Peace was fragile. Non-Indigenous men and Anishinaabe women formed kinship bonds. But, outside of family, oral testimony suggests that the "Red Coats" sometimes attacked Anishinaabe encampments without cause (Everson, 1975, pp. 54–55). Treaty #3 was, in large part, about setting the terms for ongoing, peaceable interactions.

Social justice advocates, scholars, and provincial employees have invested considerable energy in alerting Canadians that they co-habit many parts of North America as treaty partners rather than primary occupants. In 1969, Harold Cardinal demanded that Canadians recognize treaties as "the beginning of a con-tractual relationship whereby the representatives of the Queen would have lasting responsibilities to the Indian people" (1999, p. 25). Almost 50 years later, Anthony J. Hall (2001) reminded readers of the *Canadian Encyclopedia* that "treaties form the constitutional and moral basis of alliance between Indigenous peoples and Canada" (2001). Most recently, in 2016, the Ministry of Indigenous Relations and Reconciliation agreed to help fund *Gdoo-sastamoo kii mi: Understanding Our Nation to Nation Relationship*, a teaching kit designed to raise awareness of how Ontarians continue to benefit from long-standing alliances with Indigenous peoples. Each author encourages his/her reader to think about how Canada was formed, how Canada benefits from treaty, and how Canada ought to provide for its treaty partners. But treaties are not just for governments; they are for citizens. This chapter reviews Treaty #3 to see how it might apply in a university setting, and to determine how scholars (as treaty beneficiaries) can live and work rightly on shared land. We believe that:

1. Treaty #3 encourages non-Indigenous researchers to engage with Anishinaabe communities, but prohibits non-Indigenous scholars from exploiting local knowledge keepers. Non-Indigenous researchers are to participate in an information exchange (rather than extract information for personal gain).
2. Treaty #3 encourages non-Indigenous researchers to engage with systems thinking, enabling them to better identify overlap between personal research interests and community research needs.

3. Treaty #3 provides a cultural framework through which Anishinaabe youth can actively learn (and absorb) Western knowledges without fear of assimilation.

This chapter also experiments with knowledge generation and transmission in an academic setting. Anishinaabe leaders have used sharing circles to facilitate group discussion for generations. To initiate dialogue, the circle leader would present an issue (or thematic prompt) to the group. Each participant received an opportunity to speak uninterrupted on the issue. Lynn F. Lavallée (2009) has compared sharing circles to focus groups, noting that both are intended to "gather information on a particular topic through group discussion" (p. 22).[4] It seems likely that Anishinaabe leaders used a sharing circle to generate negotiating points for Treaty #3. Consider that Anishinaabe leaders deferred discussion with Crown representatives until "a large body of Rainy River and Lac Seul representatives" arrived at Northwest Angle (Morris, 1880, p. 53). Despite pressure from Lieutenant-Governor Alexander Morris to treat, Anishinaabe leaders maintained that "they had business of their own to transact, which must be disposed of before they could see the Governor" (Morris, 1880, p. 54). Negotiations with the Crown were delayed until "the Indians agree[d] amongst themselves" (Morris, 1880, p. 54). Sharing circles are rooted in an Anishinaabe "philosophical proposition" that denies the concept of absolute truth. Instead, "a speaker casts his or her words as far as his perception will enable him or her" (Johnston, 2013, p. 6). Dialogue leads to nuanced understanding. In recognition of this philosophical proposition, this chapter's findings were generated in a sharing circle.

To better understand how scholars as treaty beneficiaries can use Treaty #3, Dr. Brittany Luby called together four emerging scholars at Laurentian University: Rachel Arsenault, Joseph Burke, Michelle Graham, and Toni Valenti. Each of these students enrolled in the master of Indigenous relations program and expressed an interest in (re)shaping the practice of academic writing through Anishinaabe teachings. Independent, peer-reviewed articles are valued most highly in academia. Academic publishing expectations make it difficult for scholars to co-create knowledge in the sharing circle tradition.[5] We decided to embrace the risk of limited recognition and met face-to-face to discuss the written English version of Treaty #3 (and records of the oral proceedings). After the gathering, Dr. Luby circulated a series of questions by email, asking each author to produce a written statement about the knowledge s/he accumulated in the sharing circle. Each author responded using "Reply All" in attempt to reiterate his/her findings in an e-circle. Submissions have been edited to improve flow and reader comprehension. The authors discovered that without witnessing live interactions, it would be difficult for readers to interpret online reflections. Written approaches to sharing circle pedagogies are useful approximations, but have limitations. Editing helped to provide context and to improve flow for our reading audience.

During the revision process, we were asked to describe our socio-cultural identities. Our circle included scholars from many backgrounds: Anishinaabe, Canadian, Métis, and Portuguese-Spanish. We decided against manipulating our script to distinguish between Indigenous and non-Indigenous voices. As Bagele Chilisa (2012) poignantly articulated, "The talking circle symbolizes and encourages ... togetherness, and a continuous and unending compassion and love for one another" (p. 213). During the process, we identified most strongly as treaty beneficiaries. Whether through birth, work, or study, we each had a responsibility to define our relationship to Treaty #3. Dividing the text into Indigenous and non-Indigenous contributions, we feared, would break the circle into opposing lines. Our decision to include non-Indigenous participants is supported by Treaty #3 itself: it is our responsibility – whether Anishinaabe or Canadian – to "teach what is good" to the "Other" (Morris, 1880, p. 63). This is a unique case[6]: We have all been invited into treaty circles by our ancestors. We are bound to one another by law. This same law requires us to exchange information, but does not limit us to "Western" or Indigenous forms of communication.

Our overarching goal is to honour Anishinaabe teachings in text. By adapting the sharing circle from life to text, we attempt to challenge colonial norms that prevent Anishinaabe scholars from producing work that aligns more strongly with Anishinaabe standards of "truth" (e.g., cultural definitions of accuracy). Our findings have been presented as a script to celebrate the unique voice (or gift) of each author. It is only through conversation that we can begin to understand how Treaty #3 applies to our working lives. Headings have been provided to help organize content. We have decided not to provide section summaries. Instead, we ask you, the reader, to grab a pen, write in the margins, and join our circle. You are encouraged to participate in the construction of meaning.

TREATY #3: A CALL FOR INFORMATION EXCHANGES

Luby: In 1873, the Crown and the Anishinabeg spoke about education. The School Promise, which appears in paragraph 13 of the written English version of treaty, reads:

Her Majesty agrees to maintain schools for instruction in such reserves hereby made as to Her Government of Her Dominion of Canada may seem advisable whenever the Indians of the reserve shall desire it. (Canada, 1871–1874/1966, p. 5).

What sort of relationship does this paragraph establish between the Crown and the Anishinabeg?

Valenti: In the case of the School Promise in the written English version of Treaty #3, the federal government is the primary actor. The federal government determines which "schools of instruction" are worthy of financial support. But what type of instruction will these schools have? Who will determine the nature of instruction? The answer is unclear. A lack of specification in the School Promise, I believe, created space for the establishment of Indian residential schools in northwestern Ontario and southeastern Manitoba. The School Promise allowed the federal government to claim that residential schooling was "advisable" – regardless of Anishinaabe educational expectations and norms.

The phrase "may seem advisable" in Treaty #3 reminded me of the Medicine Chest Clause in Treaty #6 (Canada, 1876/1966). To me, both the School Promise and the Medicine Chest Clause translate as, "You can ask, and we [the Crown] will think about it."[7] As with the Medicine Chest Clause, Treaty #3 appears to provide community access to education. However, educational access is at the discretion of federal administrators.

Luby: In short, the written English version of Treaty #3 seeks to establish a hierarchal relationship between the Anishinabeg (those who demand schools) and the Crown (those who may choose to finance schools).

Valenti: Yes, that is my interpretation. The language used in the written English version of Treaty #3 allows the Crown to control if (and when) the schools receive government funding. The word "advisable" in the School Promise is powerful. Historically, the federal government manipulated the School Promise to advance its assimilation program.

Luby: It is for this reason that researchers must consider the written English version of Treaty #3 alongside records of the oral negotiations. In September 1873, a shorthand reporter from the *Manitoban* travelled to Lake of the

Woods to cover treaty proceedings. He claimed that Lieutenant-Governor Morris promised to "establish schools whenever any band may ask for them, so that [Anishinabeg] children may have the learning of the Whiteman" (Morris, 1880, p. 58). As in the written School Promise, the Anishinabeg are to request access to schools. The Crown, however, did not reserve the right to veto Anishinaabe demands during the oral negotiations.

Anishinaabe leaders may have desired the "learning of the Whiteman," but they did not necessarily associate learning with the classroom setting. The chief of Lac Seul set the following terms:

> If you give what I ask, the time may come when I will ask you to lend me one of your daughters and one of your sons to live with us; and in return I will lend you one of my daughters and one of my sons for you to teach what is good, and after they have learned to teach us. (Morris, 1880, p. 63).

Let us examine this quotation in more detail. What responsibilities does it lay out for newcomers?

Burke: Kiiwetinepinesiik Stark (2010) suggests that some of the earliest treaties in North America occurred between "indigenous peoples and the Animal and Star nations" (p. 147). These treaties are not recorded by wampum or by text, but are encoded in oral stories. Through these early treaties, we can see that the Anishinabeg identified respect and reciprocity as essential parts of nation-to-nation agreements long before European arrival.

Take, for example, the Anishinabeg treaty with Beaver: "Those who speak kindly of [and thus show respect for] the beaver will find great success in trapping one … [T]he beavers, in turn, respect the Anishinaabe by greatly loving them and giving themselves up to the Anishinaabe for food" (Stark, 2010, p. 147). To ensure a healthy and lasting relationship with Beaver, the Anishinabeg must return its bones to the river. The Anishinabeg have a responsibility to acknowledge that Beaver has given them food and, by so doing, given them life. It seems likely that the Anishinabeg would consider respect and reciprocity essential elements in later treaties with the Crown.

Education is an essential component of respect. John Curry, Han Donker, and Richard Krehbiel (2014) associate treaty making with "capacity building" (p. 295). To me, capacity building means that there must be an effort to educate parties included within the treaty. In the case of Treaty #3, the duty to build capacity should apply to both parties, the Crown and the

Anishinabeg, meaning the two must learn from each other. Knowledge is to be shared. Bones are returned to the river.

If you (re)read the written English version of Treaty #3 after the *Manitoban*, it becomes possible to reframe the School Promise. The word "advisable" suggests collaboration is a treaty responsibility. There must be some kind of dialogue between parties if the Anishinabeg are to express what is "desired" and if the Crown is to determine what is "advisable."

Arsenault: I agree that both the Crown and the Anishinabeg were to continue talking after Treaty #3 was signed in 1873. I also believe that the Anishinabeg hoped to teach "Her Majesty's subjects" to improve the flow of ideas. The Anishinabeg felt that they had valuable knowledge that would benefit newcomers. Anishinaabe leaders asked that newcomers (represented by the Crown) send their children to learn among them. Of course, when the chief of Lac Seul asked Lieutenant-Governor Morris to send "one of your daughters and one of your sons," he did not mean actual children. The chief's figurative language referred to subjects of the Crown. The Anishinabeg wanted non-Indigenous peoples to learn Anishinaabe language (Anishinaabemowin), tradition, and culture. Anishinaabe leaders hoped that newcomers would learn to respect Anishinaabe ways of being, leading to healthier interactions between treaty partners over time.

Luby: Arsenault, you make an important observation here. The request for dialogue suggests that the Anishinabeg believed their knowledge held value. To affirm this statement, I would like to draw your attention to a handwritten account of the oral proceedings by Commissioner Simon J. Dawson (Library and Archives Canada [LAC], 1873). According to his records, "Can-ta-go-wa-minny," an Anishinaabe negotiator, reminded Lieutenant-Governor Morris that "[Anishinaabe] heads are rich" (LAC, 1873). The shorthand reporter recorded similar statements for the *Manitoban*. An unidentified Anishinaabe negotiator emphasized the effectiveness of Anishinaabe mnemonic devices: "You must remember that our hearts and our brains are like paper; we never forget" (Morris, 1880, p. 69). During their four days at Northwest Angle with the Crown, the Anishinabeg emphasized their ability to retain and relay information as a nation.

Burke: It is clear that from the Anishinaabe perspective, Treaty #3 was supposed to promote capacity building through an information exchange. As

Arsenault suggested, this exchange was to improve nation-to-nation relationships into the future. In 1873, Anishinabeg negotiators realized that the Crown's failure to hire a locally trained translator put them at risk: "I would not find it to my convenience to have a stranger here to transact our business.… It is a white man who does not understand our language that is taking it down" (Morris, 1880, p. 71).

Anishinaabe negotiators did not intend to bar all "white men" from translation work. Instead, "white men" had a responsibility to learn from the Anishinabeg before claiming to represent Anishinaabe interests: "I would like a man that understands our language and our ways" (Morris, 1880, p. 71). An information exchange, learning from one another, was at the core of Anishinaabe aims – this much is obvious from the *Manitoban*.

Luby: Records of the oral negotiations suggest that non-Indigenous beneficiaries of Treaty #3 must do more than finance education. Reinterpreted in 2016, these records create space for non-Indigenous researchers to work with(in) Anishinaabe communities. Treaty #3 does not allow non-Indigenous researchers to exploit knowledge keepers. Anishinaabe teachers retain control over when (and what) material is shared with newcomers. Yet, Treaty #3 suggests that the non-Indigenous learner is responsible for (re)packaging Anishinaabe teachings for his/her audience (i.e., "to teach what is good").

Arsenault: Many researchers are writing about the challenges and prospects of intergroup collaboration. The consensus seems to be that Indigenous peoples must benefit from research studies being done by outsiders on their behalf. Edwards and colleagues suggested that this shift toward collaboration started in the 1990s:

> In the past decade [circa 1998], communities have developed strong research leadership skills, becoming active partners in research where they had previously been the passive subjects of scientific studies (Edwards, Lund, Mitchell, & Andersson, 2008, p. 187).

Treaty #3 suggests that collaboration is more than best practice: it is a treaty responsibility. Records of the oral proceedings further reveal that the Anishinabeg have a right to be actively involved in the process of knowledge creation as educators and as advisors.

TREATY #3: A TOOL FOR IMAGINING OVERLAPPING RESEARCH INTERESTS

Luby: For non-Indigenous researchers who participate in a knowledge exchange (as recommended in records of the oral negotiations), mutually beneficial research becomes easier to imagine. Anishinaabe teachers have long emphasized that all living beings are connected. In 1873, Anishinaabe negotiators understood the complex web of relations between human and natural systems in their territory. Evidence of this web exists in Creation stories (Benton-Benai, 2010; Coatsworth & Coatsworth, 1991; King, 2003). Given that Anishinaabe negotiators assumed their actions had a direct impact on the natural world, researchers must assume that words like "hunting and fishing," as they appear in the written English version of treaty, are symbolic.

Let us consider "hunting." The Merriam-Webster Dictionary (2016) defines "hunting" as "the activity or sport of chasing and killing wild animals." An English speaker is most likely to associate the treaty promise that "the said Indians [the Anishinabeg] shall have the right to pursue their avocations of hunting and fishing throughout the tract surrendered" with the right to track and to kill large game (e.g., moose and deer) (Canada, 1871–1874/1966, p. 5). However, many Anishinabeg do not distinguish between the right to hunt and the right to harvest *manomin* (wild rice). For centuries, ducks would descend on Lake of the Woods and the Winnipeg River in the fall. They came for *manomin*, which is ready to harvest in late September and early October. Anishinaabe men would hunt duck as a form of pest control, but also as a valuable source of protein for their families. Without *manomin*, there are fewer ducks. With less *manomin* and fewer ducks, the treaty right to hunt is compromised.

Treaty alerts researchers to the human and natural systems relevant to their subject group. Thus, a researcher can use Treaty #3 to develop a meaningful understanding of his/her study area.

Arsenault: Interconnectivity is not unique to the Anishinabeg. In the film *The Sacred Relationship* (Miller, 2013), Dr. Patti Laboucane-Benson discusses *wakotowin*, or the Cree doctrine of relationships. This doctrine can be visualized as a spiral with six interconnected rungs. The rungs represent self, family, clan, nation, environment, and the cosmos (or spirit realm) (Miller, 2013). There are rules that govern relations between rungs. These rules ensure that the sacred gifts of land, water, animals, plants, and all Creation are respected by the Cree. The "basic rule of survival" for the Cree is that everything is interconnected in a delicate balance (Miller, 2013). If the relationship between the self and the environment collapses, for example, the nation may also fall.

Burke: By engaging in an information exchange, non-Indigenous researchers can combat reductionist thinking (often associated with Western ways of knowing). Angayuqaq Oscar Kawagley and Ray Barnhardt (1998) quoted Fritjof Capra in saying that "reductionism seeks to break reality into parts to understand the whole, without realizing that the parts are merely patterns extant in a total web of relationships" (p. 9). By learning about interconnections that are important to the Anishinabeg, non-Indigenous researchers begin to identify overlaps between personal interest and community interest.

Luby: Burke, how might a web of relationships apply to your work?

Burke: My research focuses on the government consultation process in the Ring of Fire. The Ring of Fire is a mineral deposit "[a]pproximately 500 kilometres north of Thunder Bay, in the James Bay Lowlands" (Gravelle, 2013). It has an estimated value of CAD$30–$50 billion (Gravelle, 2013). Let us imagine that a participating community wants to learn more about water quality on-reserve. How can I serve the community (i.e., discuss water issues) and advance my interests (i.e., discuss the consultation process)? A body of ore in the Ring of Fire will undoubtedly require a process for extraction that can influence local water tables. By offering to examine this issue, I can serve both the community and the university.

Valenti: Due to the holistic nature of many Indigenous healing traditions, there are often preconceived notions that Indigenous peoples don't have science (or at least *science* as we know it within Western epistemologies) (Curtis, Reid, & Jones, 2014, p. 148). This is simply untrue. However, this misconception may have prevented previous scholars from recognizing overlapping interests. We may see change in our lifetime. For example, in the sciences, the concept of two-eyed seeing is being developed. Two-eyed seeing is the process of weaving both Indigenous and Western knowledge systems together in an applied setting as a means to create cultural safety and competency (Bartlett, Marshall, & Marshall, 2012). Two-eyed seeing was applied in the creation of the integrative science undergraduate degree program at Cape Breton University in Nova Scotia, a program that uses both Indigenous and Western sciences to explore the living environment and the web of relationships between humans, planets, and all living things (Bartlett et al., 2012). This particular program has been "on pause" since 2007 due to low student enrolment ("Academic Program," 2016). But, there is hope. What I am trying to say is that non-Indigenous researchers do not yet have a firm grasp of interconnectivity from an Indigenous perspective, but more students have been (and may continue to be) trained to see and understand webs of relationships.

Luby: If we agree to a knowledge exchange – as Treaty #3 suggests – future researchers may not require a degree in integrative science (or ecology) to identify interconnections. Engagement with treaty could better enable non-Indigenous researchers to see overlaps between community goals and individual interests by showing them how Anishinaabe thinkers define their world(s).

TREATY #3: A TOOL FOR CREATING SPACES FOR ANISHINAABE RESEARCHERS IN THE ACADEMY

Luby: Our discussion thus far has focused on how treaty should be used to create space for cross-cultural exchanges. I wonder: does Treaty #3 empower Anishinaabe scholars to participate in Western learning environments?

I raise this question because media reports have emphasized the struggles of Indigenous peoples, suggesting that they do not quite belong in university. Doubt attacks Indigenous scholars like me through the news. In *The Gradzette*, Sardana Nikolaeva (2016) argued that course evaluations put minority professors at risk of professional stagnation in (if not dismissal from) the academy. Minority professors are generally seen by students as less qualified and thus less knowledgeable about their study area. Nikolaeva (2016) concludes that "personal stereotypes, biases, and prejudices" negatively impact the career mobility of minority professors. She explains that "universities rely on service evaluations, utilizing the end-of-course student evaluations as the primary rationale for decision-making in relation to further hiring (sessional/adjunct instructors), tenure, promotions, awards, pay or recognition."

In January 2016, *The National Post* picked up a story about Lorna June McCue, an Indigenous professor at the University of British Columbia

(UBC) who was denied tenure for "failing" to publish in academic journals. She recommended that UBC "change their standards to account for 'non-traditional scholarship,' such as conference appearances, submissions to UN bodies and chapters in non-peer-reviewed books" (Hopper, 2016). UBC's tenure and promotion standards, McCue argued, "require[d] 'significant' [cultural] compromise" (Hopper, 2016).[8] Sporadic reports about Indigenous peoples in the news emphasize struggle and failure. And yet, Treaty #3 suggests that education is a right. Could teaching the School Promise make the university seem like a safer place for Anishinaabe scholars?

Burke: The initial value of teaching about the School Promise is that it aligns Indigenous rights with education. Scholars have the potential to develop a sense of empowerment from Treaty #3 by knowing that their ancestors deemed the process of education as a crucially important part of fostering an ongoing partnership with the settlers. Consequently, Indigenous scholars are more likely to find institutions like universities culturally safe places where they can learn a lot about their colonial partners (without being colonized).

Graham: I believe that there is a method for us to follow to make this possible. Culturally responsive pedagogy is a teaching method used in various parts of the world (e.g., New Zealand, Arizona, New Mexico, and northern Ontario) (Arviso & Holm, 2001; Hare & Pidgeon, 2011; Kanu, 2002; McCarty & Lee, 2014; Savage et al., 2011). This method of teaching demands that teachers connect with students "through personal and cultural strengths, their intellectual capabilities, and their prior accomplishments" (Gay, 2010, p. 26). Culturally responsive pedagogy is designed to build a better learning environment for students in the classroom.

Yatta Kanu observed students in a high school classroom in Alberta. Students commented that Indigenous teachings such as story reading, storytelling, and community support made them feel most comfortable in their learning environment. By teaching the School Promise in Treaty #3, Anishinaabe children may grow up feeling supported by their community (past and present) as they pursue their learning goals.

Burke: That being said, the teaching of the School Promise cannot stop there. For universities to be culturally safe places for Indigenous students, faculty, and staff, there must be spaces where non-Indigenous students, faculty, and staff can immerse themselves in Indigenous culture and education. In building the capacity of both camps, we can ensure that Treaty #3 is honoured in practice, and foster a partnership that is mindful of the *sui generis* entitlements of the Anishinabeg. It is possible to derive positivity from treaty language that is not very empowering for the Anishinabeg at face value.

Arsenault: By sharing treaty history with both Indigenous and non-Indigenous peoples, the intended concept of reciprocity and respect can be reclaimed and reintroduced into educational institutions nationwide. In providing this historical knowledge, a reduction in the negative encounters Indigenous peoples experience in the education system is definitely an anticipated outcome.

If we embrace treaty and begin to increase non-Indigenous access to Indigenous knowledges, as Burke suggests, we have an opportunity to make the academy a safer place. Language and culture are important to Indigenous success, as indicated in the findings from the Truth and Reconciliation Commission (2015). Once Indigenous students, faculty, and staff are reminded that they have a right to be at university, they may feel stronger demanding that non-Indigenous students, faculty, and staff also engage with their language and culture (as part of their treaty obligation). If both parties adhere to Treaty #3, for example, Anishinaabe scholars are more likely to hear Anishinaabemowin in the hallways. As more scholars hear Anishinaabemowin in the hallways, they are less likely to think of the university as a space that excludes their interests.

Valenti: In many ways, I do believe that telling Indigenous youth about their treaty rights to an education could provide a safer space in schools for them. I also believe that it is important to discuss career paths imagined by Anishinaabe negotiators for the youth. When Treaty #3 was signed, Anishinaabe negotiators believed that education could be used to train cultural liaisons. Learning this treaty goal could be very powerful for Anishinaabe scholars in Canada. I think that this emphasis affirms that they have experiences and knowledge that are important, and that need to be further privileged in Canadian society. It sets the precedent that they have something to share. This Anishinaabe understanding that their youth had a right to learn and ideally become cultural liaisons is an important teaching needed to resist both previous and current attempts at silencing Indigenous cultures.

CONCLUSION

This chapter was an experiment in knowledge generation and transmission. Our goal was to determine how, if at all, Treaty #3 applied to academics. We wanted to learn whether Treaty #3 could be used to model relationships between universities and Indigenous communities (and their representatives). Treaty #3 demands that non-Indigenous researchers collaborate with Anishinaabe communities. Collaboration, however, makes it easier to envisage overlapping interests. Non-Indigenous researchers immersed in Anishinaabe systems-thinking are more likely to identify connections between personal projects and community goals. We also discovered that Treaty #3 creates space for Anishinabeg in the academy. Anishinaabe ancestors believed that Western teachings could serve the nation – there is no sense that attendance separates Anishinaabe students, faculty, and staff from their culture.

In the process, we discovered that it is possible to pool multiple perspectives and to distill a three-part message. There is a risk, of course, to adapting the sharing circle from voice to text. As Patricia Paulis (2015) has warned, "We can get into trouble for evading templates.... And where do the lines of evasion go? Towards and away from tenure" (p. 82). In taking risks, however, we find creative ways to honour treaty in our working lives. Treaty #3 is not just for study. It is a document that can guide Indigenous and non-Indigenous students, faculty, and staff in co-creating a better, more inclusive learning environment for the next generation of treaty beneficiaries.

NOTES

1. Dr. Brittany Luby is the primary author of "Treaty #3: A Tool for Empowering Diverse Scholars to Engage in Indigenous Research." All other authors are listed in alphabetical order. Toni Valenti converted the chapter from Chicago style to APA.

2. Treaty #3 was concluded on October 3, 1873.

3. In 1793, the Hudson's Bay Company (HBC) established a post at Manitou Falls on the Rainy River. A second HBC post was erected on Rainy River in 1794. Trade increased the number of non-Indigenous workers in what would become northwestern Ontario. In 1836, a third HBC post was constructed at Rat Portage (Lund, 1975). The establishment of trade routes facilitated the movement of missionaries into the interior. Simon J. Dawson (1968) reported on missionary activity near Lake of the Woods in 1859. He had, however, been active surveying a "rough water and land route from Lake Superior to the Red River" as early as 1857–1858. Road workers followed (Lake

of the Woods Writers' Group and Kenora Centennial Committee, 1981). Other notable surveyors who passed through the territory in the 1850s include John Palliser and Henry Youle Hind (Palliser, 1968; Hind, 1860).

4. Rachel Arsenault found that Bagele Chilisa has also compared sharing circles to focus groups. However, Chilisa argues that sharing circles foster more egalitarian relationships than focus groups. The circle formation is believed to create a "collaborative, non-authoritarian relationship between members" (2012, p. 283). Chilisa (2012) maintains that the circle reminds participants of the "equality of members" – each participant is clearly visible, clearly interconnected (p. 213). Structure thus helps to prevent hierarchal relationships from forming. Toni Valenti has further noted that sharing circles are rooted in the sacred (Naibgon et al., quoted in Lavallée, 2009). Focus groups, by contrast, are secular in nature.

5. In "Tenure (Un)Secure/d: As Words Go into Labour," Patricia Paulis (2015) notes that "the count [of peer-reviewed articles] is imperative" (p. 92). Informal guidelines published for academics support Paulis' claim. Emily Toth (2009), for example, warns graduate students that "[w]ithout a publication or two, or some unique talent, you're apt to languish in the adjunct pool ... for as long as you're committed to academe ... [I]f you want to move to a liberal arts college or a research university, publication is the only path" (p. 27). Toth shares similar advice in "Ignore the Rules and Make Your Own Problems" (Toth, 2009, p. 51).

    Despite the pressure to produce single-authored peer-reviewed articles, Indigenous writers have used anthologies to resist and to circulate shared knowledge. In 2013, Jill Doerfler, Niigaanwewidam James Sinclair, and Heidi Kiiwetinepinesiik Stark published an introduction that "emerge[d] out of a conversation" (xviii). While the authors make no direct reference to sharing circles, their work is formatted like a script. The goal of their introduction (stimulating open dialogue) also reflects the goal of sharing circles. Like Doerfler, Sinclair, and Stark, we (the authors) are continuing to upset academic publishing norms and to normalize Indigenous forms of knowledge generation.

6. We have suggested that Treaty #3 invites all treaty beneficiaries to participate in sharing circles. We have also suggested that this is a unique case: the ancestors encouraged us to exchange information. They also extended an invitation to experiment with communication forms ("what is good").

    However, sharing circles are not always an appropriate form for knowledge generation and/or transmission. Some may be regarded as violating cultural norms (Chilisa, 2012). Based on his interpretation of Lynn Lavallée, Joseph Burke has suggested that sharing circles are inappropriate if none of the participants have any cultural relation to the practice *or* if the purpose of the sharing circle does not seek to embody the special relationships enshrined by treaty.

    In a case where cross-cultural exchange comes in the form of a sharing circle (as seen in this chapter), Burke suggests, some of the participants must culturally identify with the practice. This helps to maintain standards of knowledge transmission. It also helps to ensure ancestral presence, thus maintaining the integrity of the circle. We must remember that "the spirits of our ancestors and the Creator are present in the circle and guide the process. Energy is created in the circle by the spirit of the people involved" (Naibgon et al., quoted in Lavallée, 2009, p. 29).

Given ancestral presence, it is important to take spiritual precautions to ensure the safety of participants during a circle. If you are thinking of hosting a sharing circle, we encourage you to begin with two questions: "Do I have permission? Do I have the necessary skill?" If permission and/or skill is required, we encourage you to seek Elder guidance. Remember: sacred objects should never be used without sacred teachings (Alberta Education, 2005, p. 163).

7. The Medicine Chest Clause in Treaty #6 reads: "That a medicine chest shall be kept at the house of each Indian Agent for the use and benefit of the Indians at the direction of such agent" (Canada, Treaty No. 6, 1966).

8. Michelle M. Jacob (2012) suggests that female Indigenous scholars in the United States also struggle to "[maintain] their culture in the White academy." She asks, "How can we practically and respectfully serve both our communities and the institutions where we work when their values and ways of doing business are so drastically different?" (p. 247). This unresolved question appears to have negatively influenced the career of Lorna June McCue.

REFERENCES

Academic Program: Integrative Science. *Integrative Science.ca*. Accessed November 20, 2016. Retrieved from www.integrativescience.ca/Program/

Alberta Education (Aboriginal Services Branch and Learning and Teaching Resources Branch). (2005). *Our words, our ways: Teaching First Nations, Métis and Inuit learners*. [Accessed November 20, 2016]. Retrieved from https://education.alberta.ca/media/3615876/our-words-our-ways.pdf

Arviso, M., & Holm, W. (2001). Tséhootsooídí Ólta'gi Diné bizaad bíhoo'aah: A Navajo immersion program at Fort Defiance, Arizona. In L. Hinton & K. Hale (Eds.), *The green book of language revitalization in practice* (pp. 203–215). San Diego: Academic Press.

Bartlett, C., Marshall, M., & Marshall, A. (2012). Two-Eyed Seeing and other lessons learned within a co-learning journey of bringing together Indigenous and mainstream knowledges and ways of knowing. *Journal of Environmental Studies and Sciences, 2*(4), 331–340.

Benton-Benai, E. (2010). *The Mishomis book: The voice of the Ojibway* (2nd ed.). Minneapolis: University of Minnesota Press.

Canada. (1966[1871–1874]). *Treaty No. 3 between Her Majesty the Queen and the Saulteaux Tribe of Ojibbeway Indians at the northwest angle on the lake woods with adhesions*. Ottawa.

Canada. (1966[1876]). *Treaty No. 6 between Her Majesty the Queen and the Plain and Wood Cree Indians and other tribes of Indians at Fort Carlton, Fort Pitt, and Battle River with Adhesions*. Ottawa.

Cardinal, H. (1999). *The unjust society* (2nd ed.). Vancouver: Douglas & McIntyre.

Chilisa, B. (2012). *Indigenous research methodologies.* Thousand Oaks, CA: Sage.

Coatsworth, E., & Coatsworth, D. (1991). How Nanabush created the world. In E. Benton-Benai (Ed.), *The Mishomis book: The voice of the Ojibway* (pp. 1–7). Toronto: Doubleday Canada Limited.

Curry, J., Donker, H., & Krehbiel, R. (2014). Land claim and treaty negotiations in British Columbia, Canada: Implications for First Nations land and self-governance. *Canadian Geographer, 58*(3), 295–304.

Curtis, E., Reid, P., & Jones, R. (2014). Decolonising the academy: The process of re-presenting Indigenous health in tertiary teaching and learning. *Diversity in Higher Education, 15,* 147–165.

Dawson, S. J. (1873). "Notes taken at Indian Treaty Northwest Angle, Lake of the Woods, from 30th September 1873 to close of treaty." Library and Archives Canada, MG 29, C67, 35.

Dawson, S. J. (1968). *Report on the exploration of the country between Lake Superior and the Red River settlement, and between the Latter Place and the Assiniboine and Saskatchewan.* New York: Greenwood Press.

Doerfler, J., Sinclair, N. J., & Stark, H. K. (2013). Bagijige: Making an offering. In J. Doerfler, N. J. Sinclair, & H. K. Stark (Eds.), *Anishinaabeg studies: Understanding the world through stories* (pp. xv–xxvii). East Lansing and Winnipeg: Michigan State Press and University of Manitoba.

Edwards, K., Lund, C., Mitchell, S., & Andersson, N. (2008). Trust the process: Community-based researcher partnerships. *Pimatisiwin, 6*(2), 187–199.

Everson, H. (1975). *May whin shah ti pah chi mo win: Indian stories of long ago.* Alexandria, MN: Echo Printing Company.

Gay, G. (2010). *Culturally responsive teaching: Theory, research, and practice.* New York: Teachers College Press.

Gravelle, M. (2013, October 7). Developing the Ring of Fire could transform the region. *The Huffington Post.* Retrieved from www.huffingtonpost.ca/hon-michael-gravelle/ring-of-fire-development_b_4057457.html

Hall, A. (2001). Indigenous peoples: Treaties. *The Canadian Encyclopedia.* Retrieved from www.thecanadianencyclopedia.ca/en/article/aboriginal-treaties/

Hare, J., & Pidgeon, M. (2011). The way of the warrior: Indigenous youth navigating the challenges of schooling. *Canadian Journal of Education, 34*(2), 93–111.

Hind, H. Y. (1860). *Narrative of the Canadian Red River exploring expedition of 1857, and of the Assiniboine and Saskatchewan exploring expedition of 1858, Vol. 1* (pp. 99–101). London: Longman, Green, Longman, and Roberts.

Hopper, T. (2016, January 24). Law professor argues in UBC human rights complaint that Indigenous scholars shouldn't have to publish peer-reviewed research. *The National Post.*

Jacob, M. (2012). Native women maintaining their culture in the white academy. In G. Gutierrez y Muhs et al. (Eds.), *Presumed incompetent: The intersections of race and class for women in academia* (pp. 242–249). Boulder, CO: University Press of Colorado.

Johnston, B. (2013). Is that all there is? Tribal literature. In J. Doerfler, N. J. Sinclair, & H. K. Stark (Eds.), *Anishinaabeg studies: Understanding the world through stories* (pp. 3–12). East Lansing and Winnipeg: Michigan State Press and University of Manitoba.

Kanu, Y. (2002). In their own voices: First Nations students identify some cultural mediators of their learning in the formal school system. *Alberta Journal of Educational Research, 48*(2), 98–121.

Kawagley, A. O., & Barnhardt, R. (1998). *Education indigenous to place: Western science meets Native reality.* Fairbanks, AK: Alaska University and Alaska Native Knowledge Network.

King, T. (2003). *The truth about stories: A Native narrative.* Toronto: House of Anansi Press.

Lake of the Woods Writers' Group and Kenora Centennial Committee. (1981). *Through the Kenora gateway.* Kenora, ON: Bilko Press.

Lavallée, L. (2009). Practical application of an Indigenous research framework and two qualitative Indigenous research methods: Sharing circles and Anishnaabe symbol-based reflection. *International Journal of Qualitative Methods, 8*(1), 21–40.

Library and Archives Canada (LAC). (1873). *Simon J. Dawson notes taken at Indian Treaty northwest angle, Lake of the Woods, from 30th September 1873 to close of Treaty.*

Lund, D. R. (1975). *Lake of the Woods yesterday and today.* Staples, MN: Nordell Graphic Communications.

McCarty, T. L., & Lee, T. S. (2014). Critical culturally sustaining/revitalizing pedagogy and Indigenous education sovereignty. *Harvard Educational Review, 84*(1), 101–124.

Merriam-Webster Dictionary. (2016, November 14). Hunting. Retrieved from www.merriam-webster.com/dictionary/hunting

Miller, G. (2013). *The sacred relationship* [film]. Montreal: National Film Board of Canada.

Morris, A. (1880). Shorthand reporter. *The Treaties of Canada with the Indians of Manitoba and the North-West Territories, including the negotiations on which they were based, and other information relating thereto.* Toronto: Belfords, Clarke.

Nikolaeva, S. (2016, October 21). Why the University of Manitoba needs a study on white students' evaluations of minority instructors. *The Gradzette.* Retrieved from www.gradzette.com/2016/10/why-the-university-of-manitoba-needs-a-study-on-white-students-evaluations-of-minority-instructors/1782

Palliser, J. (1968). Exploration of British North America. In I. M. Spry (Ed.), *The papers of the Palliser expedition, 1857–1860* (pp. 76–79). Toronto: Champlain Society.

Paulis, P. (2015). Tenure (un)secure/d: As words go into labour. In E. Whittaker (Ed.), *Solitudes of workplace: Women in universities* (pp. 8–99). Montreal and Kingston: McGill-Queen's University Press.

Savage, C., Hindle, R., Meyer, L., Hynds, A., Penetito, W., & Sleeter, C. (2011). Culturally responsive pedagogies in the classroom: Indigenous student experience across the curriculum. *Asia-Pacific Journal of Teacher Education, 39*(3), 183–198.

Stark, H. K. (2010). Respect, responsibility, and renewal: The foundations of Anishinaabe treaty making with the United States and Canada. *American Indian Culture and Research Journal, 34*(2), 145–164.

Truth and Reconciliation Commission of Canada. (2015). *Language and Culture. Honouring the Truth, Reconciling the Future* (pp. 321–322). Ottawa: Truth and Reconciliation Commission.

Toth, E. (2009). *But will I have to publish? Ms. Mentor's new and ever more impeccable advice for women and men in academia.* Philadelphia: University of Pennsylvania Press.

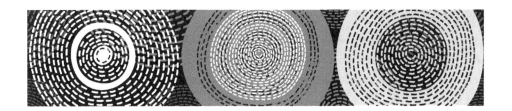

CHAPTER 13

Working to Protect the Water:
Stories of Connection and Transformation

Paige Restoule, Carly Dokis, and Benjamin Kelly

> The water always tells stories. The water is trying to speak to us because the water
> is a spirit ...
>
> *Nathalie Restoule, Dokis First Nation*

When we started our work together, it was about the water, and water has always
been a central part of everything that we have done. Although, as the experiences that we share with you remind us, our work is also about connection:
connections to lands and waters, connections between people (both between
community members and with community members and researchers), connections with family and ancestors, and connections with ourselves. Water has always
known and facilitated those connections; it has always told these stories to those
who were able to hear them. We just had to learn how to listen.[1]

What follows in this chapter are our reflections on the development of a collaborative project between university researchers and Dokis First Nation around
water quality in the community. What we offer here are stories of our own respective journeys in seeking and understanding knowledge about water, but which,
as we came to realize, also involved learning a great deal about each other and
about ourselves. Drawing on the notion that knowledge is relational, and that
our understandings flow, as Heid Erdrich (2013) reminds us, "from where we
are and from who we are" (p. 13), we recognize the importance of multivocality

in coming to terms with our respective research journeys, and have outlined here the ways in which our experiences with this project have unfolded based on our own positionalities and wider webs of relations. As Leanne Betasamosake Simpson (2011) points out, our understandings and our *(o)debwewin* (truth) are deeply personal (p. 11), and the stories that we choose to tell – the ways in which we frame or attribute meaning to a sequence of events – offer a way of ordering experience and constructing reality that is rooted in our own social and moral worlds. Though the approach to our work has been collaborative in its development, each of us came to the project with our own hopes and aspirations, fears, and ways of understanding the world, and each of us has been transformed by the project in subtle and unique ways. What we offer here is not a prescriptive map for conducting research *with* and *for* Indigenous communities, but rather a story of how we have worked toward collaboration and emergence based on the principles of respect and reciprocity, and which is also rooted in the particular relationships that we each have with places, people, ourselves, and Creation.

Our work began as an idea by a group of non-Indigenous engineers at a large university in southern Ontario to put together a project that would foster meaningful participation by Indigenous communities in water and wastewater planning and management. Benjamin Kelly, who had worked with the engineers before and had experience in understanding interactions between society and technology on issues concerning water quality, was invited to join the project, and Ben extended an invitation to Carly Dokis, who had experience working with Indigenous communities on environmental governance and the impacts of extractive industries. The project was multi-sited, and so the general research idea did not originate within any one community. Rather, the engineers invited community partners to join the project and to develop an emergent research design that reflected the specific needs and visions of each respective community. The flexibility of this approach, and of the funding that was secured to support the work,[2] fostered a space for us to collectively animate diverse forms of learning and engagement, and the engineers were very receptive to exploring methods and knowledges that fall outside of what is often called "normal science." At the same time, because the project originated outside of the community, it took time, some fumbling, and a great deal of mutual commitment to find our way. We undertook our work with good intentions, and with the understanding that how we go about seeking knowledge is often as important as the knowledge that we seek (Simpson, 2011; Wilson, 2008).

Our approach to research incorporated features identified by Brian Noble (2015) as key to anti-colonial and decolonial research praxis: consent as *peoples,* collaboration as *persons*, and "taking seriously the over-arching idea and practice of treaty as a guide to acting honorably together as *researchers, persons, and people*" (p. 411). We approached the government of Dokis First Nation in 2012 to see if they would be interested in working on a project around water quality in their community. The chief was extremely enthusiastic, and soon thereafter introduced us to Randy Restoule, the community and economic development officer, who took up the project. Together Randy, Ben, and Carly, along with the engineers, set out to develop a research plan. Randy suggested that we begin with a series of open houses where we could learn about the concerns that people had about their water, and how we might address these with our research. We learned a lot in the course of these open houses: we learned that people held a great deal of knowledge about how their water system works, we learned about the history of the water system in Dokis, and we learned that while the state had designated the community as a high-risk water system, most community members didn't see or think about the water in this way; instead, they insisted that their community has "good water." All of this opened up new ways of understanding the water, and it gave us the opportunity to hear from people about what they would like to see in a community-based project around water. A key component of this was involving the wider community membership, and especially the youth, in activities that sought to enact and maintain loving relationships with the water. These forms of engagement echo similar calls by Deborah McGregor (2013) to reorient how we relate to water to include forms of healing and action that are based on loving responsibilities – *zaagidowin* – so that this and future generations can live well (p. 73).

We knew that the development of a collaborative approach to undertaking this work would take time. Indeed, in the case of our research it has taken years.[3] Our approach was rooted in community-based participatory research, which acknowledges different ways of knowing and gives equal weight to scientific expressions of knowledge and traditional or cultural ontologies, with the goal of nurturing productive working relationships between Indigenous and scientific communities (Fletcher, 2003). Cardinal (2001) identifies another importance of this form of research, which is that it requires an understanding and adoption of the community's conditions with respect to research before beginning work with the community. We understood that building meaningful and trustworthy relationships with the community, as well as ensuring the community's jurisdiction over the research design and goals, would provide the community with outcomes specific to their well-being in both the short and the long term (Weber-Pillwax, 1999). It is in the webs of these relationships – and the conduct required for their maintenance – that learning and transformation would become possible.

We soon hired Paige Restoule as a community-based researcher and set to work to refine our research program. But we struggled to define and lay out our research questions, let alone come up with a way to answer them. We understood the importance of community-driven research, but we were uncertain of how to go about it. And perhaps because our project originated outside of the community, and was technical in nature, it felt as though people were looking to the university-based researchers to provide a clear outline of the research goals. When people would ask, "What is your research about?" we often felt unsure, except to say that it was about the water.

We began with an approach that seemed to make the most sense to us: interviews, and we supplemented these with community workshops every two months or so, during which we would gather people together to share what we were learning and seek direction moving forward. Paige conducted the interviews, and while we learned a lot about the history of the water system at Dokis, we could tell that something was missing. Paige sensed that the interviews were awkward, and while people were very generous in sharing their time, the interviews felt imposed and sterile, and failed to engage the ontological nature of people's relationships with water and with forms of learning and communicating knowledge in general. The engineers, who were very supportive of community-based work and open to diverse ways of understanding water, wanted to be in the community more frequently, but were limited in their ability to do so due to institutional commitments in the south. We fumbled around to produce some technical reports for the community, which seemed to garner only marginal interest, and our intuition told us that all of this was failing to really serve the community. It was then that we turned to story.

Much of the literature on Indigenous knowledge and Indigenous research methodologies suggests that stories are a powerful and essential form of knowledge transmission, and indeed a fundamental way in which the world is understood. As Jill Doerfler, Niigaanwewidam James Sinclair, and Heidi Kiiwetinepinesiik Stark write in their introduction to *Centering Anishinaabeg Studies: Understanding the World through Stories* (2013), "much scholarship produced by Anishinaabeg ... could be argued as different embodiments of the idea that Anishinaabeg Studies resides in and through Anishinaabeg stories – past, present, and future" (p. xvi). We began to create spaces to tell and share stories. According to Leanne Betasamosake Simpson (2011), stories are powerful because they can foster a cognitive space outside of colonality in which to remember and envision and create. Stories are also important because their exchange and telling establishes connection and strengthens relationships. As Simpson (2011) writes, "the physical act of gathering a group of people together within our territories reinforces the web of relationships that stitch our communities together" (p. 34). We wanted to foster the kinds of spaces where stories could be shared not only with us, but also between community members, so we began to hold storycircles in the community on a regular basis. We had heard the grandmothers when they told us that "water is life," and so we wanted the storycircles to reflect this knowledge and to open up ways of talking about community life – old-timer stories, personal stories, funny stories, and stories of family and community. In the end, as one grandmother pointed out, "all of these stories come back to the water." When we held storycircles, people looked forward to coming. We laughed together, and sometimes when the stories were sad ones, we cried. We shared stories of hunting, of walking in the bush, of crashing boats, and of tanning hides. We began to connect to one another through the telling and receiving of stories.

When we reflected on ways of telling and receiving stories, and of working with what has been called Indigenous Knowledge, we were also cognizant of the spaces and manner in which stories were shared. Deborah McGregor (2004) has pointed out that the acquisition of knowledge is often associated with a process of *doing*, and requires establishing relationships not just with one another, but with the lands and waters, and the spirits and beings who dwell there. With this understanding, we wanted as much as possible to situate our storytelling on the land – in the process of *doing*, not just in passively receiving. And so, a key part of our project has involved opening up spaces for *doing* – we have organized hide-scraping workshops, moose hair–tufting workshops, and an annual multi-day canoe trip around Okikwendawt Island, on which the community is situated. Importantly, these spaces for knowledge exchange have been open to all members of the community, and in this way we hope that our approach has not been one of appropriation and extraction, but rather that we have fostered exchange not only between researchers and knowledge holders, but also between community members themselves, between participants and the lands and waters upon which our *doing* has been situated, and, in recording these exchanges in audio and film, between this generation of storytellers and those who will come after.

As the stories gathered here reveal, we eventually found our way to what we think reflects a collaborative approach to a project that we hope has not only transformed each of us in different ways, but has fostered positive opportunities for knowledge sharing and engagement. The titles of the successive grant applications that we put together to fund this project themselves tell an interesting story about the transformation of our project over time, moving from our original grant application, "Sustainable Water and Wastewater Treatment Systems through a

Bottom-Up Participatory Technology-Development Process," to our most recent successful application, "Contested Waters: Exploring the Lived Experience of Water Quality Risks in an Anishinaabe Community in Northern Ontario." Yet, among each other, and with other community members, we have always referred to this project as "Working to Protect the Water," or simply "The Water Project," and we think that this is telling of how we approach our work. Water has flowed through everything we have done, from working on hides to paddling on the river, and our work on this project has brought new perspectives for each of us on the reality that water is life.

A COMMUNITY-BASED RESEARCHER'S JOURNEY TO PROTECTING THE WATER (BY PAIGE RESTOULE)

Aanii, Boozhoo, Epngishwaanmut ndizhnikaaz.
Migisi ndoodem; Okikendawt ndoonjibaa.

~

Hello, my name is West Wind.
I am Eagle Clan; I am from Dokis First Nation.

It is important for me to share who I am and where I come from. My given name, West Wind, Epngishwaanmut, was given to me after I attended my first fasting ceremony. My name describes my spirit as the one who continues to move forward with the help of her past struggles and accomplishments. Okikendawt, also known as Dokis First Nation, is the community where I was raised. My father is Ojibway from Dokis First Nation and Nipissing First Nation, and my mother is Odawa Ojibway from Wiikwemkoong Unceded Territory. I grew up playing with my family and friends, in and around the bush, swimming in the summer months and skating in the winter. Growing up, all of the families would come together and hold gatherings at our community hall, whether it was a fish fry, jamboree, traditional crafts, or carnivals. Our people are always willing to help one another when a tragedy or death occurs. I hold my community very close to me and would go the extra mile to help them be the best that they can be. The "Working to Protect Our Waters" project is one of the many ways I have been able to help my community and to ensure that the people have their voices heard. I would like to take this time to share my journey with the project and working with my community.

It has been an unforgettable journey for me. Initially, Carly Dokis approached me at the grocery store. She shared the purpose of the project and asked if I would be interested in joining the research team. I took some time to digest the request. Historically, research within First Nations communities was not conducted, documented, and shared in positive ways. Relationships were not built with community members, the knowledge was taken and not understood in appropriate contexts, and in most cases, the communities did not receive any document or results of the research in return, or if they did, it was written in a vocabulary that was too difficult to understand and the knowledge they had shared was misinterpreted. I feared that if I were to work with my community as a researcher, I would not have the same respect that I have being a community member, simply because of the stigma associated with research.

Being Anishinaabe Kwe, our role and responsibility is to take care of our water. This always came to mind when I would think of the project. I reflected on this, and came to a personal understanding that this was a calling for me as an Anishinaabe Kwe. I needed to take on the responsibility as a researcher, and help my community appreciate that their voice matters when it comes to the water that surrounds our community and the importance of safe drinking water. Today, many First Nation communities are suffering from the loss of safe drinking water and clean lakes and rivers, and most importantly of having their voices heard in water governance. I want to ensure that my community can document the importance of safe drinking water and their connection to the water. Little did I know I began my research journey the moment I was asked to join the team.

After accepting the position as researcher, we developed my roles and responsibilities; we had team meetings to become familiar with what has been happening within the community and what could be done to address community concerns. I was given a set of questions that was designed by the research team for conducting interviews, along with the appropriate paperwork that was needed when meeting with community members. I started booking interviews with family members to become comfortable asking the questions and hosting interviews. As part of the giving back, we provided the interviewees with a Tim Hortons' gift card. As I predicted, even with family members, most people were hesitant to provide an interview and even felt that they were not the appropriate people to be asked the questions. One person mentioned that she had done interviews in the past and was tired of giving information. After a series of interviews were completed, I began to notice a pattern. Most people were not truly expressing themselves; furthermore, they were sharing what they assumed I wanted to hear. One question in particular focused on sharing stories while being on the water, and most people skipped this question because they weren't sure what it was that *I* was looking for. I also began to notice that the interview participants were suggesting that we host talking circles for community members to attend in order to share their stories and personal opinions with respect to water safety. I shared this information with Carly and the research team and they felt it was a great idea.

We hosted a follow-up meeting with community members to share what the research team had been undertaking. We invited local Elders to begin the meeting with a smudge and opening prayer, and discussed the meaning of the project and how we were working toward gathering our knowledge and history of our community. We ended the session by opening up the floor to discussion. We gave the community members an opportunity to share their stories of water. From this moment forward, our research method began to unfold. Initially interviews were thought of as the best means of documenting knowledge from the community; however, in providing a safe and appropriate space where people could share, reflect, and tell personal stories, the connections between people and water became much more apparent and more meaningful, and people were making connections between each other too. Many stories arose from that one talking circle and we realized water is connected in every way possible. Individuals discussed travelling on water; harvesting food; family and community gatherings; life and death; traditional tales; economic development; how they collected drinking water; and how water has shaped their lives.

Talking circles were the answer. The research team began reorganizing and opening up doors for community members to participate and share their stories. All talking circles were scheduled on weekends and as much as possible were scheduled to not conflict with other community events. Each time, a topic was provided for the community members, although our talking circles often went in directions we never could have anticipated. After the first talking circle was held, we focused our topics on the community members' interests – for example, hunting, fishing, historical residences, traditional tales, trading, and hosting workshops. We always ensured that we gave back to the community members as much as possible, by providing them with the opportunity to discuss their topics of interest and share the stories that are meaningful to them. As the change of research was happening so organically, I began to realize that we were moving more toward an Indigenous research framework.

Indigenous research is not necessarily a new concept for me, but it is becoming more recognized within academic research. It is important to develop relationships with the community with whom you are working and to ensure you meet their expectations. After a few years of working with the community we began to develop trust by keeping the community informed of the project as well as honouring their requests regarding how the project should move forward. The community felt that an important aspect of the project was the participation of youth, to ensure their voices were heard and that they were equally included. Finally, the knowledge shared by the community members was not just about taking, it was also about what could we give back. We wanted our work to be something meaningful so that knowledge that we hold can be preserved for future generations.

Previous interviews and talking circles were recorded, but we wanted something a little more. We began documenting and filming events, workshops, and personal stories in order to create digital stories that could be shared with the wider community membership through a multi-media platform, and preserved for future generations. We shared this idea with the community and they responded with pleasing feedback. People were excited about sharing their stories, bringing in old photos and artefacts and providing feedback in order to create stories that were meaningful to them. Our first digital story that was recorded and shared was of our annual canoe trip, which takes place within the community and is geared toward the youth. Footage of the trip was documented, as well as personal interviews with the people who participated. Once we completed the video, we shared it with the community and they were very pleased. Ultimately, the digital stories cover anything and everything that reflects our connection to water. Once they are all completed they will be given back to the community and preserved; they will hold the stories that reflect the history of the people of Dokis First Nation and their connection to water. Future generations will be given an opportunity to view these documented stories visually, and hear from their family and friends about how they were connected to water and why it is important to protect our water.

As a community member and researcher working with my community, I learned a lot about our history and my family history. I learned how roads, waterways, and landmarks were given their names and the meanings behind them, as well as more about old residences that my family once maintained and where and how they travelled. One story that I will always hold close to me is how my granny and late grandpa would travel to the closest town. My granny shared how they travelled across the river in the winter by horses. One particular time, they didn't realize the ice was thin. As they proceeded over this patch of ice, they fell in. Immediately after they got out from the ice water they went to land and made a fire. They dried their clothing and stayed there for the night. The next day they continued on to town. Knowing what my grandparents endured gives me more appreciation for what we take for granted today. Nowadays, we have vehicles and roads to access shopping malls and grocery stores, whereas less than a century ago our grandparents were travelling long distances by foot or on horses.

Before tourists and boats became more common in the community, my grandparents, like most community members, used Dokis Bay on the French River for their drinking water. When they travelled by canoe to hunt or fish, as they often did, they would never need to bring water with them; all they needed was a cup. It was as simple as scooping water from the side of the canoe to quench their thirst. In today's society, with the amount of pollution in our waters, we can no longer dip our cup into the waterways to drink. Because of this change, my grandparents are no longer able to access their water from Dokis Bay; they were forced to dig a well, which was then hooked up to their home. This was also a lot of work, as my grandpa would have to ensure that the well was taken care of and always clean. Hearing these stories and the appreciation my grandparents have for the water helps me recognize the importance of taking care of our water, keeping it safe and as clean as possible.

The project has shaped me in many ways; most importantly it has facilitated my journey to protect the water. Taking a step back and letting the community guide the project has unfolded a deep connection to the water that surrounds the community of Dokis First Nation. It is important to identify the significance water has for the community and its members as the many community events, workshops, and gatherings that have taken place within the community some-how require the use of water. Helping my community preserve their stories and connection to water is important not only for me, but for the community, and for future generations. Having our youth involved in our work will ensure that the knowledge we share is passed down; it will help them understand the importance of our water, and share their stories, and ultimately, they too will strive toward keeping our water safe for future generations. Overall, the project has assisted in taking the beginning steps in the right direction toward protecting our water.

INTRODUCTIONS (BY CARLY DOKIS)

Originally from Blackfoot territory, and the territories of the peoples of Treaty 7, I moved to Anishinaabeg territory and the lands protected by the Robinson-Huron Treaty in 2008, though I had visited here for many years before that. My husband and my children are members of Dokis First Nation, and we have a camp there where we go to escape the busyness of the small city where we live. I came to this project through an invitation extended by Benjamin Kelly, who is a colleague in my department. Trained as an anthropologist, I am deeply aware of the varied ways in which our discipline has been implicated in colonial projects: its role and influence in generating Eurocentric assumptions about the nature of human societies; its proclivity for appropriating voice, for objectifying, silencing, and then speaking for an "Other"; and the ways in which anthropologists, and other non-Indigenous academics, have built their careers by making Others an object of study. Yet, I am also aware of a significant number of anthropologists, both in the past and in the present, who through their work with Indigenous communities and as political allies have made clear the injustices of the colonial order. As anthropologist Michael Asch reminded us in response to Talal Asad's challenge in *Anthropology and the Colonial Encounter* (1973), "supporting Indigenous peoples with our technical skills and exposing the harms caused them by capitalism and the settler state are ways of acting ... that are not at peace with colonialism" (Asch, 2015, p. 481).[4] As someone who is interested in the political ecology of environmental governance, and especially the ways in which institutional logics and framings of environmental management utilized by the state and extractive industries are used as instruments of power and coercion, I thought that I might have something to offer in understanding the political dimensions of water quality governance in Indigenous communities. I thought that learning more about the ways in which local people experience and know water might highlight how state management and surveillance of water quality is related to systems of coloniality and violence. It was in this spirit that I began our work. I was hoping to learn from people who I knew hold a deep understanding of, and love and respect for, the water; to learn about the ways in which colonial systems continue to interfere in these relationships; and to learn of other possibilities for our relationships with water that are not complicit in the capital-centric, object-oriented, neoliberal forms of current state water-management.

I had previous experience working in Indigenous communities; however, I recognized that each community and setting for research was unique and required attentiveness to the particular relationships, circumstances, visions, and protocols that that community presented. In my previous work, the goals and methods of my research had been well defined, but a key part of working together as *peoples* and as *persons* is the co-creation of research questions and processes. The circumstances of this project required a new approach and one that for us emerged gradually over time. Initially, we struggled to establish a research program that reflected people's relationships with water in a substantive way. We tried interviews, developing technical scenarios for water and wastewater management and planning, and even a short story that summarized technical reports about the drinking water system. In all of these cases, our research questions and direction felt imposed. In theory, we knew that our research should be co-constructed, but we wondered: how do we put this into practice? Given my prior relationships with people in the community, I got the sense that we were not really contributing anything meaningful to understanding water quality issues. For me, it was an uncomfortable place to sit.

All of this came to a head for me one night about a year into the project when Randy sent me an email to suggest that we suspend the project. He had just come from a workshop on traditional land use mapping and he too was questioning the orientation of our project. "We need to put the interviews on hold," he said, "until we can create a proper methodology. Hopefully we can start fresh with a solid plan." I called Randy the next morning feeling very anxious – I had let him down, I thought, and put the project in jeopardy. Randy was very gracious in his reception of me, and explained that after the traditional land use planning workshop, he was worried about our research not being able to withstand legal scrutiny should it be used in land claim cases.[5] We decided to speak with a local lawyer from a nearby community who could help us understand any legal ramifications of our work, and to clarify our research goals and approach. We made it clear that we were not doing a traditional land use study, which had the potential to misconstrue how community members approach their relationships to land and water, and we reoriented our work toward the embodied and sentient experiences that people have with the water. It was then that we turned to story, and to opening up spaces where knowledge could be shared, not as a means of appropriation, but for its own sake and for the purposes of bringing us all together.

This form of knowledge acquisition, and the ontological commitment that it demands of us, is not entirely unfamiliar in anthropological inquiry. Tim Ingold (2014) has pointed out that the practice of participant observation ought to be implicated in transformative learning. Citing Kenelm Burridge's concept of "metanoia," or "an ongoing series of transformation each one of which alters the predicates of being" (as cited in Ingold, 2014, p. 388), Ingold highlights this process of learning, not in the conventional sense of "education" but of "attending to a world in which things are not ready made but always incipient, on the cusp of continual emergence" (Ingold, 2014, p. 389). In this sense, the proper goal of anthropological inquiry is not elucidating the life world of an Other, but rather, as Jackson explains, "opening up new possibilities for thinking about experience" (as cited in Ingold, 2014, p. 388).

A key component of this approach to knowledge sharing is its relationality – it is situated and made possible in fellowship not only between persons in the context of storytelling, but also between persons and the world around them. As Deborah McGregor (2004) has pointed out, for Anishinaabeg people, Indigenous knowledge comes from and includes relationships with Creation, and is associated with corresponding responsibilities for maintaining relationships with the other beings that share the lands and waters. For McGregor, "Indigenous Knowledge is not just 'knowledge' per se. It is the lives lived by people and their particular relationship with Creation" (McGregor, 2004, p. 390). We became attentive to the experiential and contextual components of learning and knowledge exchange, and wanted to create spaces where people could engage with one another and also with the lands and waters in and around the community. One way in which we participated in those connections was by organizing an annual canoe trip.

The community of Dokis First Nation sits on Okikendawt Island, named for the bucket formations in the rocks that are made by fast-flowing water over long periods of time. The eastern side of the island, nearest the community subdivision and marinas that serve as a launching site for boats travelling on the Upper French River, is travelled quite frequently, but the western side of the island is far less accessible by boat and has no road access. Our intention was to gather together youth from the community and other people who wanted to travel by canoe around that part of the reserve. For many of the youth participants, the canoe trip was the first time that they had been to that part of their territory; for some of the adults, they had not been to these lands and waters for many years. We have now completed our fifth annual trip. Each year the trip is modified based on the feedback that we receive from participants. For example, on the first trip the group canoed 28 kilometres in just two days! On subsequent trips, we extended the trip to four days, often adding a whole day for swimming, fishing, and storytelling at a much-loved camping site at Five Finger Rapids. Each year we have more youth who are interested in coming. Often, we arrange to have Elders join our trip by travelling alongside the canoes in boats.

I will never forget the first time that I participated in the canoe trip. For weeks I had been nervous about the trip: What if something went wrong? Did we have enough food? Would I be able, physically, to accomplish the journey? A short blueberry season and very few acorns had brought an unusually high number of bears into the community looking for food. I was constantly worried about the bears on our trip – after all, if there were bears *in* the community, surely there would be even more bears in the bush. What if one came through our camp? I had packed my bear bangers, but maybe I should ask someone to bring a gun? I felt responsible for the well-being of the group, especially since many of them were youth. Yet, I also knew that I did not have the knowledge or experience to be of much help out on the land.

The night before the canoe trip, I had a dream. In my dream our group of canoes was paddling down the only part of the river that I had been to prior to

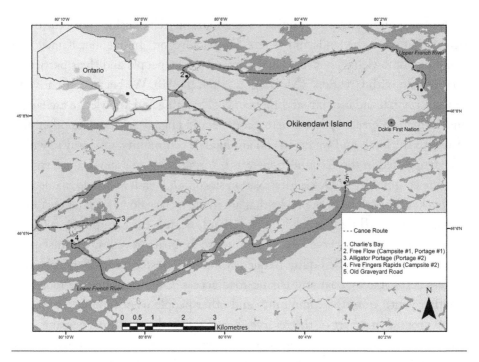

Figure 13.1: Map of the Canoe Route around Okikendawt Island

our journey – a place between Charlie's Bay and the Free Flow Rapids. The water was calm and black, and the air was heavy and wet. I could see clearly the four canoes in front of me, with two youth in each. As we paddled through the quiet, I could see something slowly emerging from the water ahead of me. I knew it was big – it was weaving its way between the canoes. As it rolled through the water, I could see its back lined with dark triangular spikes. It was a serpent. But instead of the fear that I would expect to experience in such a situation, in my dream I felt strangely serene watching the serpent's arched back slowly rising and falling as it glided along with us in the water.

I had heard people talking about horned serpents that live in the waters, though I didn't know much about them. I was scared, but in my dream it was peaceful. Still, I was worried about what the dream meant for our upcoming trip. Was it a warning? Was it a reassurance? I couldn't tell.[6] We had invited a grandmother to come and share her knowledge with us before we headed out on the water. That morning she spoke about how people were increasingly polluting the waters, dumping sewage and pollution into the waterways and garbage into Lake Nipissing. Just that week, she told us, a picture had emerged of a pickerel in Lake Nipissing with a plastic lid from a drinking cup lodged around its waist. To my surprise, she then spoke about the serpents. "You know," she told us, "there are serpents who live in the water. They travel all around everywhere and they clean the water. Some people think that they are scary, but their job is to clean the water. That's what they are doing, they are cleaning the water."

I've thought a lot about this dream and what it says about the canoe trip and the water project. I awoke from the dream with the realization that the reason people who travelled these lands and waters in the past were able to do so in companionship with other beings was that they knew each other – not in the sense that they knew of their presence, but that they knew each other intimately and by name. For me, part of my participation in the project necessarily involved making those introductions – introductions to people and communities with whom I work, but also to the bears, the waters, and the spirits and other beings who dwell there. The people who have lived all of their lives on these lands and waters know this, just as they know the beings who dwell there. Once, when a friend of mine had been away from his camp for a number of days, he said to me, "I miss the trees. I can't wait to say hello to them again." I interpret the presence of the serpent in my dream as a form of introduction, and a sign that maybe we are on a good path toward working to protect the water. Though we are still trying to refine how we approach our work, and are still continually transformed by it, I think that my dream was telling me that so long as we are open and attentive to these connections and transformations – in our research methods, and in our understandings of the nature of knowledge and of the water, and of ourselves – we can open up new possibilities for learning.

SYMBOLIC POWER, MISRECOGNITION, AND THE MYTH OF THE "UNOBTRUSIVE OBSERVER" (BY BENJAMIN KELLY)

I am from the ancestral and unceded territory of the Mi'kmaq people, and from the lands covered by the Treaties of Peace and Friendship made between the Mi'kmaq, Wolastoqiyik (Maliseet), and the British Crown. I began my academic career with an ethnographic study of a group of environmental engineers and scientists who struggle to democratize research practices so as to integrate non-experts and encourage lay involvement in all phases of technological development and environmental policy construction (Kelly, 2017). I have learned a great deal over the years from my involvement with participants, both in terms of understanding the structural obstacles that hinder negotiations with industry, government, and the public, and with the overall evolution of my sociological craft. More specifically, working with these engineers forced me to reflect on my epistemological assumptions surrounding the methodology of participant observation. My discoveries in the field revolve around three key findings: (1) given the democratic mandate that participants committed themselves to, and the environmental advocacy they expressed, I was unable to completely distance myself from their political goals, and as a result my involvement in their activities compromised my "objectivity"; (2) as I eventually became more comfortable with experiencing participants' environmental activism, a mutual influence emerged in which not only did they influence my worldview, but my sociological and social psychological toolkit assisted in the development of their democratized scientific models; and finally (3) all of this lack of objectivity and sharing of life worlds may not necessarily constitute weak ethnographic inquiry (Kelly, 2010, p. 49). Given this type of reflexive mandate, scholars can navigate the dialectic tension between full membership involvement and more traditional forms of detachment inherent in field research (Adler & Adler, 1987). I have since recognized that a naive commitment to "objectivity," pure naturalism, and ignoring one's influence in the field simply promotes what Gary Allan Fine (1993) calls the myth of the "unobtrusive observer." Fine states that "the degree to which one is an 'active member' affects the extent to which this sympathetic understanding is possible, and this is a function of one's social location.... [A]s a consequence, the presence of an observer should not be too worrisome" (p. 282). Participant observation demands that we immerse ourselves in situations in order to understand how others form their perspectives. Researchers are then affected by the way their participants negotiate their perspectives and define their situations (Becker, 1967, p. 245). Furthermore, my recent collaboration with Dokis First Nation has made me sensitive to the role of power within this hermeneutic process.

Although my experience with science-activists awakened me to the unrealistic commitment to a completely value-neutral stance toward research, I would be remiss if I did not acknowledge that the engineers and scientists I studied, including myself, are implicated in systems of coloniality that privilege settler positions relative to Indigenous peoples. Such professional individuals and organizations enjoy what Pierre Bourdieu calls "symbolic power." Bourdieu (1991, p. 169) argues that symbolic power provides its carriers with discourses of influence and competitive advantages that are unequally distributed throughout society. Moreover, social struggles over scarce resources create discourses that can legitimize symbolic categories that tend to classify the world in ways that can be misrecognized as "natural" and "objective," hiding the fact that these discourses favour the interests of one segment of society over another. Groups who have secured greater symbolic capital have the power of "world-making.... [T]he power to make groups … [t]he power to impose and to inculcate a vision of divisions … the power to make visible and explicit social divisions that are implicit, is political power par excellence" (Bourdieu, 1989, p. 23). Despite being aware of the myth of the "unobtrusive observer" (Fine, 1993), I originally approached the Dokis community from a number of epistemological and ontological assumptions rooted in my "world–making" social location. Furthermore, my view of nature was incommensurable with First Nation perspectives. The Western view of water and land as inanimate contains a *symbolic power* that I misrecognized. This bias had the potential to misconstrue my understanding of First Nation concerns around water governance and my overall participation. I have since learned that the researcher should attempt to uncover "unthought categories of thought which delimit the thinkable and predetermine the thought" – especially within themselves (Bourdieu & Wacquant, 1992, p. 40). This reflexive orientation may be even more important when attempting to understand the experience of Indigenous communities.

It was not until I started to listen to the water from an Anishinaabe perspective, and entertained another way of looking at the world, that I became even more reflexive of my settler predispositions toward nature. At no time was this progress in recognition more evident than when my seven-year-old son recently asked me if water was alive. Before working with the people of Dokis and my fellow collaborators on this paper, I would have immediately responded to my son with "Of course not!" Yet, I now see that this would have been misrecognizing my symbolic power and ultimately committing a form of symbolic violence. Bourdieu makes this clear: "Every power to exert symbolic violence, i.e. every power which manages to impose meanings and to impose them as legitimate by concealing the power relations which are the basis of its force, adds its own specifically symbolic force to those power relations" (Bourdieu & Passeron, 1977, p. 4). The answer to my son's question is firmly situated in two competing symbolic logics. On the one hand, we have a discourse corresponding to a symbolic power that has enjoyed the privilege of scientific authority. On the other, a traditional ecological logic possessing its own validity, but misrecognized and overshadowed in symbolic violence. Integrating the two to the best of my ability, I explained that water was indeed alive and that we are not only dependent on it, but the animating force that bonds the hydrogen and oxygen molecules together also binds our hearts to each other and to Mother Nature.

As one member of the Dokis community stated, "water is life, and life is water." Although the response I provided my son may not be a direct reflection of the people in Dokis First Nation that I have the honour to call friends, I nevertheless believe my evolved position is now a personal synthesis of both my scientific background and the influence Dokis members have had on my journey back to the heart of nature. And so I am slowly learning to sit comfortably within the dynamic tension that exists between two allegedly incommensurable discourses, ever cognizant of my symbolic power and careful to not let my dual membership slip back into misrecognition. It is my hope to continue to draw on multiple epistemological and ontological resources to guide not only my research methodology, but also my life.

GATHERING STORIES, GATHERING PEOPLE

As the stories collected here show, we have each been transformed by the water project in different ways – we have drawn on different sources of motivation, experienced different fears, and made meaning through our respective engagement with the project on our own terms. Yet, a key central theme that runs throughout the stories of our research journey has been a commitment to seeking knowledge in ways that are not fixed in methodology or approach, but that are reflective of the specific ontologies, lives, and visions of the community. Our approach has been to learn, as Ingold suggests, "from the crucible of lives lived with others" (2014, p. 387). And this process involves being in relation with others – in co-imagining how possibilities for learning might work, and in trusting one another to allow learning to emerge.

Water has also been a central part of all that we have done: the stories that we have gathered have often been situated on the waters in and around the community; water was essential for scraping the hides; and of course some of our most transformational learning has come through being together while travelling on the waters. But it wasn't until we let go of our focus on the materiality of water – of water as an object – and to seriously consider water as inseparable and situated in life, in the fabric of living, that we were able to see the visceral connections between people and water, between past and future, and between one another.

In one of our early interviews, Nathalie Restoule, a young Anishinaabe Kwe from Dokis First Nation, described her relationship with water:

> I was born right by the water, so I was always swimming, fishing.... It was really a gathering place when I was little, you know? Everyone would meet each other by the dock and you know, the water really gave us something to do and something to stay active. And it was really that, it gave us almost that sense of family, and that's how powerful that water is. If you go back to the cultural

teachings it talks about that healing, and it's a really powerful medicine to have. You could see what it was doing to our youth within our community and it was bringing us together actually. If you think about the ripple effect, you know? If you think about it as jumping in the water, that ripple effect was pushing us together and that's that power within that water.

Reflecting on our research journeys, it seems that the water has been working that way for us too. Though our research has seemed scattered at times, water has "pushed us together"; it has brought us together as a research team, it has brought together diverse community members who have shared with us and with one another in sharing circles, it has brought together Elders and youth, it has brought us together with the lands and waters, and through carefully creating and preserving the digital stories (and keeping those stories in the community), it has brought together this generation of storytellers and those who will come after us. We hope that it has created that ripple effect that Nathalie describes in her narrative so that the research that we have been working on does not seek to answer any specific "research question" but rather creates multifarious spaces for sharing and learning that will extend well beyond the life of the water project.

NOTES

1. The authors would like to say *Chi-Megweetch* (thank you very much) to the leadership and community members at Dokis First Nation for their support of the project and for taking the time to share their stories with us. We would especially like to acknowledge Randy Restoule, who was unable to contribute to this chapter due to other commitments, but who nonetheless has been instrumental in moving this project forward and in helping it take form.

2. This project has been aided by funding provided by a Canadian Water Network Canadian Municipal Water Network Grant, and an Insight Development Grant provided by the Social Sciences and Humanities Research Council of Canada.

3. In a study designed to explore university-based researchers' experiences with community-based participatory research, Castleden, Morgan, & Lamb (2012) describe how, when a university-based researcher was asked by her dean why she hadn't published anything two years into her project, her response was, "I spent the first year drinking tea" (p. 168), indicating the importance of developing relationships over long periods of time before research can begin.

4. Asch (2015) points to anthropologists such as Dara Culhane, Elizabeth Furniss, Stephanie Irlbacher-Fox, Dawn Martin-Hill, and Brian Noble (and I would add Harvey Feit and Paul Nadasdy, among

others), whose work has made visible the forms of violence, both historical and in contemporary times, imposed through colonial and neocolonial structures.

5.   Our work on this project began prior to *Tsilhqot'in v. British Columbia*, handed down by the Supreme Court of Canada in June 2014. This ruling, in addition to recognizing Aboriginal title to 1,900 square kilometres of Tsilhqot'in Nation lands, found that Aboriginal title could not be restricted to small, intensively used sites – or dots on a traditional land use map – but ought to extend more broadly to include all territory that the Indigenous group regularly used. Toward the beginning stages of our project we discussed undertaking a traditional land use study; however we later abandoned that idea because it did not represent the ways in which people saw their relationships to the land and water.

6.   Melissa Nelson (2013) describes how *Mishipizhu*, an underwater panther serpent, or sometimes known as a horned snake, is a mediator between land, water, and sky beings and is a protector of the water. Nelson recounts how *Mishipizhu* can be both malevolent and compassionate, and can appear to punish those who upset eco-social relations, or to provide blessings.

REFERENCES

Adler, P., & Adler, P. (1987). *Membership roles in field research.* Newbury Park, CA: Sage.

Asad, T. (1973). *Anthropology and the colonial encounter.* London: Ithica Press.

Asch, M. (2015). Anthropology, colonialism and the reflexive turn: Finding a place to stand. *Anthropologica, 57*(2), 481–489.

Becker, H. (1967). Whose side are we on? *Social Problems, 14*(3), 239–247.

Bourdieu, P. (1989). Social space and symbolic power. *Sociological Theory, 7*(1), 14–25.

Bourdieu, P. (1991). *Language and symbolic power.* J. B. Thompson (Ed.). (G. Raymond & M. Adamson, Trans.). Cambridge, MA: Harvard University Press.

Bourdieu, P., & Passeron, J. C. (1977). *Reproduction in education, society and culture.* Newbury Park, CA: Sage.

Bourdieu, P., & Wacquant, L. (1992). *An invitation to reflexive sociology.* Chicago: University of Chicago Press.

Cardinal, L. (2001). What is an Indigenous perspective? *Canadian Journal of Native Education, 25*(2), 180–183.

Castleden, H., Morgan, V. S., & Lamb, C. (2012). "I spent the first year drinking tea": Exploring Canadian university researchers' perspectives on community-based participatory research involving Indigenous peoples. *The Canadian Geographer, 56*(2), 160–179.

Doerfler, J., Sinclair, N. J., & Stark, H. K. (2013). Bagijige: Making an offering. In J. Doerfler, N. J. Sinclair, & H. K. Stark (Eds.), *Centering Anishinaabeg studies: Understanding the world through stories* (pp. xv–xxvii). Winnipeg: University of Manitoba Press.

Erdrich, H. (2013). Name': Literary ancestry as presence. In J. Doerfler, N. J. Sinclair, & H. K. Stark (Eds.), *Centering Anishinaabeg studies: Understanding the world through stories* (pp. 13–34). Winnipeg: University of Manitoba Press.

Fine, G. A. (1993). Ten lies of ethnography: Moral dilemmas in field research. *Journal of Contemporary Ethnography, 22*(3), 267–294.

Fletcher, C. (2003). Community-based participatory research relationships with Aboriginal communities in Canada: An overview of context and process. *Pimatziwin: A Journal of Aboriginal and Indigenous Community Health, 1*(1), 27–62.

Ingold, T. (2014). That's enough about ethnography! *HAU: Journal of Ethnographic Theory, 4*(1), 383–395.

Kelly, B. (2010). Exploring the dilemma of mutual influence in ethnographic research. In G. Szarycz (Ed.), *Research realities in the social sciences: Negotiating fieldwork dilemmas* (pp. 45–66). New York: Cambria Press.

Kelly, B. (2017). The social psychology of compromised negotiations: The emergence of asymmetrical boundary objects between science and industry. In B. Brewster & A. Puddephatt (Eds.), *Microsociological perspectives in environmental sociology* (pp. 192–205). New York: Routledge.

McGregor, D. (2004). Coming full circle: Indigenous knowledge, environment, and our future. *The American Indian Quarterly, 28*(3–4), 385–410.

McGregor, D. (2013). Indigenous women, water justice and Zaagidowin (Love). *Canadian Woman Studies/Les Cahiers de la Femme, 30*(2–3), 71–78.

Nelson, M. K. (2013). The hydromythology of the Anishinaabeg: Will Mishipizhu survive climate change, or is he creating it? In J. Doerfler, N. J. Sinclair, & H. K. Stark (Eds.), *Centering Anishinaabeg studies: Understanding the world through stories* (pp. 213–233). Winnipeg: University of Manitoba Press.

Noble, B. (2015). Consent, collaboration, treaty: Toward anti-colonial praxis in Indigenous-settler research relations. *Anthropologica, 57*(2), 411–417.

Simpson, L. (2011). *Dancing on our Turtle's back: Stories of Nishnaabeg re-creation, resurgence and a new emergence*. Winnipeg: ARP Books.

Weber-Pillwax, C. (1999). Indigenous research methodology: Exploratory discussion of an elusive subject. *Journal of Educational Thought, 33*(1), 31–45.

Weber-Pillwax, C. (2001). What is Indigenous research? *Canadian Journal of Native Education, 25*(2), 166–174.

Wilson, S. (2008). *Research is ceremony: Indigenous research methods*. Halifax: Fernwood Publishing.

PART V

DESTINATIONS:
WHERE RESEARCH CAN TAKE US

The tools we use to seek knowledge reflect a view of knowledge as more than just an intellectual construct. As Marlene Brant Castellano (2000) notes, "sometimes knowledge is received as a gift at a moment of need" (p. 25). Knowledge is holistic and the researcher must attend to its spiritual, emotional, and physical aspects in order to conduct research with integrity. Knowledge exists in a context, it must be experienced, and it is hard work to connect with it. Unfortunately, Indigenous knowledges have been "under assault for many years ... Aboriginal peoples have been bombarded with the message that what they know from their culture is of no value" (Castellano, 2000, p. 25). It becomes important for research to support the revitalization of Indigenous knowledges.

Furthermore, as Kovach (2009) says, knowledge must be usable: "Maybe someday we will have that luxury [of seeking knowledge for knowledge's sake], but not right now" (p. 93). The point of Indigenous research is to benefit Indigenous communities in all their complexity.[1] For communities, and the researcher too, research may promote healing, from colonialism especially. Colonialism has endeavoured to erase history, culture, and peoples. So interrupting colonialism through research is accomplished by making Indigenous peoples, especially the most marginalized and stigmatized people in Indigenous communities, visible, and empowered (Lambert, 2014), by making the voices of research participants heard. Finally, Indigenous research is a contemporary manifestation of an unbroken and ancient tradition of knowledge sharing among members of Indigenous communities.

The chapters in this section by Deborah McGregor, Nicole Penak, and Sarah Hunt grapple with the purpose of research, as does Karlee Fellner's contribution (Chapter 1).

LEARNING AND REFLECTION QUESTIONS

1. What is the overarching goal of doing Indigenous research?
2. What work counts as research in an academic context? What work counts as research in Indigenous communities?
3. How does your nation define truth? How does your nation's definition differ from or agree with how your academic discipline defines truth?
4. How do the researchers in this collection decide on research priorities?
5. How do people learn in a traditional context?
6. What is the role of intuition, revelation, and vision in Indigenous research?
7. Why is it important to acknowledge the source of knowledge in an Indigenous context?
8. Provide some examples of reciprocity in research.
9. What role does community service play in Indigenous research relationships?
10. Hunt talks about how the experiences of Indigenous women who trade or sell sex have been erased. Are there other experiences that are erased in our society? How can research counter these erasures?
11. Research can harm, but can also heal. What steps need to be taken to ensure research does not reproduce the colonial project of trauma?
12. How can research contribute to healing?
13. In your research, how is knowledge shared? What about Indigenous knowledges?
14. How do/could you live the knowledge you have learned?

NOTE

1. Delineating one's "community" is complicated and sometimes problematic, and may be done differently by Indigenous than by non-Indigenous peoples.

REFERENCES

Castellano, M. B. (2000). Updating Aboriginal traditions of knowledge. In G. J. S. Dei, D. Goldin Rosenberg, & B. L. Hall (Eds.), *Indigenous knowledges in global contexts: Multiple readings of our worlds* (pp. 21–36). Toronto, ON: University of Toronto Press.

Kovach, M. (2009). *Indigenous methodologies: Characteristics, conversations, and contexts.* Toronto, ON: University of Toronto Press.

Lambert, L. (2014). *Research for Indigenous survival: Indigenous research methodologies in the behavioral sciences.* Pablo, MT: Salish Kootenai College Press.

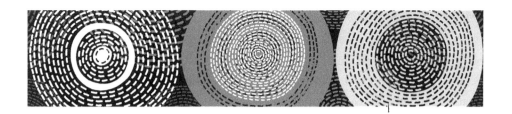

CHAPTER 14

Toward an Anishinaabe Research Paradigm:
Theory and Practice

Deborah McGregor

INTRODUCTION

As this volume attests to, in recent years there has been a remarkable emergence of Indigenous research scholarship both internationally and within Canada. Indigenous theory, paradigms, and methods inform research practices that take on many forms, reflecting the diversity of Indigenous nations. Many scholars, Indigenous and non-Indigenous alike, have sought to decolonize past and current research approaches and advance Indigenous approaches and methods of research (Louis, 2007). Some more recent efforts have focused specifically on the revitalization of Indigenous research traditions (Archibald, 2008; Kovach, 2009; Wilson, 2008). Anishinaabe research is a form of reclaiming our stories and knowledge through personal transformation while in the pursuit of knowledge. As Anishinaabe people, we have our own worldviews, philosophies, ways of being, and research traditions that account for our relationships and existence in the world. This volume represents the diversity of ways in which Anishinaabek are tackling the challenging, yet transformative, work involved in re-creating our knowledge on our own terms.

A more detailed description of the literature on Indigenous research is contained in the introduction to this volume. In this paper I offer a more specific look at Anishinaabe theoretical frameworks and practices as they are being utilized in a research project entitled "Traditional Knowledge, Aboriginal Peoples and Water Governance in Ontario," of which I am the principal investigator. Fundamentally, the approach taken in this research reflects Anishinaabe relationships to the environment (Kovach, 2009; Wilson, 2008). A "knowledge sharing" paradigm is utilized, in which researchers seek to share and learn knowledge, rather than merely extract it. The research reflects the holistic worldview of the Anishinaabe in which the economic, social, cultural, spiritual, ecological, legal, and political aspects of life are viewed, experienced, and explained as part of a whole.

For example, "storywork" (research as storytelling), a traditional form of engaging in dialogue and learning relationships with Elders as described by Archibald (2008), is currently being utilized in this research. "Theories," as they are seen through the eyes of science, do exist in Anishinaabe knowledge systems, and are contained in stories, teachings, values, beliefs, ceremonies, songs, dances, and other practices (McGregor, 2013). Research can thus be thought of as a story, and our experiences form a part of that story about our relationships with each other, with other beings, and with the earth/Creation. We are seeking knowledge that is already there, so we may tell or retell a story that often already exists, although, as Wendy Makoons Geniusz (2009), in her work *Our Knowledge Is Not Primitive: Decolonizing Botanical Anishinaabe Teachings*, points out, the source must still be acknowledged. From this standpoint, we are all part of that grand story that unfolds over time and facilitates our growth and transformation. Anishinaabe research traditions also focus on the ethical conduct required to ensure appropriate relationships with all of Creation. Proper relationships are required among all beings to ensure sustainability, not just for people, but for all of Creation. The Anishinaabe researcher's preoccupation is to learn to engage appropriately in a series of relationships with other beings in Creation to serve our nations now and into the future.

I will draw upon my own professional and personal experience as an academic and community-based researcher, where I have had to continually mediate between two (or more) different intellectual traditions over the past three decades. Many of the other contributors to this volume describe how they have managed similar challenges. As an Anishinaabe scholar, it has been an important goal of my professional life to engage in research relationships and initiatives that assist our communities in achieving *Minobimaatisiiwin* (LaDuke, 1999), that "good life," or the goals they define as requiring attention. Anishinaabe research is not just concerned with the revitalization and utilization of research traditions, but also with why we engage in these practices in the first place.

In this chapter, I will touch on four key areas that frame an Anishinaabe research process: the role of familial and community knowledge in research; the role of service in research; bridging personal, academic, and community-based practice while engaged in the research process itself; and knowledge mobilization. Prior to beginning, however, I will expand upon the idea of research as storytelling.

SITUATING ONESELF AS THE RESEARCHER/STORYTELLER

I regard research as a form of storytelling. As a researcher, sharing findings or research results often takes the form of story, whether in an oral or written presentation – Georgina Martin and Nicole Penak both illustrate this in their chapters in this volume. Our story as researchers begins with the source(s) of our knowledge, not only those direct sources that contribute to a current project, but also those individuals and life experiences that along the way have shaped who we are. In other words, it is vital that a researcher acknowledge and explain his or her perspective on the research. Wendy Makoons Geniusz (2009) states that we "must always introduce the source of one's teachings" (p. xi) in order to "explain who I am, to whom I am connected and where I come from" (p. xv). Geniusz explains that acknowledging the source of knowledge and how we came to know it is essential to Anishinaabe research practice. Often familial and community sources of knowledge go unacknowledged in our professional lives as they are taken for granted or not considered "academic." Anishinaabe ethical research protocol requires that respect be given to those who have shaped and contributed to our knowledge. Whether we care to admit it or not, community, familial, and personal knowledge greatly influence the approach that we take to research. For the Anishinabeg, cultural protocols require us to acknowledge our personal knowledge sources, just as we would cite sources from the scholarly literature.

From these personal sources of knowledge, we learn about our relationships, not only to each other, but to other beings and to Creation itself. We remind ourselves of our responsibilities, of our duties, of how we are accountable (because we are held accountable on multiple levels), and of the moral and ethical conduct required to ensure that relationships are maintained. The scope for Indigenous research is broad: it is fundamentally about our relationships, to our research topic and to the people we wish to work with, but it is also tied to our responsibilities to Creation. Over the past decades a number of scholars have articulated these very same notions as research principles. For example, Shawn Wilson (2001), Cree scholar, observes that:

> An Indigenous paradigm comes from the fundamental belief that knowledge is relational. Knowledge is shared with all of creation. It is not just interpersonal relationships, not just with research subjects I may be working with, but is a relationship with all of creation. It is with the cosmos, it is with the animals, with the plants, with the earth that we share this knowledge. It goes beyond the idea of individual knowledge to the concept of relational knowledge. (Wilson, 2001, p. 177)

An Indigenous conceptual framework views relationships, not only to what we see around us, but to all that has come before (our ancestors) and to all that comes after (those yet to be born, along with the world we leave them), as the *theory* or explanation for *why we do what we do and how we do it*. Ethically, we work to recognize and *live* these relationships. In an Indigenous research paradigm, our ethics or conduct always includes the environment (or all of Creation), as well as the spirit world, no matter what the research questions or topic. In Anishinaabe research paradigms, our original sources of information are our ancestors, who were real people living their everyday lives, as well as the places that we come from. Geniusz (2009) refers to this view of research as *biskaabiiyang*, or "returning to ourselves" (p. 9).

I have taken the concept of *biskaabiiyang* to heart in this paper and have thus chosen to share, in the brief words that follow, the personal sources of my knowledge and the places from which my knowledge is derived. I recognize my approach will transform over time as I enter different life stages, but the following is an expression of where I am currently.

My story begins with my family and community. I am Anishinaabe from Wiigwaaskinga (Birch Island, Ontario, the community at the heart of the Whitefish River First Nation), where I grew up surrounded by a large extended family, including many cousins, aunts and uncles, and grandparents. My mother, Marion, is from Wikwemikong, a large First Nation on the eastern shores of Manitoulin Island, Ontario. At age eight, she was taken to residential school in Spanish, Ontario. She retained her language and for 30 years was a schoolteacher and principal at Shawanosowe, the community school in Birch Island named after a powerful and spiritual Anishinaabe leader. My father, Murray, grew up in Wiigwaaskinga, the youngest of 12 children, and attended public school in a nearby town. His educational experience "in town" was not any better than my mother's in residential school, yet he also retained his language.

I come from a family of leaders. Both my parents served on Band Council and have been involved in First Nation politics for some time. My paternal grandfather, William McGregor, was Chief of Whitefish River First Nation for many years. My great-grandfather on my mother's side, Sam Beaucage, "knew medicine." My grandmothers, Annie Beaucage and Julie McGregor, were tireless workers, raising families while highly involved in community building; they both valued education highly. My grandparents, great-grandparents, and other ancestors on both sides of my family all flourished within Anishinaabe worldview, yet at the same time learned the language and practices of the dominant worldview, largely through varying degrees of formal education and participation in the wage economy, but mostly through religion (Christianity).

On the maternal side of my family, I come from the Mukwah (Bear) Clan, and according to the late Elder Lillian McGregor, on my father's side the Ahjijawk (Crane) Clan. There are many lessons I learned from simply growing up in this family, including the way my family and ancestors lived their lives. For example, I learned that you can still be Anishinaabe, yet learn other ways of being as well. Thus, long before I read anything about Indigenous research methods as a scholar, I was learning its central principles, ethics, and values informally from my family, community, and nation.

I am also a mother and, with my partner, am raising two Anishinaabe children in an urban context. In my community of Birch Island, we can still hunt, fish, gather medicines, and gather/pick berries. Every spring, my family opens and runs the "sugar camp." I grew up spending many long days in the bush, listening to stories, gathering sap, chopping wood, running in the woods. Though they currently spend much of their lives in the city, my children, during our frequent trips "up north," can still do these things with their cousins, aunts, uncles, and grandparents. Spending many hours at sugar camp facilitates important community and family relationships. It allows one to *just be*: to eat, work, listen, and tell stories.

In addition to relationships, it is such *places* that shape who we are and what we know, and thus our research processes. I am very fortunate that I have *place* in my life. My community is caretaker for a very sacred location, *Dreamer's Rock*. Many Anishinaabe and other nations continue to come here for spiritual and ceremonial purposes. Numerous community events and the annual traditional pow-wow are held in this place. Cree scholar Margaret Kovach (2009) discusses the importance of place for framing Indigenous research approaches, stating that "[t]he visitation of anecdotes, metaphors, and stories about place make cerebral, academic language accessible and reflect holistic epistemologies" (p. 60). Fundamentally, stories about place, about our relationships to the environment, land, and ancestors, bring deeper meaning and understanding to the research.

Before proceeding with the rest of the chapter, I should note that in the decades of research activities I have engaged in, there are many others I have learned from as well. Two people stand out who have influenced me greatly. One is Ma Chi Biness, Robin Green, an Elder who has since passed on to the spirit world, with whom I had the privilege of working both at the Chiefs of Ontario and at the Centre for Indigenous Environmental Resources, in Winnipeg. I have also had the privilege of working with Grandmother Beedawsige, Josephine Mandamin, founder of the *Mother Earth Water Walk*. I have learned much from these two magnificent teachers, not just in terms of knowledge itself, but also how to share knowledge with humility and kindness. While I cannot share here all I have learned from these two remarkable individuals, readers can refer to other writings where I share more specific insights (e.g., McGregor, 2004; McGregor, 2012a).

Recently, I remarked to a group of students that some of my most significant "a-ha" moments about Indigenous research have come through my engagement with family, community, nation, Elders, and traditional knowledge holders. Our personal sources, including places and teachers, as well as the idea of "returning to oneself," thus all form integral aspects of an Anishinaabe research paradigm (Geniusz, 2009).

THE ROLE OF SERVICE: TAKING DIRECTION FROM ELDERS AND FROM TRADITIONAL KNOWLEDGE HOLDERS AND PRACTITIONERS

There are a growing number of Indigenous scholars, including many who have contributed to this volume, who bring their community ties, responsibilities, obligations, and networks to bear on their scholarly work. Many Indigenous scholars volunteer or work with Aboriginal communities and organizations. Such service links the academy and Aboriginal communities in novel ways. In this section I will highlight how the "Traditional Knowledge, Aboriginal Peoples and Water Governance in Ontario" project emerged from working with First Nations on endeavours that later transformed into an "academic" research project.

In 2000, seven people died from E. coli contamination of the drinking water supply in the rural town of Walkerton, Ontario. An inquiry was held into the tragedy and two years later, Justice O'Connor released his report on Part 2 of the Walkerton Inquiry, outlining 121 recommendations. Key among these was the recognition that First Nations face serious problems in relation to water quality, and that the difficulty in resolving these issues is compounded by jurisdictional issues among federal, provincial, and First Nations governments

(O'Connor, 2002). The Chiefs of Ontario was asked to provide a submission to the Walkerton Inquiry. I was asked to conduct the research on the Traditional Knowledge (TK) portion of the submission and answer the question, "What was the role of TK in protecting water?" In this work, I engaged a number of Elders and TK holders in dialogue about the significance of water to First Nations people. The main finding from the work indicated that First Nations people believe TK does and can continue to play a very important role in water governance in Ontario (Kamanga, Kahn, McGregor, Sherry, & Thornton, 2001; McGregor & Whitaker, 2001). This work was expanded upon in later years through work with the Chiefs of Ontario, where the goal was to better understand the role of TK and water protection from TK perspectives (Chiblow & Dorries, 2007; McGregor, 2009). During this time, over one hundred Elders and TK holders and practitioners participated in workshops, sharing circles, conferences, dialogues, and meetings. The main directive from Elders from around the province was to find ways to protect water and define *how* TK should be appropriately and ethically considered in water governance in Ontario. The Elders felt that the best decisions were not being made about water and that TK was needed to do so. The research that followed was based on recommendations given directly from Elders.

Advocacy played a major role in this research with the Chiefs of Ontario. In 2006, Sue Chiblow, my colleague and collaborator, and I presented at the *Expert Panel to Advise on a Regulatory Framework to Ensure Safe Drinking Water in First Nation Communities*. We provided a summary of main observations and advice given by Elders, leaders, and TK practitioners. The *Expert Panel* was a commission convened by the Government of Canada and the Assembly of First Nations (AFN) to advise on the appropriate regulatory framework required to ensure clean water in First Nation communities (AFN, 2007). In 2008, the Chiefs of Ontario adopted the *Anishinaabek, Mushkegowuk, and Onkwehonwe Water Declaration*, outlining the responsibilities and duties involved in water governance in Ontario.

The service component of this project took the form of policy research and engagement with, and on behalf of, Elders, TK holders, and political leadership. Whereas research initiated by outside interests tends to benefit those interests specifically, in this case I learned a great deal about conducting research that would support First Nations policy objectives. Because of this service to First Nation communities, I did not have to try to determine First Nation research priorities; I was already working on them.

On a more personal level, the profound teachings I learned from this work completely changed my research focus. As well, they illustrate another component of the role of service in working with First Nations people: that of simply listening to, and taking appropriate direction from, TK holders. It was the fall of 2000, as I was conducting the work for the Chiefs of Ontario's submission to the Walkerton Inquiry, when I met with a remarkable group of Anishinaabe women from Bkejwanong Territory who referred to their group as Akii Kwe, or "women who speak for water." With my husband and children in tow, I met with Akii Kwe, at which time a ceremony, followed by a sharing/teaching circle, was conducted. This "meeting" had been organized by a fellow environmental professional from Walpole Island and I had no idea what to expect. I took my cue from the women, answered questions, and settled in to listen. The women shared their observations and teachings about water in their territory over the years, including their concerns and actions they had taken to protect water. The women shared teachings about water with me, many of which I had never heard before, despite many years of involvement in the TK field.

In November of 2012, I met again with Akii Kwe about the research I was conducting as part of my work as a researcher at the University of Toronto. They asked me what I had "done" with the teachings they had shared with me over a decade earlier. They were pleased their words had had a profound influence on me personally and on the work I have been involved in over the years aimed at advancing TK and women's roles in water governance. This respect for the *voice* of individuals and groups such as Akii Kwe plays a key role in effective and mutually beneficial research involving Aboriginal people.

The voice of Aboriginal women has been largely absent in the discourse surrounding water protection in Ontario. Of major concern is the general lack of recognition of the role of women and their knowledge regarding water (McGregor, 2005; McGregor, 2008). There has been in recent years at least some headway made toward correcting this situation. The Anishinabek Nation announced the creation of a Women's Water Commission aimed in part at providing input to the Ontario government on Great Lakes water issues. It was established in recognition of women's traditional role along with the need to include women as part of the decision-making processes in formal environmental and resource management (McGregor, 2012b).

Despite the importance of such community-level undertakings to effective Aboriginal research, this type of work tends to receive little if any recognition from established Western institutions. The work I had been engaged in for a decade in the Aboriginal community did not "count" as research in my academic life. This work is not rewarded in scholarly settings. In fact, I have been told more than once that such work is a "waste of time" if it does not lead directly to publication. Such a view seems to me incredibly short-sighted, as, while it may not lead immediately to publication, it certainly can lay the foundation for enriched future opportunities and outcomes. In my case, for example, this type of work formed the basis of the "Water Governance" research project, as it enabled me to reconcile my responsibilities as an Anishinaabe person with my responsibilities as an academic and community person. When SSHRC (the Social Sciences and Humanities Research Council, a major Canadian research funding agency) announced new funding for environmental issues research, I was able to submit a proposal in short order. Through my decade-long service-oriented work with Aboriginal people, I was already involved in working on high-priority environmental issues with First Nations. I had already learned to utilize approaches and methods that were acceptable and appropriate to First Nation communities. I had already worked with Elders and with TK holders and practitioners, and had already received direction and guidance from them around research questions that needed asking. With all these pieces in place at the outset, I was successful in my proposal. However, all the work leading up to its submission went entirely unrecognized. I actually had a colleague who remarked to me, "It must be nice to be able to put together such a collaborative proposal in three weeks." I replied that the proposal actually took a decade to prepare, as all the service work and relationship building, all the development of trust and my capacity as a researcher, had taken place previously. It was the many years of service and maintaining a connection to First Nation communities and organizations that enabled the research to happen.

ENGAGING THE PERSONAL, ACADEMIC, AND COMMUNITY-BASED PRAXIS

The research strategy employed in the "Water Governance" project was intended to engage Anishinaabe research traditions. This required working directly with Elders, TK holders and practitioners, and community leaders to identify challenges and opportunities for engaging TK in water governance issues. An important part of the research involved working with Indigenous women to identify how the traditional role of women in speaking for water can be appropriately addressed in water governance in Ontario (in both urban and rural contexts). This research blended my professional responsibilities as an academic researcher (conducting research, training students, sharing knowledge) with my personal responsibilities as an Anishinaabe person (protecting, caring for, and speaking for water). Through this work, I was also able to honour the direction that was given to me over the years by Elders, TK holders, and others.

In order to achieve these things, a shift from conventional research approaches was required. Over the years a consistent message from Elders and others I had worked with was, "We are willing to share knowledge with you, but really we would rather be sharing our knowledge with our own youth, children, and community members." In recognition of this sentiment, I advocated for "knowledge sharing," for us to seek to *share* and *learn* knowledge, rather than simply extract it from its original holders. This meant that through the process of learning, knowledge would be generated, transformed, and shared on the Elders' terms.

An important part of the project was therefore to learn cultural or traditional knowledge through engagement in a learner/teacher relationship with Elders and TK holders and practitioners, an approach that would not only benefit the project but would also help to revitalize TK in Anishinaabe communities. Traditional knowledge in this paradigm would remain in the community/nation with those who would otherwise have acquired such knowledge according to the methods of our ancestors. To enable this process, I worked with a young Anishinaabe woman, Sylvia Plain (Aamijwnaang First Nation), to enact the story-work process (Archibald, 2008) in an Anishinaabe context. She engaged in learner/teacher relationships with Grandmother Josephine Mandamin in an Anishinaabe immersion camp and canoe journey during the summer of 2012. Through the process of learning to build a *ciimaan* (canoe, in Anishinaabemowin), she was able to learn not only traditional knowledge, but also a process for learning and conveying such knowledge in a contemporary context. In this setting, both Grandmother Mandamin and Sylvia Plain were learners, as master canoe builder Wayne Valliere of the Lac du Flambeau Reservation taught a group of approximately 30 people through storytelling, songs, art, and hands-on experience. The teachers and learners shared and learned knowledge as a community, created relationships, and fostered mentorships and apprenticeships. Through this experience, Sylvia engaged in two disparate yet linked processes, connecting the goals of community-based scholarly research (learning about Aboriginal knowledge sharing and transmission) with those of the community (facilitating the passing on of traditional knowledge to Aboriginal community members). In this process, we are learners and teachers in the shared endeavour of *coming to know*. Knowledge sharing did not flow in one direction, but in multiple ways. As a result of this experience, Sylvia and I have given a number of presentations on Anishinaabe research process (in classrooms, at conferences, etc.). Through this project, I myself became a learner, benefiting from both Josephine and Sylvia and the teachings obtained in the canoe journey. In such a process, the line between learner and teacher becomes blurred, as noted by Archibald (2008), because to "share" implies learning, but also teaching. Sharing becomes a form of knowledge mobilization.

KNOWLEDGE MOBILIZATION

To meaningfully convey the depth of the knowledge he or she has learned, a learner in Aboriginal culture is encouraged to embody the knowledge – to enact or live out its central principles. It becomes a part of who we are. Research is, in this paradigm, both individual and collective. Certainly oral transmission remains an important form of sharing knowledge with others. As with written transmission, the form is important, but personally enacting or living the knowledge is also critical. This is something I have come to realize over the course of my own research: Anishinaabe knowledge must be lived (McGregor, 2004; McGregor, 2009).

During the journey in respect of water that this project has taken me on, I have learned from Akii Kwe, and others like them, that in Anishinaabe culture it is the women who are the voice for water. It is therefore my responsibility as an Anishinaabe woman to engage in this work. Through meeting this responsibility, I engage in what I call "Anishinaabe action research." Of course, my ancestors have engaged in this work since time immemorial. It is only recently that the scholarly community has recognized this mode of inquiry as "research" at all.

Anishinaabe people have always sought knowledge in systematic ways, engaging in protocols that included the proper ethics and conduct for doing so. This is not new. Knowledge is a gift to share for the well-being of the people and is acknowledged by other Anishinaabe scholars as the pursuit of *Minobimaatisiiwin*, or "the good life" (LaDuke, 1999; McGregor, 2013; Peltier, 2013).

Akii Kwe, in their ceremonial and spiritual life, pursue *Minobimaatisiiwin* not only for the people but for the waters and all the beings that water nourishes. The walkers that form the growing movement the *Mother Earth Water Walk*, inspired by Grandmother Josephine Mandamin, enable individuals, families, communities, and nations to carry out their responsibilities. On each journey, teachings are shared, ceremonies conducted, and responsibilities enacted. From a scholarly perspective, by living the knowledge, they are sharing and mobilizing said knowledge. Anishinaabe research, in this sense, is not just seeking knowledge, it is the way that we conduct ourselves and relate to other beings in Creation. The research that is enacted to pursue these goals is informed by an "ethic of responsibility." How we conduct ourselves matters on the physical, emotional, intellectual, and spiritual planes. Participating in Anishinaabe action research means I have a responsibility to not only learn about water, but also speak for water. As a scholar I enact this through my research projects, as well as my teaching and writing. As a community member I realize this through my policy, governance, and advocacy work with First Nation organizations (McGregor, 2012a, 2012b). As a member of my family, community, and nation, I carry out my responsibilities through my lived experience.

CONCLUSION

Aboriginal traditional knowledge is part of the lived experience of a person, family, clan, nation, or people, and even of Creation. Making this understanding of traditional knowledge a reality in the academy means that Indigenous people who are part of the academic community (faculty, students, staff, community members) must be able to live their traditional knowledge in this context.

I have, in the course of this chapter, aimed to provide some insight into what this means from a personal and a professional perspective. For this is the challenge of the Aboriginal researcher in the 21st century: to be able to integrate our personal (in my case, Anishinaabe) understandings of the world, with our professional and academic endeavours. Our research undertakings must reflect our understanding of Aboriginal ethics and worldview. Bringing these pieces of the puzzle together will not only help in resolving inner conflicts we may have experienced as we exist in these two formerly disparate spheres, but will also serve to move scientific and humanistic research in a new direction: one in which Aboriginal worldview is seen as having equal importance to that of Western science, and where it is hoped new and more sustainable relationships between human society and the rest of Creation can be developed.

REFERENCES

Archibald, J. (2008). *Indigenous storywork: Educating the heart, mind, body and spirit.* Vancouver: UBC Press.

Assembly of First Nations (AFN). (2007). *Expert panel report on safe drinking water for First Nations: Position paper.* Ottawa: Assembly of First Nations.

Chiblow, S., & Dorries, H. (2007). *Aboriginal Traditional Knowledge and source water protection. Final report.* Toronto: Chiefs of Ontario.

Geniusz, W. (2009). *Our Knowledge is not primitive: Decolonizing botanical Anishinaabe teaching.* Syracuse, NY: Syracuse University Press.

Kamanga, D., Kahn, J., McGregor, D., Sherry, M., & Thornton, A. (2001). *Drinking water in Ontario First Nation communities: Present challenges and future directions for on-reserve water treatment in the province of Ontario. Submission to Part 2 of the Walkerton Inquiry Commission.* Toronto: Chiefs of Ontario.

Kovach, M. (2009). *Indigenous methodologies: Characteristics, conversations, and contexts.* Toronto: University of Toronto Press.

LaDuke, W. (1999). *All our relations: Native struggles for land and life.* Cambridge, MA: South End Press.

Louis, R. (2007). Can you hear us now? Voices from the margin: Using Indigenous methodologies in geographic research. *Geographical Research, 45*(2), 130–139.

McGregor, D. (2004). Coming full circle: Indigenous Knowledge, environment, and our future. *American Indian Quarterly, 28*(3/4), 385–410.

McGregor, D. (2005). Traditional ecological Knowledge: An Anishinabe-Kwe perspective. *Atlantis Women's Studies Journal, 29*(2), 103–109.

McGregor, D. (2008). Anishinabe Kwe, Traditional Knowledge and water protection. Indigenous women in Canada: The voices of First Nations, Inuit and Métis women. *Canadian Women's Studies/les cahiers de la femme, 26*(3/4), 26–30.

McGregor, D. (2009). Honouring our relations: An Anishinabe perspective on environmental justice. In J. Agyeman, R. Haluza-Delay, C. Peter, & P. O'Riley (Eds.), *Speaking for ourselves: Constructions of environmental justice in Canada* (pp. 27–41). Vancouver, BC: University of British Columbia Press.

McGregor, D. (2012a). All our relations. Aboriginal perspectives on protecting water in Ontario: Ethical considerations and insights. In F. Nasti & F. Reduzzi (Eds.), *Per Una Comune Cultura Dell'Acqua: Dal Mediterraneo a l'Amerique Del Nord* (pp. 181–198). Cassino, Italy: Universita di Cassino e del Lazio Meridionale.

McGregor, D. (2012b). Traditional Knowledge: Considerations for protecting water in Ontario. Special issue on water and Indigenous peoples. *International Indigenous Policy Journal, 3*(3). Retrieved from www.iipj.org/

McGregor, D., & Whitaker, S. (2001). Water quality in the province of Ontario: An Aboriginal Knowledge perspective [unpublished report]. Toronto: Chiefs of Ontario.

McGregor, L. (2013). Children's health research in six Anishinaabe communities. In A. Corbiere, D. McGregor, & C. Migwans (Eds.), *Anishinaabewin Niiswi: Deep roots, new growth* (pp. 19–30). M'Chigeeng, ON: Ojibwe Cultural Foundation.

O'Connor, D. (2002). Chapter 15: First Nations. In *Report of the Walkerton Inquiry, Part two: A strategy for safe drinking water* (pp. 485–497). Toronto: Queen's Printer for Ontario.

Peltier, C. (2013). My Indigenous research paradigm: Staying true to my roots. In A. Corbiere, D. McGregor, & C. Migwans (Eds.), *Anishinaabewin Niiswi: Deep roots, new growth* (pp. 31–40). M'Chigeeng, ON: Ojibwe Cultural Foundation.

Wilson, S. (2001). What is an Indigenous research methodology? *Canadian Journal of Native Education, 25*, 175–179.

Wilson. S. (2008). *Research is ceremony: Indigenous research methods*. Blackpoint, NS: Fernwood Publishing.

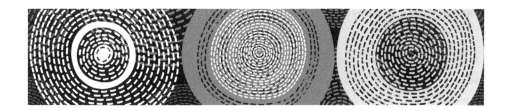

CHAPTER 15

A Story Pathway:
Restoring Wholeness in the Research Process

Nicole Penak

The sun is out, warming up the breeze as it splashes against my face. The birds are circling overhead, singing their thanks for this heat after a long winter. The waves crash into the dock and spill up over the old concrete walls. Walking helps me process, especially when I have papers to write. Gets the ideas flowing, better than sitting in front of that computer all day. As I walk the words come to me. They appear up out of the ground and I   skip   across them   like   hop   scotch. For a moment I forget where I am, I close my eyes and I am overtaken by my other senses. The feeling, the sounds, I breathe in deeply, but I do not taste that salty air I was anticipating. Of course not. I am walking along Toronto's lakeshore. This is my favourite place in the city, when it is warm out like this I walk here almost every day. There is something about being close to the water that is comforting; it reminds me of my time with my family out East, learning to fish, clam digging in the mud, running across the docks inspecting the fishermen's lobster traps, staying up late in the warm nights listening to stories, smelling and tasting that salty ocean water. *Splash!* It's that Trickster trying to find a faster way through the story   jumping   over   important lessons,   swinging from one chapter into the next, only to f

a

l

l   into the

crashing waves. Even pulling himself out of the water, he snickers at me as I move slowly along my path, stepping from word to word. But we are old friends now, he and I. Even with all the trouble we have been through together, he reminds me of how important it is to trust in my relationships that come together to form this path for me to follow. Though trying to follow the emerging story sometimes seems like a BIG leap of faith. It always seems to take me where I need to go. I guess that's the thing about stories, there needs to be some trust involved. Trust that stories do not always go in straight lines, that there may be twists and turns that take a story around in circles. Trust that what needs to be said will be said, and trust from the storyteller that the audience will take from the story what they need at that time, no more and no less.

Thomas King (2003), Native American novelist, broadcaster, professor, and Massey Lecturer, reminds us that "the truth about stories is that's all we are.... 'There isn't any centre to the world but a story'" (p. 32). The story I want to share with you takes place in my master of social work program (MSW). As you may or may not know, social work in North America is a dynamic tale of imperialism and resistance. Its story is one plagued with the reproduction of the colonial project, a *divisive* process that not only continues to isolate Indigenous people from their families, culture, and community, but one that has dismantled people's sense of self. As a First Nations woman in a school of social work, engaging this story had ripped me into pieces. It was as if every day my body was carved up and portioned in two – those pieces of me that fulfilled the social worker form, and those that filled the form of the client. My Indigenousness offered insight only into the experiences of service users and not into those of service providers. This was an experience I knew was not mine alone, as many diverse and marginalized bodies are injured by this plot of social work education. As a First Nations helping professional and educator, I have come to realize that the purpose of my work must be the restoration of *wholeness*. This is a challenging principle when embarking on a research process, considering "'research' is inextricably linked to European imperialism and colonialism" (Smith, 1999, p. 1). When imagining a research journey with other master of social work students who identify as racialized, I wondered what pathway could possibly lead us toward building this wholeness? *Drip. Drip.* I look up to find Trickster standing over me, his hands planted firmly on his hips. Soaking wet, he leans in dramatically, with one eyebrow raised. "Not *this* story?" he interrupts. I nod my head yes, and off he runs down the path, t-r-i-p-p-i-n-g and s-t-u-m-b-l-i-n-g as he attempts to soar across the words. "So I guess you will already be there, aye?!" I shout after him. You are welcome to join us as well. Come on, I am on my way through that story now.

THE STORYTELLER: SITUATING SELF

The written word has transformed the process of storytelling: "text was supposedly complete, self-contained, a thing to dissect rather than to have a relationship with" (Archibald, 2008, p. 33). However, storytelling, like Indigenous research, is an innately relational activity. As stated by Jo-ann Archibald (2008) of the Stó:lō Nation, "The story doesn't work without a participant. There has to be a participant and someone has to listen. I don't mean listening in the passive sense" (p. 33). Indigenous storytelling, which is predominantly based on oral delivery and aural reception, requires an active audience, listener, or reader. With this understanding, your contribution to this story is of great importance. I want to invite you to consider your role in this tale as participatory, actively engaging with the other beings, stories, and experiences shared in this chapter. The strength of stories is in their ability to touch us where we are, today, here, in our bodies and hearts, to challenge us to think, to examine our emotional reactions, and to reflect on a story's connectedness to our own lives and spirit and extend that connectedness to the rest of Creation. This connection is made not only through a storyteller's relationship to the topic of their tale, but also through a storyteller's ability to develop a relationship with their audience. Though this can be done through a multitude of methods, an important part of beginning any relationship is getting to know a little bit about one another.

As we walk together along this path, we have some time to get to know each other better. For me to share with you something about the context of my story and the positionality from which I tell it. You have already been to my favourite spot in this city. I live and work here in the vibrant Indigenous community of Toronto, as a social worker and social work educator. My English name is Nicole Marie Penak, I am a member of the Eagle Clan, and a Maliseet and Mi'kmaq First Nations woman with mixed Acadian and Ukrainian heritage. My family is from the territory stretching through what is now known as the Gaspé Region in Quebec and the province of New Brunswick, but I was born and raised in the Greater Toronto Area. My grandfather was the first person to bring our family story here to Toronto when he stole away on a cargo train alone and with nothing, at the young age of 15, in an attempt to start a new life. An amazing story in itself, he eventually went back to the East Coast to marry my grandmother. One summer my mother was visiting family in Toronto and met my father, precipitating her move back to the city to settle down and have me and then my younger brother. Though my family is not originally from this place, Toronto is an important part of my family's story. It is my community, where I call home, and where this story unfolds.

My traditional name, Kiishickokwe, can be understood in English to mean "Cedar Woman." It was revealed to me by my Traditional Healers, along with my path to take up our medicines to contribute to the healing of my community. To some people this may sound pretty cool, but when I heard these words I was terrified. All I could think about was whether I had flunked Grade 10 biology – *aye!* But seriously. For a long time I worried, and wondered how I would ever honour this vision. Though there was one thing that I could do, and do well – school. Now this was a curious and even troublesome talent growing up, coming from a family whose engagement with the educational system has been a source of intergenerational damage. Industrial schools, better known today as the residential school system, over time took the lives of family members and left others with deep-seated scars. Even a generation later, my family members have been failed by the Western school system and forced to drop out. For myself, bringing home gold stars eventually developed into bringing home scholarships and awards. As I packed my belongings and moved away to pursue post-secondary education, being the first person in my household to go to university made me feel farther from my family than any geographic distance ever could. Interestingly, the experience of being a First Nations woman in an MSW program was a struggle I could share with friends and family alike. Reflecting on it now, I am brought right back to that painful place.

Blink. Blink. It's hazy, but I can almost make out the wreckage. *Blink.* I stretch open my eyes and look around to survey the damage. What a mess. *Bup! Bup! Bup! Bup!* "Oooo." It feels like there's a big drum pounding inside my head. I move to hold my hands over my ears in an attempt to ease the throbbing, but only my left hand makes it. "Not again," I mumble. I have to pull myself together. Really. "Where's that sewing kit?" I see it in the back pocket of my left leg. I reach out and drag over my leg, along with my right arm, to where I am lying. "Through, over, out, over. Again. Through, over, out, over. Again." My experience in this program has been so brutalizing that the stitches don't even phase me anymore. I put down the needle and wiggle the fingers of my right hand to make sure I have my arm sewed back on securely enough. *Bup! Bup! Bup!* "Oooo." I hear his cackle, "Hee, hee, hee, hee, ayeeee." That Trickster is back again, and drumming on my head. He takes another needle from my sewing kit, stretches it into a second drumstick, and continues. *Bup! Bup! Bup!* "Augh, go!" I tell him. "Can't you see I have enough to do before the next class starts?" He moves over toward the door, holding the handle as if to leave the scene. "My friend, I ask you again, why do you endure this beating?" he says with a sly half-smile. "You have just a few minutes before the butcher – I mean teacher – arrives. Why not do as I do, and blend in or disappear?" he continues almost tauntingly. I look over the bruising along my body, and for a moment I consider his suggestion as if it were possible. Just then the door bursts open, crushing him behind it. As quickly as the students pour in, he is gone. *Blink. Blink.*

So I dragged my bruised body over to my peers to discuss this dismantling experience in the MSW program. Casual conversation amongst these fellow students began to expose a more complex and expansive shared narrative. Individual stories unearthed trails mutually travelled, and developed into a collective interest to explore the significance of these story pathways. Upon consultation with staff and peers in the program, I was able to locate a space in the school once a week to facilitate a sharing circle called "A Space for Race." The circle provided students with a place to share their experiences as racialized students and social workers, and provide peer support on various issues. Through the process we realized that somehow we needed to share our experiences from the circle with the social work program, and educational institutions more broadly. Ten dedicated peers consented to having this process transformed into an educational exercise, a research process to be precise.

I returned to friends, family, and community, to reflect on how to go about this research, or knowledge gathering, in a good way, and something hit me. It was as if all the pieces of my story were coming together around me. I had always been told that our *teachings* are medicine, and that *words* have the ability to heal, but it had taken me this long to realize that the medicines I am destined to work with are actually *stories*! I was already on the medicine path my Healers had revealed to me. My family's, community's, and my own challenging experiences with schooling flashed before my eyes. It was then that I was able to understand my vision: to bring those stories less told into educational institutions. Stories would restore the wholeness in my research process, and would guide my path from conceptualization, to process, analysis, and outcomes. Just as I travel this story pathway with you now, that is how I would come to understand this knowledge-gathering process, walking with one another through our own stories around every bend, hill, and valley. "Hey you, Trickster, a little help here please!?" I shout ahead of me. And as fast as my words reach his twisted ears he transforms his long arms into wings. I grab onto them as we fly into the sky together. "An eagle's view for my Eagle Clan friend," he says through a smile. From way up here I can see all those story pathways, where our individual trails stand apart and intersect with others' narratives. An exquisite weaving and winding of experiences laid out on the land. "What a mess!" snickers Trickster. "Well maybe we should go back down so you can appreciate the beauty and healing in the details," I wink. And D

o

w

n we go!

INDIGENOUS STORYWORK: REIMAGINING "RESEARCH"

As explained by Georgina Martin in her chapter, the term "storywork" was developed by Jo-ann Archibald to signify the importance of storytelling for Indigenous peoples and communities. These stories can restore the balance in our lives, show us "about being whole and healthy and remind us of traditional teachings that have relevance to our lives. Stories have the power to make our hearts, minds, bodies, and spirits work together" (Archibald, 2008, p. 12). However, Indigenous storytelling is not prescriptive in nature, with an index to follow to applicable solutions to life's challenges. In many cases, rather, "[o]ur teachers help us to see 'the upside down, the opposite, and the other balances of things around us'" (Graveline, 1998, p. 11).

Among many First Nations these stories take up the Trickster character – whom you have already met, in their/her/his/its many manifestations, such as Coyote, Raven, Wesakejac, Glooscap, and Nanabozo, which have all been part of Indigenous storywork since time immemorial. The English word "trickster," however, does not portray the diverse range of roles and ideas First Nations associate with the Trickster,

> who sometimes is like a magician, an enchanter, an absurd prankster ... who sometimes is a shape shifter, and who often takes on human characteristics ... one whose transformations often use humour, satire, self-mocking, and absurdity to carry good lessons.... Trickster often gets into trouble by ignoring cultural rules and practices or by giving sway to the negative aspects of "humanness".... Trickster seems to learn lessons the hard way and sometimes not at all. At the same time, Trickster has the ability to do good things for others and is sometimes like a powerful spiritual being and given much respect. (Archibald, 2008, p. 5).

Trickster stories reinforce the principal motive of an Indigenous research methodology as applied in this knowledge-gathering project: the importance of *relationships*. Trickster gets into trouble when *disconnected* from traditional teachings, family, community, nation, culture, and land (Archibald, 2008, p. i). As such, this research project sought to counter this imbalance by building relations through an Indigenous methodology that honours and upholds our connectedness.

Archibald puts forward the notion that Trickster can be as much a "doing" as a "being," and can be understood as a process that we interact with, as much as a person (Archibald, 2008, p. 6). Various expressions of Trickster have been applied in recent academic works by Indigenous scholars to explore diverse imbalances in the Western education system; from the "white man as Trickster" (Graveline, 1998, p. 11) in educational pedagogy, to Weesageechak as the tension between Canadian high schools and Aboriginal students (Bazylak, 2002) and a journey with Coyote and Raven through Canadian educational institutions (Cole, 2006). In this volume alone three of us, Nicole Bell, Amy Parent, and myself, have placed the Trickster at the centre of our research stories. This notion of Trickster is useful in reframing the idea of a "research problem" as an imbalance or disharmony that participants and/or the researcher are engaging with. The disharmony informing my knowledge-gathering project derived from my experiences as a First Nations woman within an MSW program. As echoed in the words of Absolon and Willett, "our experience as Aboriginal peoples is poorly represented in the academy. There are few places that accurately reflect Aboriginal reality, where we can see and say, 'This represents who I am'" (Absolon & Willett, 2005, p. 108). I came to this project wondering, if I am not represented, do other students who identify as "racialized" also feel unrepresented in the MSW program? It became the purpose of this knowledge-gathering process to share the stories of these students as they encounter the grand narrative of social work. Throughout this process, it became clear that the stories lived, shared, and created definitely represent a series of Trickster stories, where learning and healing could be found in even the most unlikely tales.

STORIES FROM THE CIRCLE: THE KNOWLEDGE-GATHERING PROCESS

While we walk and share together, I am reminded that Indigenous cultures, peoples, and researchers "value the journey as much as the destination" (Kovach, 2005, p. 27), and that "the process of telling a story is as much the point as the story itself" (Absolon & Willett, 2005, p. 98). From this understanding, it is important to envision methodology as the entire process of doing research, from conceptualization, to data collection, analysis, and presentation of outcomes. An Indigenous research methodology is based on Indigenous ways of knowing (Kovach, 2005, p. 28). An important distinction from dominant Euro-American paradigms is the principle of *relationality*, which is reinforced by our understanding of Trickster stories. In an Indigenous worldview, truth is not something external to be discovered but is formed out of the *relationships* that one has. Consequently, "there is no one definite reality but rather different sets of relationships that make up an Indigenous ontology. Therefore reality is not an object but a process of relationships" (Wilson, 2008, p. 73).

The conflict of transcribing an Indigenous paradigm into Western academic research systems is apparent when attempting to describe the "unit of analysis." As described previously, if reality is composed of relationships, and the purpose of research is to glean an understanding of reality, then an Indigenous research methodology studies relationships. Stories themselves are a great tool for understanding an Indigenous worldview, and by extension are an excellent Indigenous research methodology. A story is not a solid thing in and of itself, a self-enclosed or discernible point or object in the universe. It is like a constellation that presents itself in the sky, made up of the connections of light emanating from the relationship between stars, and between these stars and the sky, space, the moon, the distance from the earth, and the human eye. Stories embody this relational core of an Indigenous worldview and research, as a story, too, is a collection of relationships – between people, community, characters, context, place or setting, storyteller, audience and reader, past, present, and future – hundreds of factors forming a web of relations that we discern as "a story."

Trickster and I sat down, and I wondered out loud, "What process would best facilitate the sharing of these stories?" Trickster grumbled, "That's nice, I'm wondering what time lunch is," sucking back on his slobbery tongue. I was tempted to roll my eyes, but he made a good point. So I cooked up some snacks and put out a call for some guests. At a pilot gathering of interested participants, we tried a sharing circle format. Even with the circle being tape recorded, there was intense sharing and collective excitement and acceptance of the circle process. For this project, sharing circles appeared to be the best way to uphold the relational nature and focus of an Indigenous research methodology, as well as setting the stage for shared storytelling and collaboration that would come later in the research design. Absolon and Willett propose that a research sharing circle "is a process that generates information sharing, connections, builds capacity, and seeks balance and healing" (2005, p. 116). Sacred circle symbolism is described by Michael Anthony Hart as enacted in legends, storytelling, meetings, sun dances, sweat lodges, pipe ceremonies, feasts, and many other facets of Indigenous life and culture (Hart, 2002, p. 62). Like our Trickster stories, sharing circles remind us of the importance of balance, "when individuals work on connecting themselves emotionally, mentally, physically and spiritually" (Hart, 2002, p. 101). As further described by Fyre Jean Graveline (1998),

> Circle is based on a Traditional belief set: the connection between people in a Circle creates the threads that will weave the human species back into the Sacred Hoop of life. Traditionalists believe that the Circle contains a

recognizable power that defies superficial boundaries. To bring understanding between tribal peoples in times of decision-making, conflict resolution or healing, Circles were formed. Today we face the necessity of bridging differences between the cultures with few processes that are not based on the same individualistic philosophies that have been used to "divide and conquer." The Circle can act to deconstruct the Western dualism of individual/community by allowing us to work individually, in a transpersonal context, while building a community. Establishing a cohesive Circle is an integral part of re-establishing interconnectedness. (p. 131)

It is suggested that the embodied metaphor of sitting in the sharing circle while attending to neglected aspects of one's being can move us to an understanding of interconnectedness that goes beyond the level of conscious awareness. Though sharing circles differ from healing circles – which Elders or Traditional Teachers preside over and provide feedback on – sharing circles also carry healing effects for participants (Hart, 2002, p. 89). Circles help to break taboos about what can or cannot be shared; people are able to release long-held feelings affecting their wellness and are able to give and receive acknowledgement of shared experiences. As stated by Graveline, "there is a physical impact on the human system that happens while sitting in circle" (1998, p. 131). Participants are able to "visualize themselves as whole persons, see connections between different aspects of their lives, and determine how to balance their development" (Hart, 2002, p. 85). Moving around the circle in a clock- or sun-wise order, we honoured each person in the circle with the time and space they required to share their stories, finishing only when they chose to pass the talking stick to the person seated beside them. As topics are metaphorically placed in the centre of the circle, they are seen and spoken about from various vantage points, providing a deeper understanding (Hart, 2002, p. 90). Working collectively to understand that issue, participants are able to uncover lessons from even challenging stories. Working to create such a space with participants also provided me with a sense of community. In the sharing circle we could bring our stories of successes or challenges, people expanded on each other's experiences, new relationships between participants formed, and the relationships between their experiences began to form from these bonds. As we walked with one another along each different person's story, we found their thoughts, feelings, and spirit. Not only did we find these pathways crossing over our own stories to form an intricate web of relations, but we connected to one another in sharing our own reflections and responses to travelling along another person's path. I could feel the healing company of others travelling with me through my and others' stories. This is where the knowledge gathering happens, here on these pathways. Continuing further through our story, it was important not only to share what we had gathered so far along the way, but to have others join us on these story pathways and connect with this learning themselves. In this way others – like you – are not only reading this knowledge, but feeling and experiencing it with your own minds, bodies, and spirits. Connecting it to your own storied pathway, and knowing, experiencing, with your whole being. *Cough. Cough.* "Yeah, it sounds great until you *experience* being crushed behind a door!" *Sigh.* "Oh, Trickster."

BEING NARRATIVE: EXPLORING ANALYSIS

Shawn Wilson explains how the linear logic of dominant research paradigms looks at, or "manages," a topic by breaking it down into smaller portions. This is challenging for an Indigenous research methodology, because by breaking things down into their smallest pieces you are destroying the relationships around those things. Rather than deconstruction, Wilson describes an Indigenous research methodology as synthesis (2008, p. 121). One of the challenges with this style of analysis is when you have to try to present your findings, particularly in academic institutions. Lavallée proposes weaving points and themes back together in a collective story, keeping individual stories intact and writing about participants as characters (2009, p. 34). Likewise, Wilson puts forward the use of metaphor and symbolism in both analysis and presentation. This is a way for the audience of the research to better form a relationship with findings that sometimes feel abstract (Wilson, 2008, p. 124). Heeding this advice from previous researchers, I returned to stories as a way to uphold an Indigenous worldview.

Through both oppression and exclusion, educational systems have been one tool by which industrial forms of consciousness were and are expanded and disseminated. Blaut understands Eurocentrism as a partner of the colonial process, which

> is not just a matter of attitudes in the sense of values and prejudices, but rather a matter of science, scholarship, informed and expert opinion. Eurocentrism guides what is accepted as "empirical reality," "true," or "propositions supported by the 'facts.'" (as cited in Graveline, 1998, p. 23)

Colonial forms of education, particularly residential schools, have contributed greatly to the efforts to eradicate and replace traditional forms of knowledge, such as oral tradition, language, and storytelling (Graveline, 1998, pp. 28–29). This continues to this day, a sustained colonial assault on Indigenous consciousness.

Gerald McMaster of the Plains Cree Nation and Lee-Ann Martin of the Mohawk Nation argue that "rather than perpetuating an 'academic' colonialism, Aboriginal communities need to articulate their own scholarship that validates indigenous systems and philosophies" (as cited in Graveline, 1998, p. 12). In this way, Indigenous methodologies can work to question and displace "the construction of White/male as 'the reference point of all knowledge' [where] only one cultural reality is universalized, one language is spoken" (Graveline, 1998, p. 10). Graveline holds that "cultural knowledge is an essential component of cultural resistance … we are resisting by 'writing back,' by disrupting the European narratives and replacing them with either a more playful or more powerful new narrative style" (1998, pp. 41–42). Accordingly, teachers, students, and researchers can be agents of change, resisting the dominant colonial educational order by asserting alternative forms of knowledge.

Through the sharing circle we were able to discuss this challenge as a group, with the goal of inviting people into our stories through the use of creative writing, guiding people onto these story pathways to travel and experience for themselves through an engaging series of five creative short stories based on our experiences. After transcriptions had been made from the tapes of six sharing circle sessions, each participant was given a copy of the transcripts from the circles that they attended. The participants and myself went over the transcripts to correct any typos or misinterpretations. Afterwards, participants, aided by the transcripts, traced out their own individual storied pathways, and identified points along their journeys that crossed over or connected with others' stories. People, places, feelings, ideas, experiences became markers along each person's path. Methodologically, rather than using these connections as "key themes" to flush out of their relations and discuss in isolation, we used them as markers from which to construct a web of relations, a new, creative story pathway composed of the points of connection of all our individual stories. Though I am sure there are many more points that other researchers may glean from the transcripts, I located 32 common markers along participants' pathways. These markers included: challenges as a racialized social worker, course materials, the structure of academia, history, positioning race as a deficit, race as a positive, the inadequacies of cultural competency, experiencing feelings of guilt, extra responsibilities of racialized students, experiences of being silenced, frustration, identity, negotiating space, issues not addressed in the program, more support around placement issues, student space to discuss and debrief, race is complicated, whiteness, colonialism, fear of essentializing, professors, fellow students, solutions, lack of power, need for personal experience addressed in academia, the theory/practice disconnect, employment, reconciling experiences outside of the program, sharing circles, healing, fear for own community, and the classroom. These common markers were connected to each other to form new story pathways; they became the characters, setting, plot, conflicts, and resolutions of five creative short stories. Read together, the stories show multiple relationships between these significant points, and provide a fuller understanding as to how all points, inevitably, are connected to one another.

Relationality can also be realized through the creation of characters built out of the experiences of multiple participants. The characters are fictional in so much as they are not based on any one participant of this study, and participants contribute experiences to more than one character. The setting, plotlines, and dialogue in these stories are taken directly from the quotes, passages, and stories shared by participants. However, the experiences are not shared verbatim, but as pieces of creative non-fiction that draw not only on the content of the participants' stories, but also on the feelings and spirit expressed while people told their stories. This allows the "data" collected to maintain its relational qualities – multiple points of relation that create numerous access points for readers to enter and journey along these storied pathways with us. This is an important point for storytelling as a tool for Indigenous research. "[U]nlike quantitative work, which can carry its meaning in its tables and summaries, qualitative work depends upon people's reading it" (Richardson, 2004, p. 474). If research studies are to have an impact on people's lives, storytelling may be an avenue to reach more people with the work that has been done. Story requires a relationship with the audience, making the need for research to be engaging and accessible a significant part of our knowledge-gathering efforts. You may recall my story with Trickster in the classroom as an example of this process. Every time I read over that short story I don't simply learn about the challenges of the classroom, I experience it with my whole being. As Lee Maracle reinforces, "story is the most persuasive and sensible way to present the accumulated thoughts and values of a people'" (as cited in Archibald, 2008, p. 26).

The completed research project was entitled *(y)our stories: for an anti-colonial academia* (Penak, 2010). When reviewing the process I am reminded of my friend Trickster, how for him trouble and imbalance followed from a disjuncture in relationships. It is clear from the disharmony described by participants throughout the short stories that the relationship between social work education and MSW students who identify as racialized is significantly fractured. This project ignited new possibilities for strengthening relationships, and not only between students, and their stories, but also between us and our social work program. As these stories have taken on a new life, being presented at two research symposiums, other students, administrators, educators, and community members more broadly have had the opportunity to enter and rebuild relationships taken up along the story pathways. These stories lived, shared, and created were so impactful that the project was nominated for an award through the School of Social Work. Now five years later I have been invited back to the School of Social Work to return to where it all began, our stories. Administration and faculty reflecting on the lessons of this research commissioned me to work on a follow-up research project, connecting with Indigenous alumni and current students, in both the bachelor and master of social work programs. We have again come together in the sharing circle to share stories about our experiences as Indigenous people in the School of Social Work. Our stories shared with each other, and the program, have sparked some significant relationship building between the program and surrounding Indigenous communities, including the development of an Aboriginal Advisory Committee, knowledge-sharing workshops that bring together Indigenous community members, program staff, and students alike, as well as the development of Indigenous course content directly informed by our stories.

COMING FULL CIRCLE: CONCLUDING REMARKS

Woosh. Careful now, that's Trickster running quickly past us. Here he comes again! *Woosh.* As we have been stepping   from   word   to   word in this story, Trickster has not realized that the pathway has taken him around in circles. That's the power of stories: their ability to bring everything back together. Through what can be a divisive academic practice, stories have helped restore the wholeness in my research process. They have helped me to facilitate and develop relationships that were formerly absent or tenuous. Perhaps they have even helped me connect with you.

Though I have truly enjoyed our time together, these are solely my reflections about how stories have helped me re-imagine the research process. Like other Trickster stories, this one is not prescriptive. As our old people remind us, you can take what you need and leave the rest. Like all stories there may be, and often are, multiple understandings and lessons that come to each reader, and with each reading. For myself, this understanding mirrors the appreciation I have developed for processes – as opposed to only outcomes – as stories reveal the importance of the way we can come together, the way we share together, and the way we relate to one another. As such, I hope that *how* I have written this chapter may contribute to this understanding – not only *what* I have written. Perhaps if social workers, students, professors, schools, and researchers consider – or reconsider – process, then meaningful sharing and understanding may follow from that. I leave you now to decide how or if any of what I have shared today may help you in your own research journey. Just as our friend Trickster has continued to circle around us, I am sure we will connect again. Thank you for walking through this story with me this far. Now it is up to you to decide what pathway you will travel on.

REFERENCES

Absolon, K., & Willett, C. (2005). Putting ourselves forward: Location in Aboriginal research. In L. Brown & S. Strega (Eds.), *Research as resistance: Critical, Indigenous, & anti-oppressive approaches* (pp. 97–126). Toronto: Canadian Scholars' Press.

Archibald, J. (2008). *Indigenous storywork: Educating the heart, mind, body, and spirit*. Vancouver: UBC Press.

Bazylak, D. (2002). Journeys to success: Perceptions of five female Aboriginal high school graduates. *Canadian Journal of Native Education, 26*(2), 134–151.

Cole, P. (2006). *Coyote and Raven go canoeing: Coming home to the village*. Kingston, ON: McGill-Queen's University Press.

Graveline, F. J. (1998). *Circle works: Transforming Eurocentric consciousness*. Halifax: Fernwood Publishing.

Hart, M. A. (2002). *Seeking Mino-Pimatisiwin: An Aboriginal approach to helping*. Halifax: Fernwood Publishing.

King, T. (2003). *The truth about stories: A Native narrative*. Toronto: Dead Dog Cafe Productions Inc.

Kovach, M. (2005). Emerging from the margins: Indigenous methodologies. In L. Brown & S. Strega, *Research as resistance: Critical, Indigenous, & anti-opppressive approaches* (pp. 19–36). Toronto: Canadian Scholars' Press.

Lavallée, L. F. (2009). Practical application of an Indigenous research framework and two qualitative Indigenous research methods: Sharing circles and Anishnaabe symbol-based reflection. *International Institute for Qualitative Methodology, 8*(1), 21–40.

Penak, N. (2010). *(y)our stories: for an anti-colonial academia* (Master's thesis). York University, Toronto, ON.

Richardson, L. (2004). Writing: A method of inquiry. In S. Nagy Hesse-Biber & P. Leavy (Eds.), *Approaches to qualitative research: A reader on theory and practice* (pp. 473–495). Toronto: Oxford University Press.

Smith, L. T. (1999). *Decolonizing methodologies: Research and Indigenous peoples*. New York: Zed Books.

Wilson, S. (2008). *Research is ceremony: Indigenous research methods*. Halifax: Fernwood Publishing.

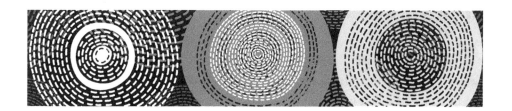

CHAPTER 16

Healing Research: Relationalism in Urban Indigenous Health Knowledge Production[1]

Heather A. Howard

The purpose of this chapter is to highlight the ways in which healing and relationalism intersect in the production of knowledge and practice in social and health services in an urban Indigenous context. First, I will briefly elaborate the multidimensional meanings of "healing research" and relationalism in the context of relevant literatures and particular location of my research. I will then provide some background and describe three specific research projects that involve diabetes education programming developed with and by Indigenous community agencies in Toronto. I have written more extensively about these projects elsewhere (Abel et al., 2011; Howard, 2011a, 2014a, 2014b; Lavallée & Howard, 2011) and refer readers there for details. My goal here is to reflect on the transformation of the personhood of researchers and of participants in these projects undertaken in a contemporary context where we are called upon to enact decolonizing structural change through research. These projects all engaged qualitative Indigenous methodologies emphasizing self-determination and culture-based assets in securing lasting resilience for individuals and the community. They developed and adhered to standards of Indigenous inquiry and collaboration that are responsive to both the sovereign status of Indigenous peoples and the importance of a community-based participatory framework.

Relationalism is grounded in an articulation of the operating system of urban Indigenous community life in which persons, organizations, and social and health programs act in relation to each other through mutual roles and responsibilities and delineate the terms of relevance and respect. Relationalism underscores the qualities of social movement, agency, and power of action in the relational engagement of emergent Indigenous community and research practices, while centring healing and decolonization in the production of knowledge. I am not an Indigenous person; however, my life has been strongly impacted by the high prevalence of diabetes in Indigenous families, and this is for me a personal journey. My reflections on research intertwine my positions in kinship and scholarship relations, and I encourage readers to similarly engage passion and curiosity with the tenacity to bring about justice and well-being through the production and application of knowledge.

HEALING RESEARCH

Health and healing research is the topical focus of this chapter in that it describes examples of the production of knowledge about diabetes by, with, and for urban Indigenous people. However, "healing research" also constitutes a process of inquiry that generates health by nurturing the socio-cultural, spiritual, emotional, and physical well-being of individuals, families, and communities. Grounded in the local pursuit of Indigenous sovereignty in the urban context (Bobiwash, 1997; Heritz, 2013; McCaskell, FitzMaurice, & Cidro, 2011, pp. 330–344), this experiential transformation is enmeshed in the work of decolonization. It is not a "settler move to innocence" or a metaphor for health equity (Tuck & Yang, 2012; see also Dei, 2013). Healing research entails a change in the order of the world (Fanon, 1963, p. 35) of the production of knowledge, unsettling community-based, participatory approaches, and the politics of recognition (Howard, 2016) through Indigenist relationalist epistemologies (Absolon, 2011; Anderson, 2011).

I align my understanding of Indigenism with the ideas of Eve Marie Garroutte (2005), who writes that it requires

> the participation of scholars who find ways to embed themselves in those communities as contributing members, who can look to traditional knowledge from a position of personal commitment, who can profoundly encounter the sacred stories and songs in the language that generated them, who contribute to conversations that the communities themselves understand to be important, and who make themselves answerable to the rules of conduct and inquiry that govern those communities. (p. 195)

Likewise, Shawn Wilson asserts that Indigenist research and pedagogy is not an approach reserved for Indigenous researchers and teachers only, but rather one from which all scholarly inquiry can improve by grounding our intellectual curiosity about the world around us in the question, "How do I behave relationally?" As Wilson emphasizes, "we *are* relationships" with each other but also with the land, the cosmos, and other beings (Adams, Wilson, Heavy Head, & Gordon, 2015, pp. 20–21; Wilson, 2017).

Moving "beyond recovery" (Lavallée & Poole, 2010), Indigenist health scholarship is resituating research as healing and as resistance (Absolon & Willett, 2005; Kovach, 2005; LaRocque, 1996). Through holistic approaches that put colonization at the centre of analyses and Indigenous cultural paradigms into practice, this body of research repositions healing and actively seeks to heal research. A significant paradigm for me comes from Anishinaabe-waki: the fundamental Indigenous context for my research. It is the land of the people of the Great Lakes region with whom I have family ties, where my place of work at Michigan State University is located, and where the cities and vibrant multicultural urban Indigenous communities with whom I live and work (Toronto, of course, as well as Lansing, Milwaukee, Mount Pleasant, Sault Ste. Marie, and Detroit) are situated. Toronto, a Wendat word often interpreted in terms of gathering, is also Wendat land, and Haudensaunee. These nations and confederacies, along with the Anishinaabek, gather, share, and steward this place as they have done for centuries. Anishinaabe-waki thus teaches us about the concept of relations and how one's conduct as a relation is a fundamental principle in this Indigenous research context.

Since Anishinaabemowin is a verb-based language, Anishinaabe-waki can only be articulated as a verb of being (Noodin, 2014), and hence in Anishinaabe-waki, people *are* earth, land, ground, country. As explained further by Lawrence Gross (2014, pp. 84–85), the language (people and land) thus emphasizes processes and events linked together through similar energies. Shared common energy is a vital principle of Anishinaabe knowledge production, and extrapolated beyond the Anishinaabe-waki to converse globally across Indigenous difference, and with non-Indigenous (glossed Western) epistemologies. Such dialogues are conditioned by the dynamics of relationships, and in the Anishinaabe-waki, by what it means to *be a relation*, a concept that encapsulates respect, reciprocity, relevance, and responsibility.

This agentive form of language intimates an Anishinaabe-centric theory of socially fortified metaphor and connected energies. Simpson (2015), for example, explains how the *concept of nation or sovereignty, Kina Gchi Nishnaabeg-ogaming,* embodies good relationships at its core. Elsewhere, Simpson (2013) draws on the Anishinaabe Flood Story, in which Muskrat, although slight and unassuming, was able to dive deeper than any of the other animals who tried, to bring a small pawful of earth to the surface and onto Turtle's back, where the new world was created. Muskrat reminds us of our "responsibility to work together to generate our new vision.... It is about knowing who you are, being responsible for the gifts you have been given, it is about being grounded in a nest of good relations" (p. 46). While these teachings are first intended for Anishinaabek, they are implicitly inclusive for all living in the Anishinaabe-waki. *Kina Gchi Nishnaabeg-ogaming* and being "responsible for your gifts" extends to open identification of a researcher's personal subjective position and recognition of the power dynamics that flow from this position in historical and contemporary relations of dominance, oppression, and resistance. Anishinaabe research theory and practice, as Deborah McGregor and Sylvia Plain (2013) write, have the power to transform Indigenous research as relational approaches become the authoritative knowledge production paradigm (see also Abel, Freeman, Howard, & Shirt, forthcoming; Ross, 2006).

While this chapter is attentive to broader Indigenous research scholarship, my goal is to highlight the enactment of an Anishinaabek paradigm of relationalism in three specific projects from several years of community-led Indigenous peoples' health and service provider research in Toronto. These will illuminate the "quadruple-entendre" of my title reference to healing research in that each example communicates four transformative dimensions of relationalist praxis. On one obvious level, the research is topically about health and healing and consequently anticipates an application of change in the lives of individuals and the community. On a second level, the examples illustrate how research should be a healing experience for participants and their communities, and reflect the principles of responsibility, relevance, respect, and reciprocity. Thirdly, Indigenist relationalist research enacts a transformation of the personhood of researchers, which implicates the fourth dimension I seek to emphasize: the healing of research itself. These latter two aspects often go under-examined and are insufficiently applied by both non-Indigenous and Indigenous researchers, albeit for different reasons.

URBAN INDIGENOUS HEALTH KNOWLEDGE PRODUCTION

As noted earlier, I refer readers to other sources for details about the culturally diverse and vibrant population of Indigenous peoples in Toronto, who form community through a strong, elaborate web of cultural, service, and other organizations and groups (Howard, 2011b; McCaskell et al., 2011; see also

Urban Aboriginal Knowledge Network, 2014). Information on the prevalence and impact of diabetes, virtually unknown among Indigenous peoples until the 1940s and now of epidemic proportion, can be found elsewhere (Lavallée & Howard, 2011, pp. 6–11). A singular important fact is more than two-thirds of Indigenous peoples live in cities and other areas outside reserves (Howard & Lobo, 2013), yet there is a virtual absence of research illuminating the inequities in health determinants of Indigenous peoples in urban areas (Allan & Smylie, 2015; Firestone et al., 2014). This is therefore an important gap my research seeks to address.

"Feeding Our Spirit, Heart, Mind, and Body": Residential School Survivors Reminiscing Circles and Diabetes Education (1999–2003)

In the first project, we recorded the memories of diet and eating behaviours experienced by survivors of residential schools. Negative relationships with food instilled in residential schools were examined as a context for understanding diet-related aspects of diabetes management, and incorporated into a workshop series (Howard, 2014a). A participant in this project summed up the significance of the research in terms of the expectation that "healing" occurs not just in health but in the relationships constructed from colonization, and which can be reconstructed through decolonization. Research was articulated as therapeutic and served as a powerful tool to shift the direction of social memory from one in which only the traumatic things about residential school were recalled, to one in which the creativity and resilience of survivors was highlighted. Survivor and intergenerational participants could think critically about the perception of failure of diabetes management and prevention in terms of structures of racism and colonialism as opposed to victimization and inevitability. The research also opened up possibilities to repair intergenerational relationships broken by the residential school experience, restorative work viewed as key to collective healing within Indigenous communities.

This research project spanned the period when my Anishinaabe partner, Rodney Bobiwash, walked on to the spirit world due to complications from diabetes when he was only 42 years old. This was a great loss still felt not just by me but by the community. Diabetes and a number of other preventable diseases continue to impact every Indigenous family and there is a great deal of suffering that continues. However, there is also tremendous strength, resilience, and ingenuity within the community, and I have dedicated much of my scholarly work to community-based research aimed at understanding how these can be mobilized toward positive change. After Rodney's death, I went away from diabetes research for a while but was compelled back to it in Toronto in 2008. I feared I had been away from it so long that a lot would have changed and perhaps I would be irrelevant. But service providers I approached knew me as a relative with responsibilities to pick up. They were particularly concerned with the growing rates of diabetes among younger and younger people. This needed to be better understood and programs adapted to stymying this phenomena. We formed an oversight committee of Indigenous diabetes educators, a youth program coordinator, and young students at the University of Toronto interested in working on this issue.

Transforming Diabetes in Urban Aboriginal Toronto (2009–2012)

In this second project, the focus was on the involvement of youth from both the Indigenous and academic communities to initiate dialogue on diabetes prevention among youth. I worked with a youth program at a local Indigenous cultural and social service centre and local Indigenous diabetes educators to gather the perspectives of Indigenous persons living with diabetes in Toronto, and of providers of health and social services that impact diabetes prevention and management in this community. This led to the creation of a web-based tool by participants in a 14-week hands-on series of activities that combined diabetes prevention with skill development in multi-media production (Abel et al., 2011; Howard, 2011a, 2014b).

A quote here from one of the participants interviewed for this project expresses several of the dimensions of healing research that resulted in the activities and tools created by and for Indigenous youth. Monica (a pseudonym as she preferred anonymity) was a 46-year-old mother of three. She described how she had been seeing an Elder to help her with recovery from sexual abuse and exploitation she had experienced as a child:

> Healing that needed to be done a long time ago that wasn't.... My diabetes is from so many things.... I think that ultimately everything is spiritual ... your physical manifestation of illnesses is a result of what's going on spiritually. That's how every diabetic should look at it because it's like you're just handing your life over to a doctor or a system that really doesn't give a shit about you. It's very demeaning and belittling for people with diabetes.... I used to be in control, but now they are in control, so I need to take it all back. I'm tired of all this invasion in my body.... Yeah, I need some proper healing.

This is particularly salient in the urban Indigenous health education contexts of my research where diabetes is often defined as a disease of colonization, and Indigenous culture-based approaches to prevention and management both decolonize and lead to the eradication of diabetes. In this respect, then, diabetes is not necessarily seen as a chronic illness, but framed within an epistemology of healing that is expressed through dialectical processes between individual diagnosis and notions of personal and community healing. While healing involves more obvious practices like the utilization of traditional medicines and guidance from Elders, it is also an expression of power and control in the production of knowledge. Healing manifests at various junctures in webs of relationships mediated by the politics of identity and culture.

For researchers interested in health education, then, the establishment and maintenance of trusting relationships that acknowledge historical relations of dominance, oppression, and resistance is essential; however, this is "easy to endorse but difficult to enact" (Ball & Janyst, 2008, p. 39). It is unlikely, but not fully off the mark, that a requirement be written into an ethics protocol that researchers do the work of establishing trust not just for the sake of conducting research but because we make a lifetime commitment to Indigenous justice and self-determination. Research is a relationship that thus entails open identification by researchers, which may be very personal and subjective, but this is already unavoidably so for Indigenous research participants, consultants, or partners. My own situated identities mediate the ways I approach research and circulate in the community (Howard, 2016; Lavallée & Howard, 2011, pp. x, 13).

Kina go Gmushkiimnaan (All Our Medicines), aka Toronto Urban Aboriginal Research Project (2011–2012)

In the third project, the funder's stated goal was to "equip the health care system with tools and appropriate knowledge to develop interventions and more relevant services that will help improve access to diabetes supports for Toronto's Aboriginal community and reduce the number of preventable interventions, and unnecessary emergency room visits." However, led by the Indigenous community health centre, Anishnawabe Health Toronto, the project was repositioned as an expression of self-determination. Research was rearticulated as a healing process, and mainstream methodologies such as concept-mapping, survey, and photovoice were transformed to engage therapeutic qualities informed by Indigenous epistemology (Lavallée & Howard, 2011). Participants in this project described how the sharing process of the research provided "healing energy," as well as practical physical results such as losing weight and keeping up with doctor and specialist visits. The research had a profound impact on the participants, and after the research ended, the sharing and peer support it generated continued as a formalized healing service offered by the community health agency. The project also impacted the researchers considerably. Each member of the team composed reflective essays on how the work transformed them, and these were included at the end of the final report.

The practices followed in this and the two other projects were at once grounded in local community political and cultural contexts, as well as in tandem with structural shifts in Indigenous research ethical practice, encoded over the course of my experience in federal guidelines (Government of Canada, 2010). As health research becomes increasingly healing research, researchers are relationally incorporated as healers. Research is shifting from the "translational" model, in which data collected for Western scientific knowledge production is shifted down to inform behavioural change, to a relational model in which the personhood of researchers is transformed as an integral part of making research relevant, respectful, responsible, and reciprocal. For example, when Ernie Sandy, an Elder hired as the Indigenous Research Integrity Advisor to assure these principles in the Urban Diabetes Research Project, referred to the honour "to be looked upon by the community as a Traditional healer," he includes the entire project and the research team as fulfilling an Indigenous culture-based and decolonizing role that repositioned the research and researchers as healers (Lavallée & Howard, 2011, p. ix).

CONCLUSIONS

In conclusion, researchers engaged in Indigenous health research enter a complex context of historically informed and elaborated processes of knowledge production. In the realm of urban Indigenous diabetes prevention and management education, my role as a person engaged in the production of knowledge intersects and continues to engage with the politics of ethics and practice of community, highlighted in the three projects I have briefly shared here. Indigenous relationalism, in which researchers are drawn into Indigenous structures of community citizenship and authority, transforms the personhood of researchers and moves health research toward broader decolonizing healing purposes. As a result, Indigenous research displaces the hegemonic authority of biomedical trajectories that have colonized diabetes education, and redefines the meanings of health and healing. Beyond the topic of health research, these projects illustrate the goals strived for in Indigenous research and the application of an Indigenist research paradigm by scholars and community participants alike as we engage in practices of healing research.

NOTE

1. This research was supported by grants from the Canadian Institutes of Health Research, and the Ontario Ministry of Health and Long-Term Care. The highest order of gratitude goes to the Indigenous youth, friends, Elders, community organizations, and leaders in Toronto with whom the research described in this article was co-produced.

REFERENCES

Abel, K., Akiwenzie, C., Dutton, J., Howard, H., Keeshig-Martin, J., & Parisee, B. (2011, February 23). *Transformations in diabetes prevention and management by and for Aboriginal peoples in Toronto*. Unpublished paper presented at Fostering Biimaadiziwin National Research Conference on Urban Aboriginal Peoples, Toronto.

Abel, K., Freeman, V., Howard, H., & Shirt, P. (Forthcoming). Indigenous women, memory and power. In M. J. McCallum & S. Hill (Eds.), *Indigenous women's histories*. Winnipeg: University of Manitoba Press.

Absolon, K. E. (2011). *Kaandossiwin: How we come to know*. Halifax: Fernwood Publishing.

Absolon, K., & Willett, C. (2005). Putting ourselves forward: Location in Aboriginal research. In L. Brown & S. Strega (Eds.), *Research as resistance: Critical, Indigenous, and anti-oppressive approaches* (pp. 97–126). Toronto: Canadian Scholars' Press.

Adams, D. H., Wilson, S., Heavy Head, R., & Gordon, E. W. (2015). *Ceremony at a boundary fire: A story of Indigenist knowledge*. Longmont, CO; Sydney, Australia: Sydney eScholarship Repository.

Allan, B., & Smylie, J. (2015). *First Peoples, second class treatment: The role of racism in the health and well-being of Indigenous peoples in Canada*. Toronto: The Wellesley Institute.

Anderson, K. (2011). *Life stages: Memory, teachings, and story medicine*. Winnipeg: University of Manitoba Press.

Ball, J., & Janyst, P. (2008). Enacting research ethics partnerships with Indigenous communities and Canada: "Do it in a good way." *Journal of Empirical Research on Human Research Ethics,, 3*(2), 33–51.

Bobiwash, A. R. (1997). Indigenous urban self-government in Toronto and the politics of self-determination. In F. Sanderson & H. Howard-Bobiwash (Eds.), *The meeting place: Aboriginal life in Toronto* (pp. 84–94). Toronto: Indigenous Canadian Centre of Toronto.

Dei, G. J. S. (2013). Critical perspectives on Indigenous research. *Socialist Studies, 9*(1), 27–38.

Fanon, F. (1963). *The wretched of the earth*. New York: Grove Press.

Firestone, M., Smylie, J., Maracle, S., Siedule, C., De dwa da dehs nye>s Aboriginal Health Access Centre, Métis Nation of Ontario, & O'Campo, P. (2014). Concept mapping:

Application of a community-based methodology in three urban Aboriginal populations. *American Indian Culture and Research Journal, 38*(4), 85–104.

Garroutte, E. M. (2005). Defining "radical indigenism" and creating an American Indian scholarship. In S. Pfohl, A. Van Wagenen, P. Arend, A. Brooks, & D. Leckenby (Eds.), *Culture, power, and history: Studies in critical sociology* (pp. 169–198). Boston: Brill Academic Publishers.

Government of Canada. (2010). *Chapter 9: Research involving the First Nations, Inuit, and Métis peoples of Canada. Tri-council policy statement-2 Canadian federal guidelines on ethical conduct for research involving humans.* Retrieved from www.pre.ethics.gc.ca/eng/policy-politique/initiatives/tcps2-eptc2/chapter9-chapitre9/

Gross, L. (2014). *Anishinaabe ways of knowing and being.* Burlington, VT: Ashgate.

Heritz, J. (2013). Urban Aboriginal self-determination in Toronto. In D. Newhouse, K. FitzMaurice, T. McGuire-Adams, & D. Jetté (Eds.), *Well-being in the urban Aboriginal community: Fostering biimaadiziwin* (pp. 43–54). Toronto: Thompson Educational Publishers.

Howard, H. A. (2011a, May 11). Healing processes in urban Aboriginal experience of type-2 diabetes. Unpublished paper presented at the annual meeting of the Canadian Anthropology Society, Fredericton, NB.

Howard, H. (2011b). The friendship centre: Native people and the organization of community in cities. In H. A. Howard & C. Proulx (Eds.), *Aboriginal Peoples in Canadian cities: Transformations and continuities* (pp. 87–107). Waterloo, ON: Wilfrid Laurier University Press.

Howard, H. A. (2014a). Politics of culture in urban Indigenous community-based diabetes programs. *American Indian Culture and Research Journal, 38*(1), 49–72.

Howard, H. A. (2014b). Canadian residential schools and urban Indigenous knowledge production about diabetes. *Medical Anthropology: Cross-Cultural Studies in Health and Illness, 33*(6), 529–545.

Howard, H. A. (2016). Co-producing community and knowledge: Indigenous epistemologies of engaged, ethical research in an urban context. *Engaged Scholar Journal of Community-Engaged Research, Teaching, and Learning, 1*(3), 205–224.

Howard, H., & Lobo, S. (2013). Indigenous peoples' rural to urban migration within the United States and Canada. *Encyclopaedia of global human migration.* New York: Wiley-Blackwell.

Kovach, M. (2005). Emerging from the margins: Indigenous methodologies. In L. Brown & S. Strega (Eds.), *Research as resistance: Critical, Indigenous, and anti-oppressive approaches* (pp. 19–36). Toronto: Canadian Scholars' Press.

LaRocque, E. (1996). The colonization of a Native woman scholar. In C. Miller & P. Chuchryk (Eds.), *Women of the First Nations: Power, wisdom, strength* (pp. 11–18). Winnipeg: University of Manitoba Press.

Lavallée, L. F., & Howard, H. A. (2011). *Urban Aboriginal diabetes research project report.* Toronto: Anishnawbe Health Toronto.

Lavallée, L. F., & Poole, J. M. (2010). Beyond recovery: Colonization, health and healing for Indigenous people in Canada. *International Journal of Mental Health and Addiction, 8*(2), 271–281.

McCaskell, D., FitzMaurice, K., & Cidro, J. (2011). *TARP: Toronto Aboriginal research project final report*. Toronto: Toronto Aboriginal Support Services Council.

McGregor, D., & Plain, S. (2013). Anishinaabe research theory and practice: Place-based research. In A. Ojiig Corbiere, M. A. Naokwegijig Corbiere, D. McGregor, & C. Migwans (Eds.), *Anishinaabewin niiwin: Four rising winds* (pp. 93–114). M'Chigeeng, ON: Ojibwe Cultural Foundation.

Noodin, M. (2014). *Bawaajimo: A dialect of dreams in Anishinaabe language and literature*. East Lansing, MI: Michigan State University Press.

Ross, R. (2006). *Returning to the teachings: Exploring Aboriginal justice*. Toronto: Penguin.

Simpson, L. B. (2013). Dancing on the back of our Turtle: Revitalizing Nishnaabeg intellectual traditions. In A. Ojiig Corbiere, M. A. Naokwegijig Corbiere, D. McGregor, & C. Migwans (Eds.), *Anishinaabewin niiwin: Four rising winds* (pp. 41–54). M'Chigeeng: Ojibwe Cultural Foundation.

Simpson, L. B. (2015). The place where we all live and work together. In S. N. Teeves, A. Smith, & M. H. Raheja (Eds.), *Native studies keywords* (pp. 18–24). Tucson: University of Arizona Press.

Tuck, Y., & Yang, K. W. (2012). Decolonization is not a metaphor. *Decolonization: Indigeneity, Education & Society, 1*(1), 1–40.

Urban Aboriginal Knowledge Network. (2014). *Research map*. Retrieved from www.uakn.org (accessed March 17, 2017)

Wilson, S. (2017, February 15). Michigan State University Global Engagement Speaker Series presentation.

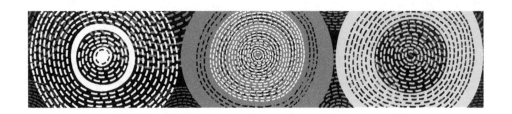

CHAPTER 17

Researching within Relations of Violence:
Witnessing as Methodology

Sarah Hunt

When I was seven years old, I took part in my first potlatch. There, I learned to dance among my aunties, cousins, and other relations as we moved around the fire together. Even though I asked over and over again for someone to show me the dance steps before the ceremonies began, I was told to watch my aunties in front of me and follow their lead. At that potlatch, and every one I have attended since then, I have been part of a shared practice of learning, teaching, creating, and continuing Kwagiulth – and broader Kwakwaka'wakw[1] – cultural and socio-legal relations. In the *gukwdzi*,[2] or bighouse, knowledge is created collectively, and its continuation relies on each person fulfilling a specific role. To learn the dances, I have had to be watchful, present, and attentive of my movements in relation to everyone else around me.

During each potlatch, payment is given to witnesses for their role in validating what they have seen. Their role of "communal acknowledgement" (Nicolson, 2013, p. 235), too, is dependent on them being present, watchful, and involved. Witnessing is part of a larger system of maintaining an oral culture, and just as the role of a dancer or singer is embodied, so too is the role of the witness. Sitting in the smoke-saturated bighouse, hearing the songs being sung in Kwak'wala, watching the movement of the dancers as they sweep across the dirt floor, witnessing requires being fully engaged. Witnesses can then be called upon to verify what has taken place, particularly if any act of business or ceremony is questioned in the future. In this way, cultural and political knowledge is kept alive in the bodies, spirits, and minds of everyone who makes up the potlatch, including witnesses.

It is in this context of active, embodied, relational systems of knowledge that my understanding of witnessing methodology has emerged. In the chapter that follows, I will share how I have developed principles of witnessing in my research on contemporary realities of violence in Indigenous communities, families, and lives. Throughout this chapter, I am concerned with a number of tensions inherent to navigating contemporary realities of knowledge production. It is often assumed that Indigenous people can take up any Indigenous issues as "insiders," yet we are at risk of replicating dominant power relations if we are not attuned to the responsibilities that come with wielding power as researchers. This is particularly true for those of us who work with members of our communities who experience most acutely the risk and vulnerability produced by ongoing colonization – those whose lives and voices are most frequently dismissed, silenced, or ignored. I have thus developed witnessing as a methodology to keep myself grounded in principles and ethics emerging within Kwagiulth systems of knowledge as I navigate these complex power relations. While witnessing has been discussed by several Indigenous scholars in relation to various aspects of Indigenous pedagogies, here I will develop aspects of witnessing methodology specific to research on gendered colonial violence. As I will show, witnessing in the context of settler colonialism comes with a set of responsibilities specific to the network of relationships within which researchers live and work. In the sections that follow, I will discuss how I have self-reflexively examined my own power as a researcher concerned with violence perpetrated against our relations who trade or sell sex in communities across British Columbia (BC), and will suggest some foundational elements of what it means to act as witness in this context.

THE RELATIONAL RESPONSIBILITIES OF WITNESSING

My work on violence is rooted within the particular history of colonial relations that shapes the network of communities in which I live and work. In the mid-1990s when I was an undergraduate student, a relative close to my age took her own life. I didn't know her very well but was close with her mother, and since her death, I have come to know her story and have been driven by the silence left in her passing. Before she died, she spoke out about abuse she suffered at the hands of a powerful man in the community. But there would be no justice for her, no legal recognition of the abuse, and limited community recognition that she had spoken out. In the days following her death, I observed that other women were speaking with one another, revealing that they knew others who had been abused by the same man. Since that time, over 20 years ago, no legal action has been launched against the offender. But the conversations among women continue. After she died, I thought of the countless youth and adults – particularly women, girls, and Two-Spirit[3] people – who have spoken out, and asked myself: who will be the voice for her silence? I felt a responsibility, as witness to her life and her death, to recount what I had seen and heard in order to ensure that she would not be forgotten. This is what it means to be a witness – stepping up to validate what you have observed when an important act is denied or forgotten.

Acting as witness responds to postcolonial theorist Gayatri Spivak's (1988) call to attend to the ways in which subaltern voices are written out of the archive, or the ways that discourse disciplines what can be heard. In other words, being a witness means sometimes creating new language, new stories, new avenues for validating those voices that are most at risk of being erased. In concluding that "the subaltern cannot speak" (p. 87), Spivak was not arguing that the subaltern woman literally had no voice, but that "if there was no valid institutional background for resistance, it could not be recognized" (Spivak, 2010, p. 228). Witnessing, then, might be understood as a methodology in which we are obligated, through a set of relational responsibilities, to ensure frameworks of representation allow for the lives that we have witnessed to be made visible.

This obligation is particularly vital in the context of normalized violence against Indigenous girls, women, and Two-Spirit people, as it has been argued that sexual violence is a central tool of colonialism, marking "the evisceration of Indigenous nations" (Million, 2013, p. 7). Michi Saagiig Nishnaabeg scholar and artist Leanne Betasamosake Simpson (2014) explains that it is not enough to recognize that violence against Indigenous women and Two-Spirit people occurs, but we must see that "it is intrinsically tied to the creation and settlement of Canada. Gender violence is central to our on-going dispossession, occupation and erasure and Indigenous families and communities have always resisted this" (n.p.). When my relative died, I felt compelled to "help" women, girls, and Two-Spirit people who had survived violence by validating their experiences through research. However, since that time, my understanding of the power dynamics of academia and processes of knowledge production have caused me to refine how I understand my role as witness to colonial violence. In part, this has been informed by seeing how research itself can work to entrench positions of power, which is so often the case with (and indeed, the goal of) academic work. While violence against Indigenous women, and the stereotypes that justify and normalize this violence, impact us all, researchers are often in positions of power or privilege relative to the people they write about. Further, as a Two-Spirit scholar, I am acutely aware of the way Two-Spirit and transgender people's experiences are often overlooked entirely in scholarly research, pushing me to further interrogate my own power in representing what comprises gendered and sexual violence.

The ethics of navigating institutional power became particularly salient as my work on violence led me to focus on issues of sex work after volunteering in the late 1990s with organizations in the Downtown Eastside of Vancouver that were advocating for police action in the unsolved murders and disappearances of women (including transgender women[4]) in that community. People who trade or sell sex are particularly targeted for interpersonal violence, and, as I have come to understand, they are also subject to the violence of erasure that is accomplished both in mainstream socio-legal relations and within anti-violence work itself. Over the years since I began working on this issue, violence targeted at sex workers has gained national and international attention through the conviction of numerous serial killers, the most well known being the murderer targeting women in the Downtown Eastside of Vancouver. Despite this increased visibility, however, the voices of Indigenous people who trade or sell sex are still being silenced. Their voices are absent from many community organizations who purport to work on their behalf, as well as from national Indigenous organizations and both scholarly and community anti-violence publications.[5] Anishinaabe activist and writer Naomi Sayers explains, even when justice is sought on their behalf, "the justice system presents this idea that Indigenous sex workers are deserving of the violence they experience and they should at minimum expect the violence they experience" (Sayers, 2016, n.p.). Only after sex workers have died, disappeared, or stopped working in the sex trade are they brought into remembrance or dialogue.

As I have become more attuned to these processes of silencing, I have seen the sensationalism that accompanies increased recognition of these issues. Academic writing and research on sex work can have a "shock and awe" (Clark, 2016, p. 1) quality that creates a buzz around this work, particularly when funders, including government agencies, decide to make this a topic of concern. As an academic talking about sex work, I am treated as brave, honourable, and edgy. Yet, at the same time, the people with whom I work in solidarity remain framed through a marginalized subject position. Violence against Indigenous girls, women, and Two-Spirit people is often treated with detached acceptance, not only in dominant society but in Indigenous communities as well. Working in diverse communities across BC, I have heard young people talk about violence as a part of daily life. For too many of our relations, violence is expected. In some of our communities, everyone knows abuse is rampant and nobody does anything, or when they do, they are silenced. In this way, talking about violence as an academic can at times feel pointless when it does nothing but advance a researcher's career, while material realities of violence remain unchanged.

These dynamics inherent to work on colonial violence, and specifically violence against people who trade or sell sex, raise important questions about witnessing. How can I step up to my obligation as a witness, recalling the realities facing our relations engaged in sex work, who are most at risk of being silenced? At the same time, how can I live up to obligations to centre the agency, voice, and self-determination of the people whose stories I seek to validate, given the institutional constraints in which I work? (See Shelly Johnson's chapter in this book for more discussion of these constraints.) And how can I remain ethically committed to the ongoing relations in which I live and work, while being called to respond to the guidelines of university ethics boards, the pressure to publish in peer-reviewed journals, and other institutional demands?

As my work unfolded over the years, I felt ever-uncomfortable with the power dynamics of trying to represent the voices of youth, women, and Two-Spirit people whose stories were most in need of retelling. Concerned with the normalization of pervasive gendered, racialized, and sexual violence against sex workers, I have remained committed to talking about the criminalization and stigmatization of people who trade or sell sex, as well as the means through which some lives – particularly those of women, transgender, and Two-Spirit people – become treated as disposable. However, I am careful in how I go about this work, given the power differences between myself and my relations in the sex trade (Hunt, 2013). As I have developed the culturally specific qualities of witnessing, it has become clear that my ego and my academic career need to be secondary as I take up this work. Indeed, the duty of a witness is not to tell their own story, but to recall what they have experienced from their own perspective in order to validate someone else's actions, rights, or stories. We must be cautious, then, of research that only serves to further validate academics who write about people who trade or sell sex, while not changing the material realities or marginalized subject positions of sex workers themselves.

In this chapter, I draw on a range of projects I have been involved with since 2001, both as a collaborator and as a solo investigator working in community, government, and institutional contexts to address violence (Clark, Bognar, & Hunt, 2002; Clark & Hunt, 2011; Hunt, 2006, 2010, 2013, 2015, 2016). My work has involved interviewing youth about experiences of exploitation and abuse, as well as adults engaged in trading or selling sex, and service providers working with youth and families in Indigenous communities and rural and urban areas across BC. I have worked in many of these same communities as an educator and support person to assist in building capacity and developing programming to address violence, particularly in contexts of ongoing intergenerational abuse. Further, when invited to do so, I take up a solidarity and support role in diverse contexts in which sex workers' voices are at the centre. As with Angela Mashford-Pringle, who describes her research in this volume, my work is dependent upon the development of a strong network of relationships within and across the communities in which I work, as well as with the people with whom I have col-laborated, laughed, shared food, and mourned. Rather than being situated solely in a professional relationship, stories are often shared within the intimate spaces of people's homes, jails and detention centres, community centres, among family and friends, and in times of emotional and physical vulnerability.

It is within this context of working simultaneously as an advocate, educa-tor, researcher, and, at times, relative, that I have become a witness to stories of violence. I have been witness to rape, sexual abuse, intergenerational violence, murder, child apprehension, and abuse of power in communities across BC and beyond. Across diverse geographic contexts, the stories often bear a striking similarity to one another, as does the response (or lack thereof) from police and other state officials. My work is driven by the responsibilities that are inherent to witnessing these realities of violence, as well as their systemic normalization and the continuation of violence in the daily lives of Indigenous girls, women, and Two-Spirit people. Rather than drawing from generalized knowledge about violence, my role as a witness emerges within the individual stories that have been shared with me, and the quiet moments I spent in close relation to women and Two-Spirit people of all ages who have experienced some form of violence. Many of the people who became colleagues in this work – often Indigenous women who are speaking out and taking action to address violence in their community – have also shared their own histories of violence and abuse. Like sitting in the *gukwdzi*, watching my relatives dance and sing around the fire, my knowledge of these issues has been embodied, emotional, relational, and life changing. Where academia attempts to train us, as Indigenous researchers, to capture knowledge in a particular way within the confines of an individual research project or paper, this kind of relational learning defies false divisions between academic knowledge and other aspects of our being. It is instead part of a lifelong journey of taking up my duties and responsibilities as Kwagiulth.

As Smith (1999) explains, Western concepts of time and space include a perception of distance that is fundamental to rational and impersonal systems of power and governance. In a research context, distance implies a neutrality and objectivity. However, Indigenous research, and specifically here, witnessing methodologies, insist on working in an intimate network of relations – an epistemologically distinct approach from this Western distancing.

Emerging from the development of this knowledge-in-relation, when I say I was witness to many stories of violence, I don't mean merely that I heard, saw, or observed these stories. As I have come to understand witnessing methodology, I view these experiences as shared with me in the context of reciprocal relationships within an Indigenous cultural framework. Therefore, in witnessing the stories, I am obligated to ensure they are not denied, ignored, or silenced. Further, if I see them being denied, it is my responsibility to recall both the truths of what I have witnessed and the ways in which their erasure is being accomplished. In my own teachings, the responsibility of witnesses to recall what they have seen is particularly important when something is called into question, or is at risk of being lost. I consider this to be the case with the normalization of violence against Indigenous girls, women, and Two-Spirit people, especially those engaged in trading or selling sex, who so often are silenced, ignored, or stigmatized when they share their experiences or advocate for change.

FOUNDATIONS OF KWAGIULTH WITNESSING METHODOLOGY

Although emerging from systems of knowledge creation, law, and governance used within diverse Indigenous oral cultures, witnessing has only recently been explored as a methodology in Indigenous scholarship. Witnessing has been discussed in such fields as Indigenous storytelling (Iseke, 2011; Thomas, 2005), child and youth care (Kovach, Thomas, Montgomery, Green, & Brown, 2007), family therapy (Richardson, 2012), and the Indigenous paradigm of insurgent research, which explicitly orients knowledge creation toward Indigenous people and worldviews (Gaudry, 2011). In each use of witnessing, Indigenous scholars draw their understanding of this approach from the cultural and institutional contexts in which they live and work. While my framework of witnessing shares similarities with some of these scholars, it is distinguished by its specific roots in Kwakwaka'wakw potlatch traditions and adaptation to account for the power dynamics of research on contemporary social issues. The principles and foundations of witnessing methodology that I discuss would therefore not necessarily be applicable to working with traditional knowledge, as my concerns emerge within the power relations of colonial violence.

Witnessing entails creating knowledge not as solitary actors (Iseke, 2011), but within a network of reciprocal relations (Nicolson, 2013). As Kovach and colleagues (2007) write, "we chose to notice – witness – the work being done within Aboriginal child welfare from our own stories" (p. 116). Yet Kwagiulth witnessing methodology differs from Kovach and colleagues (2007) in that it is inherently bound up in relations based in responsibility. I therefore experience witnessing not as a choice, but a duty, to recall something that is being questioned. Since the death of my cousin, I have felt bound by my role to bear witness to the violence she experienced within the larger network of community responsibilities that ensures the continuation of Indigenous knowledge, law, and culture.

Witnessing can involve acts of remembrance as "a powerful form of recovery from a colonial past" (Iseke, 2011, p. 312) in which we reinterpret the past in order to understand the present. Kwagiulth witnessing methodology uses a different temporal frame, as stories are recalled and enacted to make them alive in the present rather than focusing on their past use. Potlatches are about re-embodying a set of stories, ancestral claims, and "familial connection to the past, the present and the future" (Nicolson, 2013, p. 235) that make us who we are, acknowledging and respecting an ongoing, active set of responsibilities. Thus, recalling an event or story as a witness is about bringing those responsibilities into the present through confirming their power.

Witnessing has been used in the recreation of collective spaces where the contemporary experiences of Indigenous people are validated through ceremony. For example, Richardson (2012) calls on witnesses as part of marking important life events in family therapy using cultural witnessing groups. Here, witnesses are invited to be part of a contained therapeutic space, where they do not question or have conversation with those in therapy, but listen, observe, and remember. Witnessing here occurs within a set of reciprocal relations, as "there is an implicit future commitment to social justice and social change in return for the gift of the learning" (p. 72). Similarly, Kovach and colleagues (2007) use witnessing as a framework for examining resistance and resilience in Indigenous child welfare through the creation of a feast to honour community members who support local child welfare programs. Here, witnesses are called upon to "hold the memory and retell the activities of the event. The act of witnessing is an integral part of the oral tradition as it is the means by which a public accounting of the work being done will live on in the oral history of the community" (p. 98).

Given the stigma surrounding sex work and the internalized shame experienced by many victims of violence, this need for collective validation resonates with my understanding of witnessing. Witnessing can become central to undoing the harms of colonialism by humanizing, valuing, and loving sex workers, among other members of our communities and families, through acknowledging their stories, experiences, and perspectives. This collective process strengthens relationships and communication, working against the dehumanizing effects of categorizing Indigenous women and Two-Spirit people in colonial terms which have reduced us to being singularly defined by our victimization.

As I have described, my approach to witnessing emerges from my experiential understanding of the Kwakwa̱ka̱'wkaw potlatch system, in which witnesses are paid to remember what has transpired during the business of a potlatch. Building on witnessing testimony or stories (Iseke, 2011), Kwagiulth witnessing is not only a mental exercise but also includes the spiritual and physical experiences involved in a shared community process. Bearing witness in the context of a potlatch involves all the senses, not only the passing on of a story, facts, or information. Witnessing is about the affective, embodied, spiritual role that emerges from sitting among your relations in the context of a sacred place of cultural business. Thus, my role as a witness is dependent on the quality of relations within which I do my research on issues of gendered and racialized violence. This is often in tension with the values underlying academic knowledge creation within universities, their ethics processes, need for solo authorship, and rigid boundaries around the roles of researchers and research subjects. While academic institutions have begun making changes in how they engage with Indigenous communities, they predominantly continue to value and to measure knowledge that is expressed in peer-reviewed research papers and books rather than oral dialogue or shared processes that are spiritual in nature. These discrepancies create barriers for Indigenous academics like myself, who move between and across institutional and community sites of knowledge creation and validation.

As I have shown, research by Indigenous people about marginalized members of our communities can serve to reproduce colonial power dynamics in which the voices of Indigenous people must be translated into colonial language in order to be considered valid in the context of Western knowledge systems. Gaudry (2011) writes that "this translation also reinforces the colonialist assertion that Indigenous knowledges are not valuable in their own right or defensible on their own terms" (p. 115). Similarly, the voices and experiential knowledge of sex workers are often filtered through the frameworks of academics in order to provide legitimacy or validation.

While this may be true whenever we work across differences in social location, Indigenous researchers should be particularly attuned to these dynamics when bringing the stories of people who trade or sell sex into mainstream discourse. For example, with the emergence of broad recognition of the high levels of violence against residents of the Downtown Eastside, including the long-term presence of a serial killer, scholars, activists, and Indigenous organizations have sought to represent the lives of residents (especially women) in that neighbourhood. In these processes, I fear the voices of Indigenous sex workers themselves are being obscured, particularly as anti–sex work prohibitionist agendas have driven much of the work on this issue. This absence of voice has far-reaching implications, as discourse and theoretical frameworks on related issues of gendered colonial violence, sex work laws, and international human rights have been developed in the absence of these women whose quality of life is most immediately at stake. In this way, assuming others can act as "witness" on the basis that they are Indigenous women also works to silence the women whose lives we hope to witness in the first place. Power differences lie at the heart of this conundrum, as Indigenous scholars and others who have access to the tools to write about violence often centre their own perspectives, while those they seek to speak for continue to be denied the legitimacy and practical tools with which to represent themselves. Witnessing must be accompanied by actions to create welcoming spaces in which sex workers can speak for themselves and have their voices heard. As Sayers (n.d.) states, "invite sex workers to the table[,] especially sex workers who come from various backgrounds and life experiences. I say this to both sex work and non-sex work related organizations. If you are not talking about race, class, colonialism, indigenous issues, violence, or migrant rights, then the spaces you are creating are not safe to have those discussions. Start creating safe spaces to have these discussions" (n.p.). Thus, in my work, I strive to advocate for centring of the voices of sex workers while not speaking for experiences that are not my own. I have found it more in line with the ethics of witnessing to name the gaps in experience between sex workers and academics (while not assuming these are mutually exclusive groups), as well as power dynamics between these groups, rather than replicate the power dynamics inherent in academic knowledge construction by naturalizing it. In my experience, it has been more powerful to make visible my inability to resolve these power differences than to pretend I can ever fully address them.

Just as I was called to act as a witness in the death of my cousin, my obligation here is to recall the way risk, marginalization, and silencing of sex workers is produced systemically and interpersonally in our communities rather than to speak *for* anyone. In the potlatch, witnesses are called upon to collectively recall what happened, in order to reinforce, rather than replace, the individual whose political or ceremonial act was in question. As witnesses, then, we should not seek to become the voice of those whose stories are denied, but should work to make them more viable, more visible, more audible, and more deeply felt, on their own terms.

BALANCING INSTITUTIONAL DEMANDS

While Indigenous researchers may or may not be working cross-culturally when conducting research within Indigenous communities, I have illustrated here that we are nevertheless always faced with power differences and dynamics. These gaps are particularly pressing when our work is concerned with representing marginalized members of our communities, or any of those whose lives are at a greater distance from the halls of the universities and other institutions in which knowledge becomes valued and validated within dominant discourse. As Smith (1999) cautions, Western research is imbued with an attitude and spirit that at some level assumes ownership of the entire world. In other words, it assumes academics can have access to any kind of knowledge they choose from their distanced, objective, and superior position to Indigenous and other communities in which they work. As Indigenous researchers, we must be cautious not to approach our work with this same air of superiority. We must also be cautious of entering into the kinds of divisive debates that Western academia disciplines its students into. These kinds of debates only work to divide our communities and shut us off from hearing one another across our diverse experiences.

As I have outlined, Kwagiulth witnessing methodology is not akin to simply hearing, seeing, or being told something. Witnessing here is taking up a specific role in maintaining the integrity of Indigenous knowledge and community. It entails not just an obligation to recall but to act, given that violence continues to be normalized. It requires us to bear witness to the ontological violence of forgetting certain stories, as much as to the stories themselves. As academics, witnessing assumes working across a range of intersecting power relations that we must navigate as we determine how best to live up to our responsibilities. As witnesses, our role is not to take up the voice or story we have witnessed, nor to change the story, but to ensure the truths of the acts can be comprehended, honoured, and validated. Colonial violence is normalized through ongoing denial, silencing, and ontological gaps that make it impossible for Indigenous women's and Two-Spirit people's stories to be heard on their own terms, particularly individuals like those trading or selling sex who are often viewed through a dehumanizing lens of stigmatization. Thus, the need for us to step up as witnesses remains as vital as ever.

At its heart, witnessing is about the persistent reintegration of voices of people who have been pushed to the periphery in processes of knowledge creation. It is about making visible and audible those members of our communities who are being silenced, forgotten, erased, and spoken over. Witnessing emerges within the context of dominant gendered and racialized power relations in which the voices of academically trained researchers are privileged over those of other members of Indigenous communities. For this reason, we must be attuned to the responsibilities that come with our multiply situated identities (within universities, our own communities, other Indigenous communities, and so on). As my work unfolds across these spaces, I find processes of self-reflection vital to fulfilling my responsibilities as witness. In recalling the truths of violence around me, I am called to de-centre my own voice by acknowledging that my story is not the one most urgently in need of validation. Indeed, once realities of violence are no longer at risk of being denied, and once sex workers are called to speak for themselves and their lives are no longer at risk on a daily basis, the work of witnesses such as myself will necessarily change. Within this network of relational responsibilities, witnessing can thus adapt and transform as we aid one another in the healing work of decolonization.

ACKNOWLEDGEMENTS

I would like to acknowledge that this chapter was written during my doctoral studies at Simon Fraser University with financial support from the Social Sciences and Humanities Research Council (SSHRC).

NOTES

1. The Kwagiulth are part of the Kwakwaka'wakw nation, or Kwak'wala-speaking people, who live on the northern part of what is now known as Vancouver Island, in British Columbia. The Kwagiulth people of Tsaxis, or what is now called Fort Rupert, are registered with the federal government as the Kwakiutl band.

2. See Nicolson (2013) for more on the meaning of *gukwdzi* within Kwakwaka'wakw culture.

3. Two-Spirit is a term used by Indigenous people whose gender and/or sexual identity fall outside the Western gender binary and/or who identify as gay, lesbian, bisexual, queer, transgender, or otherwise non-heterosexual. It is also used to connote a specific cultural or spiritual role. In this way, Two-Spirit is used to describe diverse identities and cultural roles which cannot be captured in the English language.

4. For more, see Hunt (2015).

5. For a statement on these dynamics written by Indigenous people with experience trading or selling sex, see the Indigenous Sex Sovereignty Collective at http://indigenoussexsovereignty.tumblr.com

REFERENCES

Clark, N. (2016). Shock and awe: Trauma as the new colonial frontier. *Humanities, 5*(1), 1–14.

Clark, N., Bognar, C., & Hunt, S. (2002). Commercial sexual exploitation: Innovative ideas for working with children and youth. New Westminster: Justice Institute of British Columbia.

Clark, N., & Hunt, S. (2011). Navigating the crossroads: Exploring rural young women's experiences of health using an intersectional framework. In O. Hankivsky (Ed.), *Health inequities in Canada: Intersectional frameworks and practices* (pp. 131–146). Vancouver: University of British Columbia Press.

Gaudry, A. J. P. (2011). Insurgent research. *Wicazo Sa Review,* (Spring) 113–136.

Hunt, S. (2006). Violence in the lives of sexually exploited youth and adult sex trade workers in BC. New Westminster: Justice Institute of British Columbia.

Hunt, S. (2010). Colonial roots, contemporary risk factors: A cautionary exploration of the domestic trafficking of Aboriginal women and girls in British Columbia, Canada. *Alliance News, 33*, 27–31.

Hunt, S. (2013). Decolonizing sex work: Developing an intersectional Indigenous approach. In E. van der Meulen, E. M. Durisin, & V. Love (Eds.), *Selling sex: Canadian sex workers, academics, and advocates in dialogue* (pp. 82–100). Vancouver: University of British Columbia Press.

Hunt, S. (2015). Embodying self-determination: Beyond the gender binary. In M. Greenwood, C. Reading, & S. de Leeuw (Eds.), *Determinants of Indigenous peoples' health in Canada* (pp. 104–119). Toronto: Canadian Scholars' Press.

Hunt, S. (2016). Representing colonial violence: Trafficking, sex work, and the violence of law. *Atlantis, 35*(2), 25–39.

Iseke, J. M. (2011). Indigenous digital storytelling in video: Witnessing with Alma Desjarlais. *Equity and excellence in education, 44*(3), 311–329.

Kovach, M., Thomas, R., Montgomery, M., Green, J., & Brown, L. (2007). Witnessing wild woman: Resistance and resilience in Aboriginal child welfare. In L. T. Foster & B. Wharf (Eds.), *People, politics, and child welfare in British Columbia* (pp. 97–116). Vancouver: University of British Columbia Press.

Million, D. (2013). *Therapeutic nations: Healing in an age of Indigenous human rights.* Tucson: University of Arizona Press.

Nicolson, M. (2013). *Yaxa Uk̓wine̓, yaxa Gukw, dłuwida Awiňagwis: "The Body, the House, and the Land": The conceptualization of Space in Kwakwaka'wakw language and culture* (Doctoral dissertation). Retrieved from University of Victoria.

Richardson, C. (2012). Witnessing life transitions with ritual and ceremony in family therapy: Three examples from a Metis therapist. *Journal of Systemic Therapies, 31*(3), 68–78.

Sayers, N. (2016). #CindyGladue & unchanging truths: Whose story matters. [Blog post]. Retrieved from https://kwetoday.com/2016/09/10/6366/

Sayers, N. (n.d.). Naomi Sayers at Maggie's. *NSWP: Global Network of Sex Work Projects*. [Blog post]. Retrieved from www.nswp.org/swleader/naomi-sayers

Simpson, L. B. (2014). Not murdered, not missing: Rebelling against colonial gender violence. [Personal website]. Retrieved from www.leannesimpson.ca/writings/not-murdered-not-missing-rebelling-against-colonial-gender-violence

Smith, L. T. (1999). *Decolonizing methodologies: Research and indigenous peoples.* New York: Zed Books.

Spivak, G. C. (1988). Can the subaltern speak? In C. Nelson & L. Grossbert (Eds.), *Marxism and the interpretation of culture* (pp. 271–313). Urbana: University of Illinois Press.

Spivak, G. C. (2010). Response: Looking back, looking forward. In R. C. Morris (Ed.), *Can the subaltern speak?: Reflections on the history of an idea* (pp. 227–236). New York: Columbia University Press.

Thomas, R. A. Qwul'sih'yah'maht. (2005). Honoring the oral traditions of my ancestors through storytelling. In L. Brown & S. Strega (Eds.), *Research as resistance: Critical, Indigenous, and anti-oppressive approaches* (pp. 237–254). Toronto: Canadian Scholars' Press.

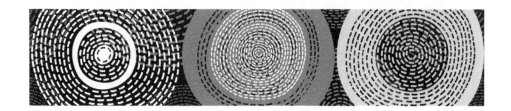

EPILOGUE

Indigenous Research: Future Directions

Deborah McGregor

Indigenous research is often viewed as a novel and recently conceived research paradigm with the aim of explicitly and actively supporting the self-determination goals of Indigenous peoples (National Aboriginal Health Organization [NAHO], 2005). While it may be "new" to academia, engaging in Indigenous inquiry, along with its resultant knowledge production and mobilization, is actually far from new. Indigenous societies, like any autonomous and sovereign nations, required regularly updated knowledge to meet existing and emerging challenges. Indigenous peoples have thus been seeking knowledge to support their existence as peoples and nations for millennia (Absolon & Willett, 2004; Cardinal, 2001; Castellano, 2000; Colorado, 1988). As Cardinal (2001) observes, "Indigenous research methods and methodologies are as old as our ceremonies and our nations. They are with us and have always been with us. Our Indigenous cultures are rich with ways of gathering, discovering and uncovering knowledge" (p. 182).

As the various contributors to this volume have elaborated upon, Indigenous nations framed their research through their own ontological and epistemological foundations and methods (Kermoal & Altamirano-Jiménez, 2016). Traditionally, protocols for seeking knowledge were about *establishing relationships*, which were not "only integrated with the natural environment around us and with our living relations, but also with the timeless past and culture of our ancestors" (Colorado, 1988, p. 55).

In such a research paradigm, one *shares* knowledge and remains account-able to that knowledge, rather than extracts or owns it. Knowledge is grounded in the richly diverse intellectual traditions of Indigenous peoples. One is not required to "separate" oneself from the research, but to approach it holistically, with the intellectual, emotional, spiritual, and physical aspects of the whole self (Absolon, 2010).

Over time, Indigenous modes of inquiry have been undermined, deemed inferior (if recognized at all), and even erased through imperial and colonial practices. As Linda T. Smith (1999) outlines in her seminal work, *Decolonizing Methodologies*, the Western scholarship that has emerged was necessary to ratio-nalize and justify the continued subjugation of Indigenous people and the taking of their lands and lives. Others have noted the trajectory research has taken since the beginning of the *terra nullius* era through to contemporary Indigenous research (Saunders, West, & Usher, 2010; Wilson, 2008). The historical course of research involving Indigenous peoples from the time of European contact begins with the Western-defined concept of *terra nullius*, in which Indigenous peoples, "if recognized at all, were viewed as part of the flora and fauna, their lands awaiting European exploitation" (Wilson, 2008, p. 48). This phase dehumanized Indigenous peoples and provided the colonizers with the necessary justification for acquiring Indigenous territories. In the early "Aboriginal research phase" that followed, Indigenous peoples continued to be "researched" and Indigenous voices remained silenced. This was the norm until more recent eras that coincided with the rise of Indigenous rights movements and Indigenous peoples asserting their voice, directly challenging Euro-Western colonial and imperial research paradigms.

Subsequent to this has been the recent "decolonizing research" phase, which has initiated the development of a distinct Indigenous research paradigm aimed at serving the interests of Indigenous peoples. In Canada, this paradigm shift can be seen as having occurred in public policy when the language used to describe Aboriginal research undertakings switched from research "on" to research "with" Indigenous peoples (McNaughton & Rock, 2004). This small but significant change in usage signalled the advent of research approaches that require Indigenous involvement from the conception of research to its conclu-sion. An example of this new policy direction can be found in the Tri-Council Policy Statement, *Ethical Conduct for Research Involving Humans* (TCPS 2), which devotes an entire chapter to ethical research involving First Nations, Inuit, and Métis Peoples of Canada (TCPS 2, 2014). This policy does not *require* collaboration or participatory approaches per se, but encourages them through the use of research agreements and ethical considerations. Moreover, it states that research that does not reflect the notion of working "with" Indigenous peoples may be called into question on ethical grounds. To support the implementation of ethical research, the TCPS 2 offers courses on various elements of the policy, including research involving Indigenous peoples. Module 9, "Research Involving the First Nations, Inuit and Métis Peoples of Canada," is offered online and includes a training webinar. Some research institutions have made these courses a mandatory requirement before undertaking research. Carleton University offers a week-long summer institute focused on Indigenous research to further advance the theory and practice of Indigenous research. The TCPS 2 espouses an approach to research with Indigenous peoples that does not exclude non-Indigenous researchers from engaging in such research, and promoting, or some in cases privileging, Indigenous modes of inquiry is not without its risks. However, engaging in research involving Indigenous peoples without sufficient grounding in Indigenous research methods may result in appropriation of Indigenous culture and other negative outcomes regardless of whether the researchers are Indigenous or non-Indigenous. The primary approach for addressing such concerns lies in the application of high ethical standards. As Keely Ten Fingers (2005) writes:

> In order to move beyond the legacy of colonialism and its effects on meaningful research, indigenous methodologies must be utilized in all research involving indigenous peoples and our territories. This means indigenous peoples must be involved throughout the research process, from design to data collection and analysis to dissemination. (p. 62)

Perhaps paradoxically, there is much research that concerns itself primarily with Indigenous peoples, but which may not be regarded as "Indigenous research" per se. Indigenous research paradigms are distinct, as explained in the introduction to this volume. There are indeed various schools of thought within the Indigenous research paradigm that speak to the conduct of such research (see McGregor & Plain, 2014, for schools of thought within Indigenous research).

In this volume, there are contributions by both Indigenous and non-Indigenous scholars. Both have employed research methods and practices supported by the community(ies) involved, thus striving to ensure the research benefits reflect community goals and needs. Certainly, there are those who will feel this approach may still leave Indigenous communities and peoples vulnerable to exploitive research and appropriation. Abenaki scholar Lori Lambert observes that if one is not from the community or nation one is engaged with in research (Indigenous or non-), one can never truly understand the stories being told (Lambert, 2014, p. 30). Researchers in this sense must be open, honest, and transparent about their own limitations, with themselves and with the communities with which they are working. In this light, the researcher's goal is not to tell the community's story, but to empower the community to tell their own story, on their own terms, for their own purpose. Self-determination in research means that, ultimately, communities will determine who they participate with in research, and what methods will be employed (Lambert, 2014).

Despite such progress over the past few decades, wherein Indigenous scholars have advanced Indigenous research theories and methodologies based on their own cultural foundations, full acceptance of Indigenous research paradigms within the academy remains elusive (Kovach, 2015). Contributors to this volume reveal that one of the barriers to such acceptance is that "unlearning" of Western modes of research seems to be a prerequisite for embracing Indigenous research. In Canada, research exists within the broader context of a society that has not yet come to terms with its relationship with Indigenous peoples. The Canadian government–sponsored Truth and Reconciliation Commission (TRC) revealed that Canada remains very much a systemically colonial and racist society in its dealings with Indigenous peoples. Academic institutions remain the primary producers of knowledge in this country, which, while logical in a sense, also serves to perpetuate the status quo, given the "academy's role in the ongoing colonization of Indigenous peoples. The academy has much invested in maintaining control over who defines knowledge, who has access to knowledge and who produces knowledge" (Mihesuah & Wilson, 2004, p. 5). As a way of bringing about change, Indigenous scholars are now advocating for space within academia for a vastly increased Indigenous scholarship, lest the academy remain a source of epistemic violence and domination (Kuokkanen, 2007; Mihesuah & Wilson, 2004). In other words, more than research methodologies require decolonizing: the academy and the institutions that support it also require explicit and purposeful decolonization processes (this includes funding bodies, identification of research priorities, etc.).

Without a doubt, many challenges remain to be addressed, but as our contributors have shared in their stories, it is possible to find expression of Indigenous research in the academy through collaborative or community-based and community-driven research efforts.

INDIGENOUS RESEARCH TO SUPPORT SELF-DETERMINATION AND SOVEREIGNTY

Indigenous peoples have not been idle, simply waiting for decolonizing processes to take place and the full recognition of Indigenous scholarship in the academy and elsewhere to occur. They have begun to set the parameters and ground rules for what respectful and ethical research will look like by developing their own research agendas, policies, processes, and ethical guidelines. Castellano (2004) further adds that "fundamental to the exercise of self-determination is the right of peoples to construct knowledge in accordance with self-determinated [*sic*] definitions of what is real and what is valuable" (p. 102). Noteworthy in this regard are the OCAP (Ownership, Control, Access and Protection) principles, developed by the Steering Committee of the First Nations Regional Longitudinal Health Survey (First Nations Centre, 2007), which state that "OCAP is inextricably linked to the agenda of self-determination for Indigenous people because it serves to guide the re-appropriation of the research activities and outcomes in research pertaining to Indigenous people and it provides the context within which the development of culturally relevant, Indigenous worldview based research paradigms are developing" (Ermine, Sinclair, & Jeffery, 2004, pp. 34–35).

The principles are "an expression of self-determination in research designed to ensure Indigenous sovereignty over their own knowledge" (NAHO, 2005, p. i). Indigenous peoples are developing their own research governance processes to ensure that research serves their goals and aspirations. In situations where the necessary Indigenous research protocols do not exist, researchers seek to establish governance bodies (through advisory committees, etc.) to guide and provide oversight for research. Several contributors to this volume (L. McGregor; Manitowabi & Marr; Howard) have offered examples of this type of governance in various contexts. Of note is the Manitoulin Anishinabek Research Review Committee, coordinated by Noojmowin Teg Health Centre. The review committee governs health research on Manitoulin Island through the Guidelines for Ethical Aboriginal Research (GEAR), an excellent example of community-based ethical guidelines that support Indigenous research self-determination. As Indigenous peoples continue to move toward self-determination and sovereignty, research that supports and realizes these goals becomes increasingly important, through OCAP and other principles (e.g., "data sovereignty" [Kukutai & Taylor, 2016]).

The application of the *United Nations Declaration on the Rights of Indigenous Peoples* (UNDRIP) in research contexts has yet to be fully explored, although it can be argued that any research involving Indigenous peoples should support Indigenous peoples' pursuit of self-determination. Article 31(1) of UNDRIP has specific implications for Indigenous research:

> Indigenous peoples have the right to maintain, control, protect, and develop their cultural heritage, traditional knowledge and traditional cultural expressions, as well as the manifestations of their sciences, technologies and cultures, including human and genetic resources, seeds, medicines, knowledge of the properties of fauna and flora, oral traditions, literatures, designs, sports, traditional games and visual and performing arts. They also have the right to maintain, control, protect and develop their intellectual property over such cultural heritage, traditional knowledge, and traditional cultural expressions. (United Nations General Assembly [UNGA], 2007)

Indigenous conceptual or theoretical research approaches and methods are fundamentally based on Indigenous worldviews (Absolon & Willett, 2004; Cardinal, 2001; Castellano, 2004; Pelletier Sinclair, 2003; Steinhauer, 2002; Wilson, 2003). This means that there will be a diversity of theoretical frameworks, methods, and applications that will reflect the variety of Indigenous traditions in Canada. Moreover, such theories, frameworks, and methods are not static: they are continually being revised and continue to evolve (Pelletier Sinclair, 2003, p. 132).

The contributors to this volume attest to the diversity of Indigenous research methods, relating a variety of ways that research has been undertaken under the guidance of Indigenous collaborators and partners. Such approaches include: ceremony (e.g., bundles, song, and dance), mentoring and apprenticeship by Elders/Traditional Knowledge holders, experience, reflection/meditation, dreams, sharing circles, talking circles, healing circles, storytelling/storywork, invoking Tricksters (Nanbusho, Raven), treaty, drums, and witnessing.

STORY AS A RELATIONAL PROCESS

In addition to being highly diverse in nature, Indigenous research is inherently contextual: the inherent "relationality" of it means that one cannot simply import theory, ways of knowing, and/or methods from one context to another, however defined (geographically, politically, culturally, etc.). In this volume, modifications of the "conversational method" (described by Kovach, 2010) and "collaborative storytelling" (Bishop, 1999) were employed as researchers conveyed the complexities and nuances involved in engaging with Indigenous research. These methods acknowledge "that the researcher is positioned as a research participant within the process of storying and restorying that creates the narrative" (Bishop, 1999, p. 6). Kovach writes that Indigenous scholars and those engaged in Indigenous research methodologies "have, to a certain extent, engaged in conversation on paradigm as form" (2010, p. 41).

Engaging in such approaches to research transforms both the research and the researcher, as the learning becomes embodied. Bishop (1999) describes this as follows: "To be involved somatically means to be involved bodily, that is physically, ethically, morally and spiritually, not just in one's capacity as a 'researcher' concerned with methodology" (p. 22). Indigenous research is not conducive to a "check box" approach, with items to be ticked off as each criterion is met. Indigenous research requires constant reflection, taking a step back, and "unlearning" in some cases. Moreover, Indigenous (and Indigenist) research is not neutral. Its aims are to support Indigenous goals and aspirations, and these aims may indeed be at odds with other interests.

This volume represents a form of *collective storytelling*, wherein contributors choose to convey their lives and experiences in research (in singing, drumming, dancing, praying, reflection, etc.). In this way, the contributors have been "researching themselves" as research "participants" to develop a "mutually constructed story created out of the lived experiences of the research participants" (Bishop, 1999, p. 2). Stories embedded in experience facilitate diversities in meaning, rather than one dominant story to be heard.

In its form and content, this volume also challenges the way in which research is communicated, creating a form of modern-day sharing circle which could help reshape the practice of academic writing. Contributors have demonstrated the divergent ways Indigenous research may be presented: some choose more creative expressions (poetry, prayer), while others adopt a conventional written approach, and others still opt for a narrative "in-between" style (Danard, 2015; Graveline, 1998; Suchet-Pearson, Wright, Lloyd, Burarrwanga, & Hodge, 2013; Wilson, 2008). The central purpose in communicating research is to empower and give "voice" (Lambert, 2014). Indigenous modes of expressing "knowing" vary just as Indigenous research practices are diverse. There is no one way to tell your research story. Abenaki researcher Lori Lambert (2014) describes the key distinction between this process and Western approaches as being in "the relationship that the research has with the story, how it is told and how the knower and researcher interpret the story" (p. 2). How the research story is told depends on who you are writing for and why you are doing so, among other considerations. There is no requirement for a formula or standardized way of writing about Indigenous research scholarship. We accepted Vanessa Watts' (2013) caution against the limitations that binaries create (Indigenous vs. academic styles of writing), and against presupposing what Indigenous research should look like, compared to what actually emerges in practice. We respected and included reflective narrative, conversation storywork, creative expression, and more conventional ways of expressing "how" research is conducted to emphasize that there is no universal Indigenous doctrine for writing about research.

The researchers' stories in this volume reveal truths about the place of Indigenous scholarship in the academy as they constantly navigate and negotiate between different realms, expectations, and obligations (Hunt, 2014; Kovach, 2010). These stories may make some readers uncomfortable, as contributors speak to their own discomfort and unease while seeking to frame research in context and place. The broader research environment is not always welcoming or accommodating to Indigenous research approaches. Indigenous scholars continue to experience instances of micro-aggression and lateral violence, as well as epistemic dominance and violence (Kuokkanen, 2007). Academic imperialism persists; systemic and institutional change are required to address the deeply entrenched colonial nature of the academy, and to ensure a safe and productive space for Indigenous scholars and scholarship. Decolonizing the academy should not fall solely on the shoulders of Indigenous researchers/scholars; the academy itself must assume responsibility for its violence.

One of the great values of the stories in this volume lies in their service as reminders that the forging of new relationships requires work and energy; it does not just happen.

INDIGENOUS WAYS OF KNOWING IN RESEARCH

Various approaches have emerged in broader research agendas to account for Indigenous ways of knowing. As one example, the Institute of Aboriginal Peoples' Health, a division of the Canadian Institutes of Health Research (CIHR), has adopted, as a central component of its Five-Year Strategic Plan for Aboriginal Peoples' Health, an Aboriginal health research program based on the Mi'kmaw principles of Etuaptmumk, or "Two-Eyed Seeing," influenced by the work and teachings of Mi'kmaw Elder and knowledge holder Albert Marshall. In this knowledge sharing model, Indigenous and Western perspectives collaborate to address health concerns in Indigenous communities. The *Five-Year Strategic Plan 2014–18*, in its "Strategic Direction #2: Transforming First Nations, Inuit and Métis Health through Indigenous Ways of Knowing," describes Two-Eyed Seeing as follows:

> Two-Eyed Seeing in research speaks to community-relevant and community-based health research that engages First Nations, Inuit and Métis Peoples in the design, implementation, analysis, data management and sharing of the research. Among its strengths, Two-Eyed Seeing in research enables the direct benefits of cultural connection, safety and control for First Nations, Inuit and Métis Peoples, achieved through ensuring involvement and a balance between "western" and Indigenous research methodologies, analysis and subsequent treatments. (CIHR, 2015, p. 26)

The concept of negotiating between different knowledge systems is gaining increasing attention, and the Two-Eyed Seeing approach itself has been taken up by a number of researchers in health fields (Hall et al., 2015; Lavalée & Lévesque, 2013). The concept recognizes that, in advocating and advancing Indigenous research approaches, paradigms, and methodologies, Indigenous peoples are not rejecting Western knowledge systems outright, but are seeking equitable consideration and application of both systems when and where appropriate. The Two-Eyed Seeing approach in fact incorporates aspects of Western systems, but does so on Indigenous terms and in ways that will serve Indigenous peoples. There are other Indigenous research models that also give due consideration to Indigenous and non-Indigenous ways of knowing, yet remain situated within Indigenous theoretical frameworks (Latulippe, 2015).

Another emerging notion with respect to the collaboration of Indigenous and non-Indigenous research methods involves the concept of research as being bound by treaty relationships. As discussed by Luby and colleagues (this volume), scholars can (and should) be seen as treaty beneficiaries, and as such they have obligations and responsibilities to uphold their part of the treaty relationship. This treaty approach may be employed to outline the roles and responsibilities of researchers to people, place, and land, and can thus be a powerful embodiment of relational accountability. The treaty approach is also elaborated upon by Latulippe (2015). Latulippe outlines the broader historical and political context in which her research is situated, identifying treaties as covenants between sovereign nations that come to bear in research endeavours, and yet which are often not considered. A research undertaking's philosophical orientation based on a relevant treaty(ies) "offers rich grounds from which to ethically approach place, people and politics" (Latulippe, 2015, p. 7). As pointed out in the introduction to this volume, Indigenous research methodologies and practices reflect such relationships to place, people, and history. Understanding the history of how we got to where we are forms an important aspect of understanding "relational accountability."

In other words, outside of specific research relationships themselves, there exist other obligations and responsibilities, and these should be brought to bear on research practices. Instead, research agendas have often been used to undermine Indigenous nations by exploiting and expropriating Indigenous peoples, lands, and identities. The treaty approach described by Luby and colleagues (this volume) and Latulippe (2015) recognizes the existence of a colonial history that continues to mar the relationship between Indigenous and non-Indigenous peoples. This broader, contextual relationship should not be ignored in research. Luby and colleagues utilize Treaty #3 (a numbered treaty in northwestern Ontario), while Latulippe draws on the Kaswentha, or Two-Row Wampum (a pre-colonial treaty), to facilitate understanding of knowledge exchange, generation, and transmission from an Indigenous perspective, and provide recognition of the fact that Indigenous and non-Indigenous partners in research, and those affected by the research, are now sharing the same space. Latulippe further reflects on the Kaswentha, stating, "Applied methodologically, separate rows [of beads in the Two-Row Wampum treaty belt] signify epistemic difference, while the shared space – the bridging rows of peace, friendship, and respect – mirrors the conceptual space shared by Indigenous and Western qualitative research methodologies" (Latulippe, 2015, p. 9).

As the basis for a research approach and methodology, treaties seek to highlight and bridge epistemic differences through mutual understanding and reciprocal obligation. Treaties also espouse a common vision and explicitly aim to reconcile differences through a covenant of relationships that requires ongoing renewal. We can also learn from the treaty approach that relationships, like research, are not intended to be "one-shot deals"; they require long-term and ongoing engagement, and they recognize that no relationship is perfect and that hard work is required to facilitate "good relations."

THE CONTEMPORARY INDIGENOUS RESEARCH LANDSCAPE

The "research landscape," internationally and within Canada, has shifted. Emergent Indigenous research approaches continue to shape broader research initiatives. In Canada, CIHR's (2015) adoption of the Two-Eyed Seeing approach is one such accomplishment. Internationally, UNDRIP (UNGA, 2007) offers a path forward for Indigenous self-determination. More work is required to determine how Indigenous research might support the realization of the goals of UNDRIP. In order to meet the obligations set out in UNDRIP, research directions, priorities, and processes will have to change considerably. For example, the requirement of Free, Prior and Informed Consent has recently become a noteworthy research topic as many struggle to determine what these principles actually mean in practice. UNDRIP nevertheless offers promising directions in research, particularly in light of the fact that until recently most research *on* Indigenous peoples was designed in such a way as to achieve the opposite of many of UNDRIP's stated purposes.

The TRC released its final report in 2015 and set out a path forward via 94 recommendations, or "Calls to Action" (CTAs). To support the goals of reconciliation, CTA 65 states that:

> We call upon the federal government, through the Social Sciences and Humanities Research Council, and in collaboration with Aboriginal peoples, post-secondary institutions and educators, and the National Centre for Truth and Reconciliation and its partner institutions, to establish a national research program with multi-year funding to advance understanding of reconciliation. (p. 8)

CTA 65 thus calls on research funding bodies to develop a research program to support the broader societal goals of reconciliation. These goals have not remained uncontested, with some scholars indicating that "reconciliation," as coined by the state, supports the goals of the state rather than the aspirations of Indigenous peoples. Ideally, however, the research directions that emerge in response to CTA 65 will result in robust dialogue around what is actually meant by "reconciliation" research and what other goals may be relevant to Indigenous peoples in this area. In fact, the CTAs, taken holistically, call for transformative change in education at all levels, including a set of principles to help guide such a process. Space must be made for different research strategies to achieve self-determination and sovereignty, beyond what may be possible in reconciliation research alone. Métis scholar Adam Gaudry (2015) asserts that the concept of "resurgence" or "insurgent" research that prioritizes Indigenous goals and aspirations is an essential strategy in research involving Indigenous peoples and communities. As the cadre of Indigenous scholars continues to grow, Indigenous scholarship will gain ground in the academy (and elsewhere). We will see in the coming years more diverse research practices and forms of producing and presenting knowledge.

CONCLUSION: CREATING ETHICAL SPACE IN RESEARCH

Working effectively in the realm of Indigenous research, while simultaneously operating within the current socio-political context of Indigenous renewal, revitalization, and resurgence, requires a keen understanding of the goals and aspirations of Indigenous peoples. Responding to the diverse yet transformative forms Indigenous research can take, this volume set out to create ethical space for dialogue on how research relationships can be negotiated and *lived*. Relationships require work, commitment, energy, communication, and continuous engagement; they do not happen just because we want them to. The importance of creating ethical space for discussion moves the consideration of Indigenous research forward, rather than perpetuating the binary notion of "Western" versus "Indigenous" research. The binary model, while helpful and necessary in distinguishing the key differences between the two systems, contributes little in terms of addressing the rapidly shifting contextual landscape that calls for innovative approaches to Indigenous research practice. Creating this ethical space, then, is necessary when two distinct societies are required to engage with each other. Ethical space is described by Ermine and colleagues (2004) as

> the idea of two spheres of knowledge, two cultures, each distinct from one another in multiple forms, [which] needs to be envisioned since the distance also inspires an abstract, nebulous space of possibility. The in-between space, relative to cultures, is created by the recognition of the separate realities of histories, knowledge traditions, values, interests, and social, economic and political imperatives. The positioning of these two entities, divided by the void and flux of their cultural distance, and in a manner that they are poised to encounter each other, produces a significant and interesting notion that has relevance in research thought. (p. 20)

As outlined by various contributors to this volume, such ethical space recognizes ongoing tensions, but also creates the space within which critical dialogue, reflection, and change may take place. Ermine and colleagues contend that ethical space is a process that unfolds as dialogue continues. Our intention in this volume has been to generate substance and depth to ongoing dialogue on how to animate mutually beneficial relations in research. It is hoped that the ethical space for such dialogue will expand into a wide variety of research areas as the work toward a sustainable future for all of us intensifies.

REFERENCES

Absolon, K. (2010). Indigenous wholistic theory: A knowledge set for practice. *The First Peoples Child and Family Review, 5*(2), 74–87.

Absolon, K., & Willett, C. (2004). Aboriginal research: Berry picking and hunting in the 21st century. *The First Peoples Child and Family Review, 1*(1), 5–17.

Bishop, R. (1999). *Collaborative storytelling: Meeting Indigenous peoples' desires for self-determination in research* (Rep.). (ERIC Document Reproduction Service No. ED467396). Retrieved from http://files.eric.ed.gov/fulltext/ED467396.pdf

Canadian Institutes of Health Research (CIHR). (2015). *Strategic Plan 2014–2018*. CIHR Institute of Aboriginal Peoples' Health. Ottawa, ON. Retrieved from www.cihr-irsc.gc.ca/e/documents/iaph_strat_plan_2014-18-en.pdf

Cardinal, L. (2001). What Is an Indigenous perspective? *Canadian Journal of Native Education, 25*(2), 180–182.

Castellano, M. B. (2000). Updating Aboriginal traditions of knowledge. In G. J. Sefa Dei, B. L. Hall, & D. G. Rosenberg (Eds.), *Indigenous knowledges in global contexts: Multiple readings of our world* (pp. 21–36). Toronto: OISE/UT book published in association with University of Toronto Press.

Castellano, M. B. (2004). Ethics of Aboriginal research. *Journal of Aboriginal Health, 1*(1), 98–114. Retrieved from www.nvit.ca/docs/ethics%20of%20aboriginal%20research.pdf

Colorado, P. (1988). Bridging Native and Western science. *Convergence, 21*(2/3), 49–64.

Danard, D. (2015). Be the water. *Canadian Woman Studies/les cahiers de la femme, 30*(2/3), 115–120.

Ermine, W., Sinclair, R., & Jeffery, B. (2004). The ethics of research involving Indigenous peoples. *Report of the Indigenous Peoples' Health Research Centre to the Interagency Advisory Panel on Research Ethics Indigenous Peoples' Health Research Centre*. Saskatoon: Indigenous Peoples' Health Research Centre. Retrieved from www.pre.ethics.gc.ca/pdf/eng/tcps2-2014/TCPS_2_FINAL_Web.pdf

First Nations Centre. (2007). *OCAP: Ownership, control, access and possession*. Sanctioned by the First Nations Information Governance Committee, Assembly of First Nations. Ottawa: National Aboriginal Health Organization.

Gaudry, A. (2015). Researching the resurgence: Insurgent research and community-engaged methodologies in 21st-century academic inquiry. In L. Brown & S. Strega (Eds.), *Research as resistance: Revisiting critical, Indigenous, and anti-oppressive approaches* (pp. 257–263). Toronto: Canadian Scholars' Press.

Graveline, F. J. (1998). *Circle works: Transforming Eurocentric consciousness*. Halifax: Fernwood Publishing.

Hall, L., Dell, C., Fornssler, B., Hopkins, C., Mushquash, C., & Rowan, M. (2015). Research as cultural renewal: Applying Two-Eyed Seeing in a research project about cultural interventions in First Nations addictions treatment. *International Indigenous Policy Journal, 6*(2). Retrieved from http://ir.lib.uwo.ca/iipj/vol6/iss2/4. DOI: 10.18584/iipj.2015.6.2.4

Hunt, S. (2014). Ontologies of Indigeneity: The politics of embodying a concept. *Cultural Geographies, 21*(1), 27–32. DOI: 10.1177/1474474013500226.

Kermoal, N. J., & Altamirano-Jiménez, I. (2016). *Living on the land: Indigenous women's understanding of place*. Edmonton: AU Press.

Kovach, M. (2010). Conversation method in Indigenous research. *The First Peoples Child and Family Review, 5*(1), 40–48.

Kovach, M. (2015). Emerging from the margins: Indigenous methodologies. In L. Brown & S. Strega (Eds.), *Research as resistance: Revisiting critical, Indigenous, and anti-oppressive approaches* (pp. 43–64). Toronto: Canadian Scholars' Press.

Kuokkanen, R. (2007). *Reshaping the university: Responsibility, Indigenous epistemes, and the logic of the gift*. Vancouver: UBC Press.

Kututai, T., & Taylor, J. (2016). *Indigenous data sovereignty: Toward an agenda*. Acton, Australia: Australian National University Press.

Lambert, L. (2014). *Research for Indigenous survival: Indigenous research methodologies in the behavioral sciences*. Pablo, MT: Salish Kootenai College Press.

Latulippe, N. (2015). Bridging parallel rows: Epistemic difference and relational accountability in cross-cultural research. *The International Indigenous Policy Journal, 6*(2). Retrieved from http://ir.lib.uwo.ca/iipj/vol6/iss2/7. DOI: 10.18584/iipj.2015.6.2.7

Lavalée, L., & Lévesque, L. (2013). Two-eyed seeing: Physical activity, sport, and recreation promotion in Indigenous communities. In J. Forsyth & A. R. Giles (Eds.), *Aboriginal peoples & sport in Canada* (pp. 206–228). Vancouver: UBC Press.

McGregor, D., & Plain, S. (2014). Anishinabe research theory and practice: Place based research. In A. Corbiere, M. A. Corbiere, D. McGregor, & C. Migwans (Eds.), *Anishinaabewin niiwin: Four rising winds* (pp. 93–114). M'Chigeeng, ON: Ojibwe Cultural Foundation.

McNaughton, C., & Rock, D. (2004). *Opportunities in Aboriginal research: Results of the SSHRC dialogue on research with Aboriginal peoples*. Ottawa: Social Science and Humanities Research Council of Canada.

Mihesuah, D., & Wilson, A. (2004). *Indigenizing the academy: Transforming scholarship and empowering communities*. Lincoln: University of Nebraska Press.

National Aboriginal Health Organization (NAHO). (2005). *Ownership, control, access, and possession (OCAP) or self-determination applied to research: A critical analysis of contemporary First Nations research and some options for First Nations communities*. First Nations Centre. Ottawa: NAHO. Retrieved from www.naho.ca/documents/fnc/english/FNC_OCAPCriticalAnalysis.pdf

Pelletier Sinclair, R. (2003). Indigenous research in social work: The challenge of operationalizing worldview. *Native Social Work Journal, 5,* 117–135.

Saunders, V., West, R., & Usher, K. (2010). Applying Indigenist research methodologies in health research: Experiences in the borderlands. *The Australian Journal of Indigenous Education, 39*(S1), 1–7. DOI:10.1375/s1326011100001071

Smith, L. T. (1999). *Decolonizing methodologies: Research and Indigenous peoples.* New York: Zed Books.

Steinhauer, E. (2002). Thoughts on an Indigenous research methodology. *Canadian Journal of Native Education, 26*(2), 69–81.

Suchet-Pearson, S., Wright, S., Lloyd, K., Burarrwanga, L., & Hodge, P. (2013). Footprints across the beach: Beyond researcher-centered methodologies. In J. Johnson & S. Larsen (Eds.), *A deeper sense of place: Stories and journeys of Indigenous-academic collaboration* (pp. 21–40). Corvallis: Oregon State University Press.

Ten Fingers, K. (2005). Rejecting, revitalizing, and reclaiming: First Nations work to set the direction of research and policy development. *Canadian Journal of Public Health, 96*(1), 61–63.

Tri-Council Policy Statement 2 (TCPS 2). (2014). *Canadian Institutes of Health Research, Natural Sciences and Engineering Research Council of Canada, and Social Sciences and Humanities Research Council of Canada, Tri-council policy statement: Ethical conduct for research involving humans.* Ottawa: Government of Canada.

Truth and Reconciliation Commission (TRC). (2015). *Truth and Reconciliation Canada: Calls to action.* Winnipeg: TRC. Retrieved from www.trc.ca.

United Nation General Assembly (UNGA). 2007. *United Nations Declaration on the Rights of Indigenous Peoples.* Geneva: Office of the Commission for Human Rights. Retrieved from http://daccess-dds-ny.un.org/doc/UNDOC/GEN/N06/512/07/PDF/N0651207.pdf

Watts, V. (2013). Indigenous Place-Thought and agency amongst humans and non-humans (First Woman and Sky Woman go on a European world tour!). *Decolonization: Indigeneity, Education & Society, 2*(1), 20–34.

Wilson, S. (2003). Toward an Indigenous research paradigm in Canada and Australia. *Canadian Journal of Native Education, 27*(2), 161–178.

Wilson, S. (2008). *Research is ceremony: Indigenous research methods.* Halifax: Fernwood Publishing.

INDIGENOUS RESEARCH RESOURCES

ETHICAL GUIDELINES AND GUIDANCE

Turtle Island: Canada – General

Assembly of First Nations: Environmental Stewardship Unit. (2009, March). *Ethics in First Nations research.* Retrieved from www.afn.ca/uploads/files/rp-research_ethics_final.pdf

Canadian Archaeological Association. (2017). Statement of principles for ethical conduct pertaining to Aboriginal Peoples. Retrieved from www.canadianarchaeology.com/caa/about/ethics/statement-principles-ethical-conduct-pertaining-aboriginal-peoples

Canadian Institutes of Health Research, Government of Canada. (2013). *CIHR guidelines for health research involving Aboriginal people (2007–2010).* Retrieved from www.cihr-irsc.gc.ca/e/29134.html

Castellano, M. B. (2004). Ethics of Aboriginal research. *Journal of Aboriginal Health, 1*(1), 98–114. Retrieved from www.nvit.ca/docs/ethics%20of%20aboriginal%20research.pdf

Ermine, W., Jeffrey, B., & Sinclair, R. (2004). *The ethics of research involving Indigenous peoples: Report of the Indigenous Peoples' Health Research Centre to the Interagency Advisory Panel on Research Ethics.* Saskatoon, SK: Indigenous Peoples' Health Research Centre. Retrieved from iphrc.ca/pub/documents/ethics_review_iphrc.pdf

Ermine, W., Sinclair, R., & Browne, M. (2005, March). *Kwayask itôtamowin: Indigenous research ethics report of the Indigenous Peoples' Health Research Centre to the Institute Of Aboriginal Peoples' Health and the Canadian Institutes of Health Research.* Indigenous Peoples' Health Research Centre. Retrieved from iphrc.ca/pub/documents/IPHRC_ACADRE_Ethics_Report_final.pdf

Estey, E., Smylie, J., & Macaulay, A. (2009, June). *Aboriginal knowledge translation: Understanding and respecting the distinct needs of Aboriginal communities in research.* Retrieved from www.cihr-irsc.gc.ca/e/41392.html

First Nations Centre. (2007). *Considerations and templates for ethical research practices.* Ottawa: National Aboriginal Health Organization. Retrieved from www.naho.ca/documents/fnc/english/FNC_ConsiderationsandTemplatesInformationResource.pdf

First Nations Information Governance Centre – Code of Research Ethics. (2010). First Nations Information Governance Centre. Retrieved from fnigc.ca/sites/default/files/docs/06._fnigc_rhs_code_of_ethics_2011_-final_3.pdf

Gehl, L. (n.d.). *Ally bill of responsibilities.* Retrieved from www.lynngehl.com/uploads/5/0/0/4/5004954/ally_bill_of_responsibilities_poster.pdf

Grenier, L. (1998). *Working with Indigenous knowledge: A guide for researchers.* Ottawa: International Development Research Centre. Retrieved from www.idrc.ca/en/book/working-indigenous-knowledge-guide-researchers

Gros-Louis Mchungh, N., Gentelet, K., & Basile, S. (Eds.). (2015). *Toolbox of research principles in an Aboriginal context. FNQLHSSC, CRDP, UQAT, and DIALOG network.* Retrieved from www.cssspnql.com/docs/default-source/centre-de-documentation/toolbox_research_principles_aboriginal_context_eng16C3D3AF4B658E221564CE39.pdf?sfvrsn=2

Kenny, C. (2004). *A holistic framework for Aboriginal policy research.* Ottawa: Status of Women Canada. Retrieved from www.publications.gc.ca/collections/Collection/SW21-114-2004E.pdf

Kishk Anaquot Health Research. (2007). *Checklist of characteristics of collaborative research relationships with Indigenous partners.* Canadian Coalition for Global Health Research. Retrieved from www.ccghr.ca/wp-content/uploads/2013/04/PartnershipChecklist_GIHR_2007_en.pdf

Manitoba First Nations Education Centre. (2014). *Guidelines for ethical research in Manitoba First Nations: Principles, practices and templates.* Manitoba First Nations Education Centre Inc. Retrieved from http://mfnerc.org/wp-content/uploads/2014/03/Ethical-Research-in-Manitoba-First-Nations.pdf

Martin-Hill, D., & Soucy, D. (n.d.). *Ganono'se'n e yo'gwilode': Ethical guidelines for Aboriginal research - Elders and Healers roundtable. A report by the Indigenous health research development program to the interagency advisory panel on research ethics.* Retrieved from www.ihrdp.ca/media/docs/lega4e54fe5d0c807-ethical%20guidelines%20for%20aboriginal%20research.pdf

National Aboriginal Health Organization. (2009, August 11). *Interviewing Elders guidelines.* Retrieved from www.naho.ca/media-centre/interviewing-elders-guidelines/

Royal Commission on Aboriginal Peoples. (1996). *Appendix E: Ethical guidelines for research* (report of the Royal Commission on Aboriginal Peoples). Ottawa: Government of Canada. Retrieved from www.collectionscanada.gc.ca/webarchives/20071124125036/http://www.ainc-inac.gc.ca/ch/rcap/sg/ska5e_e.html

MULTI-MEDIA:

Decolonizing methodologies: Can relational research be a basis for renewed relationships? (2016). Concordia University, Montreal, QC. Retrieved from www.youtube.com/watch?v=rqYiCrZKm0M

Different Knowings. (2011). *Willie Ermine: What is ethical space?* Retrieved from www.youtube.com/watch?v=85PPdUE8Mb0

Peters, W. Use of Indigenous/Indigenist research methodologies. Retrieved from https://www.youtube.com/watch?v=gSNpm9cYb2o

Tuhiwai Smith, L., & Tuck, E. Decolonizing methodologies. Retrieved from www.youtube.com/watch?v=rIZXQC27tvg

Urban Populations

Dingwall, C., de Leeuw, S., Evans, M., Krause, M., Burkitt, B. W., & West, V. (2016, March). *Urban Aboriginal research charter template: A guide to building research relationships. Developing urban Aboriginal protocols.* Retrieved from icer.ok.ubc.ca/__shared/assets/UA_Research_Charter_Template54352.pdf

National Association of Friendship Centres. (2011). *Fostering Biimaadiziwin: A national research conference on urban Aboriginal peoples: Organizational summary of promising practices, lessons learned and the journey forward.* Retrieved from uakn.org/wp-content/uploads/2014/08/Summary-of-Best-Practices-Lessons-Learned-and-the-Journey-Forward.pdf

Ontario Federation of Indian Friendship Centres. (2012). *USAI: Research framework.* Retrieved from ofifc.org/sites/default/files/docs/USAI%20Research%20Framework%20Booklet%202012.pdf

Urban Aboriginal Knowledge Network (UAKN). (2014, October). *Guiding ethical principles.* Retrieved from uakn.org/wp-content/uploads/2014/10/Guiding-Ethical-Principles_Final_2015_10_22.pdf

Women and Gender

Basile, S. (2012, June). *Guidelines for research with Aboriginal women. Quebec Native women.* Retrieved from www.faq-qnw.org/wp-content/uploads/2016/11/QNW-2012-Guidelines_for_Research.pdf, and in French from www.faq-qnw.org/wp-content/uploads/2016/11/FAQ-2012-Lignes_directrices_recherche.pdf

Fillmore, C., Dell, C. A., & Kilty, J. M. (2014). Chapter 2: Ensuring Aboriginal women's voices are heard: Toward a balanced approach in community-based research. In J. M. Kilty, M. Felices-Luna, & S. C. Fabian (Eds.), *Demarginalizing voices: Commitment, emotion, and action in qualitative research* (pp. 38–61). Vancouver: UBC Press. Retrieved from www.addictionresearchchair.ca/wp-content/uploads/2011/10/Fillmore-C.-Dell-C.-A.-Kilty-J.-M.-Ensuring-Aboriginal-Womens-Voices-are-heard-Toward-a-Balanced-Approach-in-Community-Based-Research.pdf

Fredericks, B. (2008). Researching with Aboriginal women as an Aboriginal woman researcher. *Australian Feminist Studies, 23*(55), 113–129. Retrieved from ir.lib.uwo.ca/cgi/viewcontent.cgi?article=1103&context=aprci

McHugh, T.-L. F., & Kowalski, K. C. (2009). Lessons learned: Participatory action research with young Aboriginal women. *Pimatisiwin: A Journal of Aboriginal and*

Indigenous Community Health, *7*(1), 117–131. Retrieved from www.pimatisiwin.com/uploads/July_2009/09McHugh.pdf

Meadows, L. M., Lagendyk, L. E., Thurston, W. E., & Eisener, A. C. (2003). Balancing culture, ethics, and methods in qualitative health research with Aboriginal peoples. *International Journal of Qualitative Methods*, *2*(4). Retrieved from journals.sagepub.com/doi/pdf/10.1177/160940690300200401

Pearce, K., & Coholic, D. (2013). A photovoice exploration of the lived experiences of a small group of Aboriginal adolescent girls living away from their home communities. *Pimatisiwin: A journal of Aboriginal and Indigenous community health*, *11*(1), 113–124. Retrieved from www.pimatisiwin.com/online/wp-content/uploads/2013/07/08PearceCoholic.pdf

Saskatoon Aboriginal Women's Health Research Committee, & Prairie Women's Health Centre of Excellence. (2004). *Ethical guidelines for Aboriginal women's health research.* Winnipeg: The Prairie Women's Health Centre of Excellence. Retrieved from www.pwhce.ca/pdf/ethicalGuidelines.pdf

Two-Spirited People

Nobis, T., Brennan, D., Jackson, R., & Georgievski, G. (2014). *Creating change together in Two-Spirit research: An Example from the Two-Spirit HIV/AIDS wellness and longevity study (2-SHAWLS).* Presented at the Rainbow Health Ontario 2014 Conference, Toronto, ON. Retrieved from sagecollection.ca/en/resources/creating-change-together-two-spirit-research-example-two-spirit-hivaids-wellness-and

Children and Youth

Starkes, J. M., Baydala, L. T., Canadian Paediatric Society, & First Nations, Inuit and Métis Health Committee. (2014). Health research involving First Nations, Inuit and Métis children and their communities. *Paediatric Child Health*, *19*(2), 99–102. Retrieved from www.ncbi.nlm.nih.gov/pmc/articles/PMC3941676/

Stewart, S. (2009). Participatory action research: Exploring Indigenous youth perspectives and experiences. *Indigenous Policy Journal.* Retrieved from ipjournal.wordpress.com/2009/12/16/participatory-action-research-exploring-indigenous-youth-perspectives-and-experiences/

Wilson, K., & Wilks, J. (2013). Research with Indigenous children and young people in schools: Ethical and methodological considerations. *Global Studies of Childhood*, *3*(2), 142–152. Retrieved from http://journals.sagepub.com/doi/pdf/10.2304/gsch.2013.3.2.142

Tri-Council Resources

Canadian Institutes of Health Research, Natural Sciences and Engineering Research Council of Canada, and Social Sciences and Humanities Research Council of Canada.

(2014). *Tri-Council Policy Statement: Ethical Conduct for Research Involving Humans, Second Edition (TCPS 2)*. Government of Canada. Retrieved from www.pre.ethics.gc.ca/pdf/eng/tcps2-2014/TCPS_2_FINAL_Web.pdf

Canadian Institutes of Health Research, Natural Sciences and Engineering Research Council of Canada, and Social Sciences and Humanities Research Council of Canada. (2014). *TCPS 2 – Chapter 9: Research involving the First Nations, Inuit and Métis peoples of Canada*. Government of Canada. Retrieved from www.pre.ethics.gc.ca/eng/policy-politique/initiatives/tcps2-eptc2/chapter9-chapitre9/

The Secretariat on Responsible Conduct of Research. (2012). *Chapter 9: Research involving First Nations, Inuit and Métis peoples of Canada: Community engagement, complex authority structures, capacity building and research agreements - webinar*. Retrieved from www.youtube.com/watch?v=zR61Gf1XH2A&feature=youtu.be

The First Nations Information Governance Centre – OCAP Resources

National Aboriginal Health Organization. (2005). *Ownership, control, access, and possession (OCAP) or self-determination applied to research: A critical analysis of contemporary First Nations research and some options for First Nations communities*. First Nations Centre. Retrieved from www.naho.ca/documents/fnc/english/FNC_OCAPCriticalAnalysis.pdf

The First Nations Information Governance Centre. (2014). *Ownership, control, access and possession (OCAP™): The path to First Nations information governance*. Ottawa: The First Nations Information Governance Centre. Retrieved from fnigc.ca/sites/default/files/docs/ocap_path_to_fn_information_governance_en_final.pdf

The First Nations Information Governance Centre. (2017). *FNIGC – The First Nations Principles of OCAP*. Retrieved from fnigc.ca/ocap.html

Multi-media:

Fieldworker training video #1 "Research ethics and privacy." (2015). Retrieved from www.youtube.com/watch?v=6VT9DcC2UDU

FNIGC: Data by First Nations for First Nations. (2016). Retrieved from www.youtube.com/watch?v=XAiwn0tKCIM

Understanding the First Nations principles of OCAP™: Our road map to information governance. (2014). Retrieved from www.youtube.com/watch?v=y32aUFVfCM0

Arts-Based Protocols

Anderson, J., & Younging, G. (2010). *Discussion paper on protocols*. Prepared for the Canadian Public Art Funders (CPAF) Professional Development Meeting on Aboriginal Arts: Session on Protocols. Retrieved from www.cpaf-opsac.org/en/themes/documents/DiscussionPaperonProtocols2010-07-21.pdf

Australia Council for the Arts. 2007. *Protocols for working with Indigenous artists*. Retrieved from www.australiacouncil.gov.au/about/protocols-for-working-with-indigenous-artists/

Zuckermann, G., et al. (2015). *ENGAGING – A guide to interacting respectfully and reciprocally with Aboriginal and Torres Strait Islander people, and their arts practices and intellectual property*. Australian Government: Indigenous Culture Support. Retrieved from www.zuckermann.org/guide.html http://www.zuckermann.org/guide.html

MULTI-MEDIA:

Ontario Arts Council. (2016). *Indigenous arts protocols*. Retrieved from http://nationtalk.ca/story/indigenous-arts-protocols

Turtle Island: Northern Canada/Arctic

Association of Canadian Universities for Northern Studies. (2003). *Ethical principles for the conduct of research in the North*. Retrieved from acuns.ca/wp-content/uploads/2010/09/EthicsEnglishmarch2003.pdf, and in French, Inuktitut, and Russian at acuns.ca/en/ethical-principles/

Cree Board of Health and Social Services of James Bay. (2009). *Guide for interveners and users of the Pathways to "Miyupimaatisiiun" Services*. Retrieved from http://www.creehealth.org/sites/default/files/Code%20of%20Ethics_0.pdf

Inuit Nipingit – National Inuit Committee on Ethics and Research. (2017). *Fact sheets*. Retrieved from www.naho.ca/inuit/research-and-ethics/fact-sheets/

Inuit Tapiriit Kanatami, & Nunavut Research Institute. (1998). *Negotiating research relationships: A guide for communities*. Retrieved from www.itk.ca/wp-content/uploads/2016/07/Negotitiating-Research-Relationships-Community-Guide.pdf

Labrador Health Research Advisory Committee (LAHRC) and NL Health Research Ethics Board (HREB). (2013). *Guidelines for research involving Aboriginal communities in Newfoundland and Labrador*. Retrieved from http://www.hrea.ca/getdoc/193ccb52-a88c-4454-95f5-6b455f461be7/Guidelines-for-conducting-research-with-Aboriginal.aspx

Protocols and principles for conducting research with Yukon First Nations. (2013, February). Yukon Research Centre. Retrieved from www.yukoncollege.yk.ca/downloads/YRC_FN_Initiatives_no_photos_inside_final_print.pdf

Licensing

Inuit Tapiriit Kanatami, & Nunavut Research Institute. (2006). *Negotiating research relationships with Inuit communities: A guide for researchers*. Retrieved from www.nri.nu.ca/sites/default/files/public/files/06-068%20ITK%20NRR%20booklet.pdf

National Aboriginal Health Organization. (2017). *Research permits and licenses*. Retrieved from www.naho.ca/inuit/research-and-ethics/research-permits-and-licences/

Nunatsiavut Government. (2013, May). *Research process*. Retrieved from nainresearchcentre.com/wp-content/uploads/2013/04/Nunatsiavut-Research-Process-May-20131.pdf

Nunavut Research Institute. (2015). *Research licensing applications*. Retrieved from www.nri.nu.ca/research-licencing-applications

The Aurora Research Institute. (2011, February). *Licensing*. Retrieved from nwtresearch.com/licensing-research

Community Protocols

Gwich'in Social and Cultural Institute. (2011, March 29). *Conducting traditional knowledge research in the Gwich'in Settlement Area: A guide for researchers*. Retrieved from nwtresearch.com/sites/default/files/gwich-in-social-and-cultural-institute_0.pdf

Gwich'in Tribal Council Department of Cultural Heritage: Gwich'in Social and Cultural Institute. (2016). Researcher information. Retrieved from www.gwichin.ca/researcher-information

Heron, C. (2016). *Research in the South Slave of the Northwest Territories. Northwest Territory Métis Nation*. Retrieved from nwtmetisnation.ca/wp-content/uploads/2016/02/research.pdf

Inuvialuit Regional Corporation. (n.d.). *Guidelines for research in the Inuvialuit Settlement Region*. Retrieved from nwtresearch.com/sites/default/files/inuvialuit-regional-corporation.pdf

Sambaa K'e Dene Band. (2003, February 26). *Sambaa K'e Dene Band policy regarding the gathering, use, and distribution of Yúndíit'ŏh (Traditional Knowledge)*. Retrieved from nwtresearch.com/sites/default/files/sambaa-k-e-dene-band.pdf

Turtle Island: Southern Canada

Akwesasne Task Force on the Environment. (1996). *Protocol for review of environmental and scientific research proposals*. Retrieved from www.ipcb.org/resources/archived/akw_protocol.html

Assembly of First Nations Quebec-Labrador. (2014). *First Nations in Quebec and Labrador's Research Protocol*. Retrieved from www.cssspnql.com/docs/default-source/centre-de-documentation/anglais_web.pdf?sfvrsn=2

Inter Tribal Health Authority. (2007). *Research protocol*. Retrieved from www.cahr.uvic.ca/nearbc/documents/2009/aboriginal/ITHA%20Research%20Protocol.pdf

Kahnawake Schools Diabetes Prevention Project. (2007). Code of research ethics. Retrieved from www.ksdpp.org/elder/code_ethics.php

Ktunaxa Nation's code of ethics for research. (1998). Retrieved from cahr.uvic.ca/nearbc/documents/2009/KKTC-Code-of-Ethics.pdf

Maar, M., Sutherland, M., & McGregor, L. (2007). *A regional model for ethical engagement: The First Nations Research Ethics Committee on Manitoulin Island.* Aboriginal Policy Research Consortium International. Retrieved from ir.lib.uwo.ca/cgi/viewcontent.cgi?article=1332&context=aprci

McIvor, O. (2014). *Guidelines for ethical research in Manitoba First Nations.* Manitoba First Nations Education Resource Centre Inc. Retrieved from www.mfnerc.org/wp-content/uploads/2014/03/Ethical-Research-in-Manitoba-First-Nations.pdf

Métis Centre. (2010). *Principles of ethical Métis research.* Retrieved from www.naho.ca/documents/metiscentre/english/PrinciplesofEthicalMetisResearch-descriptive_001.pdf

Mi'kmaw Ethics Watch. (2017). Retrieved from www.cbu.ca/indigenous-affairs/unamaki-college/mikmaq-ethics-watch/

Native Council of Prince Edward Island. (2014). *Research Advisory Committee: Guidance for researchers.* Retrieved from www.ncpei.com/research-ethics. (This webpage also includes a downloadable Word document titled "Application to conduct research & consultations with urban Indigenous people in Prince Edward Island.")

Noojmowin Teg Health Centre. (2003). *Guidelines for ethical Aboriginal research: A resource manual for the development of ethical and culturally appropriate community-based research within the First Nations communities in the Manitoulin Area.* Little Current, ON. Retrieved from www.noojmowin-teg.ca/Shared%20Documents/GEAR%20-%20FINAL.pdf

Nuu-chah-nulth Tribal Council Research Ethics Committee. (2008, August). *Principles for conducting research in a Nuu-chah-nulth context.* Retrieved from www.cahr.uvic.ca/nearbc/documents/2009/NTC-Protocols-and-Principles.pdf

Six Nations Council. (2014). *Conducting research at Six Nations.* Retrieved from www.sixnations.ca/admEthicsPolicy.pdf

Six Nations Council. (n.d.). *Six Nations Council Research Ethics Committee protocol.* Retrieved from www.sixnations.ca/admResearchEthicsProtocol.pdf

Turtle Island: United States

American Indigenous Research Association. (n.d.). Retrieved from americanindigenousresearchassociation.org/

Austin, D., Gerlak, S., & Smith, C. (2000, November). *Building partnerships with Native Americans in climate-related research and outreach.* The Climate Assessment Project for the Southwest (CLIMAS)/The Institute for the Study of Planet Earth. Retrieved from www.climas.arizona.edu/sites/default/files/pdfcl2-00.pdf

Becenti-Pigman, B., White, K., Bowman, B., Duran, B., & Palmanteer-Holder, L. (n.d.). *Research policies, processes and protocol of the Navajo Nation Human Research Review Board (NNHRRB)*. Retrieved from nptao.arizona.edu/sites/nptao/files/navajo_nation_research_policies_processes_and_protocol0001.pdf

Colorado River Indian Tribes. (2009). *Human and cultural research code*. Retrieved from nptao.arizona.edu/sites/nptao/files/crit_human_and_cultural_research_code0001_0.pdf

Cross, T., Fox, K., Becker-Green, J., Smith, J., & Willeto, A. A. A. (2004, February). *Case studies in tribal data collection and use*. National Indian Child Welfare Association. Retrieved from www.nicwa.org/policy/research/2005/tribaldatacollection.pdf

Gila River Indian Community. (n.d.). *Guidelines and instructions, introduction, letter of intent, sample letter and agreement*. Retrieved from nptao.arizona.edu/sites/nptao/files/gila_river_indian_community_guidelines_and_instructions_introduction_letter_of_intent_sample_letter_and_agreement.pdf

Gila River Indian Community. (n.d.). *Policies and procedures for submission of study proposals to research committee*. Retrieved from nptao.arizona.edu/sites/nptao/files/gila_river_indian_community_policies_and_procedures_for.pdf

National Congress of American Indians Policy Research Center. (2017). *Supporting Indian Country in shaping its own future*. Retrieved from www.ncai.org/policy-research-center/initiatives/research-regulation

Navajo Nation. (n.d.). *Navajo Nation human research code*. Retrieved from nptao.arizona.edu/sites/nptao/files/navajo_nation_human_research_code_revised.pdf

Navajo Nation Human Research Review Board. (n.d.). *Procedural guidelines for principal investigators*. Retrieved from nptao.arizona.edu/sites/nptao/files/navajo_nation_procedural_guidelines_for_principal_investigators.pdf

O'Neil, C., Harding, A., Harper, B., Stone, D., Berger, P., Harria, S., & Donatuto, J. (2012). Conducting research with tribal communities: Sovereignty, ethics, and data-sharing issues. *Environmental Health Perspectives*, *120*(1), 6–10. Retrieved from digitalcommons.law.seattleu.edu/cgi/viewcontent.cgi?article=1085&context=faculty

Sahota, P. C. (n.d.). *Research regulation in American Indian/Alaska Native communities: A guide to reviewing research studies*. Retrieved from depts.washington.edu/ccph/pdf_files/pdf

Aotearoa: New Zealand

Health Research Council of New Zealand. (2010). *Guidelines for researchers on health research involving Māori*. Auckland, NZ. Retrieved from www.hrc.govt.nz/sites/default/files/Guidelines%20for%20HR%20on%20Maori-%20Jul10%20revised%20for%20Te%20Ara%20Tika%20v2%20FINAL%5B1%5D.pdf

Hudson, M., Milne, M., Reynolds, P., Russell, K., & Smith, B. (2010). *Te Ara Tika: Guidelines for Māori research ethics: A framework for researchers and ethics committee members.* Health Research Council of New Zealand. Retrieved from www.hrc.govt.nz/sites/default/files/Te%20Ara%20Tika%20Guidelines%20for%20Maori%20Research%20Ethics.pdf

Hudson, M., & Russell, K. (2009). The Treaty of Waitangi and research ethics in Aotearoa. *Bioethical Inquiry, 6,* 61–68. Retrieved from www.smallfire.co.nz/wp-content/uploads/2016/07/HudsonRussell2007_ToWResearchEthics.pdf

Kaupapa Māori research. (n.d.). Retrieved from www.katoa.net.nz/kaupapa-maori

Australia

Australian Institute of Aboriginal and Torres Strait Islander Studies. (2012). *Guidelines for ethical research in Australian Indigenous studies.* Retrieved from aiatsis.gov.au/sites/default/files/docs/research-and-guides/ethics/gerais.pdf

Australian Institute of Aboriginal and Torres Strait Islander Studies. (2015). *Ethical research.* Retrieved from aiatsis.gov.au/research/ethical-research

Davis, M. (2005). *Undertaking projects and research in central Australia: CLC protocols and the development of protocols for projects and research in the CLC region.* Central Land Council and Desert Knowledge Cooperative Research Centre. Retrieved from www.nintione.com.au/resource/DKCRC-Report-8-CLC-Protocols.pdf?bcsi_scan_2687365ababd2c82=0&bcsi_scan_filename=DKCRC-Report-8-CLC-Protocols.pdf

National Health and Medical Research Council. (2003). *Values and ethics: Guidelines for ethical conduct in Aboriginal and Torres Strait Islander health research.* Commonwealth of Australia. Retrieved from www.nhmrc.gov.au/_files_nhmrc/publications/attachments/e52.pdf

Putt, J. (2013). *Conducting research with Indigenous people and communities.* Indigenous Justice Clearinghouse. Retrieved from www.indigenousjustice.gov.au/wp-content/uploads/mp/files/publications/files/brief015.pdf

Queensland Government. (1998). *Protocols for consultation and negotiation with Aboriginal people.* Retrieved from www.datsip.qld.gov.au/resources/datsima/people-communities/protocols-aboriginal/aboriginal-protocols-for-consultation.pdf

Global

Centre for Indigenous Peoples' Nutrition and Environment. (2003). *Indigenous peoples and participatory health research.* World Health Organization. Retrieved from www.mcgill.ca/cine/files/cine/partreresearch_english.pdf

DATA USE, DATA SOVEREIGNTY, AND DATA COLLECTION

Turtle Island: Canada

BC First Nations' Data Governance Initiative (BCFNDGI). (n.d.). Retrieved from www.bcfndgi.com/

Bell, C., & Shier, C. (2011). Control of information originating from Aboriginal communities: Legal and ethical contexts. *Etudes/Inuit/Studies*, *351*(2), 35–56. Retrieved from www.erudit.org/en/journals/etudinuit/2011-v35-n1-2-n1-2/1012834ar/

Bruhn, J. (2014). Identifying useful approaches to the governance of Indigenous data. *The International Indigenous Policy Journal*, *5*(2). Retrieved from ir.lib.uwo.ca/cgi/viewcontent.cgi?article=1175&context=iipj

Marshall, A., Marshall, M., & Bartlett, C. (n.d.). *Etuaptmumk/Two-Eyed Seeing: Where Indigenous and Western perspectives meet*. Presented at the Wolastoqiyik/Mi'kmaq speaker series, Mi'kmaq-Maliseet Institute, University of New Brunswick. Retrieved from www.integrativescience.ca/uploads/files/2014-two-eyed-seeing-etuaptmumk-indigenous-science-marshalls-bartlett.pdf

McMahon, R., LaHache, T., & Whiteduck, T. (2014). *Digital data management in Kahnawà:ke*. Canadian Sociological Association. Retrieved from firstmile.ca/wp-content/uploads/2015/03/2014-CSA-McMahon-Kahnawake.pdf

Mustimuhw Information Solutions Inc. (n.d.). Data governance framework: Data governance policy manual. Retrieved from static1.squarespace.com/static/558c624de4b0574c94d62a61/t/558c7c65e4b0b067ef50a4ad/1435270245149/BCF-NDGI-Data-Governance-Framework-Data-Governance-Policy-Manual.pdf

Mustimuhw Information Solutions Inc. (n.d.). Data governance framework: Framework and associated tools. Retrieved from static1.squarespace.com/static/558c624de4b0574c94d62a61/t/558c7c38e4b039169215c34e/1435270200731/BCF-NDGI-Data-Governance-Framework.pdf

Wright, A. L., Wahoush, O., Ballantyne, M., Gabel, C., & Jack, S. M. (2016). Qualitative health research involving Indigenous peoples: Culturally appropriate data collection methods. *The Qualitative Report*, *21*(12), 2230–2245. Retrieved from nsuworks.nova.edu/cgi/viewcontent.cgi?article=2384&context=tqr/

MULTI-MEDIA:

Thomas, R. (2013). *Etuaptmumk: Two-Eyed Seeing*. Presented at the TEDxNSCCWaterfront, Nova Scotia Community College. Retrieved from www.youtube.com/watch?v=bA9EwcFbVfg

Two-eyed Seeing. (2012). Cape Breton University. Retrieved from www.youtube.com/watch?v=_CY-iGduw5c

Turtle Island: United States

Indigenous Peoples Council on Biocolonialism. (2006). *The Convention on Biological Diversity's International Regime on Access and Benefit Sharing: Background and Considerations for Indigenous Peoples*. Retrieved from www.ipcb.org/pdf_files/absbriefcop8.pdf

Indigenous Research Protection Act (Template). (n.d.). *Indigenous Peoples Council on Biocolonialism*. Retrieved from www.ipcb.org/publications/policy/files/irpa.html

Kukutai, T., & Taylor, J. (Eds.). (2016). *Indigenous data sovereignty: Toward an agenda*. Acton, Australia: The Australian National University Press.

Rainie, S. C., Schultz, J. L., Briggs, E., Riggs, P., & Palmanteer-Holder, N. L. (2017). Data as a strategic resource: Self-determination, governance, and the data challenge for Indigenous Nations in the United States. *The International Indigenous Policy Journal, 8*(2). Retrieved from ir.lib.uwo.ca/cgi/viewcontent.cgi?article=1320&context=iipj

US Indigenous Data Sovereignty Network. (n.d.). Retrieved from usindigenousdata.arizona.edu

MULTI-MEDIA:

Walter, M. (2016). *American Indian Research Association 2016 Keynote #1: Maggie Walter, University of Tasmania – "Indigenous statistics: Doing numbers our way."* Presented at the 2016 American Indigenous Research Association Annual Meeting, Salish Kootenai College, Pablo, Montana. Retrieved from americanindigenousresearchassociation.org/annual-meeting/2016-meeting-report/presentations-from-the-2016-meeting/

Aotearoa: New Zealand

Commission on Human Rights. (1993). *Mataatua Declaration on Cultural and Intellectual Property Rights*. Retrieved from www.ankn.uaf.edu/IKS/mataatua.html

Global

MULTI-MEDIA:

Intellectual property issues in cultural heritage conversations: Linda Tuhiwai Smith on decolonizing research. (2015). Retrieved from www.sfu.ca/ipinch/resources/podcasts/ipinch-conversations-linda-tuhiwai-smith-decolonizing-research/

TRADITIONAL KNOWLEDGE AND TRADITIONAL ECOLOGICAL KNOWLEDGE

Armitage, P., & Kilburn, S. (2015). *Conduct of traditional knowledge research: A reference guide.* Whitehorse: Wildlife Management Advisory Council (North Slope).

Assembly of First Nations. (n.d.). *Aboriginal traditional knowledge and intellectual property rights.* Retrieved from afn.ca/uploads/files/env/atk_and_ip_considerations.pdf

Chiefs of Ontario. (2010). *Respecting our ancestors, ensuring our future: Traditional knowledge primer for First Nations.* Retrieved from www.chiefs-of-ontario.org/sites/default/files/files/TK%20Primer%20FINAL_0.pdf

Climate and Traditional Knowledges Workgroup. (2014). *Guidelines for considering traditional knowledges in climate change initiatives.* Retrieved from climatetkw.files.wordpress.com/2014/09/tks_guidelines_v1.docx

Crowshoe, C. (2005). *Sacred ways of life: Traditional knowledge toolkit.* The First Nations Centre National Aboriginal Health Organization. Retrieved from www.naho.ca/documents/fnc/english/FNC_TraditionalKnowledgeToolkit.pdf

Matsui, K. (2015). Introduction to the future of traditional knowledge research. *The International Indigenous Policy Journal, 6*(2). Retrieved from ir.lib.uwo.ca/cgi/viewcontent.cgi?article=1245&context=iipj

Métis Knowledge Environmental Knowledge Place. Retrieved from http://metisportals.ca/environment/

Native Women's Association of Canada. (n.d.). *Aboriginal women and Aboriginal traditional knowledge (ATK): Input and insight on Aboriginal traditional knowledge.* Retrieved from www.nwac.ca/wp-content/uploads/2015/05/2014-NWAC-Aborignal-Women-and-Aborignal-Traditional-Knowledge-Report1.pdf

Simpson, L. (2001). *Traditional ecological knowledge: Marginalization, appropriation and continued disillusion.* Indigenous Knowledge Conference. Retrieved from iportal.usask.ca/purl/IKC-2001-Simpson.pdf

UNIVERSITY-BASED RESEARCH ENGAGEMENT PROTOCOLS

Carleton University. (n.d). Tobacco offering protocol. Centre for Indigenous Initiatives. Retrieved from https://carleton.ca/indigenous/resources/tobacco-offering-protocol/

Carleton University. (n.d). Use of traditional medicines on campus. Retrieved from https://carleton.ca/indigenous/resources/use-of-traditional-medicines/

Queen's University. (n.d.). Elder protocol handbook. Retrieved from www.queensu.ca/fdasc/sites/webpublish.queensu.ca.fdascwww/files/files/Elders%20Protocol%20Handbook.pdf

University of Calgary. (2016). Cultural protocol guidelines: Recommended practices for First Nations, Métis and Inuit cultural engagement. Retrieved from www.ucalgary.ca/nativecentre/files/nativecentre/cultural-protocol-guideline-november-2016

University of Manitoba. (2013). Framework for research engagement with First Nation, Metis and Inuit communities. Faculty of Social Sciences. Retrieved from https://umanitoba.ca/faculties/health_sciences/medicine/media/UofM_Framework_Report_web.pdf

CIRCLE METHODOLOGY

Dudemaine, A. (1995). Healing voices. *Terre en vues, 3*(3), 7–17.

Edwards, K., Lund, C., Mitchell, S., & Andersson, N. (2008). Trust the process: Community-based research partnerships. *Pimatisiwin: A Journal of Aboriginal and Indigenous Community Health, (6)*2, 187–199.

Everson, H. (1975). *May Whin Shah Ti Pah Chi Mo Win: Indian stories of long ago*. Alexandria, MN: Echo Printing Company.

Hart, M. A. (1997). *An ethnographic study of sharing circles as a culturally appropriate practice approach with Aboriginal people* (Master's thesis). University of Manitoba, Winnipeg.

Hunter, L. M. (2004). *Traditional Aboriginal healing practices: An ethnographic approach* (Master's thesis). University of Ottawa.

Lavallée, L. F. (2009). Practical application of an Indigenous research framework and two qualitative Indigenous research methods: Sharing circles and Anishinaabe symbol-based reflection. *International Journal of Qualitative Methods, 8*(1), 21–40.

Nabigon, H., Hagey, R., Webster, S., & MacKay, R. (1999). The learning circle as a research method: The Trickster and Windigo in research. *Native Social Work Journal, 2*(1), 113–137.

Stevenson, J. (1999). The circle of healing. *Native Social Work Journal, 2*(1), 8–21.

ARTS-BASED PROTOCOLS

Anderson, J., & Younging, G. (2010). *Discussion paper on protocols*. Prepared for the Canadian Public Art Funders (CPAF) Professional Development Meeting on Aboriginal Arts: Session on Protocols. Retrieved from www.cpaf-opsac.org/en/themes/documents/DiscussionPaperonProtocols2010-07-21.pdf

Australia Council for the Arts. (2007). *Protocols for working with Indigenous artists*. Retrieved from www.australiacouncil.gov.au/about/protocols-for-working-with-indigenous-artists/

Zuckermann, G., et al. (2015). *ENGAGING – A guide to interacting respectfully and reciprocally with Aboriginal and Torres Strait Islander people, and their arts practices and intellectual property*. Australian Government: Indigenous Culture Support. Retrieved from www.zuckermann.org/guide.html http://www.zuckermann.org/guide.html

Multi-media:

Ontario Arts Council. (2016). *Indigenous arts protocols*. Retrieved from http://nationtalk.ca/story/indigenous-arts-protocols

INDIGENOUS RESEARCH TRAINING

Indigenous Research Ethics Institute. *Carleton University Institute on the Ethics of Research with Indigenous Peoples (CUIERIP)*. Retrieved from https://carleton.ca/indigenousresearchethics/

Panel on Research Ethics. (2017). *The TCPS 2 tutorial course on research ethics (CORE). Module 9: Research involving the First Nations, Inuit and Metis peoples of Canada*. Retrieved from www.pre.ethics.gc.ca/education/Module9_en.pdf

The TCPS 2 Tutorial Course on Research Ethics (CORE). *Module 9: Research involving the First Nations, Inuit and Métis peoples of Canada*. Webinar. Retrieved from www.pre.ethics.gc.ca/eng/education/fnat-pnat/

BOOKS

Anderson, C., & O'Brien, J. (2017). *Sources and methods in Indigenous studies*. New York: Routledge.

Anderson, C., & Walters, M. (2013). *Indigenous statistics: A quantitative research methodology*. Walnut Creek, CA: Left Coast Press.

Bennett, J., & Rowley, S. (2004). *Uqalurait: An oral history of Nunavut*. Montreal & Kingston: McGill-Queen's University Press.

Bird, L. (2005). *Telling our stories: Omushkego legends and histories from Hudson Bay*. Peterborough, ON: Broadview Press.

Brown, L., & Strega, S. (2015). *Research as resistance: Revisiting critical, Indigenous, and anti-oppressive approaches*. Toronto: Canadian Scholars' Press.

Chacaby, M., with M. L. Plummer. (2016). *A Two-Spirit journey: The autobiography of a lesbian Ojibwa-Cree Elder*. Winnipeg: University of Manitoba Press.

Chilisa, B. (2012). *Indigenous research methodologies.* Thousand Oaks, CA: Sage.

Cote-Meek, S. (2014). *Colonized classrooms: Racism, trauma and resistance in post-secondary education.* Halifax & Winnipeg: Fernwood Publishing.

Denzin, N., Lincoln, Y., & Smith, L. (2008). *Handbook of critical and Indigenous methodologies.* Thousand Oaks, CA: Sage.

Dokis, C. (2016). *Where the rivers meet: Pipelines, participatory resource management and Aboriginal-state relations in the Northwest Territories.* Vancouver: UBC Press.

Drugge, A.-L. (Ed.). (2016). *Ethics in Indigenous research: Past experiences – future challenges.* Umea, Sweden: Umea University, Centre for Sami Research.

Graveline, F. J. (1998). *Circle works: Transforming Eurocentric consciousness.* Halifax, NS: Fernwood Publishing.

Johnson, J., & Larsen, S. (2013). *A deeper sense of place: Stories and journeys of Indigenous-academic collaboration.* Corvallis: Oregon State University Press.

Lambert, L. (2014). *Research for Indigenous survival: Indigenous research methodologies in the behavioral sciences.* Pablo, MT: Salish Kootenai College Press.

Mertens, D., Cram, F., & Chilisa, B. (Eds.). (2013). *Indigenous pathways into social research: Voice of new generation.* New York: Left Coast Press.

Mihesuah, D., & Wilson, A. (2004). *Indigenizing the academy: Transforming scholarship and empowering communities.* Lincoln: University of Nebraska Press.

Nappaaluk, M. (2014). *Sanaaq. An Inuit novel.* Winnipeg: University of Manitoba Press.

Rimmer, M. (2015) *Indigenous intellectual property: Handbook of contemporary research.* Cheltenham, UK: Edward Elgar Publishing Ltd.

Tanaka, M. T. D. (2016). *Learning and teaching together: Weaving Indigenous ways of knowing into education.* Vancouver: UBC Press.

Tuck, E., & McKenzie, M. (2015). *Place in research: Theory, methodology, and methods.* New York: Routledge.

ADDITIONAL RESOURCES

Absolon, K., & Willett, C. (2004). Aboriginal research: Berry picking and hunting in the 21st century. *First Peoples Child & Family Review, 1*(1), 5–17. Retrieved from fncaringsociety.com/sites/default/files/online-journal/vol1num1/Absolon_Willett_pp5-17.pdf

Chartier, C. (2015). Partnerships between Aboriginal organizations and academics. *The International Indigenous Policy Journal, 6*(2). Retrieved from ir.lib.uwo.ca/cgi/viewcontent.cgi?article=1224&context=iipj

Cochran, P. A. L., Marshall, C. A., Garcia-Downing, C., Kendall, E., Cook, D., McCubbin, L., & Gover, R. M. S. (2008). Indigenous ways of knowing: Implications for participatory research and community. *American Journal of Public Health, 98*(1), 22–27. Retrieved from

www.researchgate.net/profile/Carmen_Downing/publication/5798822_Indigenous_
Ways_of_Knowing_Implications_for_Participatory_Research_and_Community/
links/

Styres, S., Zinga, D., Bennett, S., & Bomberry, M. (2010). Walking in two worlds: En-
gaging the space between Indigenous community and academia. *Canadian Journal of
Education, 33*(3), 617–648. Retrieved from www.csse-scee.ca/CJE/Articles/FullText/
CJE33-3/CJE33-3-StyresEtAl.pdf

Ten Fingers, K. (2005). Rejecting, revitalizing, and reclaiming: First Nations to set the
direction of research and policy development. *Canadian Journal of Public Health, 96*(1),
S60–S63. Retrieved from journal.cpha.ca/index.php/cjph/article/viewFile/1470/1659

CONTRIBUTOR BIOGRAPHIES

Rachel Arsenault is a master of Indigenous relations student at Laurentian University in Sudbury, Ontario. Arsenault's research responds to the First Nations water crisis in Ontario. Indeed, she seeks to provide policy recommendations to improve water quality in Indigenous communities. She is a recipient of a Canadian Institutes of Health Research Training Grant as part of the Indigenous Mentorship Network Program and works as a research assistant to the Indigenous Research Methods Working Group.

Nicole Bell is Anishnaabe (bear clan) from Kitigan Zibi First Nation. She is the founder of an Anishnaabe culture-based school for Indigenous children from junior kindergarten to Grade 12. Nicole is currently an associate professor at Trent University with the School of Education. Her research interests include: Indigenous culture-based education, infusion of Indigenous knowledge into public schooling and teacher education, decolonization and healing, and Indigenous research theory and methodology.

Joseph Burke is both staff (coordinator for international services) and student (master of Indigenous relations) at Laurentian University in Sudbury, Ontario. Using his academic background in political sciences, Burke has focused his graduate research on the role of Indigenous knowledge and perspectives in natural resource development policy-making processes. Burke is an advocate for effective dialogue on human rights issues in Canada and is inspired by international human rights law.

Paul Cormier is a faculty member in Aboriginal education at Lakehead University and a member of the Red Rock Indian Band. He holds a master's degree in conflict analysis and management from Royal Roads University and a PhD in peace and conflict studies from the University of Manitoba. His research interests include Indigenous peace building and considering research as a process for peace building in Indigenous contexts.

Erin Cusack was born and raised in a family of Irish and English heritage in Halifax, Nova Scotia, on the ancestral and unceded territory of the Mi'kmaq People. She holds a bachelor of science (honours) in health promotion from

Dalhousie University and master of arts in the Social Dimensions of Health Program at the University of Victoria. As a feminist researcher she has focused her studies on sexuality and sexual health, LGBTQ health, harm reduction, decolonizing approaches, and health equity in public health systems.

Carly Dokis is an associate professor in the Department of Sociology and Anthropology at Nipissing University, and the author of *Where the Rivers Meet: Development and Participatory Management in the Sahtu Region, Northwest Territories*. Her research interests include political ecology, anthropology of development, collaborative research methodologies, and the ethnology of northern Canada. She has worked with Indigenous communities in northern Ontario and the Northwest Territories on the social, economic, and political consequences of environmental governance.

Karlee D. Fellner is Cree/Métis from central Alberta. Her name in Cree is *miyotehiskwew* (Good-Hearted Woman). Dr. Fellner is an assistant professor in Indigenous Education Counselling Psychology at the University of Calgary. Her work focuses on Indigenous research, Indigenous curriculum and pedagogy, holistic and traditional approaches to wellness, Indigenous approaches to psychotherapy, complex trauma, and *miyo pimâtisiwin* (living a good life). Dr. Fellner centres Indigenous epistemologies and methodologies in her research, pedagogy, and clinical practices, encouraging students and professionals to bring their worldviews, traditions, beliefs, stories, and values into their work.

Michelle Graham is a master of Indigenous relations student at Laurentian University in Sudbury, Ontario. Her current research examines the effectiveness of culturally based education programs for Indigenous youth in Canada. Graham has shared her research at peer-reviewed conferences, including the Canadian Society for Brain, Behaviour and Cognitive Science.

Karen Hall is a Sahtu Dene First Nations woman, born and raised in Somba K'e (Yellowknife), Denendeh (NWT). Karen holds a BSc in health promotion from Dalhousie University and is currently a master's candidate at the University of Victoria School of Public Health and Social Policy. She also works as a senior advisor in Indigenous health for the Government of the Northwest Territories. Her research interests include improving health care access for Indigenous people in Denendeh, cultural safety, and traditional healing.

Heather A. Howard teaches medical anthropology and American Indian and Indigenous studies at Michigan State University. She also holds an appointment with the Centre for Indigenous Studies at the University of Toronto. Her research examines the processes through which authoritative forms of knowledge, identity, responsibility, and choice are produced; how these structure gendered and racialized inequalities; and how they are historicized, contested, and reconfigured in cultural, social service, and health care delivery organizations.

Sarah Hunt is a Kwagiulth activist and scholar dedicated to addressing issues of justice, violence, law, and power, working in collaboration with Indigenous communities, especially youth, Two-Spirit people, and women. Dr. Hunt has published on issues related to Indigenous research methods and ethics, decolonization, and the revitalization of Indigenous self-determination at the intimate scale of our bodies, homes, and networks of kin. She is currently a visitor in unceded Musqueam territories, teaching at the University of British Columbia.

Shelly Johnson (Mukwa Musayett – Walking with Bears) is of Saulteaux and Norwegian ancestry. She is a Canada Research Chair in Indigenizing Higher Education and associate professor in the Faculty of Education and Social Work at Thompson Rivers University, which is located on the unceded and occupied territory of the Secwepemc people. Her Indigenist research includes First Nations therapeutic jurisprudence, Indigenous culture and language revitalization, and Indigenous child welfare.

Rochelle Johnston is a PhD candidate at the Ontario Institute for Studies in Education at the University of Toronto. Working with a Guidance Circle of Indigenous academics and activists, she is researching how non-Indigenous Canadians and riverain Sudanese stand by and do nothing about genocide. Ms. Johnston has worked as a researcher, advocate, coordinator, facilitator, and popular educator with communities affected by violence in eastern Africa and Canada for over 15 years, focusing particularly on the agency of young people within these communities.

Benjamin Kelly is an assistant professor in the Department of Sociology and Anthropology at Nipissing University. His main research interests are social theory and social psychology. He has published articles on science and technology, environmental sociology, social structure, identity, and emotions. His ongoing fieldwork looks at the lived experience of scientist-activists and their concerns surrounding environmental risk in relation to industry, government, public policy, and First Nations.

Brittany Luby is an award-nominated educator from Laurentian University in Sudbury, Ontario, who joined the University of Guelph in 2017. Outside of the classroom, Luby seeks to stimulate public discussion of Indigenous issues through her critical and creative work. The Canadian Historical Association has described Luby's research as "innovative in its structure and responsive to Indigenous research methodologies." Her pieces can be found in periodicals such as the *Canadian Bulletin of Medical History*, the *Canadian Journal of Native Studies*, and *Prairie Fire*.

Marion Maar is founding faculty at the Northern Ontario School of Medicine (NOSM) and faculty coordinator for NOSM's mandatory Indigenous cultural immersion experience for medical students. Dr. Maar has collaborated on many research projects with Indigenous peoples, including research ethics, diabetes care, cancer screening, mental health, and intimate partner violence. Prior to her work at NOSM, Dr. Maar had the privilege of working as researcher for the First Nations on Manitoulin Island at Noojmowin Teg Health Centre for seven years.

Darrel Manitowabi is an associate professor in the School of Northern and Community Studies, Anthropology Program, at Laurentian University in Sudbury, Ontario. He has a PhD in socio-cultural anthropology from the University of Toronto and has published articles on Indigenous tourism and gaming, Ojibwa/Anishinaabe ethnohistory, urban Indigenous issues, and Indigenous health. He is a citizen of the Wiikwemkoong Unceded Territory and he currently resides in the Whitefish River First Nation.

Georgina Martin's ancestry is Secwepemc (Shuswap) and she is a member of Lake Babine Nation (Carrier). She developed the curriculum for First Nations Health and Wellness I & II and teaches both courses in the Community Health Promotion for Aboriginal Communities program at Vancouver Island University. Dr. Martin has over 23 years of experience with various federal and provincial government departments and in 2014, she completed her PhD research, titled "Drumming My Way Home: An Intergenerational Narrative Inquiry about Secwepemc Identities."

Angela Mashford-Pringle is an Assistant Professor and Associate Director for the Waakebiness-Bryce Institute for Indigenous Health, Dalla Lana School of Public Health, University of Toronto. She is an urban Algonquin woman from Timiskaming First Nation in northern Quebec, Canada, whose research is at the intersection of Indigenous health and education. She has held leadership and administrative positions at Peel District School Board, St. Michael's Hospital's Well Living House, and Centennial College as the inaugural Aboriginal Programs Manager. Angela worked for more than 10 years at Health Canada and the Public Health Agency of Canada managing Indigenous social programs.

Deborah McGregor (Anishinaabe) is an associate professor with the Osgoode Hall Law School and Faculty of Environmental Studies at York University. She currently holds a Canada Research Chair in Indigenous Environmental Justice. Her research focuses on Indigenous knowledge systems, water and environmental governance, environmental justice, forest policy and management, and Indigenous food sovereignty.

Lorrilee McGregor is an Anishinaabe from Whitefish River First Nation. She has been working with First Nation communities and Aboriginal organizations at local, regional, and national levels for the past 20 years. She is a PhD candidate and her research interests focus on children's health, environmental health, and Indigenous research ethics. She has been a member of the Manitoulin Anishinaabek Research Review Committee since 2002.

Nox Ayaa Wilt (Amy Parent) is from the House of Ni'isjoohl in the Nisga'a nation and belongs to the Ganada (frog) Clan. On her father's side, she is French and German. Much of her research is conducted in partnership with community organizations where she seeks to build reciprocal relations between the university and BC Aboriginal communities. She is currently an assistant professor in the Faculty of Education at Simon Fraser University.

Nicole Penak is a member of the eagle clan, and a Maliseet and Mi'kmaq First Nations woman with mixed Ukrainian and Acadian heritage. Born and raised in the GTA, Nicole lives and works in the vibrant Indigenous community of Toronto. She is a registered social worker and social work educator, and currently works at Anishnawbe Health Toronto providing individual and group counselling. Nicole is working to complete her PhD in adult education and community development at the Ontario Institute for Studies in Education.

Lana Ray, from Red Rock (Lake Helen) First Nations, is a member of the Anishinaabek Nation and muskellunge clan. She holds a master of public health degree from Lakehead University and a PhD in Indigenous studies from Trent University, and is the owner/operator of Minowewe Consulting, which specializes in Indigenous-based research, planning, and evaluation.

Jean-Paul Restoule is Anishinaabe and a member of the Dokis First Nation. He is Professor and Chair of the Department of Indigenous Education at the University of Victoria. His research is concerned with Indigenizing and decolonizing teacher education; supporting Indigenous student success; Indigenous pedagogy in online learning environments; and Indigenous research methodologies and ethics. Dr. Restoule is the lead designer of Aboriginal Worldviews and Education, a Coursera MOOC examining how Indigenous perspectives can benefit all learners.

Paige Restoule (Waasnoode Kwe) is Ojibway and Potawatomi from Dokis First Nation, Ontario. Paige graduated from Trent University with an honours degree in psychology and a minor in Indigenous studies. Currently, Paige is a graduate student at Nipissing University in the master of environmental studies program, and her research focuses on the resurgence of Indigenous land-based activities. Paige is a community-based researcher and an active community member of her school and community.

Katrina Srigley lives and works on Nbisiing Anishnaabeg territory where she is a partner, mother to two little girls, and an associate professor in the Department of History at Nipissing University. Dr. Srigley's most recent SSHRC-funded project, developed in partnership with Glenna Beaucage of Nipissing First Nation, picks up the themes of storytelling and engaged practice. *Nbisiing Anishinaabeg Biimadiziwin: To Understand the Past and Shape the Future* uses oral history and Indigenized research practice to examine the history of Nbisiing Anishnaabeg from the perspective of the community. A short documentary film based on aspects of this work, *The Nipissing Warriors*, recently premiered on the territory.

Toni Valenti is currently pursuing her master of Indigenous relations at Laurentian University in Sudbury, Ontario. She also holds a bachelor of arts in anthropology with a focus in medical anthropology. Valenti actively incorporates creative elements into her writing in an attempt to make academic research more accessible to a general audience.

Autumn Varley (Nongokwe) is an Anishinaabe researcher who recently completed the master of arts history program at Nipissing University. Her major research paper, "The Circle Is Strong: Family, Identity, and the Child Welfare System" received the highest possible grade in the program. While she calls southern Georgian Bay home, her family hails from Kitigan Zibi Anishinaabeg

INDEX